Henry Varnum Poor

Studies in Entrepreneurial History
Published in Coöperation with the
Research Center in Entrepreneurial History
Harvard University

Henry Varnum Poor

Henry Varnum Poor

Business Editor, Analyst, and Reformer

By

Alfred D. Chandler, Jr.

HARVARD UNIVERSITY PRESS

Cambridge, Massachusetts

1956

Distributed in Great Britain by
Geoffrey Cumberlege
Oxford University Press
London

Library of Congress Catalog Card Number: 56–11280

Printed in the United States of America

To my father — like his grandfather,
a man of business, of learning, and of spirit

Acknowledgments

This study of my great-grandfather's career as a business editor, analyst, and reformer is in many ways a family project. My paternal grandmother's father provided the subject; my maternal grandparents helped make it financially possible to carry out the study; while my parents gave me constant encouragement. To all I owe a great debt. To my wife I owe an even greater one. Without her there surely would have been no study at all. Among the other members of my family I wish particularly to thank my uncles, Henry Poor Chandler and Charles Lyon Chandler, for making completely available to me the large amount of materials they had on Henry Poor.

Outside the family I am most indebted to Frederick Merk, who saw that the study was properly launched, and to Arthur H. Cole who did so much to assure its completion. These two busy scholars were very generous with their time and their invaluable advice and criticism. Among the many other individuals who aided me I want particularly to thank Leland H. Jenks, William Miller, Fritz Redlich, Richard C. Overton, Thomas C. Cochran, John M. Blum, Sylvia Rice, Frederick L. Holmes, and Gerard Tonachel of Standard & Poor's Corporation. I also want to acknowledge the financial assistance I received from the Research Center in Entrepreneurial History, which helped cover the cost of research, writing, and publication. Elma S. Leavis deserves a special vote of thanks for transcribing an often close to undecipherable manuscript into a clear typescript and in so doing catching grammatical and stylistic inconsistencies and infelicities. For any errors in composition or content I am, of course, fully responsible.

A. D. C., Jr.

Contents

Henry Varnum Poor

* 1 *

The Editor

IN JANUARY 1873, Mary Wild Poor was concerned about her husband's health. He was now over sixty, she wrote their son, Henry William, and should put aside some of his business responsibilities. She hoped he would turn his energies again to writing. "The pen is his calling," Mary emphasized. "Why must he shoot about like a rocket from this place to that and find so little leisure to exercise his talents?" [1] The pen was Henry Varnum Poor's calling. When he lived by it his life was full and satisfying. When he put it aside he found work frustrating and disappointing. By the same token, when he worked with his pen Poor's career is worth recording; but, when he did not, his activities have little interest to a later generation.

As editor of the *American Railroad Journal* in the twelve years before the Civil War and of the *Manual of the Railroads of the United States* in the postwar years, Poor pioneered in the systematic collection, compilation, and dissemination of business information. Moreover, unlike most early business journalists, Poor conceived of his editorial task as a creative one. He was not content merely to report and record. Instead he used the data he compiled as a basis for analyzing the problems and suggesting changes and improvements in the industry which his periodicals served. Because he penned analyses and proposed reforms during the first great expansion of the American railroad network, Poor was one of the first Americans to examine intensively the problems raised by the coming of modern big business. A study of Poor's career as a business editor, analyst, and reformer, therefore, tells something about the impact of the railroad revolution in the mid-nineteenth century on the American economy and on American business organization. It also includes much about the development in the United States of the systematic provision of reliable business information.

Poor's editorial activities and contributions grew out of the interplay of three factors: the situation in which he worked and about which he wrote; the nature and functions of the periodicals he edited; and his own talents, education, business experience, and noneditorial activities and interests. Of these the last, the personal factor, was undoubtedly the most important. Poor's predilection for analysis and reform arose directly from his early education and his association with prominent social reformers of his day. His ability to comprehend railroad problems was conditioned by the contacts he had with railroad promoters, engineers, financiers, and managers, both before and after he became an editor. His approach to problems, the bent of his analytical thought, and many of the solutions he proposed all reflected the attitudes and values he had learned and the talents he had developed in his earlier years.

To evaluate properly Poor's writings it is necessary, then, to begin by understanding the editor, and an understanding of the editor must start with an examination of his upbringing on the New England frontier. Poor spent the first thirty-seven years of his life on the frontier, and there he learned his earliest lessons in railroading. From the frontier, too, he inherited an optimistic spirit, a faith in self-reliance, and a respect for hard work. These attitudes, so often reflected in his writings on railroads, were strengthened by his indoctrination in those vigorous, hopeful ideas which found such full expression in the New England of Channing, Emerson, and Thoreau. And his family, more than any other single force — even that of his physical environment — was responsible for indoctrinating Poor in the ideas of New England and the way of frontier life.

Henry Poor was born in Andover, Maine, on December 8, 1812, only a score of years after that village had been founded in the wilderness. His parents were pioneers.[2] His mother's family, the Merrills, had been the very first to settle in the lovely intervale on the Ellis River just south of the Rangeley Lakes. During the early 1790's the Poors and other families from Andover, Massachusetts, joined the Merrills. Hard hit by the severe economic depression which followed the American Revolution, the Poors, like so many other farmers in northern Massachusetts, decided to leave the land their family had worked since the 1630's to try their luck on the Maine frontier. For both the Poors and the Merrills the move was successful. By the time Henry's father, Silvanus Poor, married Mary Merrill, their families were the two most prosperous in Andover.

As the son of Silvanus and Mary Poor, Henry enjoyed a respected position in the town where he was born and bred. As their son, too, he was assured of a happy life at home. The few pages of Mary Merrill Poor's diary still in existence give a delightful picture of a cheerful and busy home where teas and dinners with neighbors, Sunday meetings, and visits from friends and neighbors softened the drudgery and rigors of frontier life. Children are much in evidence in the diary, for Mary was raising a large family. Henry, the next to youngest, had three brothers and two sisters. These children were devoted to their mother. She in turn instilled in them a strong sense of family loyalty which they always retained, and did much to make the family the basic educational force in the lives of the younger Poors.

From the family Henry learned the economic facts of frontier life with its requirements of constant work, responsibility, and coöperation. His earliest memories were of helping his mother and older sister spin and weave the family's clothing. As he grew older and stronger, he tended the family's sheep and cattle and aided in sowing, plowing, and harvesting the crops. Later he helped his father and brothers clear the land and gather lumber and maple syrup from the woods. During his boyhood Henry Poor came to know intimately the ways and tasks of rural America.

Yet, thanks to his parents, the constant pressure of farm work was rarely permitted to interfere with Henry's education or allowed to stunt or narrow his mind and spirit. Silvanus and Mary encouraged the children to read the books in the town library which, since Silvanus was the town librarian, was kept in their home. From an early age Henry had the opportunity to read many of the classics of English literature, as well as books on history, geography, and even economics. He had the chance to talk over what he read, for the Andover Debating Society, organized by Henry's father, met regularly at the Poors' home. In their home the Poor children met some of the most striking personalities in northern New England. Henry's uncle, Moses Greenleaf, noted geographer and statistician of Maine, Albion K. Parris, congressman and governor, Benjamin Vaughan, diplomat and veteran radical, and even the great Daniel Webster, all visited the Silvanus Poors in Andover.

Henry's father, as these visitors indicate, was an influential person in the affairs of the town he helped found. Elected town treasurer in 1804, the year Andover was incorporated, Silvanus held various town offices for the next thirty years. As one of the founders of the local church, he took an active part in the parish business, paying personally a large share of the minister's salary and the cost of maintaining the meeting house. In 1816 he also became the town doctor. That year his brother Ebenezer, the only trained physician in Andover, moved away; so Silvanus, leaving Mary to handle the farm, traveled to Philadelphia where he spent a term at the Jefferson Medical School learning the rudiments of medicine.

Silvanus' influence on his children came less from the dominating position he held in the town than from the ideas he so vigorously championed. Intellectually Henry's father was a radical. "A man of good education," a granddaughter later described him, "a strong and independent thinker; Arminian in theology; a Jefferson democrat in politics; a stern man, with a certain grim humor and immense powers of sarcasm." [3] This humor and sarcasm resulted from a long and vigorous defense of unorthodox views. Silvanus wholeheartedly accepted the doctrine of the rights and dignity of man given popular expression by the American and French revolutions. Yet he was unable to reconcile these beliefs with the Calvinistic dogmas of original sin, election, and predestination. Such dogmas, he therefore insisted, must be rejected. To his cousin, Deacon Samuel Poor, and many other members of Andover's Congregational church, Silvanus' ideas were heresy. For many years a bitter theological controversy raged in Andover dividing the town into two hostile camps. In time Silvanus' views won out.

Though Silvanus and his friends were able to weaken the traditional ways of thought, they had difficulty in replacing them with new positive tenets. One minister found his Andover congregation "disgruntled with the orthodox preaching which they have had here, and willing and glad to hear something more liberal and rational from the pulpit. . . . [But] in their theological notions they are very crude and unsettled." [4] Silvanus reacted more with constructive action than with theological reasoning. His work in founding the Sunday School, the Debating Society, and the Temperance Society, indicate his belief that men are improvable and that efforts should be made to improve them by social action. Henry Poor's sympathy for the reform movements of his day stemmed in part at least from watching and participating in his father's activities in Andover.

The views the Poor children learned from their father were admirably reinforced and supplemented by the teachings of the local minister, Thomas Treadwell Stone. Silvanus was responsible for having Stone ordained minister in 1824, despite the vehement protests of the conservative members of the church. The young pastor lived with the Poors, became the children's regular teacher, and eventually married Henry's sister, Laura. Stone, no ordinary frontier preacher, had graduated from Bowdoin with high honors in 1820. He was destined to become a prominent Unitarian and one of the early Transcendentalists.[5] "A freer, more childlike, more beautiful mind, I never met with," a colleague, Christopher Cranch, once said of him. "He is fragrant with the very warmest bloom of the true transcendentalism — a true Christian Pantheist, a man with a soul. . . ." [6] Stone taught the young Poors that God was a God of kindness, love, and beauty. Such a God favored no one sect or group. He came equally to all and He was manifest everywhere and in everything. Nowhere, Stone stressed, did He reveal Himself more gloriously than in the natural beauties of Andover's intervale and mountains. Wordsworth was Thomas Stone's literary hero, Channing his religious mentor, and Emerson was to be his contemporary ideal.

The teachings of Thomas Stone and Silvanus deeply impressed young Henry Poor, a sensitive and somewhat introspective youngster.[7] Throughout his life he retained a fundamental belief in the rights and dignity of human beings and the universality and goodness of God. His dislike of the dogmatic, the sectarian, and the traditional also reflected his early education in Andover. But Henry at Andover was only a boy. He received impressions of and approaches to thought rather than any real understanding of specific ideas or definite beliefs. His mind needed training and discipline before his basic concepts were to be clarified and crystallized.

Stone did as much to train Henry's mind as to stimulate it. He taught him, with his brothers and sisters, the fundamentals of good writing and good speech as well as mathematics, Latin, a little natural science, and more history. A pamphlet that Stone wrote in 1831, entitled *An Address on the Introduction of Historical Studies into the Course of Common Education,* presenting some remarkably modern ideas on the teaching of history, shows what an effective teacher he must have been.[8] It suggests also why Henry and his brother John Alfred had a lifelong interest in history. Stone continued to mold Henry's mind even after they both left Andover. In 1829 Stone, forced out of the Andover church by Deacon Samuel Poor and the conservative faction, became the preceptor at Bridgeton Academy. Henry, who had just begun studying at Hebron Academy, transferred to Bridgeton. After a thorough training there in Latin, elementary Greek, algebra, and geography, he passed the entrance examination for Bowdoin, where he matriculated in the fall of 1831.

Henry was the first in his family, indeed the first boy from Andover, to go to college. In the summer of 1831 Silvanus, deciding to retire from active farming, turned his farm over to his oldest son, Silvanus, Jr. Young Silvanus then paid each of his brothers a "portion" to cover their share in the family land. Thus Henry, unlike his older brothers, had money available in time for a college education. Yet even with this money and with what he earned by teaching school during vacations, he still needed financial help from his father and Silvanus, Jr. Henry was always grateful for this aid, although in later years he often expressed doubts as to whether the sacrifices of his father and brother were worth while.[9]

There was nothing interesting or exciting, Henry later maintained, in Bowdoin's old-fashioned, orthodox, sectarian course of instruction. Indeed Bowdoin, a stronghold of conservatism, was at this time actively combating the ideas Silvanus Poor and Thomas Stone so heartily espoused. Yet Poor probably received more from his college years than he was willing to acknowledge. Four years of Latin, Greek, and mathematics undoubtedly helped train him to think logically and clearly; while the required themes and declamations gave him valuable experience in expressing his ideas. Moreover, from Samuel P. Newman's lectures and readings in civil polity and political economy, he received his first initiation into political and economic theory.[10]

Newman, a forceful teacher and ardent admirer of Adam Smith, thoroughly indoctrinated his students in the ideas of classical economics.[11] From him Poor learned, in a far more systematic and convincing way than most of his contemporaries, about the "natural laws" of supply and demand and of competition. Although in later years Poor questioned many of the teachings of the classical economists, he accepted almost without reservation their basic assumptions. He remained sure that uncontrolled competition between individuals seeking to maximize profit provided a nearly automatic regulator for the economy, made for the most effective allocation of capital, labor, and resources, and stimulated the developments of new and more efficient techniques of production. Newman was even more enthusiastic about the future of the United States of America than he was about the teachings of Adam Smith, and his sanguine vision of the nation's enormous and yet untapped economic resources must have fired the imagination of Henry Poor and his classmates.

Bowdoin had something to offer socially as well as intellectually. Though somewhat shy, Poor made many friends at college and was an active member of the Peucinian Society, the "more aristocratic" of the college's two rival literary and social organizations.[12] After graduation he enjoyed returning to Brunswick and in later years took part in the Bowdoin Alumni Association. Undoubtedly Bowdoin gave him the social poise and assurance, not easily developed on a frontier farm, which was to be so useful in the coming years in Bangor and New York.

II

On graduating from Bowdoin in 1835 Henry entered the law office of his uncle, Jacob McGaw, in Bangor, Maine. In Bangor, New England and the frontier were uniquely blended. Rough lumbermen relaxing from cruising or chopping in the woods, merchants buying lumber and selling supplies, speculators trading in land, lawyers settling claims, all gave the town a frontier atmosphere. Here, too, was the intellectual and cultural atmosphere of New England, for Bangor was a town of libraries, lyceums, and churches. The minister of its Unitarian church was Frederic Henry Hedge, a close friend of Ralph Waldo Emerson and an influential figure in the intellectual flowering of New England.

When Henry came to Bangor, the town was in the throes of "the Great Speculation." [13] Warrants, rights, and titles to timber lands were rapidly changing hands amid enthusiastic bidding engendered by wildly optimistic hopes. Strangers were pouring into town, rooms were impossible to obtain, prices were soaring. Washtubs of champagne shipped in from New York completed the classic picture of a frontier boom town. The disastrous collapse came quickly, wiping out fortunes both paper and real. The Bangor lumber trade did not recover until the 1840's. From observing the exciting climax and the catastrophic results of Bangor's land boom, Henry Poor learned a vivid lesson in the dangers of overoptimism and speculation so characteristic of the American frontier. This lesson he recalled in the 1850's and again after the Civil War when he repeatedly warned against similar speculations in railroad construction.

Of more immediate importance to Henry's education than the Great Speculation was the close friendship he formed during these first years in Bangor with the Reverend Frederic Henry Hedge and his family. When Henry moved to Bangor, he lived with his older brother, John Alfred Poor, who, having been made in 1835 a partner in his uncle's firm, was already one of the rising young men in the state bar. After his wife's sudden death in 1837, John Alfred asked Hedge and his family to move in with Henry and himself.[14] Henry was especially pleased when the Hedges accepted his brother's offer. Now after a long day with the law books of McGaw and Poor, he could look forward to a pleasant evening with Mrs. Hedge and her delightful children, and an occasional talk with one of the ablest scholars in all America.

Henry Hedge, by introducing Americans to German literature, thought, and scholarship, was making during his residence in Bangor a significant contribution to the intellectual growth of the United States. The son of Levi Hedge, professor of logic at Harvard, he had at the age of thirteen gone to Germany with young George Bancroft. After studying for four years at German universities, Hedge returned to Harvard, graduating high in the class of 1825. He then went on to the Divinity School, where he and his fellow student, Emerson, became close friends. At his first church in West Cambridge, Hedge, as "a fountain of knowledge in the way of [the] German," began to play an important role in furthering the new ideas then stirring in New England.[15] After he moved to Bangor he continued to have a strong influence on Transcendental and Unitarian thought. The celebrated Transcendental Club which included Emerson, George Ripley, Bronson Alcott, James Freeman Clarke, Margaret Fuller, and Elizabeth Peabody was also known as the Hedge Club, since its meetings were made to coincide with Hedge's visits from Bangor.

Hedge, who became one of Poor's lifelong friends, had a lasting influence on the future editor's intellectual development. From him Poor learned the importance of careful study and critical evaluation of data in the analysis of problems, whether philosophical, economic, or business. Hedge's keen sense of history increased Poor's appreciation of the need to set events, issues, and problems in their broader perspectives. Even more important, he helped Poor to formulate and define his basic ideas, to clarify and crystallize the impressions he had acquired from his father and from Thomas Stone as a youngster in Andover.

Poor's basic philosophical ideas, which began to take clear form under the influence of Henry Hedge, can be summarized in this fashion: God is good. He expects man whom He made in His image to become like Him. In man's mind God gave him the means for this perfection. The mind is more powerful than any man-made institution. It can, therefore, reshape those institutions which have permitted sin and evil to flourish. It can also create new institutions to assure man of a better life on earth. Yet the mind, if it is to conquer evil and work toward perfection, must be intellectually and morally trained and disciplined.[16] These basic views reflect the dominant ideas of the day. Henry Poor's father introduced to him the ideas of the French enlightenment; Thomas Stone, those of English romanticism; Hedge provided the integrating and crystallizing concepts of German idealism. But all three streams of thought were naturally modified and tempered by the environment of frontier America in which Poor lived.

Such a thorough impregnation with the optimistic and romantic thought of the early nineteenth century significantly affected Poor's later writings on industry and technology. He ardently believed in the ability of man to progress toward perfection, even before he came into direct contact with the amazing technological developments of the last century. The coming of the transportation and industrial revolutions was, indeed, a magnificent verification of his basic beliefs. Here men, by creatively applying their minds to labor-saving machinery, were making strides towards that physical perfection which in his mind was the first necessary step to intellectual and moral perfection. Of all the new technical instruments furthering the progress of man, the railroad, Poor was soon to believe, would have the most profound effect.[17]

Henry Poor's faith in American industrial and business growth was a positive faith. It had little in common with those ideas which later found their fullest expression in Herbert Spencer's social Darwinism. For Poor there was little certain or automatic about progress. Progress resulted only from an active effort, a forceful drive, a rigorous application of the mind to the machine, and not from the automatic operation of mechanistic forces. Nevertheless, this progress did take place within the framework of "the natural laws" of classical economics. Competition and the law of supply and demand provided a useful, if not essential, stimulus to individual effort.

Hedge thus helped provide Poor with a theological and philosophical framework which not only gave his later writings spirit and force but, more important, assured him of a fuller intellectual and spiritual life. Moreover, Poor had the Hedges to thank for introducing him to Mary Pierce. In the fall of 1838 Mrs. Lucy Pierce Hedge invited her youngest sister to visit them in Bangor. Henry and Mary, a pert, attractive, and intellectually mature girl of seventeen, were quickly drawn to each other. There was a long engagement of three years, until Henry finally felt himself financially established. Then in September 1841 the two were married.

Henry and Mary were ideally suited to each other, if one might judge by their correspondence of over half a century. Mary's friendly outgoing nature helped offset Henry's diffidence and mild shyness. Intellectually they had similar backgrounds. As the daughter of John Pierce, one of New England's foremost clergymen, Mary was even closer than Henry to the Unitarian and Transcendental thought of the day. She knew personally William Ellery Channing and his brother Dr. Walter Channing, as well as Emerson, Clarke, Ripley, Theodore Parker, John S. Dwight, Margaret Fuller, Elizabeth Peabody, and others. When she was still a girl in her teens, she joined these liberal thinkers in their discussion meetings and carefully read their works.[18] Through Mary, Henry soon met and came to know many of America's leading intellectuals, and she, with her background, shared and reinforced her husband's faith in the progress and perfection of man.

While they were in Bangor the Poors kept in close contact with the intellectual and social life of Boston through visits and letters. They also took an active part in local Bangor affairs. They regularly attended meetings at the Unitarian Circle and church discussion groups and fully enjoyed the parties, concerts, lectures, and talks at the Lyceum that brightened the long winters of this northern town.

Henry himself gave an occasional talk on political and economic subjects from the Lyceum platform. Children soon began to enliven the Poors' household; Agnes, Henry William, and Robert, were born before the family moved to New York. It was a full and satisfying marriage, which made Henry's life emotionally stable and psychologically secure.

His marriage also helped enhance Henry's social position. In New England, where the clergy still enjoyed the highest social prestige, Mary's father was one of the most prominent ministers. John Pierce, who was pastor at Brookline for more than half a century, secretary of Harvard's Board of Overseers for thirty-three years, first secretary of the Massachusetts Bible Society, secretary of the Massachusetts Convention of Congregational Ministers, a member of the Massachusetts Historical and the Massachusetts Statistical societies, and officer and member of other similar organizations, was close to many of the leading men of his native state.[19] Moreover, Mary's mother was a Tappan and Mary's Tappan uncles — Benjamin, senator from Ohio, Arthur and Lewis, merchants in New York and leaders in the antislavery movement, and Charles, a successful Portland businessman — were all eminent men of their day. By marriage, then, if not by family lineage, Poor acquired a social status which was useful in obtaining easy access to intellectuals in Boston and established merchants in New York.

Through his connection with the Pierces, Poor came to know a number of New England clergymen more intimately. Three of John Pierce's daughters married clergymen, of whom two — Hedge and Thomas B. Fox — like Poor's sister's husband, Thomas Stone, became leaders in the Unitarian church. Poor considered the work of his brothers-in-law important. Yet in the new industrial age he thought their work and their social position were overrated. He was prompted, therefore, in his writings during the 1850's to call for a reëvaluation of the American social structure.[20] A new aristocracy was rising, he emphasized, which should be given recognition. The man of science, the man of mechanical ingenuity, the "practical man of affairs," was, by applying his mind to the new machines, advancing mankind far more effectively than those who merely applied their minds to books and abstract ideas. These new leaders, thought Henry, must soon be granted their rightful place in the social scale above the older, but now less socially useful representatives of the "learned professions."

Poor included his own vocation, the law, among the learned professions still overrated by society. He had been admitted to the Maine bar in 1838, and shortly afterwards, when his uncle Jacob McGaw retired from active practice, Poor joined in partnership with his brother, John Alfred. The firm of J. A. and H. V. Poor, as successor to McGaw and Poor, had a profitable practice, but although the law provided him with a comfortable living, Poor never really cared for his profession.[21] He especially disliked the aggressive, pushing, combative life in the courts.

In spite of his dislike for it, however, Poor's practical experience as a lawyer proved quite useful to him. In editing the *Journal* he was often called upon to discuss railroad matters involving complex legal problems. In fact, he devoted a special section in the *Journal* wholly to railroad law. Of more importance, the law trained him to understand the value and nature of concrete evidence. He learned the difficulties of testing evidence and the ease with which evidence could be twisted and distorted, a training which he found especially useful in his later efforts to provide accurate business information. In the same way the law helped strengthen the careful and critical approach which marked his analytical studies of railroad problems. "The most sagacious man," he wrote in 1850, "is the most diffident as to the correctness of his conclusions, or rather perhaps, the most cautious in asserting their correctness. Upon every subject about as much can be said upon one side as the other. It is the *balance* of evidence that turns the scale." [22] The law, like the teachings of his father and Hedge, increased Poor's distrust of the dogmatic and the opinionated.

In his legal practice Poor came in constant contact with the business life of Bangor. Moreover, the relatively light demands of his practice permitted him to participate actively in Bangor's major business, which was lumbering. In 1845, when the return of prosperity throughout New England and especially in Maine's shipbuilding industry drove up the price of lumber, the young lawyer with a few Bangor associates undertook some fairly large lumbering operations.[23] In 1845 and 1847 Poor purchased timber lands, supervised logging operations, and sold both logs and finished boards. The boards he had manufactured at a mill in nearby Orono in which he had a financial interest. These ventures, which until the depression of the late forties proved quite profitable, gave Poor many practical lessons in the ways of business.

III

But far more valuable to Henry Poor than the business experience he acquired in either his legal work or his lumbering operations was the training he received during his Bangor years in railroading. Nearly everything Poor knew about railroads when he became editor of the *American Railroad Journal* he learned, during his last five years on the New England frontier, by watching the railroad activities of his brother, John Alfred.

John Alfred Poor, more than any other single person, was responsible for the creation of the Maine railroad system during the second half of the 1840's. Henry's brother not only conceived and aggressively pushed forward plans to build the Maine system, but he also played a key role in the organization, promotion, construction, and financing of the individual roads. John Alfred's initial ambitions and achievements were impressive. The first and most important of his ventures, the railroad from Portland to Montreal, was one of the first of the great trunk lines designed to connect the Atlantic seaboard with the West. At its inception it was one of the largest railroad construction projects yet proposed in the United States. Moreover it was to cross as rugged and wild country as any railroad which had at that time been constructed. The difficult terrain, combined with the paucity of local capital in this semifrontier state, forced John Alfred and his colleagues to transform conservative New England practices of railroad finance and construction into techniques which were very much like those used in the Western states in the following decade. John Alfred attempted, to an even greater degree than the promoters of other trunk lines, to integrate his road into a transportation system designed to benefit and expand the economy of his particular state.

John Alfred's personality and special talents helped make him an effective promoter and, by the same token, a poor manager and administrator. He had the vivid imagination, the convincing tongue, the unbounded energy, and the incurable optimism so essential to the initiating of a bold economic enterprise. Like so many of the successful railroad promoters of his day, he conceived of his work as much more than a business venture. His railroads, he was completely convinced, were laying the basis for the future commercial and industrial growth of his community. They would in a short time make Maine one of the richest states in the union.[24]

The story of John Alfred's railroad ventures will be only summarized here, since they have already been described in some detail elsewhere.[25] Moreover, Henry played only a relatively small active part in the building of the first Maine railroads. The law and lumbering remained his primary occupations. Yet as his brother's law partner and his agent on railroad matters in Bangor, Henry Poor was in an incomparable position to watch the beginnings of a railroad system. Here he had the opportunity to observe the working out of a great railroad project from an idea into the reality of an operating road, and at the same time to obtain an understanding of the many practical difficulties involved in achieving this transformation.

The story of John Alfred's railroads begins in Andover. By the 1830's the town had stopped growing.[26] Like so many American frontier communities, its markets, and therefore its prosperity, depended wholly on improving transportation facilities for its surplus lumber and farm products. To the farmers of Andover the appearance of the steam locomotive in the early 1830's offered a means of salvation. In the spring of 1835 the town sent Silvanus Poor to Augusta to bring pressure on the state legislature to grant financial aid for the proposed railroad from the Maine coast to the Canadian border.[27] The collapse of the lumber boom early the next year, and then the depression years after 1837, however, cut short all Maine's plans for internal improvements.

With the return of prosperity John Alfred Poor revived the town's plan of placing Andover on the main line of transportation from the Maine seaports to the towns in the valley of the St. Lawrence. At first his plans were modest. In June 1844 he petitioned the state legislature for aid in the building of a stage road from the northern part of Oxford County to Sherbrooke in Canada.[28] But his horizons broadened when later that summer he visited Sherbrooke in Canada, as well as Colebrook, New Hampshire, and other American towns on the proposed route. At Sherbrooke he learned of a scheme being promoted by Boston merchants to connect their city with Montreal by a railroad which was to pass through that Canadian town. John Alfred's immediate response to this plan was to devise one of his own which would make Portland rather than Boston the terminus of a Montreal to tidewater railroad. Within a week he had won the support of the powerful British-American Land Company. Its commissioner, Alexander Tilloch Galt, who then was residing in Sherbrooke, accepted with little hesitation Poor's arguments that Portland was two hundred miles closer to Montreal than Boston and that a railroad to Portland would run through much more of the company's lands than one terminating in Boston.[29]

John Alfred went from Sherbrooke almost directly to Portland. There he quickly convinced the Portlanders that their city's destiny lay in becoming Canada's winter port. In articles printed in the Portland papers and in conversations with its leading citizens he argued that a railroad to Montreal would not only open the Canada trade to Portland but, through the construction of the Welland and Rideau canals, would give Portland access to the grain crops of the American West. Moreover such a road was essential to reviving older semifrontier communities and opening up unsettled country in western Maine.[30] At a special city meeting held on September 25, 1844, less than a week after Poor arrived, the voters of Portland authorized city funds for the financing of a preliminary survey and the dispatching of two prominent Portlanders to Montreal to check on the support the proposed line might have there.[31] By the following January a provisional committee to organize the road had been created and the Maine legislature had granted a charter to the Atlantic and St. Lawrence Railroad Company.

John Alfred, however, still had to convince Montreal. In February he made a dramatic dash to that city in subzero weather, traveling through a raging blizzard in order to prevent the Board of Trade from giving official backing to the road to Boston.[32] Not only was he able to turn the board in favor of the Portland project, but, with the assistance of Judge William P. Preble who arrived from Portland late in February, he obtained the backing of the Canadian Parliament. Before Poor left Montreal towards the end of March, the Parliament had by an almost unanimous vote chartered the St. Lawrence and Atlantic Railroad Company to connect Montreal with the terminus of the Maine line at the Canadian border.[33]

With the successful chartering of the line between Portland and Montreal, Poor and his colleagues enlarged their plans. They now envisaged a state-wide system with the Atlantic and St. Lawrence as its central axis. In the spring of 1845 they chartered the Androscoggin and Kennebec and the Penobscot and Kennebec, to connect Lewiston, on the projected Montreal line, with Bangor. In the following year they chartered the York and Cumberland to run from Portland south to Portsmouth, New Hampshire. Still later they chartered the Androscoggin and Buckfield Branch railroads. In order to give this system a unity of its own, and to hinder the movement of Boston-bound traffic over its tracks, John Alfred gave these roads, despite strong opposition in both Maine and Canada, a broad 5′6″ gauge. But the price for giving the Maine system a unique unity proved a heavy one. For the next twenty years the "war of the gauges" disrupted railroading and politics in both Maine and Canada.[34]

While on a second visit to Montreal early in the fall of 1847 to win the Canadian government's backing for the broad gauge, John Alfred began to see the Maine railroad system in a larger continental setting. The Canadians by this time were becoming excited about railroads, and one of the most talked-of proposals was a line to connect Montreal with the maritime provinces. Poor's suggestion that the Maine roads might be used to make this connection won immediate support in both Montreal and New Brunswick.[35] Bangor was the key town in Poor's new scheme. She must organize, John Alfred wrote Henry, and help build a railroad eastward to the New Brunswick border. At the same time she must push construction of the line already chartered westward to Waterville and Lewiston. Although Henry Poor worked hard to get the men of Bangor to support the road, they, because they enjoyed excellent water transportation, saw little reason to invest in a railroad plan that offered little immediate benefit. Furthermore, money was hard to come by in 1848, for all New England was suffering from the repercussions of the current severe British economic depression.[36] The only immediate result of this project was to bring John Alfred Poor one step closer to the boldest of his transportation dreams — the vision of joining Europe and North America.

In 1850 John Alfred brought forth a magnificent design to provide rapid transportation between New York and London.[37] The plan called for the building of the European and North American Railroad from Bangor east to St. John and then continuing it by separate branches to Halifax and Louisburg. With the completion of this road, a traveler could go by express train to either Halifax or Louisburg. From there a fast steamer, "the Atlantic Ferry," would carry him to Galway in Ireland. Here he would take an express train to the Irish Channel, go by steamer to Holyhead, and then, again by express, to London. The whole journey, which then took a dozen or so days, would be reduced to six or seven.

A brilliant transportation scheme, the European and North American Railroad was in 1850 a thoroughly impractical business proposition. Local traffic in the almost unexplored region between Bangor and St. John was virtually nonexistent. Nor was there any certainty that trans-Atlantic passengers and shippers would pay the high rates the road would surely have to charge if it were to make a profit on its construction and operating costs. Therefore, in spite of an ambitious promotional send-off in the summer of 1850, neither private individuals nor the towns of Bangor and St. John offered any substantial financial backing. John Alfred was to spend the rest of his life trying to transform this last of his railroad schemes into a reality.

John Alfred's bold, imaginative, though increasingly impractical railroad projects deeply impressed Henry Poor. In his brother's work Henry had a specific and striking example of a mind being applied to the potentiality of the machine. John Alfred, through the railroad and the steamboat, would raise the standard of living of the Andover farmers and the Portland merchants, and also would provide the peoples of Europe with cheaper food, and the farmers of the western United States with cash for their many needs. At the same time,

Henry came to appreciate that more than vision, enthusiasm, and promotional ability were required to build a railroad.

John Alfred's work also introduced him to the many problems of building a railroad in a new country. The first and most pressing of these problems was finance. James Hall, the surveyor, had estimated the cost of the Atlantic and St. Lawrence at two and a half million dollars. No business undertaking in Maine had ever required anything like this amount of capital. In a search for funds, Preble and Galt had gone to London and John Alfred Poor to Boston. All were unsuccessful — Poor primarily because the merchants and financiers of Boston saw little reason to finance a railroad intended to build up a rival port.[38] So John Alfred and his colleagues were forced to turn to Maine.

During the spring and summer of 1845 the managers of the Atlantic and St. Lawrence carried on a spirited campaign to raise funds locally.[39] The campaign was similar to those carried on in many an American city in the mid-nineteenth century — in Baltimore, Charleston, Savannah, and New York in the 1830's, the Midwestern cities in the 1850's, and the trans-Mississippi West after the Civil War. Meetings were held; petitions and declarations signed. The Portland press, both Whig and Democratic, fervently endorsed the road. Newspapers throughout the state were filled with statistics and other information provided by John Alfred Poor and others which attempted to prove that the projected road would channel a vast amount of trade through the state of Maine and the city of Portland. In Portland these efforts were supplemented by a carefully organized door-to-door canvass in search of stock subscribers. That city, the chief beneficiary of the proposed railroad, took by far the largest portion of the 10,019 shares sold. Bangor, having little to gain from the project, subscribed, despite the strenuous efforts of John Alfred and Henry Poor, to only 150 shares.[40]

With the initial capital raised, or at least promised, the incorporators of the Atlantic and St. Lawrence on September 27, 1845 formally organized their company.[41] John Alfred was the only non-Portlander elected as a director. In the following year in order to be closer to his primary business interest he moved from Bangor to Portland, leaving Henry to handle in northern Maine the interests of the Atlantic and St. Lawrence and its allied lines.

The new board was at once faced with the many problems of construction. First came the selection of the route.[42] This task proved to be, as it did in most parts of the country, as much a political as an engineering problem; for every village in the vicinity of the probable route expected the line to pass through it. Fortunately for the company one of the three routes surveyed was patently so superior that the company was able to convince almost everyone that the route had been selected for technical reasons alone. Ironically enough, the route by-passed both Andover and Colebrook, two of the communities which had originally sponsored the road. While these surveys were being made, the contracts for the construction of the first twelve-mile section were let out to Wood, Black and Company, local contractors.

With the surveys completed, the company next had to obtain charters from New Hampshire and Vermont and then make arrangements about construction, future traffic, and other matters with its Canadian partner. The first of these tasks called for a great deal of time and effort on John Alfred's part, for the local roads in New Hampshire and Vermont, oriented as they were to Boston, did their best to block the Maine company's charter in their respective legislatures.[43] The second task was much easier. In July 1846 after several days of negotiation, the American and Canadian firms signed the "convention and fundamental articles of agreement" which among other things arranged for Alvin C. Morton, the Maine company's engineer, and Wood, Black and Company, its contractors, to do the same work for the Canadian railroad.[44]

After completing the legal arrangements and the letting of the construction contracts, the next job was to purchase rails and equipment. This task fell to John Alfred Poor, the chairman of the directors' committee on construction. He visited and then continued to correspond with such manufacturers as Hinckley, Gray, Baldwin, and Norris asking for data on the types, prices, and probable dates of delivery on locomotives, cars, and other equipment.[45] He also wrote importers about procuring English rails. His main source of information, however, was David A. Neal, the president of the Eastern Railroad, to whom he wrote a lengthy letter asking every type of question about railroad equipment. Poor, after receiving replies to this extensive correspondence, made a thorough report to the board on the needs and estimated costs of equipping the road.

In this report John Alfred urged the company to manufacture its equipment locally. Shops would soon have to be built to service and repair the road's equipment. These shops, he stressed, should be built large enough to permit the company to make its own locomotives, cars, and other necessary items. The savings over purchasing this equipment from Philadelphia and New York were, he was certain, quite substantial. When the more conservative directors turned down John Alfred's suggestion, he then, with the help of the veteran locomotive builder Septimus Norris, organized the Portland Company.[46] This company, incorporated in the fall of 1846, soon had a plant covering eight acres. It built nearly all engines and machinery for the Atlantic and St. Lawrence, and also made locomotives for other railroads in New England and Ohio. The firm became at once and long remained the largest manufacturing establishment in Portland. Poor's plan of building large repair and manufacturing shops to equip and service a road operating at a distance from existing shops was widely followed in the West during the 1850's. Indeed, it was through such railroad shops that industry first came to much of rural America.

Early in 1848 finance again became the Atlantic and St. Lawrence's primary problem. Because a business depression struck New England late in 1847, the directors found it difficult to collect assessments from its present stockholders and impossible to find men willing to buy new shares.[47] To meet the crisis the directors permitted farmers on the road's western extension to pay for stock in promises of labor and material — a practice soon to be used extensively in the West.[48] For a time they considered issuing bonds, a procedure then quite novel to New England. The majority of directors decided against the plan on the grounds that the issue could only be sold at a heavy discount, thus injuring the company's credit and driving down the value of its stock.[49]

The directors instead looked to public support. Portland was the obvious source of assistance. State aid was prohibited by a recent amendment to the Maine constitution; and, as yet, there was little indication that the national government might be a source of financial help. John Alfred, therefore, in a series of newspaper articles, appealed to Portland.[50] In the fall of 1848 her citizens, by more than a two-thirds vote, authorized the issuance to the railroad of a million dollars worth of municipal bonds to be paid in three nearly equal installments.[51] The loan, secured by a first mortgage on the road, with a carefully constituted sinking fund, marked the beginning of large-scale municipal support to Maine railroads — a policy which made possible the completion of nearly all the railroads in the state and one which became standard practice in the West in the early 1850's. In the following year Montreal and the Canadian Parliament provided similar assistance to the financially desperate St. Lawrence and Atlantic.[52]

The next step was to convert municipal aid into actual construction work. This John Alfred finally arranged at a conference held in Lebanon, New Hampshire, in July 1849.[53] Here Poor, representing the Maine line; Galt, acting for the Canadians; Morton, the engineer; and John M. Wood, the contractor, formulated one of the earliest examples of the "gross" contract which was later used so extensively to finance construction in the West. By this contract Wood, Black and Company agreed to do "the whole work of constructing the Road . . . under the supervision and direction of Engineers, employed and paid by the Company." [54] The railroad was to pay the contractors "$26,200 a mile, one half payable in Cash, one quarter in the Bonds of the Company on twenty-years with semi-annual interest, and one fourth part in the Stock of the Company at its par value." The Canadian company was to pay one quarter in the company's stock at par, one quarter in Montreal bonds (for which Montreal would take an equal amount of the company's preferred stock) and one half of the company's bonds guaranteed by the colonial government.[55] To pay for the costs of the contract and for equipping the road, the Atlantic and St. Lawrence in the next two years increased its capitalization from three to four million dollars, issuing a second mortgage bond issue for $1,500,000, and received $500,000 more in bonds from Portland.[56] With payment in this way assured, the contractors completed their work on schedule. By January 1853 the line from Portland to Montreal was finished; by that July trains were running between the two cities. By then, too, the branch lines which Poor and his colleagues had earlier chartered to Waterville, Leverence Falls, and the Saco River had been completed.

Although he observed more than he participated in these operations, Henry Poor came to know intimately the difficulties of financing railroad construction. He learned also of the methods by which to equip a railroad and to contract for its construction. He acquired an understanding of the techniques of organizing railroad companies. He became wise in the ways of railroad promotion, saw the value of the press and the speaker's platform to win essential political and financial support for a railroad, and learned of the difficulties of chartering a road in three states and two nations. By observing the fight for charters, he saw how important urban rivalries were in stimulating railroad construction and became aware of the necessarily close connection between railroads and politics. Henry Poor observed too how the Maine frontier forced a modification of New England methods of railroad organization, construction, and operation. Since the problems John Alfred and his colleagues had to solve were much closer to those faced by the railroad builders in the West during the 1850's than to those raised in the construction of the first American roads during the 1830's and 1840's on the Eastern seaboard, and since the great railroad expansion of the 1850's was to be concentrated in the Middle West, Henry Poor's experience proved to be extremely useful when he became editor of the *American Railroad Journal.*

IV

By the same token the railroad experience which Poor had acquired by working with his brother would have been of comparatively little value to him if he had remained a Bangor lawyer and lumber merchant. Nor would he have been able to make the most of the intellectual training and stimulus which he had received from Silvanus Poor, Thomas Stone, and Henry Hedge, and from Bowdoin College. Nor could he have as effectively employed his understanding of the needs of the American frontier which he had learned from his Andover boyhood. It was only after he moved to New York early in 1849 that Poor was able to make full use of the business training and the cultural education he had received on the New England frontier. In New York he applied his broad intellectual background and his railroad experience to make the *American Railroad Journal* one of the most influential business journals of the day. There, too, he and Mary were able to play a far more active role than they had in Bangor in working for the progress and perfection of man through social reform. In New York they both enjoyed a thoroughly satisfying and rewarding way of life.

Yet the move from Maine had been completely unanticipated. In the spring of 1848 the Poors considered themselves so permanently settled in Bangor that they purchased a large and comfortable house to meet the demands of a growing family.[57] The depression of 1848 changed their minds about Bangor. By the summer of that year hard times had brought Henry's railroad enterprises almost to a standstill. That fall the price of lumber dropped precipitously. The depression, and then the news of California gold discoveries caused many of the Poors' closest friends to leave Bangor. Already dissatisfied with his own profession, and now receiving setbacks in both his other business activities, Poor, like these friends, was ready to move. Thus when in the very last days of 1848 John Alfred, because of a series of unexpected circumstances, was able to offer his brother the editorship of the *American Railroad Journal*, Henry immediately accepted the proposal.

John Alfred's offer, like Henry's acceptance, resulted directly from the current business depression. Hard times caused D. Kimball Minor, the editor and proprietor of the *Journal*, to think about selling his paper. Before 1848 Minor had had difficulty in meeting his costs. By the fall of 1848 he was finding it almost impossible. During that September and October he made an extended tour of the middle states and New England, hoping to collect debts and to enlarge his subscription and advertising lists.[58] In Portland he talked with John Alfred. He asked the Maine railroader, with whom he was already acquainted and whose activities his paper had actively supported, to write a series of articles for the *Journal* on Maine railroads. John Alfred welcomed the editor's suggestion, for he was anxious to convince a wider audience of the value of his temporarily financially distressed railroads. Minor may very well have discussed the sale of the *Journal* with John Alfred at this time. But if so, nothing definite was done.

The news from California precipitated the sale. Minor, a few days after the President's annual message to Congress early in December confirmed the gold discoveries, wrote John Alfred that he wished to sell the *Journal* so he could be off to the gold fields. John Alfred, after conferring with Henry, went to Philadelphia and there he and Minor quickly came to terms. John Alfred agreed to pay $2,500 for the paper, a part to be paid in cash and the balance in four six-month installments.[59] The Poors were to take over the *Journal* after Minor moved it to New York, where it was to be published by John H. Schultz, a New York printer to whom John Alfred sold a third interest. Henry Poor probably also took at this time a third interest, although the evidence is not clear. In any case, John Alfred soon sold his share to his brother and throughout the fifties Schultz and Henry Poor jointly owned the *Journal*.[60] Besides his financial interest in the paper, Henry received a salary of twenty dollars a week.

When Henry Poor arrived in New York on February 10, 1849, John Alfred and the printer, Schultz, had already put out their first issue. Henry went right to work learning his new profession. From the first he and John Alfred were certain they could succeed where Minor had failed. They had had much more actual railroad experience than Minor. Their friends in railroading were highly encouraging about their venture. Moreover, both had complete faith in the rapid growth of the American railroad system. "The field is good," Henry wrote Mary, "all [that] is needed is a cultivator." [61]

Although he found his work hard, Henry enjoyed it thoroughly. He and John Alfred, Henry assured Mary, would have the paper running smoothly by late spring, when John Alfred planned to return to Portland and the Atlantic and St. Lawrence railroad. In one long letter home, Henry, after telling of his plans for moving the family to New York, described his editorial work in some detail:

> I am now in my office in Wall Street. We have two offices which open into each other. They are very pleasantly situated, back from the street so that even in this great Babel I have no more noise and tumult than I had in my office in Bangor. . . . The office of publication is but a short distance from the printing office. My duties are to prepare copy as the printers term

it and have a general supervision over financial affairs of the paper. . . . My business is very congenial to my feeling, suits my turn of mind exactly. I think too that I have every prospect of success. All assure me that I can do well. The subscription list has gained quite fast since I have been here and I have received some commendations from those whose opinions I value. I think I can have by the end of the year at least 1200 at $5 each besides an advertising list of $1200 per annum. I shall enjoy this business vastly better than the law.[62]

Preparing copy for and supervising the finances of the *American Railroad Journal* remained for twelve years Poor's major occupation. From the spring of 1849 until the outbreak of the Civil War, he considered himself wholly accountable for the paper's content and its editorial policies. Although during the first years of his editorship, he hired assistant editors to handle special departments of civil, mechanical, and mining engineering, they, like most contributors, signed or initialed their articles. Poor took full responsibility for the unsigned material in his paper.[63]

An editorial assistant normally helped Poor put out the paper. This assistant, usually one of his nephews, read proof, culled the newspaper exchanges, and, once in a while, penned an editorial.[64] On occasion when her husband was caught short, Mary herself lent a capable hand in the editorial office. Thursday evening was the deadline for the completion of the weekly copy. On Fridays Schultz printed the paper, putting it in the mails that evening. Thus, on Saturday mornings local subscribers received the latest news of the railroad world in the octavo-sized periodical of sixteen pages measuring 8½ x 10½ inches.

The editor's financial duties were primarily handling the monies from advertising and subscription, the business accounts of the paper, and the funds needed to run his small office. This office he moved twice, first to Nassau Street, then in 1854 to nearby 9 Spruce Street, where it remained for many years. Occasionally he made an extended trip away from New York to collect debts, solicit advertising, and encourage new subscriptions. Much to Poor's relief, Schultz took over a large share of this onerous traveling.[65]

Even with this meager assistance Poor, probably because he did much of his editorial writing at home in the evening, found time for many business, social, and intellectual activities. He occasionally acted as an agent for railroad supply houses.[66] Toward the end of the 1850's he became a director in a firm which quarried and shipped building stone from Nova Scotia to the United States. At different times he helped to promote and finance railroads in the South and West. He published elsewhere a few articles and statistical compilations on railroads. Yet, except possibly for a trip to England in 1858, he never, before the fall of 1861, let these business activities interfere with his primary task of editing the *American Railroad Journal,* for nearly all of them were in fact closely related to his editorial concerns, as were the social and intellectual pursuits he and Mary enjoyed in their new home.

V

The Poors found their new life stimulating and satisfying since New York, socially and intellectually, offered a good deal more than Bangor. Henry found fresh opportunities to develop his interests in history, geography, and statistics. Mary was particularly delighted by the chance she and her husband had to participate more actively in the great social reform movements of the day. These noneditorial activities had a significant impact on Poor's editorial writings. By providing him with interests and ideas which differed from those of his acquaintances in the business and journalistic world of Manhattan, they did much to make Poor one of the first American business editors to conceive of his editorial task as a creative one where his major concern was the analysis of problems and suggestions for improvements and reforms.

"I feel much happier than I have in a long time," Mary wrote her sister Lucy Hedge not long after she had come to New York, "because there is work to do and I can do it with all my energies." [67] During the first years in New York the Poors' energies found their outlet primarily in work at the church. Shortly after their arrival, they joined Thomas Lake Harris's First Independent Christian Church. They were first attracted by Harris's liberal doctrines. That remarkable man, a Universalist turned Swedenborgian, a poet and a spiritualist who eventually became one of America's best known mystics, had founded this nonsectarian church in 1848. Although Mary, in writing the Hedges, explained that their new minister "sympathises more nearly in religious sentiment with Mr. Channing than anyone else," Harris was certainly far to the theological left of the accepted Unitarian position.[68] After Harris left his congregation to help found a combination of an antislavery, spiritualist, and communistic society at Mountain Cove, Virginia, the Poors returned to the Unitarian fold. But as Unitarians they much preferred Henry W. Bellows, an advanced social reformer, to the theologically and socially more conservative Samuel Osgood. When a third Unitarian minister, Octavius Brooks Frothingham, was ordained in New York City, the Poors were immediately drawn to the church of that unorthodox disciple of Theodore Parker.[69]

The Poors, besides being attracted to Harris's theological views, liked the "many unaffected and real people" in his congregation. In this "society of earnest minds," including such reformers as Horace Greeley, Elizabeth Peabody, Catharine Sedgwick, and Elizabeth Blackwell, Mary quickly found her place. "I have entered most actively into the ladies' society and am secretary and on several committees," Mary wrote her sister Lucy.[70] Besides conducting Sunday School classes and taking an active part in the sewing society and church fairs, Mary worked hard with Catharine Sedgwick at the House of Industry, a home founded in 1853 in the depressed Five Points area of the city to help rehabilitate women who had been released from the local jails. She also helped that distinguished reformer and author to organize the Women's Prison Reform Association. Later Mary aided Elizabeth Peabody and Elizabeth Blackwell, the first modern woman doctor of medicine, to found one of the earliest hospitals built especially for women.[71]

Henry enthusiastically approved of his wife's social work.[72] He also encouraged Mary to work energetically for women's rights. Both Poors were members of the New York Anti-Slavery Society—the organization founded many years before by Mary's uncles, the Tappans. Both supported the temperance movement. Moreover, the Poors counted the leaders of the different reform movements in and about New York among their close friends. Not only did they see these reformers at church and at home in the winter, but they also spent the summers with them, first at Horace Greeley's North American Phalanx at Red Bank, New Jersey, and later at Theodore Weld's settlement at nearby Eagleswood.[73]

The Poors continued to maintain their contact with New England; such liberal clergymen and intellectuals as Bronson Alcott, Charles Weld, James Freeman Clarke, Walter Channing, Thomas B. Fox, and Henry Hedge often stayed with them when they visited New York.[74] In the late 1850's the visits from the two brothers-in-law were especially stimulating, for in 1857 Fox had purchased the *Christian Examiner*, the leading Unitarian periodical, and had made Hedge and Edward Everett Hale its editors. Immediately Fox and Hedge became the most influential spokesmen of the liberal wing of the church.

In New York, then, Henry, Mary, and their associates were energetically pushing mankind along the road to perfection. There the Poors were among those pacing the advance of that spirited, sanguine, romantic movement of mid-nineteenth century America, the Humanitarian Crusade. Inevitably much of the spirit of this crusade was reflected in the editorial pages of the *Railroad Journal*.

If Poor's enthusiasm for the reform movements of his day underlined his belief in man's progress and perfection, so his close association with the American Geographical and Statistical Society reflected his interest in and his enthusiasm for the collection of accurate information. In 1852 Poor helped found that society whose purpose was the systematic collection and diffusion of geographical and statistical information in the United States. As long as he lived in New York, he helped the society carry out its aim, serving at various times during the fifties and early sixties as librarian, secretary, councilor, and as a member of numerous committees. In 1859 he became the editor of its first organ, *The Journal of the American Geographical and Statistical Society,* one of the more important early scientific journals published in the United States.[75]

The editor rarely missed a meeting of his society. There he and Mary — for Henry often brought his wife to hear the lectures and papers — thoroughly enjoyed seeing old friends and making new ones. At these meetings the Poors talked with Henry Grinnell, Alexander Isaac Cotheal, William C. H. Waddell, Marshall Lefferts, Archibald Russell, and other prominent New York men of business. There the Poors saw regularly the Reverend Joshua Leavitt, a close friend of uncle Lewis Tappan and the editor of the *Independent,* an outspoken journal of reform; Hiram Barney, one of Lewis Tappan's sons-in-law, and an associate of William Cullen Bryant on the *Evening Post;* and George Bancroft, the historian, who long ago had chaperoned Henry Hedge through Germany. Besides talking with these business and literary men, Henry Poor at the meetings met such geographers as Matthew Fontaine Maury and Arnold Guyot, such explorers as Elisha Kane, and such cartographers and statisticians as John Disturnell and J. Calvin Smith.[76]

Henry Poor became almost at once the society's most active cartographer. In 1854 he was given charge of constructing a large 15 x 30 foot map of the United States on which the proposed routes of the Pacific railroad were to be depicted. The map, drawn to the scale of six inches to a degree, was executed, under Poor's supervision, by George Schroeter, the society's first paid assistant. It was complete enough by June 1854 for Poor to use it to illustrate a paper he delivered to the society on the Pacific railroad. In 1855 Poor traced on a revised copy of this map all the railroads then in operation or under construction in the United States, listing in the margin the names of these roads and giving their lengths. This map, regularly revised, undoubtedly became the master chart for the railroad maps of the United States which Poor published annually as a supplement to the *Railroad Journal.*[77]

Besides giving Poor a useful training in map-making, the Geographical Society helped him to keep abreast of current statistical developments. Its library was at that time one of the best sources of statistical information in the United States. Moreover, in the society's quarters Poor often consulted with some of the very few professional statisticians, compilers, and gazetteers in America, including Disturnell, J. Calvin Smith, Richard S. Fisher, and one of the earliest theoretical statisticians in this country, Archibald Russell. Poor's interest in geography, cartography, and social statistics strongly affected the caliber and content of the *Railroad Journal,* and in turn his editorial work for the *Journal* quite naturally stimulated his interest in geography and statistics. Poor was one of those fortunate men for whom the line between vocation and avocation is slim. Both reflected what he liked to consider one of his major objectives in life — the acquisition of useful knowledge to be applied to useful ends.

Poor's wide range of interests and activities as well as his place in the business and social world of the day can best be summarized by describing briefly the four-month trip he took to England in the summer of 1858. What he did there, who he saw, the comments he wrote home all help to delineate the full dimensions of the man and to emphasize again the close interrelation between his avocations and his vocation. In this way the story of the journey provides an opportunity to review Poor's qualifications as a business editor.

The editor owed his trip to the directors of the Mississippi Central Railroad. Unable to raise funds to purchase the rails needed to complete their road, they asked Poor to obtain the money and purchase the rails in London.[78] He accepted their invitation readily. At that moment he could hardly turn down a chance to earn some extra income, for the depression of that year had cut down or postponed payments from subscriptions and advertising in his paper. Moreover he had long hoped to visit Britain and had a particular desire to study her railroads.

The business for the Mississippi Central took only a little of the time he had in England. The road was conservatively financed and at least two of its promoters, Walter H. Goodman and Uriel A. Murdock, were, like Poor himself, well known in London financial circles.[79] The major difficulty was, Poor wrote his wife, that "Englishmen have been so taken in by American R.R. projects. The road I represent, however, has paid cash for whatever they bought, and propose to pay in money after a little credit for the purchases I wish to make." [80] After a month of negotiating with George Peabody and his associate Curtis Lamson, two shrewd Yankee-bred London bankers, Poor arranged a contract by which Peabody agreed to deliver 6,500 tons of rails at New Orleans within a year.[81] He then had to await the arrival of the road's president, Walter Goodman, to sign the contract, after which the two planned to raise more funds for the road in England and on the Continent.

During the first two months of his stay Poor spent most of his time talking to railroad engineers and financiers. His first interview, which took place only a day or two after he reached London, was with Robert Stephenson, the dean of British railroad engineers, with whom he spent an afternoon discussing the role of government in controlling transportation facilities.[82] He learned much from several long sessions with his friend Douglas Galton, probably the most knowledgeable man on railroads in England. He spent two evenings with Sir Charles Fox, the developer of the railroad switch and the engineer who, after building the London and Birmingham, pioneered in railroad construction in India, France, Australia, Canada, and South Africa. Later Fox, who had been knighted for his work in designing the Crystal Palace, took Poor for an extended tour of this impressive edifice. The American editor spent another enlightening day visiting the offices and shops of the Great Western Railway with Daniel Gooch, its superintendent of motive power and one of England's most distinguished locomotive designers. From his talks with these and other men, and from the many government and private railroad reports and statistics he collected, Poor wrote a series of articles on British railroad administration for his *Railroad Journal*.

Britain's railroad financiers and financial experts interested Poor as much as did her railroad builders and administrators. He talked with and dined at the homes of James Wilson, the editor of the *Economist* and Financial Secretary to the Treasury under Palmerston, and Marmaduke B. Sampson, the internationally known financial editor of the London *Times*. These two men appear to have been as anxious to learn Poor's views on the ability of American railroads to recover from the 1857 crisis as Poor was to get information from them on the finance and profits of British roads. Poor's views on American railroad finance also interested bankers and brokers like Robert Benson, Thomas Smith, Henry Thomas Hope, William Lance, and Joseph Fisher, with whom the New York editor spent many hours conferring, either at their offices in the city or at their town houses, and on weekends at their country places.[83]

Poor also had to attend to Geographical Society business. At the request of the Royal Geographical Society in England, he had brought with him for exhibition his huge 15 x 26 foot railroad map of the United States, revised to include the vast amount of new information disclosed by the government surveys of routes for a railway to the Pacific coast. The American society had further commissioned Poor to protest against the remarks made in a recent meeting of the British society impugning the accuracy of statements made by Elisha Kane. The American society had a direct interest in the achievements of this Arctic explorer since it had helped promote and finance his expeditions.

Poor carried out both these tasks at a meeting of the Royal Geographical Society held on June 14. There the American delivered a paper describing his map and the sources for his cartographical data, and then gave a brief account of the topography of the United States. After this the society's president, Sir Roderick Impey Murchison, handsomely apologized for the misunderstanding about Kane, explaining that it had been caused by inaccurate newspaper reports.[84] Two weeks later Poor was a guest of honor at the society's anniversary dinner. Seated between the affable Sir Roderick and a charming and amusing dabbler in poetry and politics, Richard Monckton Milnes, Poor enjoyed himself immensely. The only dinners equaling this one, Henry wrote Mary, were George Peabody's celebrated affairs, three of which he had attended within six weeks of his arrival.

By the end of July Poor began to find time a little heavy on his hands. Most of his railroad and business friends had left London for the summer, but the editor, waiting for Goodman, was forced to stay close to the city. He, therefore, turned his attention to social reform. On his arrival Poor had been struck both by the need for improvement in Britain's political and social structures and by the ambitious efforts which were being made toward reform. "In England, there are vast abuses to be reformed," he told Mary, "abuses that have stood 1,000 years and which still rear their hoary heads." Yet in spite of the size of the task, "the gallant set of knights that is meeting the challenge do more than we are doing at home." [85]

Poor's interest in reform and in the work of fellow reformers led him to collect data on British social and legal organizations. For, as he emphasized in his letters home, only when the nature of the institutions creating social inequities was thoroughly known could an effective program of improvement and reform be created. He began buying volumes of statistics from parliamentary and government offices and searched bookstores, libraries, and the large collections in both the Royal Statistical and the Royal Geographical societies for additional information. These written data he supplemented by talking to leading reformers. He called on John Bright, Milnor Gilson, and James Wyld, prominent advocates of reform in Parliament. He spent several evenings with Edwin Chadwick, whose brilliant work in revising the poor laws and factory acts made him an expert on law as well as on the conditions of the depressed classes, and whose activities on the Sanitary Commission made him an authority on England's health,

Poor spent even more time with the Reverend Samuel Martin, who impressed him as much as any man he had met in England. Martin showed Poor the "Ragged School" for the children of the destitute, the "Reform School" for the rehabilitation of released prisoners, and other social innovations he had made in his parish, located in one of London's dreariest slums.

Poor never found time to make a careful analysis of the mass of information he had collected.[86] Still his concern for and approach to learning about reform in Britain reveal much about the ways of his mind. The inequalities of wealth and status in England disturbed Poor primarily because he thought they forced wickedness and evil on society. To eliminate such causes of evil, the editor believed, was one of man's most important tasks. The basic prerequisite to this reform was, in his opinion, an understanding of the broad institutional framework of society. And the initial step to such an understanding was the collection of accurate factual data. By applying reason to this information, the ways to improve man and to eliminate evil could be found. "The race progresses through *reason,*" he reminded Mary, "not through the sentiments or affections. Men become humane as they become intelligent. Sympathy never created hospitals nor restrained the power of a tyrant or a church." [87]

Here then is Henry Poor as he appeared in the year 1858, a reformer, geographer, statistician, journalist, man of business, and an accepted expert on American railroad finance and operation. He enjoyed the friendship and often the confidence of many of the social, intellectual, and business elite of his day; as a journalist who had little innate talent for writing or specific training in journalism, he learned to evaluate and analyze data effectively, and to present his findings clearly. As an editor who was not an original thinker, he was fully aware of the major intellectual developments of the day and wholeheartedly accepted the current optimistic faiths in reason, progress, and the perfectibility of man. He was quite convinced that through his editorial work, the collection and dissemination of information and ideas, he would help his fellow men to move along the road of material and moral progress.

Intellectually and psychologically well equipped to be a forceful business editor, Poor had less actual business experience than he might. He knew at first hand, before coming to New York, the problems of railroad promotion. At his office on or near Wall Street he came to learn intimately the problems, methods, and intricacies of railroad finance. Yet not until after he left the *Journal* did he serve in a position of authority and responsibility in a railroad or any other large business corporation. Poor, therefore, rarely had the sobering experience of making critical business decisions. He never really faced the difficult task of making irrevocable decisions on the basis of insufficient information between confused or unclear alternatives. Lacking this type of experience and being morally certain of the need for and value of improvement and reform, Poor in his editorials tended to criticize a little too indiscriminately and to suggest too simple and easy answers to some very complicated problems. As a result his reforms, while they usually had a valid basis, often failed to achieve immediate tangible results. Like so many editorial commentators Poor's therapy frequently had less value than his analysis. Still, compared to other nineteenth-century business editors, Poor was quite experienced in business matters. No other of these journalists had carried heavier business responsibilities than the editor of the *Journal.* And even though some had taken part in railroad promotion, very few had had Poor's close acquaintance with railroad finance.

In many ways, in fact, Poor's background, training, and talents differed from his fellow editors.[88] They were not businessmen or lawyers who became editors, but in most cases were trained journalists who turned to business journalism when the expanding opportunities of this new specialty grew apparent. Very few of these men had gone to college. Still fewer had Poor's close association with the intellectual and social reform movements of the day. Yet, oddly enough, none had been raised as close to the frontier as had this friend of many American intellectuals, reformers, and businessmen. Only in his concern with the compilation and publication of economic information did Poor have much in common with the editors of other business and trade journals. Three other business editors were, for example, members of the American Geographical and Statistical Society. What differentiated Poor from other trade journalists also set him apart from the railroad managers and entrepreneurs about whose work he wrote. Comparatively few of these railroad men were college graduates or were raised on the frontier, and almost none were concerned with social reform.[89]

Such dissimilarities in interests and education helped Poor to understand the problems and needs of the railroad industry differently from most of his competitors and from the railroad operators themselves. This uniqueness may have accounted for the occasional original insights Poor had into railroad problems. In any case his education, his talents, and his wide range of interests all contributed to make him one of the country's most distinguished pioneer business editors and to maintain the *American Railroad Journal* as one of the leading business periodicals of its day.

⁎ 2 ⁎

The American Railroad Journal

POOR'S EDITORIAL WORK and writings were more than the product of his special abilities, his education, business experience, and other interests. They were shaped also by the nature of the paper he edited. When Poor became its editor the *American Railroad Journal* had been for seventeen years one of the best known trade and business papers in the country. During that time policies had been set which Poor would continue to follow. These policies, however, had been determined less by the efforts of previous editors than by the needs of the business and railroad world. An examination of these needs which led to the flowering of business journalism in the mid-nineteenth century and an account of the specific history of the *American Railroad Journal* before 1849, is, therefore, necessary for an appreciation of the framework in which Poor exercised his talents and put to use his training.

Although Poor pioneered in business journalism, he was certainly not the first editor or journalist to meet the rapidly growing demand for business and trade information during the mid-nineteenth century. By that time there was a plethora of periodicals being published in the United States. Many of these — the news, literary, political, religious, educational, and reform papers — helped to entertain, inform, educate, and culturally broaden the American reader. Others provided him with more practical information useful in the carrying out of his daily business. Of the papers providing business information in the broadest sense there were by mid-century four important classes, the commercial, the agricultural, the scientific, and the industrial journals.[1]

Of these four, the commercial papers had the longest history.[2] The earliest colonial newspapers included commercial news. During the rapid expansion of American shipping and commerce after the War of 1812 commercial information began to fill the pages of the newspapers of the larger cities. Some newspapers like the *Com-*

mercial Advertiser, the *Mercantile Advertiser,* the *Daily Advertiser,* and the *Journal of Commerce* of New York; the *Daily Advertiser* and the *Commercial Gazette* of Boston; the *North American and Daily Advertiser* and the *Commercial List and Maritime Register* of Philadelphia and those even more specialized periodicals, the *Prices Current* and *Shipping Lists* printed in New York, Philadelphia, Baltimore, and New Orleans concentrated specifically on providing business information. They listed prices of wheat, flour, provisions, fish, textiles, and a large number of other products and commodities. Besides local prices, quotations were given for other American cities and important foreign ports. Shipping movements were carefully described. The editors of these papers often commented on fluctuations and differentials in prices and occasionally gave brief analyses of changing market and trade conditions.

In the first half of the nineteenth century magazines as well as newspapers and the weekly *Prices Current* carried commercial news. The most famous of the nation's early weeklies, *Niles' Weekly Register* devoted some, though surprisingly little, space to comments on commercial conditions and development.[3] The mid-century regional periodicals like *De Bow's Commercial Review of the South and West* and the *Western Journal and Civilian* provided more general commercial information; although, like *Niles',* these papers concerned themselves chiefly with local industry, transportation, agriculture, politics, and literature. In 1839, however, two journals were founded specifically to provide information of interest to the merchant and shipper. One, the *United States Commercial and Shipping Register,* established by Samuel Hazard in Philadelphia, lasted only three years. This failure probably resulted from the fact that Hazard supplied much the same type of data as the daily papers and the several *Prices Current.* The other, *Hunt's Merchants' Magazine,* founded in New York by Freeman Hunt, was eminently successful. Hunt printed reports and documents of more than day-to-day interest to men of commerce. He also published articles of general interest to businessmen. These included detailed accounts of different cities and ports, discussions of current economic and political problems and issues — particularly those concerning trade and finance, and even biographies of influential businessmen.

In 1846 two other important periodicals concerned with commerce and finance were founded.[4] One of these, the *Dry Goods Reporter and Commercial Glance,* concentrated at first on information concerning textile importation but later, when Thomas Prentiss Kettell became its editor and changed its name to the *United States Economist,* it dealt with a much wider range of commercial and financial matters.

Kettell more than Hunt analyzed current developments in the money and commercial markets.

The second, founded in 1846, was the *Banker's Magazine.* Although two earlier attempts by such famous editors as Condy Raguet and William B. Gouge to start periodicals devoted to finance and banking were short-lived, I. Smith Homans' *Bankers' Magazine* immediately obtained and maintained a profitable subscription list. Homans, like Hunt and Kettell, not only provided valuable information to his readers, but acted as spokesman for the bankers and merchants on issues of political and economic interest. These last three periodicals, *Hunt's Merchants' Magazine,* Kettell's *United States Economist* and Homans' *Bankers' Magazine,* all provided during the 1850's a good deal of information on railroads and, therefore, competed to a degree with Poor's *Railroad Journal.*

The other two classes of business journals, the agricultural and scientific periodicals, while not in competition with the *Journal,* are significant to the background of its story; for the first constituted the largest class of business or service papers published in the 1850's and the second was the direct forerunner of the industrial journals of which Poor's paper was the oldest and best known. By 1850 over thirty agricultural periodicals were published in different sections of the country.[5] Though most were published as commercial ventures, a few appear to have been at least partially subsidized by private and state agricultural societies. A number of the leading farm journals were published in New York City, where one of the foremost agricultural editors, John S. Skinner, published *The Plough, the Loom and the Anvil* for many years at 9 Spruce Street in the office adjoining Poor's. The primary purpose of these papers was to act as a clearing house for agricultural information. As such they carried a mass of data written by the editors, by contributors who were almost always unpaid, and by subscribers and others in their letters to the editor. These writings dealt with soils, farming techniques, fertilizers, new types of seed, breeds and plants, agricultural chemistry, farm machinery, drainage, and so forth. Besides this major function, the journals often spoke for the farmer by advocating state and national aid for agricultural improvements, for education, for improved transportation, and once in a while for a tariff on farm products. They offered on a small scale a means by which land agents, commission merchants, farm suppliers, and agricultural manufacturers could advertise their goods and services.

The scientific and mechanical journals, which were as old as the agricultural periodicals, were like them in many ways. Benjamin Silliman founded the *American Journal of Science* in 1818, the year before John Skinner began the pioneer American agricultural periodical, the *American Farmer*.[6] Silliman's journal, while concerned first with developments in the natural and physical sciences, included much practical information on applied science and the uses of new techniques and processes in American industry, transportation, and agriculture. The two other most significant scientific periodicals, the *Journal of the Franklin Institute,* founded in 1826, and the *Scientific American,* started in 1845, concentrated even more on the development of new industrial and engineering methods and inventions. The mechanics' journals which flowered after the 1820's were almost wholly concerned with describing useful gadgets and inventions for the home, shop, and farm. Like the agricultural papers the mechanics' papers were aimed at the ordinary man and served as a significant channel for providing and interchanging information on ways to improve the products and expand the production of the artisan and farmer. Like the farm papers, too, they were often connected with an organized group, a society like the New York State Mechanics Association or a more learned one like the Franklin Institute. As shops expanded into factories and as artisans were replaced by machines, these scientific, technical, and mechanical periodicals began to find readers among the owners, managers, and foremen in the rising textile, iron, and railroad industries. As such they were the direct forerunners of the industrial periodicals.

With the business boom of the 1850's the industrial periodical came into its own. In 1849 when Poor became editor of the *American Railroad Journal* there were only two or three other industrial periodicals being published in the United States. By the end of the decade of the 1850's, however, the iron, the mining, the textile, the printing, the carriage, the harness, the shoe and leather, the gas-light, the telegraph and the insurance industries all had one or more trade papers.[7] Railroad journalism was particularly active in that decade. Within ten years after Poor became editor, five weekly and two monthly railroad periodicals were begun; and all but two had a comparatively long life.

The industrial and especially the railroad journals had much in common with the other types of service periodicals. This close connection is demonstrated by the fact that Minor, when he founded the *American Railroad Journal* in January 1832, was editing or publishing a newspaper, the New York *American,* besides two agricultural papers, the *New York Farmer and American Gardener's Magazine* and the *Plough Boy,* and a mechanics paper, the *Mechanics' Magazine.*[8] The latter he incorporated into the *American Railroad Journal* in 1838. Also Minor and later Poor printed information taken from nearly all the journals mentioned here, and they in their turn borrowed a good deal of material from the *Journal,* for most of the service papers were interested in one way or another in railroads.

The industrial journals carried out functions similar to the other papers. Like the farm and commercial periodicals they acted as spokesmen for the occupational interests of their readers. They pled for government aid and protested against government interference. They did much to promote their industries in general and some, especially the railroad papers, to encourage individual companies. Also, like the farm journals, the industrial periodicals acted as a means by which the various firms in the industry and their suppliers could advertise their wares and their services. Their most important function, however, was, like that of all other types of service periodicals, to provide information useful to their readers in carrying on their trade or business.

II

The importance of providing useful information is particularly well illustrated by the *Journal's* history, since it was the oldest industrial and one of the oldest mechanical papers in the United States. The early story of the *Journal,* besides helping to make clear the nature of the first trade papers, indicates the type of policies and programs Poor inherited, shows some of the problems the American railroads faced in the years before Poor became a railroad analyst, and tells a little about the compilation of railroad information and statistics before Poor began his work of collecting and publishing accurate data on American railroads.

Probably the most significant fact about the *American Railroad Journal* when Poor became its editor was that it had existed for seventeen years. At any time during the nineteenth century this was a long life for a periodical; but in the years which included one of America's longest and severest economic depressions, it was most exceptional. Periodicals were short-lived primarily because in these years they had to rely on subscriptions to meet their cost. Except for a few agricultural journals and organs of scientific or technical associations, few service papers were subsidized. Only a small portion of their income came from advertising. In 1849 Poor estimated the advertising income of the *Journal,* which was probably larger than most, at $1,200 a year as compared to an estimated $6,000 from subscriptions.[9] To stay alive the *Journal,* like most other trade and business periodicals, from the very first had to supply enough useful information to persuade its readers to pay a comparatively high subscription rate.[10]

When D. Kimball Minor decided to publish in the last days of

1831 a journal devoted to railroading, that means of transportation was in its very infancy.[11] Still the thought of rapid cheap overland transportation had captured the imagination of many Americans, much as the airplane and air travel did in the first decade of the twentieth century. Minor, experienced journalist that he was, undoubtedly saw a chance to capitalize on the enthusiasm for the new machine. He soon, however, became thoroughly convinced of the future of the new method of transportation.

From the beginning the *Journal* was the spokesman for the new industry. Minor printed letters, reprinted articles, reports, newspaper exchanges, and once in a while wrote an editorial, all of which were intended to show the superiority of the railroad over the canal and the turnpike as a means of transportation. As spokesman for the industry, the *Journal* emphasized the need for assistance from the national government through mail subsidies, tariff exemptions for rails and equipment, the use of army engineers for surveys, and for direct financial assistance from the states. Minor printed much to help promote individual companies as well as the industry as a whole. For example, he concentrated on the promotion of New York's railroads, particularly the Erie. He was able to obtain a little advertising, some of which came from suppliers of railroad and engineering equipment, but more from the railroads themselves. The roads used the *Journal* both as a place to display their schedules and fares and to advertise for bids on contracts for construction. The *Journal,* after Poor became its editor, continued to carry on these functions of spokesman, promotor, and advertiser.

Yet Minor's promotional activities and his services as spokesman of the industry were not in themselves enough to attract the number of subscribers needed to make the paper a paying proposition. What did permit the *Journal* to survive, particularly during the depression years of the late 1830's and early 1840's, was the engineering and technical information it provided. The supplying of technical information came less from Minor's initiative than from the imperative need for such data in the railroad world. Almost immediately after the appearance of the first issue of the *Journal,* a civil engineer working on the Baltimore and Ohio wrote Minor:

> Something of the kind has for a long time appeared necessary as a means by which the variety of information connected with this subject may be collected and disseminated. Rail-roads unlike other means of internal communication, have various modes of construction. Canals and turnpikes differ very little under any circumstances. But you will scarcely find two of all the numerous projects of Rail-roads now in progress in this country, whose construction is after the same plan. Even on the same work a variety of modes is sometimes used, as, for instance, on the Baltimore and Ohio

AMERICAN RAILROAD JOURNAL.

STEAM NAVIGATION, COMMERCE, MINING, MANUFACTURES.

HENRY V. POOR, Editor.

ESTABLISHED IN 1831.

PUBLISHED WEEKLY, AT No. 136 NASSAU ST., NEW YORK, AT FIVE DOLLARS PER ANNUM IN ADVANCE.

SECOND QUARTO SERIES, VOL. IX., No. 5.] SATURDAY, JANUARY 29, 1853. [WHOLE No. 876, VOL. XXVI.

PUBLISHED BY J. H. SCHULTZ & Co., 136 NASSAU ST.

PRINCIPAL CONTENTS.

American Railroad Journal.

Saturday, January 29, 1853.

Considerations addressed to Foreigners who wish to invest in Securities of American Railroads.

We have recently received numerous applications from Europe, from parties wishing to invest in their stocks and securities, for information respecting our railroads, the rights secured to companies by their charters, the relation they sustain to the governments and laws of the several States, in fine, for all such information as would enable a person in England or Germany, to form a correct idea as to the value of our roads, as investments of capital. The low rates, and the difficulty of finding employment for money, in England particularly, has turned the attention of capitalists to this country, and should the favorable opinion now entertained of our railroads be confirmed, a large amount of capital would at once flow hither for investments, not only in their securities, but stock; and we are happy to take this opportunity and mode of replying to the queries addressed us, intending to convey an entirely correct idea of the *legal* relations sustained by our companies, and hoping to present a view of the objects, uses, and probable value of our roads, that will be sufficiently understood.

It is probably pretty well understood, even in Europe, that all the charters of railroads in this country proceed from the several *State* governments; the general government never claiming to exercise, if it possesses, this power, which is generally denied. As an ordinary rule, a charter for a railroad is granted as a matter of course, and in a number of States, there are what are termed "*General Railroad Laws*," which provide for the organization of railroad companies, and the construction of railroads, without application to the Legislature. In either case, there is little difference in the privileges conferred; the object of the *General Laws* being to save the necessity of application to the Legislature in each particular case, and to place all companies on an equal footing.

A charter for a railroad necessarily carries with it all the powers essential to the construction of a road, the company is a unit as far as its legal relations are concerned. Its property occupies the same relations to the government, as does that of the individual citizen; the government, in the former case, retaining only such control over the companies, as is necessary to provide for the safety, and protect the rights of the community and the stockholders. It has no (we now speak of all the States) control over their management (with the exceptions stated), dividends nor property, any more than it has over the conduct or property of the individual citizen, which can only be taken in an imminent necessity, such as war, and then only by making full compensation.

The *special* charters frequently designate the leading points on the route. A few of those first granted in several States limited the dividend to 10 per cent per annum, and their legal existence to a certain period. But as a general rule, both *special* and general charters are perpetual in their duration, and are unrestricted in their dividends.

In accordance with the tendency in this country to *general*, instead of special legislation, and to provide an uniform mode for the organization of companies, which have the same general characteristics and objects, many of our leading States have enacted such *general* laws, authorising the construction and providing for the management of railroads. New York was the first to take this important step in liberal legislation, and the leading features of her law have been copied by the other States which have followed her example. This law provides that any number or company of her citizens may associate themselves for building a railroad, and upon subscribing at the rate of $1000, and the payment of $100, per mile for the length of the road, into the treasury of the company, and on filing in the office of the Secretary of State the articles of the association, which set out its objects, the route, the title of the company and the capital stock proposed to be raised, the Secretary of State, as a matter of course, issues a charter, conferring legal authority to carry out the objects of such association. Under this authority the company may proceed to the construction of the road, and do every necessary act for this purpose. Such company may build their road when and where they choose, and parallel to those already in operation, whether constructed under a general, or special, charter, may borrow whatever money, and upon such rates of interest, and upon such time, and declare such dividends, as it may deem proper. The law entirely ignores the expediency of protecting rights which are based on priority in point of time, but throws open the construction of railroads to the competition of the public, and makes this right the common privilege of all, as is the building of ships, steamboats, or manufacturing establishments.

There can be no doubt whatever that the public interests are immensely benefitted by *general* laws. Instead of stimulating the building of railroads beyond the wants of the community, they only promote their healthy progress. When the right to build a railroad always exists, and can be exercised as well at one time as at another, and when no advantages are forfeited by delays, parties will take a suitable time for reflection before they act.—Where, too, every road is exposed to the liability of having a parallel rival road upon its immediate route, those constructing it will be very certain to avail themselves of the strongest of all monopolies, and which is secured by adopting the *best* and *cheapest* route. Men do not go into ship building unless with a good prospect of making money, which cannot be the case provided the ships already built have sufficient capacity, and are sufficiently adapted to the business for which they were constructed. So with railroad construction in New York. If an existing road meets the wants of the country traversed, there is little disposition, or danger, that a rival will be constructed; and to ward off such danger, it is necessary that such road should be well built and well managed. We have therefore the constant and immediate corrective of

The format of the *American Railroad Journal*

RAILROAD SHARE LIST, including Mileage, Rolling Stock, etc., etc.

An *asterisk* (*) occurring in the column headed "Rolling-Stock," signifies that the cost is included in that of "Railroad and Appurtenances." A *dash* (—) signifies "nil." Running *dots* (.....) signify "not ascertained." Land-Grant Railroads are in "*italics*."

Years ending	Railroad: Main Line	Railroad: Lateral and Branch Lines	Railroad: 2nd Track and Sidings	Road in progress or projected	Equipment: Engines	Cars: Passenger	Cars: Freight, etc.	Companies	Property and Assets: Railroad and Appurtenances	Property and Assets: Rolling-Stock	Property and Assets: Invested in foreign works	Liabilities: Share Capital paid in	Liabilities: Bonded and Mortgage Debt	Liabilities: Floating Debt	Balance Total, incl. all other assets and liabilities	Road operated, incl. road leased, etc.	Mileage run by locomotives with trains	Earnings: Gross	Earnings: Net	Dividends	Price of shares
	M.	M.	M.	M.	No	No	No.		$	$	$	$	$	$	$	M.	M.	$	$	p. c.	p. c.
								NEW YORK.													
30 Sep. '59	—	—	—	140.0	—	—	—	Albany and Susquehanna	406,952	—	—	404,950	—	31,135	436,085	—	—	—	—	—	....
30 Sep. '58	32.9	—	3.3	—	5	12	53	Albany and Vermont	1,557,502	136,038	—	439,005	1,575,099	60,000	....	32.9	93,894	84,119	11,215	—	....
30 Sep. '59	38.3	—	34.0	—	—	—	—	Albany and West Stockbridge	2,392,984	*	—	1,000,000	1,932,984	....	2,392,984	oper. by Western.			....	6	100
30 Sep. '59	34.9	2.6	....	73.6	4	6	39	Black River and Utica	1,156,148	81,405	—	804,648	700,000	8,158	1,512,806	37.5	36,838	62,941	32,962	—	....
30 Sep. '59	14.8	—	1.6	—	—	—	—	Blossburg and Corning	496,661	—	—	250,000	220,000	....	....	14.8	20,647	26,858	13,429	5	....
30 Sep. '59	142.0	—	13.6	18.5	28	32	386	Buffalo, New York and Erie	3,150,762	*	164,200	680,000	2,592,221	252,142	4,206,709	235.0	487,589	541,249	172,321	—	....
30 Sep. '59	68.3	—	18.0	—	28	34	312	Buffalo and State Line	2,467,258	312,736	449,000	1,934,850	1,049,000	161,263	3,145,213	87.8	370,488	848,327	419,378	10	120
30 Sep. '59	24.6	—	38.1	—	—	—	—	Cayuga and Susquehanna	1,067,629	37,971	—	687,000	411,000	....	1,098,000	34.6	61,435	59,266	10,398	4½	....
30 Sep. '59	17.4	—	2.1	—	—	—	—	Chemung	400,000	*	—	380,000	70,000	....	450,000	oper. by N. Y. & E.			24,000	6	....
30 Sep. '59	46.8	—	2.9	—	10	8	83	Elmira, Jefferson & Canand.	500,000	*	—	500,000	....	....	500,000	oper. by Receivers.			30,000	6	....
30 Sep. '59	—	—	—	63.2	—	—	—	Erie and New York City	287,357	*	—	352,741	14,000	28,716	395,457	—	—	—	—	—	....
30 Sep. '59	—	—	—	15.0	—	—	—	Genesee Valley	329,225	*	—	75,689	165,000	62,500	329,225	oper. b. B. N. Y. & E.			....	—	—
30 Sep. '59	17.3	—	0.5	—	4	3	50	Hudson and Boston (West'rn)	148,000	27,000	—	175,000	—	—	....	17.3	57,065	63,803	11,999	6	....
30 Sep. '59	144.0	—	106.5	—	52	107	542	Hudson River	10,205,906	1,182,372	—	3,758,466	8,842,000	414,644	....	150.0	700,224	1,842,636	770,096	—	41
30 Sep. '59	—	—	—	73.8	—	—	—	L. Ontario, Auburn & N. York	74,203	—	—	75,771	....	....	....	—	—	—	—	—	....
30 Sep. '59	—	—	—	182.0	—	—	—	L. Ontario and Hudson River	3,497,538	178,320	—	2,715,186	870,000	115,856	....	—	—	—	—	—	....
30 Sep. '59	84.0	2.5	10.1	8.5	18	37	129	Long Island	2,211,659	354,611	1,000	1,852,715	636,997	17,559	2,567,270	101.5	248,123	334,195	147,084	—	11¼
30 Sep. '59	297.8	258.1	313.8	—	211	237	3,171	New York Central	25,164,200	5,257,077	588,980	24,000,000	14,333,771	—	40,366,005	655.9	3,945,128	6,200,848	2,791,419	7	78½
30 Sep. '59	448.0	19.0	282.5	—	219	194	2,763	New York and Erie	31,148,015	4,172,192	1,311,385	11,000,000	25,326,505	2,074,795	38,401,300	495.0	3,019,000	4,282,149	1,404,837	—	16½
30 Sep. '59	130.8	2.1	30.9	—	33	93	576	New York and Harlem	7,303,339	634,777	—	5,717,100	5,151,287	147,640	....	152.9	621,747	975,853	358,792	—	12
30 Sep. '59	118.0	3.8	17.7	—	28	8	417	Northern (Ogdensburg)	4,097,208	702,079	—	3,077,900	1,500,000	....	4,799,287	121.8	347,800	382,932	120,850	—	....
30 Sep. '59	35.9	—	2.2	—	7	6	44	Oswego and Syracuse	675,215	100,462	—	396,340	213,500	10,875	....	35.9	69,759	109,152	60,829	8	....
30 Sep. '59	75.4	—	2.0	—	6	4	33	Pottsdam and Watertown	1,527,072	67,884	—	665,419	911,000	192,748	1,769,167	75.4	107,046	100,047	47,571	—	....
30 Sep. '59	25.2	—	2.1	—	5	13	70	Rensselaer and Saratoga	743,968	157,057	—	610,000	140,000	—	901,025	46.2	61,900	235,902	108,769	6	....
30 Sep. '59	18.4	—	1.3	32.6	—	—	—	Rochester and Genesee Valley	652,151	1,776	—	557,560	150,000	23,496	731,056	18.4	135,000	44,220	24,661	2	....
30 Sep. '59	18.0	—	1.0	—	—	2	32	Sacketts Harbor and Ellisburg	371,556	17,714	—	167,485	278,400	56,810	....	18.0	17,620	12,025	—	—	....
30 Sep. '59	21.0	—	1.6	—	2	3	10	Saratoga and Schenectady	480,684	*	—	300,000	85,000	—	385,000	oper. by Ren. & Sar.			30,150	7	....
30 Sep. '59	40.9	6.6	3.9	—	9	12	84	Saratoga and Whitehall	820,518	74,904	—	500,000	395,000	—	895,000	54.5	107,506	154,099	7,493	—	....
30 Sep. '59	—	—	—	13.2	—	—	—	Staten Island	114,015	*	—	50,603	41,200	22,686	114,489	—	—	—	—	—	....
30 Sep. '59	11.0	—	....	—	—	—	—	Brooklyn and Jamaica	369,856	—	—	284,850	85,000	—	....	oper. by Long Isl.			37,560	9	....
30 Sep. '59	81.3	—	7.1	—	13	12	117	Syracuse and Binghampton	2,851,292	*	—	1,200,130	1,643,125	146,079	2,989,335	81.3	176,273	196,402	112,155	—	....
30 Sep. '59	27.2	—	3.2	7.7	10	6	76	Troy and Boston	1,366,826	143,687	—	604,911	806,500	247,676	1,659,087	51.0	194,921	218,680	103,010	—	....
30 Sep. '59	6.0	—	0.1	—	—	—	—	Troy and Greenbush	294,731	—	—	275,000	—	....	294,731	oper. b. Hud. River.			....	6	....
30 Sep. '59	2.1	—	2.1	—	—	—	—	Troy Union	732,114	—	—	30,000	680,000	....	732,114	oper. by other Co's.					....
30 Sep. '59	96.8	—	11.0	—	7	11	288	Watertown and Rome	1,839,787	319,715	—	1,498,500	685,000	65,683	2,249,183	96.8	219,280	362,994	154,752	3	....
								NORTH CAROLINA.													
.. .. '58	95.2	2.0	....	—	....	....	....	Atlantic and North Carolina	1,850,000	*	—	1,600,000	400,000	....	....	95.2	....	....	....	—	....
.. .. '58	223.0	—	....	—	....	....	....	North Carolina	4,235,000	*	—	4,000,000	....	....	....	223.0	....	....	....	—	....
.. .. '59	97.0	—	....	—	....	....	....	Raleigh and Gaston	1,240,241	*	—	973,300	126,200	....	....	97.0	....	206,917	108,541	—	....
30 Sep. '59	161.0	—	17.1	—	22	20	144	Wilmington and Manchester	2,586,238	*	201,500	1,127,511	1,060,000	111,856	2,892,969	171.0	....	487,043	209,793	—	....
30 Sep. '59	161.9	—	....	—	24	32	144	Wilmington and Weldon	2,869,223	*	107,000	1,340,213	791,055	102,391	3,114,954	171.0	323,069	477,554	235,201	8	....
15 Mar. '58	—	—	—	43.0	—	—	—	Western North Carolina	190,793	*	4,700	290,212	—	70,860	364,072	—	—	—	—	—	....
								OHIO.													
.. .. '58	—	—	—	....	—	—	—	Atlantic and Great Western	613,231	....	—	866,939	—	77,294	....	—	—	—	—	—	....
31 Dec. '58	118.2	—	....	—	17	12	208	Bellefontaine and Indiana	3,008,919	*	11,000	1,879,370	1,274,828	39,028	3,370,281	118.2	....	332,226	146,812	—	....
1 Aug. '59	137.0	—	....	—	41	39	508	Central Ohio	5,579,508	922,670	106,133	1,628,356	3,673,000	1,126,458	6,810,432	141.0	....	597,622	71,356	—	....
31 Mar. '59	60.3	—	....	—	22	28	432	Cinc., Hamilton and Dayton	2,648,266	504,892	26,500	2,155,800	1,411,000	32,918	3,650,716	60.3	....	489,437	249,666	7	66
.. .. '59	37.0	—	....	62.1	—	—	—	Cinc. and Indianapolis Junc.	....	....	—	....	—	—	....	37.0	....	—	—	—	42
1 May, '59	131.8	—	....	31.0	16	10	332	Cinc., Wilmington and Zanesv.	6,250,841	*	—	2,441,176	3,032,000	228,973	....	131.8	304,168	190,745	19,180	—	....
31 Dec. '58	135.4	5.8	....	—	42	31	439	Cleveland, Columbus and Cinc.	4,087,571	684,955	67,422	4,746,100	38,000	8,242	5,343,275	141.2	....	1,113,639	575,159	7	92
31 Dec. '59	67.0	—	....	18.0	10	6	205	Cleveland and Mahoning	1,920,953	*	—	580,000	1,202,300	161,200	1,943,500	67.0	183,973	285,140	182,282	—	....
31 Dec. '59	95.4	1.2	37.9	—	31	39	453	Clev., Painesville & Ashtabula	3,431,732	555,343	541,503	3,000,000	1,667,000	35,500	4,812,201	96.6	402,935	1,111,353	646,057	15	111
30 Nov. '58	101.0	102.5	....	—	42	....	....	Cleveland and Pittsburg	9,320,288	*	—	3,942,368	4,918,325	653,821	9,661,102	203.5	646,413	772,093	332,083	4	8
30 Apr. '59	109.2	79.4	....	—	32	52	430	Cleveland and Toledo	6,729,056	458,194	258,424	3,343,812	3,842,720	358,605	7,858,918	188.6	....	798,155	414,456	6	29
31 Dec. '58	61.4	—	....	53.0	5	6	99	Clev., Zanesville and Cincin.	1,574,693	*	—	369,673	575,250	632,486	....	61.5	75,120	68,128	19,763	—	....
31 Dec. '58	72.0	—	....	31.0	6	9	103	Columbus and Indianapolis	2,555,000	*	—	750,000	1,600,000	205,000	....	72.0	144,000	84,000	17,760	—	....
30 Nov. '58	54.5	—	10.4	—	—	—	—	Columbus and Xenia	1,376,250	392,909	112,734	1,490,000	290,700	50,500	1,965,539	oper. w. Lit. Miami.			170,795	8	84
31 Dec. '58	72.0	—	....	72.0	....	....	....	Dayton and Michigan	3,746,000	*	—	1,620,000	2,126,000	....	....	72.0	144,606	124,559	66,779	—	....
31 Aug. '58	36.6	—	....	—	5	3	87	Dayton and Western	930,262	104,912	—	289,692	700,000	90,482	1,080,174	36.6	....	125,940	66,253	—	....
31 Aug. '58	16.0	—	....	47.0	3	2	21	Dayton, Xenia and Belpre	860,496	*	—	437,838	422,658	....	....	16.0	40,064	64,000	33,000	—	....
31 Dec. '58	45.0	—	....	—	6	5	72	Eaton and Hamilton	1,101,744	79,022	62,630	469,762	728,853	152,694	1,358,867	45.0	105,304	151,866	44,615	—	....
.. .. '59	36.0	—	....	84.0	....	....	....	Fremont and Indiana	....	....	—	....	....	....	....	—	—	—	—	—	....
31 Aug. '58	32.0	—	....	—	6	5	68	Greenville and Miami	888,000	*	—	500,000	473,000	75,000	....	47.0	60,901	63,141	13,573	—	....
30 Nov. '58	13.0	—	....	34.0	1	2	56	Iron	172,830	*	—	118,865	50,000	3,965	....	13.0	24,000	31,126	10,460	—	....
30 Nov. '58	83.5	—	37.8	—	39	32	602	Little Miami	3,451,179	785,817	438,857	2,981,293	1,399,000	34,196	4,709,137	138.0	637,855	1,200,499	341,591	8	86¼
31 Dec. '58	173.8	21.6	....	—	33	26	523	Marietta and Cincinnati	9,517,551	1,115,662	574,000	3,477,705	7,405,917	1,754,220	13,202,262	195.4	556,732	374,198	45,452	—	....
30 Apr. '59	192.3	—	....	—	48	34	628	Ohio and Mississippi	18,635,[illegible]	*	*	6,584,681	9,880,000	2,330,030	18,794,721	192.3	....	881,957	312,441	—	....
31 Aug. '58	117.0	8.0	....	—	17	16	238	Pittsburg, Columbus and Cin.	4,772,951	*	—	1,906,736	2,400,000	466,215	....	125.0	....	....	....	—	....
30 Jun. '59	153.9	52.0	....	—	39	27	365	Sandusky, Dayton and Cinc.	5,988,154	605,900	197,967	2,697,090	2,134,000	439,261	5,508,257	205.9	....	577,958	211,894	—	....
30 Dec. '58	116.0	9.0	....	—	13	20	206	Sandusky, Mansfield & New'k	2,141,811	*	—	828,583	1,402,572	132,301	2,363,456	125.0	155,006	209,918	51,371	—	....
30 Nov. '58	55.6	—	....	74.0	7	3	64	Scioto and Hocking Valleys	1,163,975	*	—	403,975	500,000	100,000	....	55.6	70,000	110,200	53,100	—	....
31 Aug. '58	19.5	—	....	23.5	—	—	—	Springfield and Columbus	346,500	—	—	193,000	150,000	3,500	346,500	oper. by C., C. & C.			....	—	....
30 Nov. '58	49.8	—	....	62.2	5	6	62	Springfield, Mt. Vern. & Pittsb.	2,205,000	*	—	1,000,000	1,050,000	200,000	2,250,000	49.8	222,000	....	....	—	....
.. .. '58	243.0	—	....	—	35	18	580	Toledo, Wabash and Western	10,542,000	*	—	3,573,000	7,650,000	—	11,223,000	250.0	....	676,022	159,769	—	19¼
								PENNSYLVANIA.													
30 Nov. '59	45.0	—	3.0	136.2	4	6	97	Allegheny Valley	1,700,000	65,200	—	1,660,000	400,000	20,000	2,080,000	45.0	....	87,940	45,000	—	....
31 Aug. '59	20.5	—	23.2	—	15	2	1,005	Beaver Meadow	966,792	290,000	—	1,410,900	2,000	....	1,412,900	20.5	....	311,201	164,554	10	....
31 Aug. '59	63.5	—	3.0	—	22	13	282	Catawissa, Williamsp't & Erie	3,518,785	364,571	—	1,700,000	2,271,536	436,228	4,407,764	119.0	....	337,257	90,438	—	....
30 Sep. '59	52.5	—	3.2	—	11	8	66	Cumberland Valley	1,225,971	*	—	981,900	245,500	55,643	1,299,194	52.5	142,944	169,125	94,311	6	....
31 Dec. '59	110.8	2.3	36.0	—	....	....	....	Del., Lackawanna and West'n	8,831,707	*	505,000	3,360,872	6,070,125	569,190	11,064,413	202.0	....	1,430,512	881,609	—	82
30 Nov. '59	36.3	—	2.3	—	3	3	—	East Pennsylvania	900,000	16,617	—	386,121	365,500	188,515	940,136	36.3	....	—	—	—	....
30 Sep. '59	18.6	—	4.0	—	....	....	....	Erie and Northeast	700,000	....	—	600,000	400,000	....	1,000,000	oper. b. Buf. & S. L.			....	10	....
31 Aug. '59	36.9	18.6	21.9	—	—	—	—	Harrisburg and Lancaster	1,882,555	....	—	1,087,100	661,000	....	1,883,343	55.5	....	[illegible]	166,852	6	54
31 Aug. '59	32.3	—	1.2	44.1	3	2	17	Hempfield	1,388,168	*	—	1,809,563	....	....	1,809,563	32.3	....	[illegible]	7,267	—	....
31 Aug. '59	30.9	11.3	4.6	—	6	3	1,000	Huntingdon and Broad Top	1,354,724	*	—	425,015	1,000,000	206,550	1,631,565	42.2	....	84,017	3,413	—	....
30 Sep. '59	68.9	—	2.2	11.1	10	6	318	Lackawanna and Bloomsburg	2,057,393	107,000	—	710,000	1,100,000	167,303	2,164,303	68.9	—	116,200	67,600	—	....
30 Nov. '59	45.7	—	....	20.2	15	6	....	Lehigh Valley	....	*	—	1,966,250	1,500,000	....	....	45.7	....	525,846	333,896	6	25
30 Nov. '59	28.0	5.0	13.5	....	9	....	....	Little Schuylkill	3,299,600	*	—	2,256,100	942,500	85,000	3,299,600	oper. by C., W. & E.			....	—	....
1 Dec. '59	20.0	—	4.0	—	....	....	....	Lehigh Coal and Navigation	1,380,000	....	4,455,000	2,470,900	3,619,304	231,532	9,291,156	....	....	695,857	503,660	6	52½
30 Nov. '59	24.5	74.8	45.5	1.5	28	2	3,026	Mine Hill and Schuylk. Haven	2,594,228	266,838	....	2,800,000	....	....	2,991,150	72.3	....	556,192	379,976	10	....
30 Nov. '59	55.6	10.1	9.7	—	16	15	531	North Pennsylvania	5,449,061	398,997	—	3,155,829	2,787,060	377,818	6,320,638	65.7	....	347,302	188,398	....	8½
1 Dec. '59	330.0	56.0	350.0	—	213	98	2,492	Pennsylvania	23,009,849	2,974,473	862,762	13,249,125	16,932,517	....	31,356,832	388.0	....	5,362,355	2,221,617	—	75
30 Sep. '59	12.0	—	0.3	67.0	1	1	1	Phila. and Baltimore Central	264,000	10,000	—	—	250,000	50,000	....	20.0	....	1,637	—	—	....
30 Sep. '59	17.0	7.0	....	—	16	....	....	Phila., Germant'n & Norrist'n	1,422,977	228,555	—	1,208,500	374,800	104,720	1,742,333	24.0	....	288,657	167,194	—	....
30 Nov. '59	147.4	4.0	61.0	—	149	57	5,697	Philadelphia and Reading	19,390,868	2,121,010	20,180	11,737,041	12,195,950	1,125,000	26,057,991	151.4	....	2,724,293	1,245,816	....	41
1 Dec. '59	28.0	—	—	—	—	—	—	Philadelphia and Trenton	1,000,000	—	—	1,000,000	—	—	1,000,000	28.0	oper. by Cam. & Amboy			....	....
30 Oct. '59	98.0	6.0	....	—	31	60	487	Phila., Wilmington and Balt.	7,788,786	*	78,962	5,600,000	2,498,435	370,078	8,468,513	—	11 mos.	1,086,168	437,499	6	48½

A page from Poor's Stock and Bond List

Rail-road, where four different methods of *construction,* or more definitely of laying rails have been pursued. If engineers or other persons feeling sufficient interest in the matter, were to make communications from time to time, imparting such information in relation to the work on which they may be engaged, as would lead to a knowledge of the manner of construction noting defects, suggesting improvements, and in a word, giving any statements which would be collected, and through your useful paper disseminated, that would lead to results in the Rail-road department of Engineering highly important and advantageous to the public.[12]

Other engineers were interested. Many wrote Minor in the next few months heartily endorsing their colleague's suggestion. They soon began to contribute as well as subscribe to the *Journal.*[13] As the contributions increased, the paper became more and more an engineers' journal. Its technical content was further expanded in 1836, when George Schaeffer, an experienced New York civil engineer, joined in partnership with Minor and took over most of the work of editing.[14] In 1838 Minor was away from New York most of the year; and in 1839, discouraged by the effect of the depression on the subscription list, he sold his interest in the *Journal* to Egbert Hedge, the printer, leaving Schaeffer as the sole editor. Before Minor's return to the paper in 1843, Schaeffer had made it one of the leading technical journals in the United States, if not the world.

The need for information on engineering, which was so well expressed in the letter from the Baltimore and Ohio official to Minor, arose fundamentally from the experimental nature of railroad construction. American railroad builders had few precedents to rely upon. In the United States, there were, as compared to Europe, few trained or qualified engineers. Moreover, in this country personal communication between engineers was far more difficult than in Europe. As a result, the *Journal* not only supplied essential information, but became probably the most important formal channel of communication between railroad builders. In this way it helped prevent, in the words of an able American engineer, Benjamin H. Latrobe, the wasting of "a vast deal of sterling talent and precious time . . . in reinventing what has already been invented and applied." [15]

The *Journal,* under Minor, Schaeffer, and later Henry Poor, filled the need for technical engineering information first of all through the articles and letters written by prominent engineers. These contributions, for their authors were never paid, indicate, like the other sources of information, the amount and the nature of the data exchanged, and also suggest the changing types of engineering and technical problems which faced the railroad builder during the 1830's and 1840's. In the early years, the *Journal's* contributors concentrated first on problems of surveying, alignment, and curvature. Then they turned more to problems of construction — the building of the permanent way, bridges, and tunnels. By the late 1830's and early 1840's their major concern was with rolling stock and included such a wide variety of items as braking, axles, cranks, and lubrication. Finally many engineers, and none more enthusiastically than Charles Ellet, highly successful railroad and bridge builder, turned to examining questions of rates, rate-making, and operating costs.[16] These contributors, who included nearly all the leading engineers in the United States, also wrote on a number of technical matters other than those directly concerned with railroads.[17]

A second source of technical information provided by the editors of the *Journal* was reprints taken from newspaper exchanges and from other railroad and technical papers which, except for the *Journal of the Franklin Institute,* were published abroad. Especially useful to American engineers was the republication in installments of professional tables, texts, and treatises, including the works of such important European writers as Peter William Barlow, Nicholas Wood, and Peter Lecount on rails and road beds, and F. M. G. de Pambour on locomotives.

Even more valuable, however, were the railroad reports printed regularly in the *Journal.* Some of these annual reports, statements of engineers on survey and construction, and reports on operations and experiments with equipment, were provokingly vague and general. But others, much more detailed, accurate, and thorough, like those of J. Edgar Thomson of the Georgia Central and Benjamin H. Latrobe of the Baltimore and Ohio, provided engineers throughout the world with firsthand information on the working out of complex problems of railroad construction and operation. Minor undoubtedly reflected the views of many a railroad builder when he wrote of the reports issued by the officers of the Baltimore and Ohio:

> [We] cannot refrain from here expressing our own and we believe we do not say too much when we say the thanks of the whole *Railroad* community, as well in *Europe* as in AMERICA, for the candid, business-like and liberal manner in which they annually lay before the world the result of their experience.
>
> It will not be saying too much, we are sure, to denominate them the *Railroad University* of the United States. They have labored long, at great cost, and with a diligence which is worthy of all praise, in the cause; and what is equally to their credit, they have published annually the result of their experiments and distributed their reports with a liberal hand that the world might be cautioned by their errors and instructed by their discoveries.[18]

Certainly the European engineers did praise the reports of the Baltimore and Ohio and other American railroads,[19] for during the experimental period of railroad construction, the conditions the Continental engineers faced both as to terrain and traffic were closer to those in the United States than those in Britain. In learning from the American experience, these Europeans undoubtedly acquired much useful information from the pages of the *American Railroad Journal*.[20]

Poor, when he became editor of the *Journal*, continued to print the articles, letters, reprints, and reports which his predecessors had. However, more than Minor or Schaeffer, Poor compiled these data into a compact, usable, and often statistical form. If the earlier editors failed to do this, it was not because they were not urged. Engineers, both American and European, complained repeatedly of the difficulty of using American railroad reports to make meaningful comparative studies. They found it especially hard to compile adequate data from enough roads to draw up authoritative analyses of construction and operating costs of American railroads. Benjamin Latrobe was echoing the complaints of Charles Ellet, Franz Anton von Gerstner, and other engineers when he wrote the editors of the *Journal* in December, 1843:

> The collection and arrangement of railway statistics has heretofore met serious obstacles in the irregular and incomplete manner in which most railroad reports are presented to the public. Many details essential to the derivation of general principles and practical results from the working of the railroad system are altogether wanting in their reports, and those particulars which are given, are often expressed and arranged so as to be useless, or available only at the expense of much time and labor.[21]

As one method of removing obstacles in the way of collecting railroad statistics, Latrobe urged Minor and Schaeffer to send copies of a questionnaire, which he forwarded with his letter, to all the roads in the country. After the railroads had filled out and returned these forms covering their "character, cost and operations," Minor and Schaeffer might then compile annually a complete and accurate statistical summary of the railroads of the United States. The editors failed to act on Latrobe's suggestion. They may have thought that Latrobe was overoptimistic about the railroads' coöperation in this plan. More likely, they shied away from the work and cost involved in such an ambitious program. In any case, regular and systematic collection of railroad statistics in the United States was left for Henry Poor to begin a decade later.

Railroad journalism developed in Europe quite differently from the way it did in the United States, undoubtedly because the British and Continental railroad builders who used the *Journal* to advantage in learning of the American experience, had in their own lands other more formalized means for the interchange of information. In Britain, the engineering societies, the Institution of Civil Engineers and the Society of Mechanical Engineers, provided highly effective channels of communication. On the Continent, the great schools — the École Polytechnique and the École Centrale des Arts et Manufactures in Paris, and the Royal Polytechnic Institutes in Berlin and Karlsruhe — were even more important than the professional societies in the dissemination and exchange of engineering data.[22] The European railroad journals, therefore, found little demand for technical information among their readers. The first of these papers, the *Railway Magazine,* a monthly founded in London three years after Minor began publishing the *Railroad Journal* in New York, concerned itself primarily with defending the railroads from the attacks of canal and turnpike operators, property owners, and conservative-minded persons throughout the kingdom. When the able and spirited John Herapath, a man with engineering training, took over this periodical in 1836, he printed many articles on technical matters, most of which he wrote himself. Before the end of 1839, however, he had transformed it into a weekly financial paper. The success of the *Railway Times,* founded in 1837 to provide financial news only, convinced Herapath that in England the need for financial news far outweighed the call for technical information. By the mid-1840's, when railroad construction reached boom proportions, and when the capital invested in railroads had increased tremendously, a half dozen railroad journals were being published in England.[23] Across the English Channel, the same pattern held. The *Journal des Chemins de Fer,* the leading Continental railroad paper, founded in 1842 under the editorship of the economist, Adolphe Blaise, was far more interested in railroad promotion and finance than in technical matters. It was not until the publication of the *Archiv für Eisenbahnwesen* in Berlin in the 1880's that a European railroad periodical began to concern itself primarily with the technical problems of railroading.

The editor of the *American Railroad Journal,* watching the success of the British financial papers, decided that his paper should follow suit. In November 1845, only a few months after Schaeffer resigned as coeditor, Minor told his readers that the time had come for the publication of a weekly paper concerned with the management and financial affairs of American railroads. The subject matter of the paper during the past years, Minor reminded his readers, "has kept our circulation almost entirely among engineers." To increase his circulation, Minor proposed:

> To bring out a weekly paper which shall not only be useful to the Engineer, but we hope indispensable to that large portion of the community who look to railways as offering a safe, permanent and productive invest-

ment of capital; or, we may say briefly, that we aim at a Railway Journal for *stockholders,* and those taking a general interest in the progress of railways and other public works, as well as for Engineers who have the superintendence of construction and the management of railroads.[24]

Minor's attempt to make the *Journal* a financial paper was premature. In the United States no large portion of the community yet looked to the railroads for investment. For a time Minor did run an "American Share List" similar to those in the British periodicals, but the data he included were fragmentary and he made little attempt to keep it up to date. Within a year, Minor had dropped the list from the paper.

Unable to make his journal a financial paper, Minor now failed to maintain it as an engineering organ. He only occasionally printed articles on technical matters, and made few attempts to encourage engineers to contribute. After 1845, the paper's primary function became what Minor had considered it to be when he first began publication—that of spokesman for and promoter of railroads. The editor delighted in encouraging new projects by printing their prospectuses, reports, articles by their promoters, and occasionally by writing laudatory editorials on their behalf.[25] Yet even here, Minor put himself at a disadvantage by moving the paper from New York to Philadelphia in 1846, at a time when railroad construction was concentrated in New England. As these changes in policy and location were soon reflected by a drop in circulation and continuing loss of income, Minor was happy late in 1848 to sell the *Journal* and depart for the California gold fields.

For the seventeen years before Poor became its editor, then, the *American Railroad Journal* had carried on many of the major functions of a modern trade paper. Minor had made it the spokesman for and promoter of the industry. In its columns individual roads and promoters had made known their projects; while on its advertising pages the railroads, railroad suppliers, and engineers had displayed their wares and services. Most significant of all, the paper, through articles by contributors, letters, reports, reprints from books, other periodicals, and occasionally editorials had provided information of real value to railroad men. That this information in the early years of the *Journal* was largely technical indicates the nature of the first major problems the railroad industry had to face and solve. It also reflects the experimental nature of the early railroad building and the lack of other channels such as the professional society and the engineering school for the collection and dissemination of technical and engineering information.

In providing information and other services, the editors, both

Minor and Schaeffer, played an essentially uncreative role by printing information they received from subscribers and unpaid contributors and by culling pretty much at random from newspaper exchanges, periodicals, and technical books. They made little effort to systematize the compilation, collection, and publication of information, nor did they attempt to provide data of their own through their editorial columns or to synthesize and analyze their material in occasional editorials.

III

After Poor became editor of the *American Railroad Journal* he not only carried on its earlier functions, but as the decade of the 1850's passed, he increasingly came to speak for the railroad investor in particular. For a while, at least, he helped promote individual roads as well as the industry as a whole. At the same time he revived the *Journal's* position as an engineering organ, and in the mid-1850's he succeeded, where Minor had failed, in making the *Journal* a financial paper. Further, he expanded the paper's role as an advertising medium. Most important of all, Poor enlarged the editor's function by playing a more active part than his predecessors in the systematic compilation and collection of business information, and using these data to write weekly editorials on developments, problems, and needed reforms in the railroad industry.

One of the first things Poor did as editor was revive the *Journal's* technical content. Realizing he was not competent to write on technical matters, he hired in July 1849 M. Butt Hewson, a well trained engineer recently arrived from England, to be assistant editor in charge of engineering. Hewson immediately began to fill the *Journal* with articles on the technical aspects of railroad construction as well as on other professional subjects such as bridges, canals, water works, dams, and river drainage.[26] At the same time he collected and reprinted engineering information from reports and other journals, papers, and books. This increase in the *Journal's* technical content encouraged engineers, who since Schaeffer's departure had lost interest in the paper, to contribute regularly again.

The articles now sent in by John A. Roebling, Benjamin H. Latrobe, John F. Winslow, Thomas A. Rogers, George L. Vose, Zerah Colburn, and other engineers were concerned almost wholly with bridges, rails, locomotives, and railroad machinery. As this new emphasis indicated, the major problems of American railroad construction had been solved by the early fifties. The success of the construction engineers, symbolized by the almost simultaneous completion of four east-west trunk lines in 1852 and 1853, only intensified the problems of the bridge builders and mechanical engineers. The steeper grades, longer hauls, and heavier loads required them to develop larger, more efficient locomotives, rolling stock, and equipment, as well as heavier rails and stronger bridges.

To meet the changing situation, Poor converted his civil engineering department into one for mechanical engineers. Some time after Hewson left New York for a position in the Southwest, Poor asked Zerah Colburn to take over the new department. Colburn, though only twenty-one when he began writing for the *Journal* in 1853, was already one of the best-known mechanical engineers in the country.[27] Trained in the textile machine shops in Lowell, he had worked as a superintendent at the Souther locomotive works in Boston, and for Rogers, Ketchum and Grosvenor in Paterson, New Jersey. In 1851 he published *The Locomotive Engine, Theoretically and Practically Considered,* one of the earliest handbooks on American locomotives. In his articles for the *Journal,* Colburn continued his studies of the locomotive, considering the latest developments in boilers, valves, drivers, axles, wheels, tires, and so forth. He made comparative studies of engines operated on different roads or manufactured by different firms, occasionally illustrating his comments with finely executed engravings. He described the most recent technical improvements which effectively reduced costs, and he often chastised conservative managements, especially in New England, for failing to make use of improved machinery and new methods of operation.[28]

Colburn remained with the *Journal* only a little over a year. He and Poor apparently clashed violently on some matter, for Colburn left the paper in anger, and relations between the two men remained acrimonious for some time.[29] After breaking with Poor, Colburn immediately set up in New York City his own paper, the *Railroad Advocate,* a weekly journal "addressing itself to master mechanics, machinists and engineers." [30] Although ably edited, first by Colburn and then jointly by Colburn and Alexander P. Holley, another brilliant young engineer, the *Advocate* failed to make money. The loss of advertising during the panic of 1857 finally put the paper out of business.[31]

With Colburn's departure, Poor discontinued his special engineering department. He did, however, continue for two more years to pay such competent engineers as Theodore Krauch and Thomas Stetson, a former editor of *Appleton's Mechanics Magazine,* to write on technical subjects.[32] For a time, too, engineers continued to contribute unpaid articles to the paper. By 1857, however, the *American Railroad Journal* had almost completely dropped its technical content. Colburn and Holley's *Railroad Advocate* had become between 1854 and 1857 the primary source of technical information for the American railroad industry. After the *Advocate's* demise, the *Railway Times*, a small regional and financial paper published in Boston, helped fill the demand for these types of data by hiring as an editor George L. Vose, one of the most articulate American engineers of the day.

In 1849, when he began editing the *Journal*, Poor envisaged his paper as of use to other engineers besides those in the railroad industry. In the late spring of that year he began a department for "manufactures and mechanic arts," with Charles T. James as editor in charge, and a department for "mining and metallurgy," headed by James T. Hodge. The first of these departments lasted only a few months, for James, a successful and vocal Rhode Island textile manufacturer, stopped writing for the paper after the summer of 1849. The mining department was more successful. Until 1851 Hodge, a geologist and mining engineer experienced in mining exploration, regularly carried out his function of describing "the various mining districts and smelting operations of the United States . . . including geological descriptions of localities, as well as accounts of actual mining operations and treatment of ores." [33] Hodge, like Hewson and Colburn, kept his readers up to date on developments in their profession by reprinting relevant information on mining engineering which he found in American and European newspapers and periodicals. Poor further strengthened the *Journal's* position as a mining paper by purchasing in June 1849 the *Mining Journal and American Rail-road Gazette.* This weekly, founded in New York in 1847, a weak imitation of the London *Mining Journal,* was a small four-page affair consisting primarily of reprints from other newspapers and periodicals.[34]

In 1851, however, Poor decided to drop the mining department. Hodge had made the *Journal* a spokesman of the iron industry, especially in its demands for an increased tariff.[35] Though Hodge's stand on the tariff probably increased the *Journal's* circulation among iron manufacturers, it antagonized the railroads. In 1850 and 1851 a great construction boom was getting under way, and the last thing the railroad industry wanted was an increase in the cost of rails and other railroad iron, nearly all of which was imported from England. Since the *Journal* was the leading railroad organ in the country, and since Poor sincerely believed that cheap iron was essential for the construction of railroads and hence for the economic good of the nation, he felt obliged to let Hodge go. After 1851 the technical content of the *Journal* concerned itself only with the problems of railroad engineering.

In the early years of Poor's editorship, the information published on railroad engineering appears to have affected significantly his ideas about railroads. From talking with many eminent American engineers, and from reading copy on engineering matters, he acquired a competent layman's grasp of the technical aspects of railroad construction and operation. Besides increasing his understanding of railroad problems, this intimate contact with the engineering profession reinforced his careful, analytical approach.[36] All in all, Poor, by serving the engineers, became more competent to paint the portrait of the railroads as a young industry and more able to provide railroad managers and investors with essential business information.

Besides reviving the technical content of the *Journal,* Poor in his first years as editor made a concerted effort to expand its advertising columns. From the very beginning of its publication by Minor, the *Journal* had relied on three main sources of advertising. There were the railroad companies themselves who had used the *Journal* to give their time tables and rates of fare and to advertise for bids for construction contracts.[37] During the 1850's, with the rapid increase in the number and size of railroad guides published specifically to give train schedules and fares, the roads dropped this type of advertising in the *Journal.* However, with the building boom of the early 1850's, the space devoted to advertising for construction bids increased.

A second source of advertising income was from the civil engineers and firms and institutions which serviced that profession. The engineers kept their names before the railroad managers by having their "cards" placed in the advertising columns of the paper. Often too they advertised their availability for new positions. Publishers of engineering books, makers of instruments, and even such educational institutions as the Harvard Lawrence Scientific School exhibited their wares in the advertising pages of the *Journal.*[38] In the latter part of the 1850's, when the *Journal* became more of a financial paper, this source of advertising also dwindled, but it was replaced by banking and brokerage houses who wanted to display the securities they had for sale.

Firms which manufactured and commission merchants who supplied a large variety of railroad equipment constituted the third type of advertisers. It was this source on which Poor concentrated. Partly because of his efforts and partly because of the rapid growth of the railroad supply business in the 1850's, these companies soon provided the major portion of the *Journal's* advertising income. In encouraging the suppliers to use his columns Poor pioneered in the advertising of producers' goods. Advertising, the editor often repeated in the

1850's, was just as important to a locomotive works as it was to a soft drink manufacturer. In 1855, in an article entitled "Philosophy of Advertising," he remarked:

> This is a philosophy which is but imperfectly understood. There are a few truths connected with it which should always be borne in mind. *First:* — the *object* of advertising is to keep the NAME, LOCATION and BUSINESS familiar to the minds of that class of people to whom we look for patronage. *Second:* the CHANNEL best adapted to the attainment of the above object. . . . *Third:* the QUANTITY AND QUALITY of matter which is best adapted to secure CONFIDENCE in the community. . . . *Fourth:* What *length of time advertising should be continued to give the best effect?* The answer is plain and reads thus: *Until the business is given up.* . . . If a man wants car springs does he not at once think of Ray; if equipments, of Bridges; if engines, of Rogers, or Danforth, or Blandy, or Breese, or Norris, or Hinkly, or Mason or Swinburne, etc.? Certainly, and because their names are inseparably connected with their business just as much as is that of Townsend with Sarsaparilla, or Barnum with the Museum, or Genin with Hats, or Brandreth with Pills, or Goodyear and Day with Rubber. It is just this having one's name and business so familiarized to the public mind, and the two so connected that the mention of the *one* immediately suggests the other that constitutes the success of advertising.[39]

As the number of firms wanting to display their goods to railroad men grew rapidly, Poor was able to increase both the rates charged and the space devoted to advertising. In 1849 the rates were three dollars a column and eight dollars a page, with sizable reductions for long term insertions.[40] By 1854 the rates had risen to ten dollars a column and twenty-five dollars a page, where they remained for the rest of the decade. These rates were above the average prices charged by the other types of magazines in the 1850's and, except for the *Railway Times* of Boston, were much higher than those charged by most other railroad periodicals.[41] At the same time the space devoted to advertising nearly doubled. After 1851 eight unnumbered pages of advertising were added to each issue.

Nevertheless Poor's major source of income throughout his editorship remained his subscription list. In spite of the many railroad papers, seven in all, which were founded in the decade after he became the *Journal's* editor, he maintained the high subscription rate of five dollars a year. All but two of his competitors charged the then more standard rate of three dollars a year. These two exceptions, Colburn's *Railroad Advocate* and the *United States Railroad and Mining Register*, actually asked only two dollars a year.[42] Despite his higher rates, Poor rarely found cause to complain, although his competitors did repeatedly, about unpaid subscriptions; nor did he have to make special offers for long term subscriptions or for reducing rates on orders of two or more subscriptions.[43] Moreover, he appears to have increased his circulation in spite of the growing competition. When he took over the paper he counted on a subscription list of 1200.[44] By 1854 he claimed a fourfold increase in circulation with a total of 30,000 readers and according to this claim sold between 4000 and 5000 copies weekly.[45] He then lived in large part on the income from his paper and, since he could afford a substantial home, two or three servants, summer vacations away from New York for the family, and private school and college for the children, these claims seem quite credible.[46]

Poor's financial success was adequate testimony to his abilities as an editor. Although he had revived the paper's circulation among American engineers and expanded his income from advertising, his financial success came primarily from attracting new readers. Businessmen, investors, and railroad managers began subscribing to the *Journal* in the early 1850's largely because of the quality of the information they found in its pages. But also, most certainly, they did so because of Poor's weekly editorial analyses of the current developments in the railroad industry and his outspoken editorial policies urging careful, conservative expansion of the industry and all possible improvement and reform.

* 3 *

Initial Editorial Policies

IN 1849 three matters particularly concerned the railroad world: the depression in New England, the building of a railroad to the Pacific, and the growing construction boom in the South and West. On these topics Poor concentrated his editorial attention during his first year or so as editor of the *American Railroad Journal.* His initial editorials, besides describing the railroad situation at mid-century, help make clear what he considered at the beginning of his career to be the functions of a specialized industrial periodical and the duties of its editor. Furthermore, they emphasize many of his basic ideas about railroads and the collection of business information.

Poor's articles on the railroad depression in the Northeast provide a particularly useful introduction to his editorial writings because New England's experience in the 1840's proved to be a foretaste of what would occur in the rest of the nation in the 1850's. During the mid-forties New England enjoyed one of the most prosperous periods in her history. Shipbuilding boomed, the output of the textile industry nearly doubled, and construction was begun on a large number of railroads.[1] Then, after the region's surplus capital had been heavily invested in textile mills and railroads, came the worldwide business recession precipitated by the collapse of the British railroad boom of 1847. The resulting financial crisis in New England forced her railroad managers to think about problems of finance and operation which railroad men of the rest of the nation did not have to face until the depression of 1857. In investigating the causes and suggesting remedies for the New England railroad crisis, Poor first came to grips with those problems of railroad finance and management to which he would later, during the middle and late 1850's, devote so much of his editorial attention.

To Poor most of New England's railroad troubles were the result of inexperience and a lack of reliable business information. Inadequate data, he contended, encouraged the construction of many railroads unwarranted by existing commerce. Too many New Englanders, Poor pointed out, failed to analyze realistically the potential traffic of a projected road. They merely accepted the financial success of the first New England railroads as a guarantee that "any road proposed was sure to pay." [2] In Poor's opinion, the most flagrant case of commercially unsound construction was the line of roads running from Massachusetts to Lake Ontario, including the Vermont Central, the Vermont and Canada, and the Northern. These lines, Poor correctly predicted, would have the greatest difficulty in competing with the Western Railroad and the Boston and Worcester for the trade of the West.[3] Nor would they have enough local traffic to meet the costs of construction and operation. More information and more understanding about the realities of geography and commerce, Poor maintained, would have saved the supporters of these roads a great deal of money.

Yet in writing about Maine railroads, Poor himself refused to face such realities. During his initial years as editor he enthusiastically endorsed his brother's roads, especially, after 1850, the European and North American.[4] Few roads in the United States had poorer prospects for local business or more problematical prospects for through traffic than the European and North American. Poor's support came partly from family loyalty; but also he had become quite convinced by his brother's and, indeed, by his own arguments. The *Journal's* editor would undoubtedly have been incensed at the suggestion that men often refuse to act on information, no matter how reliable, if they choose not to do so. Yet Poor consistently refused to consider the facts in his support of the European and North American.

Uninformed assumptions about railroad traffic of projected roads were, Poor stressed, only one cause of New England's difficulties. Even more serious was the inability of the managers of many roads already in operation to obtain an accurate picture of the financial situation of their companies. Before the depression in late 1847, New England railroad directors had tended to declare excessive dividends and issue overly sanguine reports. Such dividends and reports had in turn both encouraged the construction of unnecessary roads and forced the price of railroad stocks far above their true value. In their optimism about the profits of their roads, these railroad managers were not, as many critics were arguing, incompetent or dishonest. They had been misled, in part, Poor maintained, "from want of experience in these matters [of financial management] which, it is not to be expected, could keep pace with the very rapid development of railroads." [5] But, just as important, they lacked adequate information.

In the New England states, directors too often failed to consider fully enough the costs of continuing construction, or of repairs and renewals. "In this country," Poor pointed out, "every road of any considerable magnitude requires the united strength of those interested in its construction to build it." [6] Yet, as in the case of the Atlantic and St. Lawrence, the united financial strength was frequently not enough to meet the cost. Since many a road was, therefore, built as cheaply as possible, "the work of repairs must be commenced almost as soon as it goes into operation." Furthermore, the desire for income "causes them to be put into operation before they are fitted to receive their equipment." Yet the amount spent "to put them in this condition is put out to the world as their ultimate cost, and the proportion that their earnings bear to this cost is taken as the rate of dividends that they are capable of paying."

If the managers of the newer roads failed to account for what amounted to continuing construction costs, Poor further pointed out, those on the older roads rarely put enough money aside to meet the expenses of renewals and replacements. Still more rarely did they give thought to the less obvious problem of long-term depreciation. Too many directors apparently believed that "all surplus earnings over the cost of running the road" should be issued as dividends. "There can be no greater mistake," the editor warned. "There should always be set apart, before making a dividend, a reserve fund equal to the annual wear of the road, though the amount reserved may not be required to be laid out for years." [7] Moreover, Poor was convinced that on the very few roads which had depreciation funds the amount set aside was too small. Using British experience to judge the American conditions, he estimated that 6 per cent of their annual initial cost should be set aside for rails, and on most railroads, the additional depreciation "in their equipment, in the various kinds of wood work used, runs all the way from 10 to 20 per cent." [8]

There was an obvious connection, Poor believed, between this inadequate understanding of railroad accounting and the depressed condition of railroad stock on the Boston market. He analyzed the current low price of railroad securities in the following way. After 1845 the recently opened roads found themselves spending nearly all their income to pay for construction, repair, and renewal charges. At the same time the older roads were forced to expend increasingly large funds to replace rails, ties, locomotives, rolling stock, and other equipment. To meet these expenses, many of which they considered only temporary, most New England directors issued more stocks or borrowed money on short-term notes in preference to a curtailment of dividends. Then with the money stringency of late 1847 and 1848, the market for new stocks collapsed and the cost of borrowing money soared. Unable to raise funds either locally or in the Boston market, most roads were driven to cut their dividends drastically. Uninformed investors, startled by the unexpected decrease or even cessation of their dividends, sought to sell their shares, pushing the price of railroad stocks down still further. In this way the prices paid for stocks in 1849 and 1850 were as far below the true earning value of that stock as the prices paid in 1846 and 1847 had been above this value. It is little wonder, then, concluded the editor of the *Railroad Journal,* that in 1849 unhappy stockholders on so many railroads were instituting investigations and raising the cry for economy and reform.[9]

To Poor the basis for reform was reliable information. This must be provided, he insisted, before the other suggestions for curing New England's railroad troubles could be effective. Therefore he wrote little about the continuing controversy over the ways to determine the most profitable rates. Although he favored low fares, he thought rate changing would have little immediate effect on the railroad depression.[10] Nor did he at this time say much about the "gross" construction contract, the mortgage bond, municipal aid, and other new techniques New England roads were adopting to meet their financial difficulties. Instead Poor looked for ways to assure the publication and general dissemination of the facts about railroad finance and operation.

To obtain more reliable data Poor first called for more accurate reports from the railroad companies themselves. He urged the state legislatures to follow the example of Massachusetts and New York and require annual reports for all roads operating within their territories. At the same time, taking his cue from John Herapath and editors of other British railroad papers, he began to analyze reports of New England roads, pointing out omissions, discrepancies, and undocumented claims.[11] To guarantee with even more certainty the collection and publication of reliable statements, Poor suggested that:

Each State institute a commission, composed of men of acknowledged character and reputation as engineers, whose duty it shall be on the opening of any road, or any section of it, of 20 miles or more in length, to make a thorough examination into the affairs of such a road and report — 1st. The actual amount expended on the portion opened. 2nd. The sums necessary to complete the road, or such portion as may have been opened. 3rd. The amount of indebtedness of the road. 4th. The character of the work, and the probable amount that will be annually required for repairs and depreciation of property and deterioration of way; and such further information as may be necessary to give a full and accurate knowledge as to the condition and value of such road, it being made obligatory upon directors to furnish under proper sanctions all the information required of them.[12]

The commission should also be empowered to obtain similar data from the roads already in operation. Such information, Poor reminded his readers, would be of inestimable value to railroad managers. It would also help prevent violent fluctuations of railroad stock prices and the exploitation of these fluctuations by a "designing director" or "gambling speculator." [13] Since railroads "would soon become our leading monetary interest," Poor urged the state legislatures to act quickly on his proposal.

As the New England railroad depression continued, Poor began to call for operational as well as financial reform. Here again the primary difficulty was inexperience and insufficient information. As Poor pointed out, the preoccupation with construction problems during the rapid expansion of the New England railroad system had allowed very little time for the study of the economics of operation. New England must, he stressed, quickly give serious thought to improving operating methods. For, "while the cost of many items of construction has been reduced from 50 to 100 per ct., the result of our increased experience, the cost of running roads regularly increases." [14]

Efficient management depended first of all on well-trained managers. Yet such men were hard to find. "The demands of new works increase much faster than they can be met by engineers of experience," Poor emphasized. "Their superintendence must, therefore, be entrusted to those who qualify themselves for their duties as they go along." [15] The qualifications were rigorous because few occupations in Poor's opinion required a more thorough preparation in and broader knowledge of engineering, business, and handling of men. By the end of 1850 Poor was convinced that the caliber of the railroad manager, and with it the efficiency of railroad operation, could best be improved through a more formal systematizing of the "intercommunication of ideas and experience." [16]

In words which were quite similar to those used by Benjamin Latrobe a few years earlier, Henry Poor pointed out the many obstacles currently hindering this essential interchange of information. The engineer, who by training and inclination disliked to write, all too rarely recorded his experiences. Moreover, in the United States there was no obvious central place like London or Paris where the annual reports of railroad companies might be collected, or where the results of railroad experiments might be filed. In this respect the British, Poor wrote, with their professional and scientific societies, "are greatly in advance of us."

In the United States a first step in the right direction had been the formation of the New England Association of Railroad Superintendents. This organization was founded in April, 1848, by the managers of leading New England roads in order to provide a channel for essential intercommunication. "The Association has been formed to meet the wants of Railroad Superintendents," read one of its early reports,

> to collect and preserve facts; to combine the results of individual experience; to discuss opinions; to compare expenditures; to communicate the results of experiments; to examine inventions; to devise and mature plans for the protection of life and property; to agree on uniformity of action when desirable; and generally, its end and aim is to study to render Railroad operations safer and more profitable, by a systematic investigation of all questions relating to the management of Railroads.[17]

The association by 1850 was carrying out many of these functions. It had reading rooms and a library in Boston. Its committees had studied and reported on technical improvements in car springs and couplers, track sprinklers, rails, on systematizing procedures for the handling of freight and passengers, on the hiring and firing of employees, on taking care of claims and losses, on setting a standard time for synchronizing schedules, and so forth. Effective as it was, the editor of the *Railroad Journal* considered the New England association's value limited. Only a few of its reports were made public. Also it lacked the funds to carry out many of the experiments suggested at its monthly meetings.

Poor therefore urged the railroads of the whole country to "form an association for mutual instruction and improvement," similar to the one then existing in New England.[18] Such an association, financed by the railroads, each paying in proportion to its total capitalization, would have, he maintained, many advantages. In the first place it could act as the agency for the rapid collection and distribution of information needed on any important railroad problem.

> All its members, therefore [Poor reasoned], would be in a position to be educated up to the highest point of excellence of any individual one. The aggregate of all would become the property of each, and this alone would place the profession as a body vastly ahead of its present condition. But this would constitute but a small part of the advantages of such an association. It would at once erect a higher standard of excellence, and stimulate to vastly greater exertions. New ideas are evolved by bringing members of the same profession into contact with each other. When a person exhibits himself before his associates, he of course puts his best foot forward.

Another advantage would be that the association could provide "the means for carrying out a thousand experiments, beyond the ability of any individual to make." And, finally, it might help bring uniformity and system into the operation and management of railroads throughout the country.

The association properly conducted could in a thousand cases give to right ideas and proper system of management, that prominence and influence which is now withheld from them, from jealousy, from supposed interests, from a lack of moral courage, or fear of consequences. It would become the common arbiter in disputes between different companies — a sort of Congress of nations, whose opinions, usages, and modes of proceedings, would, among railroads, as among nations, ultimately be recognized as of the same binding force as positive law.

Except for this rather Utopian and grandiose scheme for an association of railroads, Poor was not suggesting especially novel reforms. Even here, as in his recommendations for other improvements, the editor was primarily advocating a more general adoption of reforms which were already being urged and put into effect in New England. During 1849 and 1850 New Englanders were talking and writing about the need for better accounting methods and more publicity of accounts as well as improved channels of communication. The stockholders and managers of such important roads as the Eastern, the Old Colony, the Boston and Maine, the Western, and the Vermont and Massachusetts all made, during the months after Poor became editor, recommendations for more systematic and careful accounting of continuing costs of repairs, depreciation, and even obsolescence.[19] At the same time the New England Association of Railroad Superintendents was pressing for legislation requiring detailed and uniform reports of railroad operations and finance. Also in 1849 and 1850 New Englanders were watching reforms in accounting and publicity being carried out in old England where the current depression had set off investigations into all aspects of railroad management. In writing about the New England railroad situation Poor was then defining, popularizing, and expatiating upon reforms and improvements already proposed and under consideration.

During the early 1850's some improvement did take place, although to Poor and many New Englanders the results must have seemed disappointingly limited. More accurate accounting procedures were adopted by many roads. Still, less than a handful bothered to calculate and submit figures in the column of the annual reports required by the Massachusetts legislature asking for the amount allotted to depreciation over and above cost of renewals.[20] By the mid-fifties all the New England states required their railroads to submit annual reports. By then all these states except Massachusetts had set up railroad commissions. The commissions, however, did not carefully examine the financial and operating conditions of the roads, as Poor had suggested. Nor did the required reports supply the information that he and others considered essential.

Possibly if Poor had continued to advocate his reforms for New

England railroading, more might have been done. But after 1850 he concentrated his attention on the great expansion of railroad construction in the South and West, leaving the publication of New England railroad news and developments to the *Railway Times*, a four-page quarto-size weekly founded by John A. Haven in Boston in November 1849. Although Haven did occasionally speak for better accounting and even more for the publicity of accounts, he concerned himself much less than Poor with reform.[21] In the late 1850's Poor once again turned to examining the reforms he had discussed in 1849 and 1850. This was, however, only after the great railroad boom of the 1850's had run its course, and when the railroad men of the rest of the nation first began to face problems which had confronted the New Englander a decade earlier.

II

If Poor's editorials on New England popularized current ideas, those he wrote in 1849 and 1850 on the railroad to the Pacific ran strongly against the popular view. Those on New England reflected rather than shaped public opinion, but those on the Pacific railroad seem, insofar as editorials can, to have influenced and changed opinion. In both cases Poor believed he was carrying out a major function of his paper — to analyze and evaluate the issues and problems of most concern to the railroad world. Carrying out this function in connection with an issue of such widespread interest as the Pacific railroad helped more than any other single factor to acquire for Poor a reputation as an outspoken and influential editor.

In 1849 no subject excited railroad men more than the plans to build a transcontinental railroad. Nor was any railroad topic of more vital interest to the public in general. Although there had been some discussion and planning for a road to the Pacific before 1849, it was the discovery of gold and the rush of the forty-niners to California that dramatized this need. During the spring and summer plans to build the road were perfected and publicized; the press and periodicals were filled with articles on the different proposals. That fall two large Pacific railroad conventions were held in St. Louis and Memphis and one at Philadelphia in the following April. The projected road even received attention in the President's annual message to Congress in December 1849 and was seriously considered by Congress in the following session.

The excitement and enthusiasm for the Pacific railroad disturbed the editor of the *American Railroad Journal*. Not that he had any doubts about the essential value, both commercial and military, of a railroad to the Pacific, but he was seriously afraid that too few Americans appreciated the enormously difficult engineering problems involved in building a transcontinental railroad. There was a real danger, Poor warned, that the public and Congress would endorse some ill-considered though plausible scheme. The inevitable failure of an oversanguine plan could, by turning public opinion violently against the idea, delay construction for over twenty years. For this reason Poor was skeptical of the proposals of Asa Whitney, Peter P. F. De Grand, Thomas Hart Benton, and others for building a railroad quickly and cheaply from the Mississippi Valley to the Pacific Ocean.[22]

Of these plans, Poor became the most critical of Asa Whitney's for the very reason that it was the most popular. As early as 1845 Whitney, a New York merchant, proposed to build a railroad from Lake Michigan to Puget Sound via South Pass with funds acquired from the sale of lands in a strip sixty miles wide running along the proposed line of road from Wisconsin to Washington Territory. This strip he asked Congress to sell him for ten cents an acre. Whitney so energetically publicized his plan that by the summer of 1849 he had the endorsement of eighteen state legislatures and the support of most of the press and of such influential periodicals as *Hunt's Merchants' Magazine, De Bow's Review,* the *Democratic Review,* edited by Thomas Prentiss Kettell, and the *American Review.* D. K. Minor's *American Railroad Journal* had by January 1848 endorsed Whitney's scheme.[23] Whitney considered the continued support of the *Journal* important for, according to the new editor, he sought Poor's backing "in favor of it as strong as any person's could be."[24] Yet the more Poor considered Whitney's project, the more impractical it appeared. Finally in July 1849 he came out emphatically against it.[25]

The trouble with Whitney's plan was, Poor maintained, that "from the beginning to the end, everything has been *assumed* that should have been *proved.*"[26] In the first place, his assumptions as to the road's future traffic were absurd. Whitney expected that the wealth of the Far East would flow over its tracks en route to Europe; and, like Horace Greeley, one of his most ardent champions, he was certain that the road would carry the grain of the Mississippi Valley to the semistarved hordes of Asia. Given the relatively high cost of rail transportation, Poor insisted that such expectations were mere fantasies.

Nor were Whitney's estimates of the costs of construction more realistic. He claimed that he could build a road thousands of miles from the source of supplies and equipment, and across some of the most rugged terrain in the world, at a cost of $60,000,000, or about $20,000 a mile. This estimate was, Poor pointed out, less than half the average cost per mile of railroads in New England, where the cost of equipment was the lowest in the United States and where labor was readily available. Moreover, Poor thought Whitney's proposal to use settlers living along the line of the road as his labor force would greatly increase rather than lower the total cost. The pioneers available at any one time would be far too few to carry on sustained construction. Also, as railroad experience had demonstrated, the specialized contractor and his crew could build a road far more cheaply and efficiently than part-time untrained workers.

Finally, Poor challenged Whitney's assumption that the cost could be met from the sale of the lands along the line of the road. If Whitney managed annually to sell tracts equivalent to as much as a quarter of the total amount sold by the federal government in 1848, he would receive a maximum of $400,000 a year. Thus, even if he could build the road for $60,000,000, it would be some 150 years before he covered his costs. So utterly impractical did Whitney's scheme appear to Poor that he began to suspect that it was merely a front for a vast land-grabbing scheme. After all, the editor suggested, the purchase of the vast tract from the government would give Whitney control of some potentially very valuable land, especially at the terminal areas of Puget Sound and Lake Michigan. Such suspicions were quite unfair to the honest, though in this case unrealistic Asa Whitney.

Facts determined by trained engineers, not the imaginative assumptions of dreamers or schemers, Poor insisted, must be the basis for any realistic planning about the Pacific railroad. No competent engineer, he reminded his readers, had yet endorsed any of the current plans. "Let us have the opinions of such men as Mr. Latrobe, or J. Edgar Thomson, or Mr. Kirkwood, or Mr. Morton, or Mr. Seymour, or some other eminent engineer," he urged. "Let us hear what they say." [27] Poor especially feared that Congress might approve Whitney's plan before examining it carefully. In his very first editorial on Whitney's proposals he emphasized:

> The first step that Congress should take, should be to institute a suitable commission for the purpose of ascertaining the distance, grades, nature of the soil, and the capacity of the country over which the road is to pass, to sustain a population, and furnish materials for building and sustaining the road, the obstacles interposed by water courses, etc., etc. In fact, the government should do just what a prudent individual or company would do, before commencing work; first ascertain precisely what is to be done, and then determine whether the result accomplished will justify the outlay. Individuals who should adopt any other course would instantly lose all the confidence of the community. The great mistakes that have been committed in connection with our public works, have arisen from a want

of thorough and critical surveys before commencing work. Yet in the discussion of this subject, both in and out of Congress, these considerations seem entirely lost sight of, and every person having fixed upon what he considers the proper termini, looks upon all the intervening space as mere plastic materials in his hands, to be moulded by the action of his will, into such form as he may wish to give it.[28]

The editor of the *Journal*, for somewhat different reasons, considered the plans of Peter P. F. De Grand and Senator Benton almost as dangerous as those of Asa Whitney. De Grand's plan, supported by New England railroad men and often called the Boston plan, proposed that the national government lend a private corporation chartered in Massachusetts $98,000,000 to build the road within five years. The company would then raise $2,000,000 on its own account. The defects of this proposal were, in Poor's opinion, obvious. First, to build the road in five years was an engineering impossibility; second, such a huge loan would create a serious stringency in the American money markets; and third, Congress in this time of sectional conflict would hardly agree to finance a private company whose members nearly all came from one section. His strongest argument against De Grand's plan, however, was that it gave a private concern control of the nation's most important single transportation route:

If the road should be private property, it would be in the power of individuals to impose, in the shape of tolls, such a tax upon merchandise, and travelers passing over it, as they might choose. Such a road could not for a long time at least have any competition. We have a right to suppose, that in such a case, the owners of the road would make the most money possible out of their property, and thus the trade and commerce of the United States, and as the enthusiastic believe, of the world, would be subject to all the burdens that individual cupidity could impose. There is, therefore, the same and an equal objection against making this work private property, as there is to giving to individuals the sole privilege of navigating the Pacific, for reasons too evident to be pointed out. Public rights of such vast magnitude should never be surrendered to the control of individuals.[29]

Poor just as vigorously protested against Benton's plan to have the national government build and operate a railroad to the Pacific. The editor of the *Journal* feared both that government operation would be wasteful and that the road would quickly become a patronage plum.

We believe [Poor maintained] . . . that the general government should have as little connection as possible with the construction and management of the road; for the reason, that government cannot directly construct it without an enormous waste of money, and that if under its immediate control, it might be made the instrument of vast political power, consequently of corruption.[30]

Since neither the national government nor a private corporation could be trusted to build the road, Poor suggested that the task be undertaken by the states. In a plan of his own outlined in the September 29, 1849, issue of his paper, he proposed that Congress authorize each state to appoint one of its citizens as a director of the Pacific railroad.[31] These directors, selected by the state legislatures for a term at a salary set by Congress, would have "those powers in the construction and management of the road, as are usually possessed by the directors of railroads thro'out the country." Their meetings would be public and they would report fully at stated intervals to Congress.

The cost of the road, Poor believed, must be met, first, from land sales, and he further urged that all proceeds from such sales be set aside as a special fund for this purpose. Popular opinion was so strong on this point that Poor was sure "no other source will be resorted to till these shall be found to be inadequate." Fearing that these would be inadequate, he suggested that the directors be allowed to borrow funds for construction from the general government on the security of future land sales. Poor further recommended that a corps of engineers rather than a single man be charged with the actual construction. Each member was to be responsible for completing one section of the road while collectively they might work out the larger problems of construction.

Poor claimed many advantages for this plan. Since the general government would not be directly involved in construction, it could hardly use the road as an engine of political patronage. The diversity of sectional and party interests represented on the board precluded improper influence by the states. Since private gain was ruled out, careful construction and fair rates were more certain. Furthermore, Poor expected that the board, which he believed would include the nation's most able railroad men, would be able to compromise on a route far more quickly than the politicians in Congress. Finally he pointed out that this road, owned and operated by the various states, might well become a significant unifying and nationalizing force at a time when the slavery issue was so dangerously dividing the nation. In the editor's opinion:

> The railway systems of each State would be gradually connected with this as a great trunk line, and thus the bonds of our union would receive all the strength that mutuality of interest could give, while the care and management of this great work, requiring the co-operation of all the States, would promote a more intimate acquaintance between the different sections of the country — a more frequent interchange of the kind offices and hospitalities of life — and, more than all, an uniformity of ideas, which is the true bond of all political union.[32]

Poor expected too much. This administrative machinery, while large enough to prevent undue political influence, was much too cumbersome to permit efficient management. Nor was there any assurance that political and sectional differences would not divide the directors and block action as effectively as such differences did in Congress. Still Poor's plan, as sound as any proposed at this time, was well received. In the fall of 1849 Captain Albert Pike incorporated its main features in his proposals, which were strongly supported in the South and West. In the following April similar proposals were favorably received by the Philadelphia convention on the Pacific railroad.[33]

Poor did not energetically pursue this plan. Editorially he was much more concerned with preventing the adoption of any other plan until the potential routes and the over-all costs of construction had been given more expert attention. He remained especially unhappy about the enthusiasm of the press, public, and politicians for Whitney's scheme, but as the months passed, Poor's fears on this score became progressively allayed. At the Pacific railroad conventions held in Memphis and St. Louis in October 1849, the delegates agreed, as did those at the Philadelphia convention held the following April, that any further meaningful discussion must await a survey of the possible routes by responsible engineers. To Poor's great satisfaction, the Secretary of Interior in his annual report and the President in his annual message to Congress made the same point. Finally, in March 1850, Congress shelved the bill to enact Whitney's proposals, although it was endorsed by both the House and the Senate committees on Roads and Canals. "We earnestly opposed it in face of the united support it received from nearly the whole press of the country," Poor wrote when he heard the news, "and think we may claim to have done something toward bringing the public mind to view it in a true light."[34] This appears to be a fair claim. Certainly, nearly all other influential periodicals eagerly endorsed Whitney's plan. Even those few who did oppose it because they favored some other route and plan, accepted Whitney's engineering and financial assumptions.[35]

During the following decade the same pattern continued. The *American Railroad Journal* regularly reiterated its views on the difficulties and expenses of constructing a railroad to the Pacific, while *Hunt's Merchants' Magazine*, *De Bow's Review* and the *Western Journal and Civilian* continued to print optimistic articles on the ease of construction.[36] Also sanguine were Haven of the *Railway Times* and Edward D. Mansfield of the *Railroad Record* after its founding in 1853.[37] The major concern of the other railroad editors was not the feasibility but the location of the route. Mansfield advocated the southern route through Texas while Haven and his associate editor, George Vose, argued for the central route from St. Louis to San Francisco via South Pass. Poor, too, had his favorite route, the northern one which was surveyed by his close friend and fellow Geographic Society member, Isaac I. Stevens.

But even for a road built along this route, which he was sure had the easiest terrain, Poor estimated the cost and time of construction far more conservatively than did his fellow editors. Only for a brief period in 1853 did he consider construction of the transcontinental road an easier task than he had thought it in 1849.[38] The reports of the five government surveys completed in 1854 and his own investigations for the American Geographical Society in the same year convinced him that he had in 1849 actually underestimated the difficulties of completing the road. From this time on, he constantly stressed two points: First, he insisted that more accurate information about the prospective routes must be known before any intelligent positive action could be taken. Throughout the 1850's he urged Congress to appoint a commission of able engineers to follow up the hurried and most incomplete preliminary surveys made in 1854.

Next, Poor urged the nation's legislature to think more realistically about costs. By the mid-1850's he had become certain that even under the most favorable engineering conditions the cost of a well built transcontinental road would be over $100,000 a mile. At such a cost, proceeds from land sales could never pay for the road's construction. For one thing, much of the land along the line of any railroad to the Pacific was almost worthless. Moreover, as the experience of the Illinois Central was showing, several years were required before a railroad received any sizable amount of revenue from the sale of even the best lands. Nor did the editor of the *Journal* expect private capital to make up the balance of the funds required for construction. He was quite certain that the road, once in operation, would be unable to make enough beyond its necessarily heavy running expenses to meet the interest charges on any large loan from private individuals. The road would, he feared, "never become a channel of commerce — not even for the 'Teas and Silks of China.' Its business will be mainly confined to passengers, the mails and the precious metals."[39] Important as such traffic was to the nation, it would hardly provide the large volume of trade necessary to make a railroad profitable.

By 1858 Poor had reluctantly decided that the Pacific railroad must be financed and built by the federal government. Although government construction "will necessarily increase its cost and delay its completion," Poor saw no other way to obtain this essential link between East and West. Also, if the road was able, as he hoped it might be, to help unify the nation, then its construction by the government would be well worth the extra cost. "We have little nationality, and are fast losing the little that we have," Poor wrote in January 1858. "In a railroad to the Pacific we have a great national work, transcending, in its magnitude, and in its results, anything yet attempted by man. By its execution, we are to accomplish our appropriate mission, and a greater one than any yet fulfilled by any nation." And this mission was to establish "our empire on the Pacific, where our civilization can take possession of the New Continent and confront the Old."

Poor's faith in the Pacific railroad as an agent in America's "Manifest Destiny," combined with his caution and conservative approach to the problems of its construction and finance, and his own writing and cartographical work on the road for the Geographical Society gave him a reputation as an expert on the subject of a railroad to the Pacific. It appears most probable that this reputation had much to do with his appointment in July 1862 as one of the five government commissioners to the newly chartered Union Pacific Railroad Company and his election as the company's first secretary in the following September.

III

Poor's editorials on the expansion of railroad construction in the South and West were even more imbued with his belief in the railroad as an agent of progress than his editorials on the Pacific railroad. This conviction undoubtedly helped make his articles more persuasive and more convincing, and permitted the *Journal* to carry out very effectively its traditional role as the promoter of American railroads, collectively and individually.

During 1849 and 1850 Poor's editorials on the South and West found many readers, since outside New England the year 1849 was for railroad men one of great expectations. During the second half of the 1840's American farmers and planters, after nearly a decade of hard times, were enjoying good crops; and more important, the Mexican War, the famines in Ireland and Germany, and the repeal of the British Corn Laws had rapidly increased the demand for their products. Moreover, war, famines, and free trade had, by stimulating the trade of the Atlantic ports, increased the wealth of the eastern cities, and consequently the supply of liquid capital in the United States. At the same time the large-scale immigration, precipitated by the European famines, offered an ample supply of cheap labor.

Again the dramatic discovery of gold in California made a new export available to pay for imports of rails and other equipment needed for any widespread railroad building in the United States. For these reasons, then, during the last years of the 1840's, farmers, planters, and businessmen in the East, South, and West began to revive old schemes and to develop new ones for the construction of railroads which would help meet the new demand for agricultural crops by providing better transportation to and from the older farming areas and by opening up new territory to commercial farming.

This renewed interest in railroads began, apart from New England, first in the commercial seaports of the East. In 1847, the same year which marked the beginnings of New England's railroad troubles, construction was started in New York on the Hudson River and the New Haven railroads and recommenced on a large scale on the Erie and the Harlem.[40] In 1847, too, Philadelphia celebrated the chartering and the beginning of construction on the Pennsylvania Railroad, the road by which she hoped to regain from New York much of the trade of the West. To the south, the Baltimore and Ohio began during that same year to make surveys and let contracts for the continuation of its line over the mountains toward Wheeling. In the lower South, work was resumed in 1847 on the Macon and Western and the state-owned Western and Atlantic, which were to connect Savannah and Charleston with the Mississippi Valley. Poor, who enthusiastically described the progress of these east-west trunk lines, devoted comparatively little space in the *Journal* to promoting them.[41] They had, he believed, the necessary support from their terminal cities and the communities along their routes. Instead, he used their rapid construction as one of his major arguments for promoting railroads in the West.

When Poor became editor of the *Journal* in 1849, there were less than eight hundred miles of railroad in operation west of the Alleghenies — less mileage than was then in operation in Massachusetts alone. Yet few areas in the country or even in the world more urgently needed railroads. In the Old Northwest, some of the richest agricultural land in the world, though open to settlement for nearly a generation, still lay unused. Heavy rains turned the unsurfaced roads in the rich soil into seas of mire so that farms and cities like Indianapolis, which could not be reached by steamboat, were practically mudbound for months at a time. As long as the farmer depended on the horse and wagon to haul his crops to market, Poor pointed out, "the cost of transportation is greater than the value of the article after it reaches a market. The most fertile lands are consequently worthless, or nearly so."[42]

From the very first the Western farmers, like those on the Maine frontier, saw the railroad as the solution to their transportation difficulties. During the 1830's Western hopes ran high. Michigan, Indiana, Illinois, and Kentucky all embarked on ambitious schemes for state-owned and state-operated railroad systems; while Ohio amply supported her road by guaranteeing to purchase two thirds of the railroad company's stock. The panics of 1837 and 1839 shattered the early railroad schemes. Unable to raise money, disillusioned by the heavy expenses incurred in building a few hundred miles of unfinished roads, Western legislatures sold their uncompleted roads at great loss to private companies and passed laws prohibiting further state aid to railroads.[43]

In the 1840's railroad construction was largely limited to completing the few roads which, started with state support, had been purchased or refinanced by private companies. During 1848 and 1849 five such roads were finished: the Mad River and Lake Erie, the Little Miami, and the Mansfield and Sandusky in Ohio; the Madison and Indianapolis in Indiana; and the Michigan Central in Michigan. Their completion, in addition to the revival of the east-west trunk line construction, led to a spate of railroad chartering and the revival of older companies in the Old Northwest.[44] The depression of 1848, short-lived outside New England and Pennsylvania, only temporarily delayed construction. In the spring of 1849, the West appeared to be on the verge of a railroad boom.

Still many Westerners held back. They vividly remembered the expensive failures of the great majority of the early state-supported roads. Farmers and merchants hesitated to put their limited surplus funds into railroad stock or to approve of increased taxes to pay for county or town support of local roads. Many wondered whether private companies could succeed where the states had failed so miserably. Others, especially those living near rivers or the few canals, questioned whether any railroad was really worth the cost involved. Late in 1849 Poor came to consider one of his major editorial tasks to be the resolving of these doubts.

With an enthusiasm engendered by a profound faith in the railroad as an agent of progress and tempered by an understanding of the problems involved in building frontier railroads, Poor began to point out the tremendous benefits the railroad would bring the West. A railroad, he argued, was certainly worth its initial heavy cost. In the first place, it assured the farmers a greater cash return for their labor. Besides enlarging their local markets, it would permit them to compete with the farmers of the East and even of Europe in the agricultural markets of the world. "A railroad opens every market in the world to every man whose door it passes, and gives him access to them at all times."[45] To answer the men who were satisfied with existing water transportation facilities, Poor stressed that with the railroad they would no longer be at the mercy of winter ice, spring floods, and summer droughts. The advantages of the railroad, Poor further indicated,

> will be much greater than the mere saving in expense of transportation. Every farmer and planter can hold his own produce to meet the demand. He is now compelled to forward when the rivers are navigable. The whole mass is thus thrown upon the market at the same time. The natural tendency of this is to diminish the demand, consequently the price. If the producer wishes to hold on for a rise, he is subjected to heavy expense at a distant port. With a railroad, he stores his own crop, and forwards it to market only when he can realise a fair price. The convenience of a railroad to the country merchant is equally great. When his means of communication are open only one half the year, he must lay in a sufficient stock for the balance. This involves the necessity of having a much larger capital than if he could supply all his wants at will.[46]

The businessman in Western cities likewise had much to gain from railroads, Poor continued. The railroad would increase the size of his community, the value of his lands, and the volume of his business. Since much of the West was financially in the same position as Maine, that is, with state aid prohibited and private capital limited, Poor urged Westerners to follow the Maine practice of relying on town and county support of local roads. Surely no right-minded citizen, the editor reasoned, could object to having his community help finance a railroad when he realized how much the Eastern towns and cities had benefited from their railroads. In Boston, for example, the population during the 1840's, the decade of Massachusetts' greatest railroad construction, had jumped from 94,000 to 139,000, and the value of real and personal property from $94,600,000 to $188,000,000.[47] Certainly the railroad could do for Cleveland, Cincinnati, Indianapolis, Chicago, and St. Louis what it had done for Boston.

To encourage railroad construction in the West, Poor concentrated even more on describing the individual roads than on writing general promotional editorials. His descriptions were supplemented by articles sent to the *Journal* by individual promoters telling of the prospects of their roads and the advantages they would bring to the areas through which they were to pass. In promoting individual railroads, Poor gave space to nearly all the new roads being planned in the West. He did, however, tend to favor certain lines, especially those on the "Great Central Route" running from Pittsburgh to St. Louis and beyond to Independence, Missouri.[48] Through his support of the roads on this route, Poor soon came to know some of the most influential railroad and businessmen in the West, including John Brough, Oliver H. Smith, James F. D. Lanier, Chauncey Rose, John H. Goodman, and General William Robinson. By the end of 1850, the *Journal's* pages were crowded with articles by such men which, together with editorials by Poor about other Western roads, took up the largest share of the *Journal's* pages.

The editor of the *American Railroad Journal* was as anxious to encourage railroad construction in the South as in the West. Not only were railroads "indispensable to the progress of the South," but they also, Poor hoped, might, by mitigating the South's economic handicaps, help to allay the ominous sectional controversy.[49] If the editor devoted more pages to the West than to the South, it was only because more railroads were being built at this time in the West. As the need for railroads lasted much longer in the South, Poor continued to encourage the construction of Southern roads long after he stopped writing promotional articles for Western railroads.

The revival of railroad construction in the South paralleled closely that in the North, with the renewed building in the eastern section coming after 1847 and in the western part after 1849. In Virginia, between 1847 and 1849, four important roads were organized and work was resumed on two others.[50] In North Carolina these years saw the chartering, with state financial support, of the North Carolina Central and the revival of plans to connect Wilmington to the South Carolina roads. During the late 1840's the Camden branch of the South Carolina Railroad was begun and construction started on the first railroads in that state organized independently of the South Carolina Railroad.

Georgia paced railroad development in the lower South. With the completion of her two great roads, the Georgia and the Georgia Central, she had by the mid-1840's twice as much mileage as any other state in the South and as much as all the states in the Old Northwest together. After 1847, besides renewing work on the Macon and Western and the Western and Atlantic, the western extension of the two main lines, Georgians organized three new companies, the Southwestern, the Muscogee, and the La Grange, all pointing towards the Alabama boundary and all partially financed by the Georgia and the Georgia Central.[51] Georgia's activities led to a new interest in railroads in both Alabama and Tennessee. Just before 1850 work was taken up again on the Montgomery and West Point, and started on the Alabama and Tennessee, the East Tennessee and Georgia, the Nashville and Chattanooga, and the Memphis and Charleston. A final important Southern railroad project which started in the late

1840's, the Mobile and Ohio, stimulated plans for railroad construction in both Mississippi and Louisiana.

Railroad builders in the South relied much more than did those of the West on state aid. This was in good part because the first Southern roads, unlike the early Western roads, were completed before the depression of the late thirties became acute. With some notable exceptions such as the ill-fated Louisville, Cincinnati and Charleston, the states of the South suffered little from their initial financial connection with railroads. Therefore in Virginia the railroad promoters in the late 1840's, pointing to the dividends the state was drawing from its investments in the older lines, had little difficulty in persuading the legislature to authorize the state to purchase three fifths of the stock of the new roads.

Poor in 1849 wholeheartedly endorsed state aid to the Southern railroads. Such financial assistance was, in his opinion, more essential to the South than to other parts of the country, because "the sparse population which exists in most sections renders . . . [railroad] construction beyond the ability of private means."[52] Poor was especially pleased with Virginia's "comprehensive liberality," which he hoped would set the pattern for postdepression state aid throughout the South.[53] By 1851, when North Carolina, South Carolina, and Alabama had purchased stock in their new roads, Poor began to advocate the more conservative plan of the endorsing of railroad bonds. He urged the states to guarantee the principal and interest of the bonds of roads which met fairly rigid financial and engineering requirements. Poor was more than satisfied with the Tennessee law, passed in 1852, issuing 6 per cent state bonds to the extent of $8,000 a mile to help cover the cost of rails and equipment in return for a carefully protected first mortgage.[54] Although Missouri and Florida were the only states to follow Tennessee's plan, every state in the South did give financial aid to its railroads during the 1850's. Such aid, Poor later maintained, not only helped provide the South with essential transportation services, but also permitted, in striking contrast with the Western roads, a sounder, more conservative financial development of the individual roads.[55]

Poor advocated national and municipal aid as well as state financial support for the Southern railroads. He supported bills before Congress granting public lands to railroads in the South and West. Of the two sections, he felt the South most needed land-grant assistance. And, in his opinion, the three most deserving projects were the Mobile and Ohio, the Memphis and Charleston, and the Alabama and Tennessee.[56] At the same time, he praised Charleston, Savannah, and Mobile for the financial support they had given their railroads, and urged New Orleans to follow suit. Unless New Orleans began immediately to encourage her railroads, Poor warned in 1851, she would lose her trade, not only to the more railroad-minded ports in the South, but also to New York City, already her most formidable rival for the trade of the Mississippi Valley.[57]

While urging government aid, Poor insisted that such aid should stimulate and supplement, but never supplant, private capital. His articles on New Orleans were directed as much to encouraging private citizens to invest in railroads as to urging the loan of city credit. The initiative for organizing a road, the major share of its cost, and the responsibility for its operation should, Poor believed, come from individuals living on the line of the road. The example he urged both Southerners and Westerners to follow was the Atlantic and St. Lawrence, "a happy combination of public credit and private capital," initiated and managed by private individuals.[58]

In stimulating local interest in railroads throughout the South, Poor used arguments very similar to those he used in promoting Western railroads. Once again he tended to favor certain lines. He was especially enthusiastic about the roads on the north-south routes from the Gulf to the Great Lakes and those on the "Great Central Route between North and South" running from New Orleans to New York by way of Chattanooga, Knoxville, and Lynchburg. Again, as in the case of the Western lines, Poor soon came to know personally many of the men promoting these roads. John Childe of the Mobile and Ohio, Walter H. Goodman of the Mississippi Central, Lewis Troost of the Alabama and Tennessee, and Thomas Jefferson Boyd, John Roberts McDaniels, and Charles F. M. Garnett of the Virginia and Tennessee, all wrote much for the *Journal* about their roads, and when they came to New York for money, rails, and equipment, they called on the editor.[59] Besides giving them his fullest editorial support, Poor played an important role in helping both the Mississippi Central and the Virginia and Tennessee, the road he considered "the *Moses* which is to lead Virginia out of Egypt into a better land," to raise money in the New York and London money markets.[60]

One reason Poor became personally involved in these companies was that he was impressed, indeed overimpressed, by the commercial prospects of the north-south lines. These roads, he noted, "coincide with the natural lines of internal trade" just as the east-west roads "are more intimately connected with our foreign commerce." [61]

In a country like ours [Poor wrote], producing the fruits of the tropics, as well as those of higher latitudes, where everything that enters into consumption is produced within our own limits, the natural course of trade is from north to south and south to north. Each section forwards its surplus products which are peculiar to, or most easily produced on its soil, to the other, and receives in return the appropriate products of the latter. The lines of communication, therefore, which run at right angles with the parallels of latitude, must be the great channels through which the products of these different latitudes shall be diffused and scattered over the whole.[62]

To the editor of the *Railroad Journal*, Southern railroads were much more than just good business ventures, for he was convinced that their construction might help to heal the bitter sectional controversy then threatening to disrupt the nation. Poor, in spite of his close connection to the Tappans and the antislavery movement, considered the issue between North and South an economic, not a moral one. He found the cause of conflict in the rapidly growing economic imbalance between the two sections rather than in an uncompromising clash between personal liberty and slavery, between a dominant nineteenth-century ideology and the Southern solution of race relations.

The necessary economic balance could only be restored, Poor was certain, by bringing railroads and industry to the South. Until the South was equal in economic wealth and industrial power, she would continue to look on the North as an aggressor and an exploiter. Poor shared the views of many of his closest Southern friends, including John Roberts McDaniels, James D. B. De Bow, and Matthew Fontaine Maury, and of his fellow New Englander and one-time assistant editor, Charles T. James. These men, among the most vocal advocates of industrializing the South, often talked with the editor of the *Journal* about ways and means of encouraging Southern railroads and industries.[63] As a result of one conversation with De Bow in October 1850, Poor wrote an editorial entitled "The Importance of the Railroads and Manufacturers to the South," in which he summarized many of his sanguine views on the economic solution to the sectional issue. After describing the imbalance in the wealth and population of the two sections, Poor wrote:

The steps necessary to restore this equilibrium, we are glad to see, are now being taken by the South in earnest. The subject of the development of the resources of that part of the Union, are [*sic*] now engrossing the attention of its people. Railroads, the pioneers of all other improvements, are projected in every quarter, and many of them are in progress. Wherever they run by a waterfall, an iron or coal mine, someone will be sure to be found who will be ready to turn all these to account. The improvement of these sources of wealth will react upon agriculture. A market will thus be opened for a very large amount of products, which may be made the basis to support a home population, but which cannot be exported. The South then can raise something to sell besides *cotton*. *Farming* to some extent will then take the place of *planting*. The agricultural sections will fill up. A mutual demand will grow up between all classes for the respective products of each; in fine, we see at the South the same state of things which we witness in every community whose industry is devoted to different objects.

So much for restoring an equilibrium based upon equality of numbers. Similarity of pursuits, while they will secure what may be termed *physical* equality, will create at the same time a much stronger bond of union, similarity of interests and ideas. Under this influence local distinctions will be forgotten. The words North and South, East and West, will cease to stand for terms representing different parts or interests. Every part of the country will occupy an equal place in each person's affections.

Let us do our utmost to promote that state of things which shall not only be productive of the greatest *material* good to all, but which at the same time shall work an effectual cure for the political ills which threaten.[64]

For Poor, then, the railroads had an essential role to play in reintegrating the South into the national pattern of economic, social, and political growth. Not until the outbreak of hostilities in 1861 did he realize that the railroad had failed to fulfill his hopes. Only then did he understand that the moral and ideological issue divided the two sections far more deeply than the economic imbalance.

Poor's editorial arguments for construction of railroads in the West and South were in 1849 and 1850 quite valid. Most railroad men or economists would have agreed that the railroad would give "commercial value" to vast areas of Western land; would open markets for Western farm products; would increase the value of the land and the prosperity of the community; and would do all this because in so many areas the railroad was a more efficient means of transportation than the river, lake, or canal. A few might have qualified these views by pointing out, as Poor would do in a short time, the dangers of building or overbuilding in areas where potential traffic was comparatively light. Although these arguments were fairly obvious, Poor developed them more logically, used more statistical information, and repeated them more often than Minor had done before or than the other railroad editors, with the possible exception of Mansfield of the *Railroad Record*, would do in later years.

It is, of course, almost impossible to say just what effect Poor's editorials had on those Western and Southern farmers and planters to whom these arguments were not obvious or on those who were uncertain whether the advantages of a railroad outweighed its cost. Poor's comments were repeated in the annual reports and prospectuses of the new roads. They were also undoubtedly copied in local newspapers and quoted by local promoters, much as John Alfred Poor and the Portland newspapers had used Minor's favorable remarks about the Atlantic and St. Lawrence between 1845 and 1848.

In any case the *Journal's* editor was convinced of the value of his and other papers in crystallizing public opinion. "The editor of an influential journal can often effect more for a public work than a dozen leading men in a community," Poor commented. "No individual or company can hope to succeed in any great enterprise, without the aid of the press." [65]

It seems quite certain that the leading men in Western and Southern communities who were promoting local railroads felt that the *Journal's* support carried weight. During 1850 these men came increasingly to the great port city of New York. The roads they had started now needed funds that could only be obtained in the Eastern money markets. Their visits, and his own belief in the supreme importance of building the new roads in the South and West, convinced Poor late in 1850 to make his paper the representative of the Southern and Western railroads on Wall Street.

⁎ 4 ⁎

Representing the Railroads on Wall Street

FROM THE FALL OF 1850 until December 1852, Henry Poor considered that the primary mission of his journal was to represent the railroads on Wall Street. He carried out this objective in three ways. First, he reported on and analyzed almost weekly the condition of the New York market for the securities of Western and to a lesser degree Southern railroads. In these analyses he often gave advice on when and how to sell and what type of securities to bring to the money market. In so doing he also advocated improvements to provide for more efficient and equitable marketing of railroad securities. Finally he devoted much editorial space to making the Western and Southern securities better known to Eastern and foreign investors.

The services Poor provided were fairly unique. Railroad men could get brief reports and occasional analyses of the general condition of the security markets from *Hunt's Merchants' Magazine* and the *Bankers' Magazine*. They might obtain even more detailed reports and analyses from the financial columns of the New York daily papers, especially the *Tribune*, and, after the spring of 1852, from Thomas Prentiss Kettell's weekly *United States Economist*. Although both the *Tribune* and the *Economist* paid a good deal of attention to railroad securities, their editors were not, as was Henry Poor, primarily concerned with the interests of the railroads, particularly those of the South and West. They, therefore, rarely carried information on when and how to market new railroad issues. Nor did any New York periodicals and papers try, at least before 1852, to popularize the securities of the more distant roads. Moreover, the Southern and Western roads were able to get little comparable information from the *Railway Times*, the only other railroad periodical published at this time, for that paper continued to concern itself largely with New England railroading.

By the late summer and fall of 1850 it had become obvious to Poor that finance was rapidly replacing promotion as the major problem for railroad men in the West. No longer did Western farmers and merchants need to be urged to support their local railroads. "The public feeling in the West, upon the subject of railroads, is excited to an extraordinary degree," wrote Poor in November 1850. "The people of every town and county in the great valley, are now putting forth all their means to secure to themselves the advantages of railroads." [1] Gone were the doubts as to the practicability of immediate large-scale railroad construction. The net receipts of the Michigan Central, the Little Miami, and the Madison and Indianapolis proved the worth of the Western railroads as business ventures. The unexpectedly heavy traffic in wheat, pork, and other farm products demonstrated their usefulness as common carriers.[2] The prosperity of Detroit, Cincinnati, and Indianapolis attested to the value of the railroad for the larger Western communities. As a result, by late 1850 Cleveland, Cincinnati, Louisville, St. Louis, Milwaukee, Pittsburgh, and Toledo, such smaller towns as Evansville, Jeffersonville, and La Porte, and many Ohio and Indiana counties had given financial aid to railroads.[3] Having obtained local support for their roads, Western railroad presidents now began to come East to New York City.

The reasons the Western railroad presidents came East, Henry Poor pointed out, were quite obvious. Local stock subscriptions, both private and municipal, permitted most Western railroad companies chartered in the late 1840's to survey, clear or "grub," grade, ballast, and bridge the lines of their roads. In other words, these companies were able to prepare their roads for rails with local resources; but, with very few exceptions, they were unable to raise enough money near home to purchase rails, locomotives, and rolling stock. Taking one state as an example, Henry Poor wrote:

> In looking at the State of Indiana, for instance, we see that her people find no difficulty in constructing their numerous lines of railroad in progress, until they come to the purchase of the iron — their difficulties then commence. All before that is easy work. What is the reason of this? It is not because her people have not an abundance of property, but they have no money. They have labor and abundance of food for the support of this labor. A substantial farmer, therefore . . . without any embarrassment, can devote one-fourth of his time and an equal amount of his surplus products, to the work of constructing railroads, and receive in exchange its stock. There are great numbers of people on every line who would be glad to do this, and in the Southern States in particular, large amounts of stock in their railways are subscribed to by planters, with an understanding that they are to work out their assessments. If instead of the road being constructed by those who take stock in it, it is let to contractors, the result is pretty much the same. The proportion of profits to the work performed bears but a very small percentage. The money paid for work returns immediately to those who contributed it, for supplies of provisions, lumber, labor, etc. But little goes out of the country. It changes hands, but soon

returns to the hands of its original possessor for articles he can very easily produce, but which he could perhaps never sell, except for the opportunity thus afforded.[4]

The West was indeed long on land and short on cash. The reports of the early Western roads show that payment for shares of stock by land and labor was a standard practice. In 1849 the stock subscription of the Indianapolis and Bellefontaine, according to its first annual report, stood at $90,425 in cash, $155,449 in land, and $33,425 in labor and material; while the first annual report of the Indianapolis and Cincinnati showed $130,000 in cash, $125,000 in real estate, and $57,000 in labor and materials.[5] To obtain funds to pay for their rails and equipment the roads issued bonds. Usually rail, locomotive, and equipment manufacturers would take part of their payment in bonds. But they demanded some cash. Also they accepted the bonds only at a heavy discount. It was, then, to obtain funds through the sale of bonds that the presidents of Western and Southern roads first came East in 1849, 1850, and 1851.[6]

Much more complex were the reasons why, when these men came East, they went to New York rather than to Boston or Philadelphia. Between 1849 and 1852 New York, as a result of a variety of complicated and interrelated factors, began to replace Boston as the nation's financial capital. This shift, which was of profound significance for American businessmen, especially railroad managers, received a good deal of attention in the pages of the *American Railroad Journal, Hunt's Merchants' Magazine* and the *Bankers' Magazine.* An understanding of the importance of this shift for American railroad and business history as well as of its effect on Poor's editorial policies and services, requires a brief summary of the development of early American railroad finance.[7]

Throughout American railroad history the scarcity of local capital was a primary problem for railroad builders and managers. Except in New England, American railroad promoters from the very first looked to the distant investor for funds to help build their roads. The need for outside funds had two results. First, American railroads, again excepting the early New England roads, were financed more by bonds than by stock, for throughout the nineteenth century the investor almost always preferred what appeared to be the secured principal and the guaranteed interest of a bond issue. Secondly, middlemen were required to market these bonds to investors scattered overseas and in the few large American coastal cities. In the 1830's the men who marketed these securities lived primarily in Philadelphia, in the 1840's in Boston, and only after 1850 in New York City.

During the 1830's there were two types of securities sold to distant investors to provide funds for the construction of American railroads and canals. One was the government bond, both state and municipal. It was used to finance the ambitious and costly east-west transportation projects in Massachusetts, New York, Pennsylvania, Maryland, Virginia, South Carolina, and Georgia, and nearly all the railroads and canals in the Western states. The other, the mortgage bond of private corporations, was used to help pay for the building of the larger coal roads and the north-south lines running from New York City to Wilmington, North Carolina. The promoters of these roads preferred private rather than public methods of finance primarily because these roads, which were less ambitious engineering projects and which connected some of the largest towns in the nation, were much more certain of making an income for both promoters and investors than the great east-west lines. The long-term twenty- to thirty-year bonds secured by mortgage on the road's property and convertible into stock at the holder's option, which were issued in the 1830's by the Reading, the Camden and Amboy, the Philadelphia, Wilmington and Baltimore, and the Virginia roads, remained throughout the nineteenth century the standard type of security used to finance railroads.

During the 1830's many of these private mortgage bonds were, like government bonds, issued in sterling denominations specifically for the London market. Some of these sterling issues were taken directly to England, while others, like so many of the state bonds, were sold through the British mercantile houses in New York and Boston. The largest number of railroad and canal corporation bonds, however, were marketed through Philadelphia. Here the most active private firm was Thomas Biddle and Company. But it was overshadowed, as indeed were all other individuals and firms handling issues of new roads, by the magnitude of the marketing operations of that financial colossus, Nicholas Biddle's Second Bank of the United States, particularly after it was rechartered in 1836 as the Bank of the United States of Pennsylvania.

As long as the British investor continued to consider American securities a good buy, the sterling mortgage bond and the state issues financed a large number of America's railroads and canals. And as long as this faith in the United States lasted, railroad construction was concentrated in the states south of New York. When, however, the depression precipitated by the financial crises of 1837 and 1839 destroyed British confidence, railroad building in this area almost ceased. With the coming of the depression, with the cessation of railroad construction, with the failure of Biddle's bank, with the loss of the foreign investment market, Philadelphia lost a primacy in American railroad finance which she was never again to regain.

Only in New England did railroad men avoid the catastrophes of the depression. The New York railroad men, who until 1837 had relied much less than those to the south on the mortgage or state bond, were forced to turn to state aid to see them through the worst of the depression. When in 1842 the state legislature passed a law prohibiting further state support, railroad construction in New York, like that to the south, almost stopped. But in New England, where, unlike much of the rest of the country, stock subscriptions had built nearly all the early railroads, financial self-reliance paid off. With few debts to meet, and with profits coming in from textile mills and railroads completed before 1837, New England rapidly recovered from the world-wide economic shock of the late 1830's. By mid-forties, when the economy of the rest of the country was still recuperating from the earlier business paralysis, she was enjoying high prosperity.

During this prosperous period Boston became the center of American railroad finance. Not only did she finance the new roads in the industrial valleys of the Connecticut, Blackstone, and Merrimac rivers and across the mountains of New Hampshire and Vermont to Lake Ontario and the St. Lawrence Valley, but she also provided essential capital to many important railroad enterprises operating outside New England. Before the end of the decade Bostonians including John and Nathaniel Thayer, David A. Neal, Nathan Appleton, and William Sturgis had refinanced and come to control the two large Pennsylvania railroads, the Reading, and the Philadelphia, Wilmington and Baltimore. Farther to the south New Englanders had provided management and capital for the railroad from Norfolk to Richmond; while, with a group of New Yorkers, other New Englanders did the same for the Macon and Western of Georgia.

At the same time railroads in central New York and in the West turned to Boston for funds. By the mid-forties John E. Thayer, John Murray Forbes, Nathan Appleton, and John P. Cushing were investing heavily in the roads that would in 1853 become the New York Central. These men, too, joined with Erastus Corning, the leading railroad man in central New York, to purchase the dilapidated Michigan Central from the state of Michigan and finance its construction. In the meantime the Ohio roads, like the Little Miami, the Mad River and Lake Erie, and the Mansfield and Sandusky, which originally had been largely state-supported, were refinanced by Boston capital through the agency of Nathan Hale, Samuel Henshaw, William Ward, and David A. Neal. The only road in the West to raise funds for its construction before 1849 in New York rather than in Boston was James F. D. Lanier's Madison and Indianapolis.

The railroad promoters to the south and west now acquired most of their funds in Boston, as did the New Englanders, through the sale of stock shares. These shares were sold primarily through personal contacts rather than through specialized middlemen, although by the end of the decade John E. Thayer and Brother, and Henshaw and Ward were beginning to emerge as specialists in the marketing of new securities. Yet even Thayer, Forbes, and other New Englanders who raised the money for the Michigan Central, Boston's largest single Western railroad venture, began doing so by seeking out personal friends, relatives, and business associates.

The depression which struck New England so hard in late 1847 radically altered these patterns of railroad finance. Bonds rapidly replaced stock as the usual instrument to raise capital for Boston-financed railroads. Before the end of 1849 the larger new roads still under construction, such as the Michigan Central, the Vermont Central, the Vermont and Massachusetts, the New Haven and Northampton, and the Northern of New York, had all made their first long-term bond issues.[8] Such financially weak older New England roads as the Old Colony quickly followed suit, and by the end of 1850 even the oldest and the soundest Massachusetts roads, such as the Boston and Providence and the Boston and Worcester, were using bonds as the most satisfactory way to raise money.

Moreover, as the depression deepened, the market for railroad securities almost disappeared in New England. The roads of that area now had to look to the distant investor. They turned to New York to market their new bond issues, for there interest rates for both long- and short-term loans remained from 1848 until 1852 from 1 to 3 per cent lower than in Boston. "The peculiar condition of the Boston market," *Hunt's Merchants' Magazine* reported in the fall of 1849, "threw on the New York market not only the notes given by New Yorkers for goods purchased there, but also much local paper in addition to obligations of railroads and corporations, which could not be placed in New England."[9]

For, while Boston was suffering, New York was prospering. As the nation's leading port, she profited most from the rapid expansion of American exports from 1847 on which was precipitated by the Irish and German famines and further encouraged by the repeal of the Corn Laws. At the same time, the current depression abroad, by forcing down prices of finished goods, especially railroad rails, was stimulating the import trade through the port of New York. Expanding profits from the rapidly growing international trade made it easy for

New York to recover quickly from the depression of 1847 and the short but sharp financial stringency in the spring of 1849. They also provided New York merchants, bankers, and brokers with funds available for long-term investment at the very time when Boston no longer had surplus capital to invest in railroad construction.

In reporting and commenting upon the resulting differential in interest rates between Boston and New York, the editors of *Hunt's Merchants' Magazine,* the *Bankers' Magazine,* and the *American Railroad Journal,* while agreeing on the general pattern, emphasized, quite naturally, different causes. Hunt stressed the commercial aspects, not only the increases in trade and bank deposits, but also New York's better adjustment to the dislocation of trade caused by the California gold rush.[10] Homans, who had moved his *Bankers' Magazine* from Baltimore to Boston shortly after its founding in 1846, blamed Boston's plight on overstrict banking laws, on too rigid legal limitations on interest, on the great expansion of commercial deposits in New York City, and on overinvestment in Western lands, Michigan mines, and in textiles and railroads.[11] Poor, as might be expected, emphasized the last reason. Writing in April 1850 he pointed out:

> The condition of the money market in Massachusetts affords a good illustration of the influence of railroads in absorbing the capital of a community. That State has built more railroads than any other, but she is vastly richer in proportion. She is the most commercial of any, and commerce is the parent of wealth. Her floating capital has been almost entirely invested in railroads and manufacturing establishments. She has not enough left to carry on with ease her ordinary business. She is compelled to borrow from others, till she can, by industry, create sufficient to supply the place of that which she has, for all present practicable purposes, lost. This great scarcity of money has depressed the price of her railroad and manufacturing stocks . . . [to] a ruinous degree, and has placed it out of her power to continue the construction of railroads as formerly, even if she desired to do so.[12]

Since Massachusetts could no longer provide funds for railroad construction, the railroad companies in the South and West had almost no alternative but to turn to New York. This was all the more true because Philadelphia was suffering from the collapse of the iron market caused by the dumping of railroad and other iron in the United States by British manufacturers who had lost their home market with the curtailment of British railroad construction after 1847. During 1848 the Alton and Sangamon, and possibly the Galena and Chicago Union and the Little Miami, unable to obtain funds in Boston, turned to New York. In 1849 the Cleveland, Columbus and Cincinnati, the Cincinnati, Hamilton and Dayton, and one or two other Western roads, went directly to Wall Street for capital. By the end of 1850, the older roads that had developed close financial ties with Boston, like the Mad River and Lake Erie, the Little Miami, the Seaboard and Roanoke, the Reading, and even the Michigan Central, as well as a rapidly growing number of new roads, were relying almost entirely on New York for funds.[13] By that time New York was financing most of America's railroad construction. "If the money had, during the past season, ruled as high in New York as Boston," Poor concluded in October 1850, "thousands of miles of railroad now in successful progress, would have been discontinued."[14]

II

To help the railroads raise the money in New York so essential for their completion, Henry Poor in his first issue of 1851 announced a new editorial policy. He would now devote more space "to new enterprises either in progress or projected and to the diffusion of such information as may be useful to those engaged in their prosecution."[15] To do this he planned to write weekly "a carefully prepared monetary article." This article would list the current prices of railroad stocks and bonds as well as railroad iron. Since, however, reported prices of securities were unreliable and often gave a deceptive picture of the situation on Wall Street, the editor also planned to analyze the changing situation in the New York bond market, "a matter in which all companies, however remote they may be from the commercial centers, are deeply interested as almost every company is obliged to resort to loans." At the same time he promised to make Western securities better known to investors.

In advising the railroads about the condition of the New York money market and in popularizing their securities, Poor's editorials between 1850 and 1852 reflect three major business phenomena. The first was the rapid fluctuation of the business economy from the 1848 recession, to a second severe recession in 1851, to the high prosperity of 1852. The second was the rapid institutionalizing of the nation's money market in New York City; and the third, the change in demand for railroad securities, particularly Western bonds, from a situation in 1850 where there was little or no demand to one of the greatest popularity in 1852.

Even before Poor's announcement early in January 1851, he had begun to give advice on what and when to sell in the New York security market. He had already warned railroad men that they could not hope to sell shares of stock in New York as some of them had previously done in Boston. They would now have to rely on New York. New York merchants and capitalists had less interest in financing Western railroads than the Bostonians had had a few years before. The New Yorkers were unimpressed by the argument, which had carried weight in Boston, that they, as men of commerce, would greatly increase their trade and markets by the construction of railroads in the West. "Our citizens," Poor explained to his out-of-town readers, "have too much business constantly on hand, to feel the importance of taking any steps to add to it. They have consequently remained in indifference as to the importance of railroads." [16] When New York does put money into railroads, Poor continued, "her loans are based on railroad securities, and not in the shape of *subscriptions* to stocks; and are made for the purpose of investment rather than any design to promote the progress of these works." Even preferred stock would not do. In 1848 and 1849 managers of several railroads, including the Michigan Southern, experimented for almost the first time with using preferred stock as more than a temporary emergency financial measure. Yet, as there was little demand for these shares, they all returned to a reliance on the mortgage bond.[17]

In 1850 New Yorkers, Poor further pointed out, were skeptical about buying the bonds of Western railroads. They had plenty of the securities of the best known Eastern roads to choose from. Not only were Pennsylvania, New Jersey, and New England roads offering 7 per cent mortgage bonds, but also the Erie, the Harlem, the Hudson River, and the central New York lines had all made, for the first time, large bond issues to pay for new construction or to replace their strip rails with all iron ones in compliance with a New York law passed in 1847.[18] In such a market, Poor advised the Western and Southern railroad companies to sell bonds of counties and municipalities issued to them, rather than their own bonds. Or if they needed more money immediately than could be raised on public bonds, he recommended that they persuade the municipalities to guarantee their corporate bonds. The investor, he reasoned, often preferred a security backed by public taxation rather than by the still unproven earning ability of a private company. These municipal securities, he reminded investors, "represent a mere fraction of the ability of those issuing them" to pay. Their payment, he added, "may be readily enforced by law, and the aggregate property of a whole community may be seized in discharge of the debt." [19] Yet in 1850 even Western municipal securities could be sold only at a discount.

Early in 1851, however, the market for all types of securities expanded rapidly. Poor was soon advising Western railroad managers to bring to New York their own corporate mortgage bonds as well as those of county and city.[20] After the money markets had recovered from the sharp but brief financial recession of the fall of 1851, bonds of railroads and other corporations were again in great demand — so much so, that early in 1852 Poor began urging Western railroads to issue bonds convertible into stock.[21] Convertibility, he suggested, would give the issues more appeal in a market fast becoming speculative and in which the values of railroad stocks were beginning to rise rapidly. It also would help bring reduction of a road's debt and interest charges. Poor further urged the Western roads to insert in town and county issues clauses permitting them to be converted into company stock. This would not only reduce a municipality's interest charges, but also allow it to withdraw more quickly from its financial and corporate connections with its railroad, which, in Poor's opinion, would benefit all concerned. Finally, Poor advised the roads to make their municipal bonds more marketable by guaranteeing their interest payments. This was, indeed, a far cry from the situation in 1850 when most railroad bonds needed to be guaranteed by municipalities if they were to sell at all.

Poor's advice on what to sell was closely related to his views on when to sell. Moreover, the editor devoted much more space in his monetary articles to a consideration of long- and short-term prospects for the sale of new railroad securities than he did to indicating the most salable type of security.

Although Poor continued to write in his money-market column during much of the fifties, only his initial market analyses need be described in any detail. They illustrate clearly enough the nature of these analyses and also provide a useful background for other Wall Street developments about which he was concerned. When the editor first began to write his money-market articles for out-of-town railroads, many railroad and financial men were troubled by the long-term prospects of the New York investment market. They feared that overinvestment of liquid capital in railroads would lead New York to a financial crisis similar to those which both London and Boston had so recently suffered. In the fall of 1850 and winter of 1851 Poor thought otherwise. He maintained that the future of the sale of railroad securities was comparatively bright because the current railroad construction differed from that financed by Boston and London in three significant respects.[22] First, the railroads which New York was financing in the West cost much less than those in old or New England; therefore the drain caused by this investment was that much less. Secondly, there was in New York's case much less of a time lag between initial investment and returns on the investment. As the experience of the Western roads was already showing, by the time a railroad in that section was but partially completed, it began to enjoy heavy traffic in corn, wheat, hogs, and other agricultural products. In Britain and New England, on the other hand, where existing water transportation was good and where railroads generally connected industrial and commercial centers, few roads became productive until they were fully completed. A third advantage, in Poor's opinion, was that New York's investments were, unlike those of Boston and London, being made in bonds rather than stocks. The purchasers of Western railroad bonds would receive a steady return on their investment rather than, as happened in old and New England, unwarrantedly high dividends for a short period followed by years with no dividends at all. The regular payment of interest on Western bonds, Poor contended, lessened the financial stringency in New York City. Since the railroads in the West promised to be productive, and since they made careful provision to pay their interest, there was little reason why the interest charges should not be met.

There were, however, other dangers resulting indirectly from the rapid increase in railroad construction. The opening up of new areas by improved transportation meant heavy local investment in houses and other construction and also increased the market for many finished goods. This new demand, Poor believed, was reflected in the heavy importation of textiles, hardware, and other manufactured products as well as rails from Europe and especially from Britain. This importation, by requiring in turn an excessive export of bullion and specie necessary to balance the payments, threatened to create a dangerous contraction of credit.

In Poor's opinion, two fortuitous events, the discovery of gold in California and the political upheavals in Europe, prevented the unprecedented amount of imports from causing a serious specie shortage. "If we can not export our breadstuffs to the extent to be desired [to balance the imports]," the editor wrote, "the receipt of gold from the new state of California will prevent any pressure in the money market, which might have proved disastrous but for this new resource." [23] If the supply of California gold should fall off, Poor warned his readers, "we may then begin to look out for a panic." [24] He also considered important "the vast amount of foreign capital seeking investment in this country on account of the low rate of interest, and the threatened political commotion, in Europe." [25] Foreign capital, besides easing the strain of excessive imports, was also relieving the pressure caused by the investments in railroad construction; for, although foreigners in 1850 were purchasing government securities almost exclusively, the resulting rise in the price of public bonds made railroad and municipal bonds more attractive to American buyers.

During 1851 Poor kept a close watch on the New York money market as he reported to the Western roads the fluctuating short-term demand for their securities. In the first weeks of the year he noted that money was plentiful and urged the roads to make the most of the growing market for Western bonds. By the end of March, however, he reported that, although money was still abundant, the demand for railroad bonds had dropped off. For besides the municipal and corporate securities brought to New York by the Western roads, the Baltimore and Ohio, the Hudson River and the New Haven had all put large blocks of bonds on the market. Therefore Poor wrote:

We would advise our country friends to keep out of the market for the present. In a short time the immense amount of bonds which have been recently thrown upon the market, will gradually find their way to the holders for investment, and thus create an opening for a new supply. A few weeks we believe will witness a favorable change, of which we will give our readers timely notice. The quickest and surest way to improve the market, is to guard against overstocking it.[26]

The market remained overstocked throughout April and May, and Poor continued to advise the Western roads not to bring their securities to Wall Street even though the abundance of money in New York and rapidly rising prices of stocks and real estate gave the general impression of highly favorable selling conditions. One major reason for the prolonged oversupply, Poor reported, was that during "the last season" brokers buying for resale, had "completely *gorged* themselves with securities." [27]

During June, however, the demand for securities momentarily improved, and Poor advised the Western railroad managers to sell their bonds. Then the general condition of the money market in New York took a turn for the worse.[28] Bankers, becoming uneasy over the continuing export of gold, began to call in their loans. This in turn forced brokers, who by 1850 were beginning to rely on call loans to finance their speculations, to sell securities in order to meet the bankers' demands. The result, as Poor reported, was a precipitous drop in stock prices and a rapid rise in interest and money rates. Before the end of September, many brokerage and banking houses had failed, including the most notorious of the speculating firms, Jacob Little and Company. The depression, however, was surprisingly short-lived. During the fall Poor was advising the railroads to keep out of the market at all costs. "Many companies can much better afford to suspend work than pay the rates for money now asked." [29] Yet it was only a few months later that he was recommending the sale of convertible bonds to meet the demands of a booming security market.

The editor gave California gold and foreign capital, the two factors that had delayed the financial stringency of 1851, the credit for New York's swift recovery. Cancellation of orders and the resulting reduction of imports relieved for the moment the greatest pressure on the money market. Yet in 1852 imports again increased so rapidly that the total excess of imports over exports was larger for 1852 than for either 1850 or 1851.[30] The continued heavy influx of California gold helped balance the payments. What may have been even more significant, the New York merchants and bankers were no longer troubled by a heavy export of specie. In Poor's opinion, one real cause of the panic had been psychological. "We have been so long accustomed," he wrote late in 1851, "to apprehend disastrous consequences from the exportation of large amounts of the precious metals, [that] it will take us some time to outgrow the habit and look upon the shipment of our surplus coin in the same light that we do the exportation of corn and flour." [31] Poor, more than the other business editors and many financial men, was concerned with the effect on business of gold as a new export crop rather than as a base for credit expansion within the country.

As important for New York's prosperity in 1852 as the shipments of gold, Poor believed, was the large export of securities. Heavy purchases of American securities, stimulated by the influx of foreign capital resulting from the uncertainties created by Napoleon III's *coup d'état* in December 1851, not only provided a balance for the payment of imports, but, since foreigners began to purchase railroad bonds, eased even more than before the pressure on the domestic investment market. Because foreign capital was beginning to flood the New York security market, the theme of Poor's advice to Southern and Western railroad men during most of 1852 was to make the most of the opportunity.

III

During 1851 the editor of the *Journal* wrote almost as much on how to market as on when and what type of securities to sell. Besides hoping to provide useful business information, Poor wrote these editorials because he was firmly convinced that better methods of marketing securities were one of the most important needs of the Southern and Western roads. This need had resulted largely from the New Yorkers' lack of interest in Western and Southern railroad securities in 1849 and 1850. The presidents of the country roads, therefore, had no well-known men or institutions, as they had in Boston and Philadelphia, to which they could turn for financial assistance. The few merchant capitalists interested in railroads, like James Boorman, William E. Dodge, and Moses Taylor, were wholly involved in the Hudson River, the Erie, the New Jersey Central, and other railroads close to New York. The few established foreign exchange houses, like Ward and Company and Brown Brothers, who had earlier, as embryonic investment bankers, marketed state securities in the 1830's, were willing to be agents for Eastern roads, but they had little reason in 1850 to incur the risks involved in handling the securities of unknown Western railroads.[32]

When the Western and Southern presidents first came East, almost the only New Yorkers interested in taking securities were either stock and exchange brokers who specialized in trading on the New York Stock Exchange or an occasional merchant who handled Western accounts. The stock brokers first became involved in marketing new bond issues in the early 1840's. At that time such firms as Jacob Little and Company; Drew, Robinson and Company; Winslow and Perkins; and Rogers, Ketchum and Bement had bid for state bonds which the incorporated banks and mercantile houses then handling such securities were no longer willing to take. In 1850 these houses, and others like John Thompson; Gilbert, Cobb and Johnson, and such commission merchants as Gibson, Stockwell and Company; Spofford, Tileson and Clark; and Henry Coit and Sons were willing to take a similar risk on Western corporate and municipal bonds. Purchasing sparingly at first, they were by the late fall of 1850, Poor noted, already buying "in large quantities . . . for the purpose of selling again in smaller lots." [33] These firms normally purchased the bonds outright. The transactions were, to use the language of the day, "negotiated" at "private sales."

The alternative to dealing with a stock broker or commission merchant was to sell at public auction. The auction, long a standard method of buying and selling securities in New York City, was also first used for the marketing of new issues in the early 1840's, when states like Ohio, forced to raise funds to meet current debts and unable to negotiate an issue, turned to the auction as the last resort. In the early 1850's, the auctioning of new railroad securities became a regular practice. The auctions were handled by professional auctioneers like Simeon Draper of Haggerty, Draper and Jones or Wilmerdings and Mount, and, after 1853, by Albert H. Nicolay, either at the instigation of the railroads themselves or by the brokerage house handling their securities.[34]

For Poor, both the public auction and the private sale to stock and exchange brokers were highly unsatisfactory ways of selling securities. In the first place, the editor had only distrust for the "money broker" whose primary business was speculating on the exchange. "Speculation in stocks," Poor fumed, "is the worst form of gambling, and is only tolerated upon the principle, that 'one murder makes a villain — thousands a hero!' If similar combinations should be formed for the purpose of putting up the price of provisions or ordinary merchandise, which are an everyday occurrence on the stock exchange, the parties would be ridden on a rail, or indicted as nuisances." [35] The legislature should in fact, Poor urged, make selling "on time" an indictable offense.

The *Journal's* editor was especially disturbed by the brokers' eagerness to speculate in the securities of the new roads. "The favorite footballs in the stock market are those whose value is *problematical.*" [36] Here the Wall Street bulls and bears have "plenty of scope; the one in exercising the imagination in inventing plausible reasons to convince people of its value, and the other to show that it is utterly worthless." Railroad managers must use, Poor warned, every means to prevent the securities of their roads from becoming speculators' footballs. Not only was it fatal to the "character" of a stock for it to become involved in such operations, but "in the end too often it becomes fatal to the value of the property which it represents." [37]

Yet even the broker who did not use for speculation the issues he helped market was still the wrong sort of middleman. After all, wrote Poor, since he is buying for resale, "the money broker and the company have exactly opposite interests: the former to buy as low and the latter to get as much as possible." [38] The broker is only satisfied if he can buy at 75 and sell at 100. Even if he was purchasing for a customer on commission, "a broker buys at a low figure, upon an order, [since] his principal may wish to sell again as the value of the security rises in the market. This gives him a chance for a second commission, which he would lose if he gave in the outset all the security was worth." Poor, indicating the difficulties involved in negotiating with Wall Street brokers, gave a picture of how such a sale was transacted:

> When securities are disposed of at *private* sale, the broker or operator to whom they are committed, makes up a *party* of his friends, among whom they are divided, each taking 5, 10, or $20,000; for, notwithstanding we have some pretty capacious maws in Wall Street, it can boast of but few individuals who severally could comfortably digest a mass of bonds of $500,000 without having the functions of his business stomach somewhat deranged. Even such a person prefers a variety of dishes to a surfeit of one. As soon, therefore, as the seller, with the greatest secrecy and confidence, imparts his scheme to the money lender or broker, he communicates with an electrive [sic] despatch the same to some twenty or thirty others.[39]

Once the scheme is known, other brokers with securities of their own to sell do their best to force the price down by criticizing the road, its management, and its financial prospects. If the brokers can prevent the securities from being "'placed' soon after they come into the market, the inference is, that there is some intrinsic defect in them which has prevented a sale. The securities in this way become *shop-worn,* and must be sold as second-hand goods."

Public auction was, in Poor's opinion, a somewhat better way to sell new issues. Yet it was both costly and risky. At an auction, Poor warned:

> The great mass of operators will of course unite to break down the sale; and will do so, unless it is strongly supported. A few strong names must be selected to lead off, to puff and blow, and manufacture a public sentiment in favor of what [is] to be sold; to form the nucleus, and start off in the race, and the number and spirit of those that will follow, will bear an exact proportion to the apparent zeal and confident assertion of the leaders. After the public sentiment is brought up to the proper point, the managers must attend the sale, start and sustain the bids at a proper point, and take for the sellers what cannot be disposed of *bona fide.*

If because the managers mishandle the bidding, the bids are low, "the security loses *caste* and must then be disposed of as a second-hand article."

Poor advocated two improvements in the marketing of Western railroad securities. For one thing he urged the roads to sell their bonds on commission rather than directly to the brokers. Select a reliable agent, a banker or merchant who is not one of the broker fraternity, he recommended, "a man who shall bring the seller and purchaser for investment together, and who shall be entitled to a proper commission for his services." [40] However, Poor's major reform was, characteristically enough, publicity. All private and public sales, he wrote, "should be *publicly* reported and the exact price obtained stated. This course would at once reduce matters to a system, and securities would soon sell at their fair value, in the same manner as other kinds of merchandise. Purchasers for investment would investigate for themselves, and the information which is monopolized by a few persons would, as it were, become common stock of the whole community." [41] If the low prices that, for example, had been paid for the bonds of Milwaukee in 1850 and for the bonds of several well located Western railroads in 1851, had become more generally known, competition among buyers, Poor maintained, would have driven up the prices of such securities closer to their true value. On the other hand, if the price received was so low that its publication might injure the credit of a road or a municipality, then such bonds should be taken off the market. No road, Poor warned, could succeed financially if it paid "exorbitant shaves" on its loans. Also Poor stressed that the railroads would gain much more from such publicity than from their present misguided policies of reporting overly high prices paid at private sales or from "the vast amount of *sham* resorted to in almost every public sale; we mean the fictitious bids put in and the various tricks practiced to sustain the bidding." [42] Since the public is well aware of these shams, such practices only discredit the railroad companies and depress the value of their securities.

Poor was asking too much. Very few brokers or railroad companies would have voluntarily made public the prices paid for their new railroad issues. However, during 1851 an increasing number of new railroad issues were sold through the sealed bid system, which the federal government and some states had used since the 1820's to sell their bonds.[43] By this method, the closest practical realization of Poor's ideal, notices were placed in the daily press several weeks before the sale. They first described the bond issue in detail and then announced that bids would be received until a specified hour of a certain day. On the day following the sale, all bids, successful and unsuccessful, were listed in the newspapers, with the name of each bidder and the amount taken. In some but not all of the early sales made by this method, the bids could be opened any time before the final hour, thus permitting manipulation of the bids. By the middle of the decade, however, most advertisements read that the bids would remain unopened in the hands of the agent making the sale until the given day and hour, and "then opened in the presence of the President or some other authorized agents of the Company." [44]

During 1851 one firm, Winslow, Lanier and Company, was bringing to the marketing of Western railroad securities the order and the system that Poor so desired. This firm was all that Poor required of a New York agent for Western railroad companies. It was a respectable banking house, selling new securities primarily on a commission basis, and, more than any other firm, was responsible for the introduction of the sealed bid method of marketing railroad securities. Although Richard H. Winslow, a former partner of Winslow and Perkins, had the taint of being a Wall Street broker, the other senior partner, James F. D. Lanier, was a banker of the highest respectability.[45] Lanier first made his reputation by guiding the state bank of Indiana successfully through the financial storms of the late 1830's. In 1847 he further enhanced his reputation by negotiating a satisfactory resettlement of the state's debt with European bondholders. While in Europe, he met and gained the confidence of the Rothschilds, Pierre Labouchere of the Dutch house of Hope and Company, and Horsley Palmer, president of the Bank of England. Such contacts became of immense value to the Indiana banker after he and Winslow formed their banking firm in January 1849.

In 1849 Lanier was one of the few bankers in New York with confidence in Western railroads. He had, in fact, first met his partner, Winslow, when he came from Indiana to New York in 1845 to negotiate a loan with Winslow and Perkins for funds necessary to complete the Madison and Indianapolis.[46] Lanier's company had been the only railroad between 1840 and 1847 to raise a sizable amount of money in New York instead of Boston. During 1849 and 1850, Winslow, Lanier and Company purchased and helped market bonds of Cleveland, Pittsburgh, Indianapolis, and other Western municipalities issued for local roads. By the beginning of 1850, the new firm was acting as agent for the Michigan Southern and several Ohio and Indiana roads, including the Cleveland, Columbus and Cincinnati, the Indianapolis and Bellefontaine, and the Cleveland and Pittsburgh.[47] As 1852 opened, the banking house was handling the securities of nearly a majority of the Western railroads.

As a railroad company's fiscal agent, Winslow, Lanier and Company had many duties.[48] It marketed the company's corporate and municipal bonds, normally at a 5 per cent commission. The corporate bonds it usually sold by sealed bids, although quite often it sold them directly to investors or financial institutions. When, for example, the bids on a million-dollar issue of the Little Miami were unsatisfactory, the bonds were disposed of at private sales. On the other hand, nearly all the county and municipal bonds, which were usually issued in small amounts, were negotiated by private sales rather than by sealed bids. Occasionally the firm took all or part of an issue on their own account instead of selling it on a commission basis. Also as a railroad's fiscal agent, it usually paid the interest and principal on a company's bonds; often its partners became trustees and registration agents for later issues. Besides these functions, the firm paid dividends, acted as a stock transfer agent, and occasionally purchased iron and equipment for a road, or forwarded railroad iron and materials which the company had purchased abroad.

Poor had only the highest regard for this banking firm, which was bringing efficiency and system into the marketing of new railroad securities. He had come to know the senior partners when he and they set up their respective enterprises during the early weeks of 1849 in adjoining offices on Wall Street. Throughout the 1850's there appears to have been a close personal relationship between the editor and the bankers.[49] As the decade progressed his editorial columns increasingly reflect their attitudes and opinions. In 1851 they certainly saw eye to eye with him on the importance of systematizing the methods of selling Western railroad securities. At that time too Winslow, Lanier and Company must have heartily approved of Poor's campaign to popularize Western bonds.[50]

IV

In January 1851 the editor of the *American Railroad Journal* promised Western railroad men that, besides providing a weekly analysis of the New York investment market, he would do his best to make their securities better known. Already in 1850 he had pointed out that, because the Eastern investor knew so little about the West and Western securities, the bonds of prosperous cities in the Mississippi Valley were selling at a discount, while those of Eastern cities were being taken at a premium. "The difference in the price of these securities is in part owing to the shortness of time they have been on the market," Poor had written. "They have attracted so little attention that the public have not become impressed with their true value." [51] For the same reason, Poor advised his Western and Southern readers, the mortgage bonds of Western railroads were bringing much lower prices than those of Eastern companies. "The market value of securities," Poor again emphasized, "depends upon their *reputation* rather than intrinsic worth." [52] The reason 6 per cent bonds of the Boston and Worcester would sell at 106, 16 per cent higher than the average Western bond, was, Poor continued, because "a capitalist does not so much look at the amount of income which a security yields, as its safety and convertibility." Yet, Poor pointed out, "time is necessary to invest securities with such attributes, and those of our Western friends that are in the market now must make the sacrifice due to their position. They pay a penalty for no other reason than that of being pioneers in railroad construction. Time will bring with it that general confidence and reputation, the want of which is now so severely felt." From 1850 through 1852, Poor determined to do his best to decrease the time needed to give Western securities the reputation they deserved.

In his editorial efforts to popularize Western railroad bonds, Poor played steadily on one basic theme: the tremendous need of the West for better transportation would undoubtedly make its railroads a profitable investment.[53] The Western canals, lakes, and rivers, essential as they were, in no way fulfilled the transportation requirements of the Mississippi Valley. Because of ice and drought, the service they offered was often irregular and undependable. Even more serious, large areas in the West were too far from rivers or lakes to make use of water transportation. As the dirt roads of the West were totally inadequate, only the railroad could carry economically the crops and agricultural products either to the rivers and lakes or directly to the Eastern markets. In the future, then, Poor was absolutely certain, the railroad must carry the lion's share of the commerce of the West. Already the early Western roads were having difficulty in meeting the call of the farmers along the line of their roads to carry wheat, corn, hogs, and other agricultural products to the Ohio River or Lake Erie. The completion of the many roads currently under construction would, by opening up direct rail routes to the East, immeasurably increase the traffic of all the Western roads.

This need for improved transportation facilities not only assured a heavy traffic for the new roads, but also helped lower the cost of their construction. Westerners, eager for the new transportation, were happy to give railroad companies a right of way and terminal locations at almost no cost. For the same reason, Western counties and cities levied few and often no taxes on railroad property. With lowered costs of land and taxes, and the relatively flat terrain in the Western states, construction costs in this area would be, Poor was certain, as cheap as in any part of the country. Enjoying such low costs and heavy freight, these roads could hardly fail to be profitable.

The Westerners' keen interest in improved transportation would, Poor further maintained, assure competent management of the new roads. In the West, in contrast to England and even to the East, the directors and managers of the roads resided in towns along the lines of the roads and had a direct stake in their success as providers of transportation. They, in turn, were carefully watched by the local farmers, whose economic well-being depended on the efficient management of the road. Thus, in Poor's opinion, there was comparatively little danger of that exploitation by unscrupulous directors and officers who lived in distant cities, which had so often occurred in England and was beginning to occur in New England. Finally, the strong desire in the West for railroads, Poor reasoned, prevented the danger of the antirailroad sentiment which, when expressed politically, occasionally harassed the railroads in the East and in Europe.

To make the investor more aware of his opportunity, Poor printed a great deal of factual data on Western railroads, both individually and collectively. He wrote articles on the railroad systems of the different Western and Southern states and gave careful descriptions of the individual roads. These descriptions discussed the territory through which the road passed, giving its population, current crop production, and probable freight traffic; indicated the amount and type of local financial support; and concluded with a statement or two on the value of the road as an investment.

In describing the Western roads, Poor concentrated on those coming into the New York market for the first time. Once a road had successfully sold its securities and had completed the major portion of its construction — that is, once its securities had become well known

— it received little attention in the *Journal.* Similarly, Poor kept comparatively silent about, or at least did little more than briefly describe projects concerning whose future he was somewhat skeptical. Until the middle of 1852, however, most railroads coming into the New York investment market were assured of having their present condition and future prospects attractively presented to the investor in the pages of the *American Railroad Journal.*

Poor's editorials on Western railroad bonds differed from the type of literature which had hitherto appeared in the *American Railroad Journal* and local newspapers promoting railroad construction. Earlier promotional articles appealed to farmers and merchants to purchase stock in a local railroad venture. The call for local support had to be bold and imaginative. It must convince the local community that the proposed railroad would bring economic prosperity and new commercial opportunity. The investor, on the other hand, cared little about indirect benefits of community growth. Interested almost wholly in a certain and steady return on his investment, he was more likely to be persuaded to help finance a distant road by objective, analytical articles describing a road's prospects in terms of statistics of population, of agricultural production, and of current river and canal traffic. Poor, already experienced in writing for the local farmer and merchant, quickly excelled in appealing to the Eastern investor. His interest in the collection of data, his respect for facts, and his analytical approach all helped him sound convincing. So also did his sincere belief in the value of the railroad as an instrument of economic progress.

This faith in railroads too often made the *Journal's* editor overoptimistic and unskeptical about the costs, potential traffic, and future management of many Western railroads. Still, Poor's sanguineness was shared by many of the shrewdest businessmen and engineers of his day. After 1850, such hardheaded merchants, bankers, and manufacturers as Joseph Alsop, Azariah C. Flagg, Amasa Stone, Abram Hewitt, and Joseph Sheffield, and such competent engineers as John B. Jervis, William N. Roberts, and James Kirkwood made even more enthusiastic claims than Poor about railroads in the West and invested their own time, money, and often their future careers in these roads. In a surprisingly short time, however, Poor was to alter his views and his editorial policies on Western railroads. He was soon to become more realistic about their value as investments and more selective in the roads he endorsed.

V

Before changing his policies, Poor, however, devoted a large amount of editorial space to making railroad securities, especially the bonds of Western roads, acceptable to the foreign as well as the American investor. It was for the foreign investor that many of Poor's editorials were explicitly written in 1852. As the year passed, the content and tone of these editorials changed. As the foreign investor began to purchase more and more American railroad securities, Poor turned from popularizing the railroad bond to advising foreign investors on how to buy and even on what securities not to buy. This shift in emphasis Poor believed was necessary if his paper was to continue to serve the best interests of the American railroad industry.

Poor first began to address the foreign investor in January 1852. The sharp depression of the preceding months had persuaded him of the vital importance of foreign capital for the railroads of the United States. He had become convinced that only a steady flow of foreign funds would permit New York to avert a financial fate similar to that of Boston.[54] Poor began his campaign to popularize American securities abroad by directing his editorials at the Continental investors, for they, rather than the British, were the largest buyers of American securities in January 1852. The revolutions of 1848 had created, for the first time since the 1830's, a real demand in Europe for American securities. German and French investors, frightened by the political upheavals, had first purchased large amounts of United States government bonds. These bonds, largely Mexican War bonds, they bought either through the Barings or Rothschilds or directly from the Washington firm of Corcoran and Riggs, the largest contractors for the war issues.[55]

Although some of these government issues were later returned by the European investors, the Continental demand for securities continued after 1848. In 1849 and 1850, as the supply of government bonds became limited, the Europeans began to take the bonds of the financially sound states, especially those of New York, Massachusetts, and Ohio. Here again, the heavy buyers for foreign accounts were the correspondents of the Barings and Rothschilds, including Ward and Company, Watts Sherman, and August Belmont. When this demand drove the price of most state securities above par for the first time in over a decade, the foreign investors turned to railroad securities, usually taking the bonds of the finished roads in the East.[56] By 1851, they began to buy cautiously the securities of the Western roads.[57]

The buyers of railroad securities for the foreign customer tended to be foreign exchange, importing, and shipping firms that were agents or correspondents of Continental business houses rather than the better known private bankers in New York like John Ward and August Belmont, who purchased large blocks of public securities for the European market. Of these firms, De Launay, Iselin and Clarke was the heaviest buyer of Western railroad bonds; but Cammann and Whitehouse; Delano, Dunlevy and Company; De Coppet and Company; Meyer and Stucken; Moran and Iselin; De Rham and Moore; and Philip Speyer and Company were by the beginning of 1852 starting to send railroad bonds to Europe.[58] All these firms, except perhaps Delano, Dunlevy and Company, had been and still were active importing houses. They had, as an adjunct to their commercial work, a foreign exchange business; and by 1850 some already considered their financial business more important than their importing trade.[59] All these firms had family and business ties on the Continent, primarily in Switzerland and Germany. The Iselins, Adrian and John, were from an old Basle family, and their firm continued to have close connections with Geneva and Basle bankers until well into the twentieth century. The Morans, Charles and Theodore, also apparently had connections in Switzerland. De Launay had business ties with Le Havre; while the De Coppet firm was agent for business houses in Germany and Paris. Meyer and Stucken were the correspondents for Gogel, Koch and Company of Frankfort, and enjoyed business contacts with Bremen; the Speyers had Frankfort and Bremen alliances; while Cammann seems to have kept in contact with his relatives in Bremen and Hamburg.[60]

In 1851 and early 1852, as the columns of the *Railroad Journal* noted, these firms were bidding regularly for the bonds of Western roads, though usually they took but a small amount of any one issue. They also purchased bonds from the houses handling these securities, especially from Winslow, Lanier and Company. Thus by 1852, several issues marketed by Winslow, Lanier and Company, including those of the Ohio and Pennsylvania, the Cleveland and Pittsburgh, and the Cleveland, Painesville and Ashtabula, were already being traded on the Frankfort exchange.[61] These foreign exchange and importing houses may also have purchased securities directly from the railroads themselves, for before the end of 1852 De Launay, Iselin and Clarke, Delano, Dunlevy and Company, and one or two others were acting as fiscal agents for Western railroads. It was to these firms and their customers, then, that Poor turned his editorial attention in January 1852.

In bringing Western railroad bonds to the notice of the Continental investor, Poor used many of the same arguments he had made to the domestic investor. In addition, he stressed the difference between the United States and Europe as a field of investment. In the United States, the editor began, there was little danger of a political revolution similar to those which had so recently disturbed many European investors. Conveniently forgetting for the moment the tensions between North and South, he maintained:

We are the only people in the world that have a system of government which every citizen, high and low, rich and poor, regard as best adapted to promote the particular advantage of each. . . . No man among us can imagine a radical change, which shall be for the better. All, therefore, from choice, are conservitors of [the] existing state of things, while in Europe, a vast *majority* in nearly every State, are discontented, and plotting the overthrow of all existing institutions which they regard only as instruments of oppression.[62]

Nor were there in America standing armies, established churches, governmental bureaucracies, or a large leisure class to drain off the returns from investments by heavy taxes, rents, and annuities. Here, too, was one of the fastest-growing populations in the world, eager to develop the vast and as yet largely untouched stocks of agricultural and mineral wealth.

In the United States, with its growing and satisfied citizenry, and its untapped natural resources, transportation was the key to economic development. The farmer and manufacturer, Poor pointed out to the European man of means, had far more need of the railroad in America than he did in Europe. "Take England, for example," Poor wrote. "*There* a railroad may be built without necessarily increasing the value of property or the profits of a particular interest." For one thing, since the British cities are scattered, nearly "every farmer in England lives in sight of a market." [63] In the United States, on the other hand, "we have no market for our produce in the vicinity of its growth." The Western farmer, for example, "has no home demand for the wheat he raises, as the surplus of all his neighbors is the same in *kind*." [64] Since the domestic market for Southern and Western products is largely confined to a narrow belt on the Eastern seaboard north of Baltimore, and a large share of the market for the Eastern manufacturers is in the Mississippi Valley, "nearly every product of our industry requires to be transported to a great distance to find customers." [65] As the railroads must supply the major part of this transportation, railroad securities should, Poor told the foreign investor, become among the safest and most productive of American investments.

Of all the areas in the United States, the West, where the roads were so poor, the canals so few, and the rivers so unreliable, had the greatest need for foreign capital. In the West, unlike the East, little or no surplus capital was available; and, unlike the South, all the states except Missouri prohibited state aid. Investment in the Western railroads, Poor was certain in his own mind, would surely be mutually beneficial to the foreign investor and the railroad. Most Americans wanted capital at this time, he maintained, for legitimate and productive projects. "Our people do not ask for . . . [capital] for any speculative purposes, but for such only as will vastly increase our means and bear the most careful scrutiny. We wish to make up in a few years the time lost in not discovering this continent a few centuries sooner. . . . With accumulated capital, which represents *time,* we can in fifty years reach a point which, without it, it would take us two hundred to attain." [66] Or, to put it another way, outside funds permitted American capital which must otherwise be used for railroad construction to go into the building of farms and cities in the areas the railroad was opening to commercial agriculture. By releasing funds from railroad building, the foreign investor was therefore assuring more traffic for the very roads he was helping to finance.

To demonstrate to the foreigner the soundness of Western railroads as investments, Poor pointed to actual operating results.[67] The recent profits of the completed roads in the West showed clearly that they could easily meet interest and sinking fund charges. As Western roads usually borrowed about $10,000 a mile to complete construction, they had to net at least $1,500 a mile over operating costs if they were to meet a 7 per cent interest charge and 8 per cent toward a sinking fund for the retirement of the issue. According to their most recent annual reports, Poor noted that the Little Miami had earned $3,541 per mile; the Columbus and Xenia, $2,778; the Michigan Central, $2,116; the Madison and Indianapolis, $2,378; and the Cleveland, Columbus and Cincinnati, for six months only, $1,710. Thus local traffic, as most of this was, netted them much more than they needed to meet the cost of borrowing money. As the railroads pushed west and opened new areas to commercial agriculture, and as the through routes between East and West were completed, the business of both old and new railroads must increase still more.[68] Moreover, the need for railroads was so great, Poor maintained, that overconstruction and the resulting ruinous competition was a danger which, if it materialized at all, would only do so in the distant future.[69]

By the summer of 1852, many foreign investors had obviously come to agree with the *Railroad Journal* on the value of American railroad bonds. Not only were New York firms buying heavily for Swiss, French, and German investors but, for the first time since the late 1830's, British capitalists began to purchase American securities in large amounts. Before 1852, the ordinary British investor, recalling his unhappy experiences with American securities in the 1830's and the disastrous results of the more recent railroad boom at home, shied clear of buying the bonds of any American railroads, and took federal and state securities only very sparingly.[70] Between 1848 and 1852, a few railroad bonds seem to have been purchased for British accounts by Ward and Company and one or two importing houses, like John Ferguson and possibly Delano, Dunlevy and Company. More were taken by London firms, like McCalmont and Company and George Peabody and Company; but the McCalmonts were handling almost wholly the securities of the Reading, and Peabody, the Baltimore and Ohio — roads in which each firm had long been financially involved. Also, after the beginning of railroad expansion in the late 1840's, American railroad bonds reached England to pay British iron manufacturers for rails, but were usually sent to Switzerland, Germany or returned to New York for sale.

In 1852, prosperity, a low interest rate, and the rapidly rising prices of British securities combined to break down the British investor's prejudices against American securities. That spring, when the Bank of England reduced its interest rate to 2 per cent, the lowest in its history, the 7 per cent mortgage bonds of American railroads proved irresistible. In the summer and fall, British capital began to flood the American investment market; and by the end of the year, several of the bonds of Western roads, some of which had already appeared on the Frankfort exchange, were listed on the London exchange.

Poor was actually more disturbed than pleased by the British investor's sudden interest in American railroad securities. He feared that the amazing abundance of capital and the sharp demand for railroad bonds was tempting the speculator into railroad construction. "We are exceedingly anxious that nothing should be palmed off upon foreigners that has not a real and intrinsic value," he told the Western railroad promoter. The amount of future European investment depended, Poor warned, "entirely upon the confidence felt in our securities, and . . . this confidence must result from an *experience* of their value."[71] Therefore during the summer and fall of 1852 Poor's editorials were almost more concerned with advising the foreigner how and what to buy than with appealing to him to purchase American railroad bonds. This advice was, for the most part, directed at the British investor.

As a primary "condition of safe investment," Poor urged the British to follow the practice of the French, Swiss, and German buyers, of placing orders for American securities "through responsible American houses."[72] The reasons for purchasing through American firms "of the highest respectability" were, in his opinion, obvious. With the firm of Winslow, Lanier and Company undoubtedly in mind, Poor advised the British investor that:

> A person residing in New York, and competent to conduct a banking house, can hardly make a mistake as to the character of a project before the public. He is, or can make himself acquainted with the route of a road, its local resources and the relation it bears to the commerce of the country. He knows, or can easily know, the persons who have charge of the work, their integrity, and capacity to manage its affairs properly and successfully. He can also avail himself of the opinion of others who have, from their position and relation to the work, and the parties connected with it, the best means of forming a correct opinion in reference to it; and lastly, he has all those aids to the forming of a correct opinion which can only be picked up in a thousand different ways, by a person having daily and hourly intercourse with the parties themselves, and moving within the sphere where all public projects are daily discussed, and all their weak points, if they have any, exposed and laid open.

Moreover, a New York house acting as an investor's agent can "apprise him of any change that may threaten in the value of his security, thus giving him an opportunity to dispose of it, should the retaining it involve present or prospective loss."

The German investors used another safeguard which, Poor stressed, the British would be wise to follow. They sent out competent men to study the financial position of the railroads, their management, and the territory through which they passed. "The consequence is, that knowing what they are purchasing, they take our choicest securities, leaving the others to the less fastidious or less informed buyer."[73] Finally, Poor pointed out that the Continental investors were as careful about quantity as quality of the bonds they bought. The Swiss and German houses, he noted, "adopt another precaution of great service to us as well as to themselves. They purchase only what they have immediate use for. They do not load themselves with three or four times the amount for which they have orders, for the purpose of speculation on future demand."[74]

The British investors, on the other hand, paid much less attention either to the quality or the quantity of their purchases. This was, in Poor's opinion, primarily because British investors and banking houses tended to avoid the American middleman. The individual investor in England nearly always purchased through a London house; and, often as not, the London house failed to scrutinize carefully the securities it handled. By placing his orders in London rather than in New York, the investor was cut off from an important channel of information about the changing conditions of the American investment market. More serious, Poor remarked, was the fact that "in this case the *Banker* in fact represents the seller, repeats his statements and representations, and knows only so much about the affair as the principal, who is anxious to sell, communicates to him. Of course all information is drawn through interested and consequently unsafe channels."[75] Too often the British banker, taking the American railroad promoter at his word, did not bother with a further investigation of the securities he agreed to negotiate. To make matters worse, London houses usually took a larger amount of securities than the current demand warranted, and so had to unload bonds, often of uncertain value, on their unsuspecting customers.

This failure of many British houses and investors to buy through agents in the United States made them an easy target for glib bond salesmen with second-rate securities to sell. Poor, describing the weaknesses of the British ways of investment, suggested:

> Now John Bull is being a little humbugged in this business of bond-selling, and will very likely be a good deal so, before it is through with. Having made some bad bargains in times past, he has adopted as a general maxim, that the great mass of our securities are good for nothing, and will not take the trouble to inquire into their character, nor inform himself as to their real merits. He consequently remains in almost entire ignorance of what we are doing, of the mode in which our works are constructed, and of their success when brought into operation. The shrewd operator, knowing his frame of mind, goes to him, humors his way of thinking, blows up in the English papers our whole system of doing things, echoes every sentiment and whim of the old fellow, until he has secured a strong hold on his good graces. John Bull begins to think his new acquaintance a mighty fine fellow; and so much like himself, that his opinion can certainly be relied upon. Having got into *position*, the operator tells him that his opinion of our securities is correct, quite correct, entirely correct; that too great caution cannot be used in reference to them, and winds up by gently suggesting that there are some things that *are good*, one of which he has, out of great regard, brought with him, for Mr. Bull's special use, "*seeing it's him.*"[76]

Poor emphasized that, while some securities taken directly to London were undoubtedly sound, the majority "are taken abroad [because] they will not sell at *home*." Neither domestic purchasers nor houses buying on foreign account would take them. "Shut out from our own market, the holder goes in quest of one abroad, where his project is not so well known, and where his statements cannot be so readily disproved, as at home."

To the British banker or investor who insisted on buying American securities in England, Poor offered a rule of thumb by which to evaluate American railroad bonds. If the sum to be borrowed was more than half the amount of capital already raised through the sale of stock locally, the road was a speculative project. For, unless the people living along the line of the road were able to contribute at least half the cost, "the construction of a road is not demanded by the business of such section, and will not probably *pay*." [77] There might, of course, be exceptions to this rule. However, Poor argued, "these exceptions better remain at home, where the character of the project, and the men managing it, are well understood, and [where] the value of these securities depend upon causes that cannot be appreciated abroad. We have, too, an abundance of first class securities, so that there is no necessity for foreigners taking those about which there shall be the least risk." Poor then told both the European capitalist and the Western railroad manager that he would point out when and how an American security for sale in foreign markets failed to meet this criterion. "If *our* people will purchase them, possessing the fullest means of informing themselves, it is their concern, not ours. If we do not think well of a security, this is no reason why *we* should condemn it. Our convictions may be wrong; and where we do not *know*, we are duty bound to be silent."

In the summer of 1852, Henry Poor began to speak out strongly against the issues of the Illinois Central, the Erie, and one or two other companies that were being taken directly to London for sale. The Erie bonds of 1851 and 1852, he noted, were only income bonds unsecured by any kind of a mortgage. In fact, large issues of first and second mortgage bonds had already been sold and took priority in payment over the new issues. More serious was the fact that, of the total capitalization of the road — $27,000,000 — only $6,000,000 was represented by stock.[78]

The securities of the Illinois Central, Poor maintained, were even more unsound. In the first place, the company was being managed as a speculation. For some time before the summer of 1852, Poor had been condemning the financial methods of its promoters.[79] The state of Illinois, he contended, had virtually sold the land granted to it by the national government to finance the road to a small clique of New York capitalists. These men, after estimating the cost of construction at $17,000,000, had issued $1,000,000 worth of stock to themselves and $17,000,000 worth of bonds secured by the land grant. In other words, wrote Poor, outsiders were to pay for the road while the insiders reaped the profits at no risk to themselves. Poor was incensed to find the first of the government land grants, which could prove so beneficial to the development of American railroads, being used more for "private aggrandizement than to the public good." [80] He was as distressed by the fact that a huge loan had been authorized before any construction was begun and before any bona fide stock had been subscribed. During the winter of 1851–1852, the company, as Poor had earlier predicted, had failed to market its bonds abroad. The following summer, however, its agents were back in London; and this time, owing partly to the new demand for American securities and partly to an extensive propaganda campaign, they were meeting with success.

Although many financiers and railroad men held the same opinion as Poor of the speculative nature of the Illinois Central, the road had strong support in the business press.[81] In New York Thomas Prentiss Kettell's *United States Economist* gave it enthusiastic backing; while in London *The Times,* which had been condemning most American securities, gave the issues of the Illinois company emphatic and repeated editorial endorsement. Kettell, who had just become editor of the *Economist,* had been writing money articles since the 1830's in the New York press which were said "to have had oracular authority with statesmen and merchants." [82] His editorials, therefore, carried almost as much weight both here and abroad on American business situations as did the most influential British paper, the London *Times.* Poor feared that it was just this type of propaganda that led investors, especially the British, to buy speculative and unsound securities.

In giving such warnings to the foreign investor Poor became increasingly aware of the uncertain quality of the railroad bonds coming into the New York investment market. He now urged Western railroad companies to delay coming to New York for funds until they could "show an undoubted subscription list equal to one half the cost of the road." Unless they did so, he warned, they must "expect to submit to sacrifices in proportion to their weakness." [83] When they did come with a substantial subscription list, he advised them to make their financial position clear in a detailed and carefully drawn-up prospectus.[84] At this same time, he began to deplore the practice among some Western roads of declaring excessively high dividends in order to attract investors.[85] Such dividends, he maintained, instead of creating confidence in a project, created a suspicion of an extravagant and speculative management.

These warnings in turn caused Poor to reconsider the value of the services he had been rendering the railroads since the fall of 1850. Business conditions had in two years changed phenomenally. Where in late 1850 railroad bonds could only be sold at a heavy discount, in the summer of 1852 they were going at a premium. By the fall even the stocks of the Western roads were selling at well above par.[86] New conditions called for a change in editorial policy. No longer was it necessary to popularize Western railroad securities. Nor was it necessary to explain to distant railroad managers the intricacies of the New York investment market. Moreover the new situation raised new problems for the railroad industry. Because of these new conditions Poor, at the end of 1852, announced a new editorial policy. The *Journal* would now devote more space to pointing out and helping to prevent the dangers arising from overconstruction and less to aiding Western railroads to market their securities on Wall Street.

5

Warning Against Overconstruction

FROM DECEMBER 1852 when Poor announced his new editorial policy until the summer of 1862 when he severed his connection with the *American Railroad Journal,* he repeatedly stressed the necessity for retrenchment and reform within the railroad industry. During 1853 and much of 1854 Poor's editorials emphasized the need for retrenchment and warned against the dangers of overconstruction. After the sharp but short financial recession of 1854, the editor concentrated on the need for financial and administrative reform. In urging retrenchment and reform, Poor still continued to publicize the value of American railroad securities as investments. It was his intention that these editorial policies would help make such investments more sound and productive.

In carrying out his new editorial program Poor had little support from the railroad and business press. The railroad periodicals particularly disliked the *Journal's* policy of retrenchment during 1853 and 1854, although later in the decade they, too, joined in warning against overconstruction. Commercial papers like *Hunt's Merchants' Magazine* and the *Bankers' Magazine* and to a lesser degree the *United States Economist* saw dangers in the growing railroad boom. Yet since their major interest lay elsewhere, they only sporadically discussed the need for retrenchment; and, at least until 1854, they often commented favorably on the rapid expansion of railroad construction. The uniqueness of Poor's conservative editorial policies attracted a rapidly growing new business group — the purchasers of private corporate securities. From 1853 on the *Railroad Journal,* therefore, became increasingly an investor's paper.

In the issue of December 11, 1852, Poor wrote a long editorial announcing the reasons for the major changes in the *Journal's* policy. Like Homans, Hunt, and Kettell, he had begun to point out that the high prosperity of the past months was breeding speculation in urban real estate, Western lands, banking, coal mining, and railroads.[1] The *Journal's* editor was, quite naturally, concerned particularly by the railroad boom. "Railroads are the great topic of the country," he began his editorial of December 11, "the most attractive of all others to capital, to enterprise and to adventure."[2] For this very reason, Poor warned, "our real danger has just commenced." Where capital had been doled out slowly and cautiously, millions were now being offered. The danger thus threatening the railroad industry was "that taking advantage of the confidence known to exist in railroad investments and the abundance of money, some projects not entitled to aid from their inherent strength, and others of a purely speculative character, may succeed in effecting large loans, involving not only great risk of loss, but bringing discredit and suspicion upon the whole railroad interest, and productive of the most injurious consequences."

> This change in the condition of our railroads, [Poor continued] and of the credit attached to them, must be met on our part, by an altered tone of our Journal. Where a year or two since, we were only called upon to help a struggling interest, it is now our duty, as it is equally for the interests of railroads and the public, to point out the dangers to which we are exposed from an excessive investment in these works, to expose merely speculative schemes, which are encouraged by the ease with which money is had for anything like a railroad, and to effect the necessary reforms in the style of railroad accounts and exhibits. As a great interest, our railroads possess sufficiently the public confidence, to secure to them all the aid and support they deserve. Their great success has relieved us of the necessity of insisting upon their general value and importance. These being admitted, the duties now devolving upon us is [*sic*] to point out the conditions entitling new projects to aid, to present a faithful record of the operations of our roads, and to urge the adoption of such measures as shall be productive of the greatest advantage not only of those, but of all interested in them.

Poor intended to carry out these duties in two ways. He promised to analyze and evaluate carefully the prospectuses and reports of the railroads bringing securities to the New York investment market. The *Journal* would no longer, as it had in the past, remain silent about projects "when we could not speak approvingly." Instead, if these exhibits were unclear, or included misstatements or "any important omissions" the editor would "not hesitate to refer to such in direct terms." In the second place, he planned to supplement these analyses of the condition of individual roads by writing articles which examined and described the more general practices creating speculation and the overconstruction of American railroads.

The abrupt shift in the *Journal's* editorial policies did, indeed, reflect the astonishing changes that occurred in the New York investment market in 1852. For the events of that *annus mirabilis* of railroad history, 1852, did make Poor's previous services less necessary and create a demand for a different editorial program and new types of information. "The past season," Poor exclaimed in January 1, 1853, "has been one of extraordinary prosperity both with our works in operation and in progress." [3] "No year in the history of the country," echoed Homans in the *Bankers' Magazine,* "has exhibited more activity than this in the creation of new lines and the extension of old." [4] This prosperity which clinched Wall Street's position as the nation's primary investment market, also assured, Poor pointed out, "the *closing up* of our isolated, and hitherto unconnected roads, into one grand system." [5] For by the end of 1852 enough money had been raised to complete the major Western lines. "The present season has been the turning point in their favor." Our basic railroad network, Poor confidently predicted, "may now be said to be out of harm's way, as far as any commercial or financial revulsion is concerned." [6]

At the beginning of 1852 no city west of Buffalo had direct rail connections with the Eastern seaboard. By the summer of the following year Cleveland, Sandusky, Toledo, Columbus, Dayton, Indianapolis, Terre Haute, and most important of all Chicago, enjoyed rail transportation to New York, Boston, Philadelphia, and Baltimore. In those months not only had many lines in the West been completed, but the Baltimore and Ohio and the Poor-sponsored Atlantic and St. Lawrence had been finished, and a third trunk line, the New York Central, had been formed by the consolidation of eight small lines. By 1854, when the Pennsylvania had its own line from Pittsburgh to Philadelphia, railroads had reached the Mississippi in several places. By then too every city of any size in the upper Mississippi Valley had not one but several railroad routes to the seaboard.

This phenomenal growth had been made possible by and had, in turn, made possible the rapid systematizing and centralizing of the American investment market in New York City.[7] The year 1852 was as memorable for Wall Street as it was for the West. During the year a large number of banking, brokerage, and importing houses had begun to take part in the marketing of railroad securities. Among the heaviest of the new buyers who purchased on their own account or on commission for European customers were such Germany-oriented firms as Louis Von Hoffman and Company, H. Gelpcke and Company, G. Vombaur and Company, Charles Luling and Company, William Schall and Company, the Holland-connected firm of Schuchardt and Gebhard, Marie and Kanz with Frankfort and Geneva ties, and the recently formed Duncan, Sherman and Company, correspondents of George Peabody in London.[8] In that same year a smaller number of domestic firms began for the first time to buy and sell railroad securities. They included such well established private bankers as Brown Brothers, Strachan and Scott, G. S. Robbins and Son, stock brokers like William and John O'Brien, Alfred and Legrand Lockwood, and Wadsworth and Sheldon, and commission merchants like Morris K. Jessup and Company.

During 1852 and the following months many of these firms as well as those commercial and banking houses which had purchased securities before 1852 began increasingly to make the buying and selling of railroad securities a major part of their business.[9] Like the pioneer firm of Winslow, Lanier and Company these houses marketed the bonds of roads either on commission at private or public sale, by sealed bids, or by taking large blocks of bonds outright. Each firm normally handled the bonds of only two or three roads who in turn tended to rely almost wholly on that one house. The marketing firm would then act as the road's fiscal agent, handling the transfer and registration of its securities, paying its interest and dividends, and acting as trustee for new issues.

The new middleman provided as useful services to the investor as he did to the railroad manager. The foreign-connected houses played a particularly significant role, for not only did they represent British and Continental bankers and brokers but also purchased directly for European investors. Poor mentioned, as an example, "one intelligent capitalist of Bremen, Germany," who before August 1852, had bought forty different security issues through one New York house.[10] The importers and stock brokers who turned to investment banking, besides buying for their customers, advised them, as Poor had suggested, on the changing values of the different securities and about the over-all fluctuations of the New York investment market. The banking firms also became the investors' agents in the collection of dividends and interest and acted as their representatives in actions resulting from the road's failure to pay its interest or meet other obligations.[11]

To protect their own investments, as well as those of their customers, many bankers and brokers during the 1850's took a continuing interest in the roads they helped finance. A number of bankers, including James F. D. Lanier, Richard H. Winslow, Lewis H. Meyer, Frederick Schuchardt, Frederick C. Gebhard, Charles Butler, and Nathan Stockwell, became directors of the roads for which they had raised funds, as did such New York merchants as William Aspinwall, Joseph Alsop, Frederick A. Delano, and several others.[12] Some bankers, as directors, stockholders, trustees, or chairmen of bondholders' committees, kept a close watch on the affairs of their railroad companies. Others took only a passing interest, until the financially difficult years at the end of the decade threatened their investments and those of their customers. In the financial reorganizations of railroad companies after the crisis of 1857, the New York bankers played as important a role as they did later in the reorganizations of the 1880's and 1890's.[13]

In the early years of the 1850's, then, the investment house took much of its modern form. These New York firms were not fully specialized investment banking houses according to Fritz Redlich's definition, in the sense that they were not yet the exclusive marketers of new securities.[14] During the 1850's, individual investors and speculators could buy bonds directly from the issuing railroad. In nearly every other aspect, however, the firms that followed the lead of Winslow, Lanier and Company in the marketing of railroad securities carried on almost all the functions of an early twentieth-century investment banking firm. The changes in investment banking after the 1850's were ones of degree, not of kind. They were connected with the development of more effective techniques, especially those of interfirm coöperation, such as syndicating and underwriting, which were necessary for the marketing of the massive government issues during the Civil War and the much larger railroad issues after the war.

Middlemen had, of course, played a major role in the marketing of securities in the United States since the 1790's and had been particularly important during the boom times of the 1830's. It was the size and the nature of the financial operations of the 1850's that made those years so significant in the history of investment banking. During the 1850's many more securities were sold than in the 1830's.[15] Moreover, where the bulk of the securities sold in the 1830's had been the bonds of less than a score of states, those marketed two decades later were largely the bonds of private railroad corporations plus a sizable portion of bonds issued by cities and counties for these private corporations. There were, then, many more issuing units in the fifties than in the earlier decade. Also, the major issuing units, the railroads, needed the continuing services of the middlemen as much, if not more, than did the state governments. Finally, the heavy demand for American securities on the Continent as well as in Britain meant that more European middlemen and investors were buying American bonds in the 1850's than in the 1830's. The sudden need by a large number of railroads for capital combined with the sharp demand of foreign capitalists for American securities during the early years of the 1850's turned many an importer, commission merchant, stock broker, and commercial banker to specializing in investment banking; and this in turn helped make Wall Street the nation's financial capital.

The rapid growth of the specialized investment house in New

York City made less necessary the services Poor had been rendering the railroads from his office just off Wall Street. Since the marketing of securities was becoming systematized, the railroads no longer needed information on what and how to sell. They could now obtain information on when to sell from their New York agents. Moreover, in the fall of 1852 Thomas Prentiss Kettell was beginning to provide useful summaries of the condition of the New York money markets in his *United States Economist.* Nor was there, of course, after the spring of 1852, any real need to make Western securities better known to the investor.

On the other hand, the new investors and many of the new middlemen welcomed information about the securities coming on to the market. They cordially received Poor's analyses of railroad reports and prospectuses. Investors and many of the established banking firms also approved of Poor's new editorial policies of retrenchment and reform. These investors, both at home and abroad, not only became subscribers in increasing numbers to the *Journal*, but they paid close attention to what its editor wrote. During 1853 and 1854 their representatives, including such investment houses as Hessletine and Powell of London and Meyer and Stucken in New York, began writing Poor about matters concerned with railroad investments.[16] By 1855 Poor's pen carried enough weight to cause John Murray Forbes, president of the Michigan Central, to write John W. Brooks, his superintendent, to advertise in the *Journal* because its editor was said to be "very influential with foreign circles." [17]

II

Although his new editorial policies appealed to the investor more than to the railroad managers and promoters, Poor considered himself to be speaking for the best interests of the railroad industry as a whole. The editor still wanted to see the United States provided as soon as possible with an efficient transportation system. This end, he now insisted, could be achieved only by an orderly, healthy expansion of the railroad network. It would be seriously endangered by abnormal growth stimulated by overoptimism or speculative greed.

> It is much better [Poor reasoned] for us to proceed with an uniform and regular, though what may seem to be a *slow* pace, for it is quite certain that our progress under any circumstances will be quite as rapid as in a *healthy* growth. . . . Everything is so new . . . that precedents may throw little light upon our course. By proceeding slowly we can each day use to a certain extent, the *result* of the *preceding*, and in this way make the greater haste though with less apparent speed.[18]

In the years after 1852, Poor stressed the vital and continuing need for capital for legitimate projects — for railroads that were wanted and would pay. Many important commercial routes still lacked rail transportation. Many recently completed roads on strategically located routes required large sums to expand their facilities to meet the ever-growing demand for transportation along their lines. Thus while Poor was conducting a campaign for retrenchment and reform, he continued to appeal to investors, especially foreign investors, to place their funds in American railroad securities.[19] He emphasized again and again that the continuing demand for better transportation in the United States was certain to make the bonds of properly managed railroads on important commercial routes a profitable investment. For evidence, in the years before 1857, he pointed to the rising earnings of American roads and large interest and dividend payments made through their New York bankers. Winslow, Lanier and Company alone, Poor reminded investors, as the fiscal agent for several Western roads, paid over a million dollars every six months in interest on railroad bonds.

The real need, then, was to channel available funds into legitimate projects; and the real problem was to prevent capital from being drained off by speculative or "illegitimate" construction. To this problem Poor devoted many of his more general editorials warning against overconstruction. "To distinguish a legitimate from an illegitimate project, we must look in the first place," Poor advised, "to the parties who are engaged in their construction." [20] If a railroad was projected by persons living along its line for the purpose of "the income to be derived from it with its *incidental* advantages," and if the locality was able to prepare the road for rails, then it was — as Poor had contended earlier — a legitimate project and most probably a safe investment. If, on the other hand, it was promoted by persons living off the line of the road, or if the locality failed to raise through stock subscriptions enough funds to meet the cost of grubbing, grading, and bridging, it was, in Poor's opinion, an illegitimate project and one to be avoided by investors.

Throughout the 1850's the editor was particularly concerned with the amount of local traffic available to a new railroad. "It may be laid down as one of the fundamental principles of railroad economy," he maintained, "that a road dependent on through business *never* pays." [21] To prove his point Poor cited the unhappy financial history of the Long Island, the Stonington, the Vermont Central, the Rutland, and the Ogdensburg, all constructed primarily to carry through freight and passengers.[22]

As a major part of his program against the construction of non-legitimate projects, Poor after December 1852 wrote many editorials condemning the building of lines unwarranted by local traffic and describing the practices which led to unnecessarily rapid construction of the railroad system. Because of his belief in the need for local freight and passengers, Poor had little use for "air lines" or "rival roads." [23] The editor questioned the validity of the plans to build a direct line between Cincinnati and Cleveland, or between Cleveland and St. Louis. Such roads, even if they carried most of the through traffic and a good share of the local traffic, could hardly pay a profit to investors. At the same time, by depriving already completed roads of essential local trade, the latter would be forced into bankruptcy. Few routes in the United States, Poor cautioned, could yet provide enough business for two railroads. For the same reasons Poor decried the projected lines which paralleled the existing roads from Utica and Schenectady, Utica and Syracuse, Cincinnati and Dayton, and elsewhere. He deplored the proposals to build two different railroads to connect the central New York lines to the St. Lawrence River and praised the agreement signed by the Marietta and Cincinnati and the Cincinnati, Hillsborough and Parkersburg to join forces to construct one instead of two lines across southeastern Ohio. For somewhat similar reasons Poor protested against the use of the 6-foot gauge then being introduced in the West.[24] This new gauge, besides hampering the efficient movement of passengers and freight, would lead to a wasteful duplication of railroad facilities.

On the other hand, Poor warned, few railroads could live on local traffic alone. The editor advised investors to avoid buying securities of small "interior" railroads.[25] He cautioned railroads or local promoters against building branch lines and lateral extensions. The experience of both old and New England had demonstrated, Poor wrote, that

> Railroads should be constructed only upon great routes of commerce. Upon such only will they *pay*. The feeders to such routes are the *ordinary* roads, over which a railroad will *not* pay. To build such is to incur for a *part* the same expense per mile, as for a *whole*. In addition, the *trunk* will get all, or nearly all, the business brought to it by branches, whether they be built or not.[26]

The *Journal's* editor blamed several groups for the construction of unnecessary railroads. First, there were the local promoters. Every hamlet wanted its own railroad depot, every town its railroad terminal. Yet local promoters could accomplish little without the encouragement and financial support of railroad contractors, Eastern financiers, or managers of completed roads. Of these Poor, particularly before 1854, considered the railroad managers the worst offenders. For one thing, many of the Western railroads continued to pay oversized dividends. Such excessive payments not only endangered the financial future of the companies issuing them, but also fanned the flames of railroad speculation.[27] The practice of putting funds into dividends, funds which should have been placed aside for maintenance and depreciation, made Western railroading appear to be much more of a bonanza than it really was.

Even more serious, in the editor's opinion, were the railroads' overzealous programs for expansion. Many recently completed roads, especially in the West, anxious to reach near-by trade ahead of their potential competitors, had begun to build or to help finance the construction of branches, feeders, and spurs. To Poor such competitive construction was wasteful. It was "foolish rivalry," costly for both the railroads and the local communities. The editor, though he must have winced at its prose, fully agreed with the view of the New York Railroad Commission:

> This increase of cost, growing out of a departure from the objects aimed at in the original construction, and a chase after the phantom of 'through business,' 'westward connections,' 'tributary roads,' while by the expenditures of further sums for 'more equipment,' 'larger depots,' 'steamboat connections,' and 'material aid' to connecting roads, an aggregated capital has accumulated, the interest of which will impose a tax upon its local business, inasmuch as for its through business, it is compelled to maintain a competition with rival lines, who can or do perform it at a minimum profit.[28]

Other men experienced in railroading heartily agreed. Railroad president John Murray Forbes wrote with satisfaction that his Chicago, Burlington and Quincy was not "cursed by branches."[29] Railroad engineer John B. Jervis warned against the dangers of branch lines and "amalgamations," while railroad financier James F. D. Lanier at a stockholders meeting of the Ohio and Pennsylvania forced through a resolution prohibiting the directors "to construct any branch roads, nor to make any additional subscriptions of stock to any other company, nor to give any aid to any other railroad without the consent of the stockholders, previously obtained at a regular annual meeting, after 30 days notice by newspaper publications in Pittsburgh, Philadelphia and New York."[30]

Poor, the commissioners, and the railroad men were in large part right. Competitive construction did lead to the building of unprofitable roads and did raise the over-all cost of transportation in many areas. Still these men were not yet fully aware of the almost irresistible economic forces which compelled even the most conservative railroad presidents to seek to increase their traffic through new construction.

The railroads were the first American businesses to face the problems of heavy fixed costs. Since the costs of interest, taxes, maintenance of roadbed, equipment, and facilities, and even a large portion of the operating expenses remained constant, any sizable loss of traffic meant a complete loss of profits. Conversely, any sizable increase in traffic was not accompanied by a comparable increase in total operating costs. With every new train load carried, then, the net profits increased. Since a comparatively small change in traffic meant either rapidly increasing profits or near bankruptcy, the new roads were under constant pressure to build or finance feeder and branch lines in order both to expand their own traffic and to prevent its diversion to a competing line. This is one reason why John B. Jervis' Michigan Southern encouraged the construction of the Rock Island, the Chicago, Alton and St. Louis in Illinois, the Cincinnati, Logansport and Chicago in Indiana, and the Missouri and Mississippi in Iowa; and why John Murray Forbes as president of the Michigan Central accepted at the urging of his operating managers, John W. Brooks and James F. Joy, the promotion and construction of the lines that became the Chicago, Burlington and Quincy, the Burlington and Missouri, the Hannibal and St. Joseph, and the New Albany and Salem. While this almost unavoidable rivalry proved costly, especially to the Michigan Southern, it was hardly foolish.

After 1854, Poor increasingly laid the blame for construction of "illegitimate" projects on the contractors.[31] From the very beginning, railroad companies, following the example of the canals, had their roads built by contractors. The early contractors were usually small operators who generally bid for the construction of only one or two short sections of a road. It was only after construction was begun in the more sparsely settled areas, in northern New England and in the West, that the contractor who built an entire railroad under a "gross" contract became a major factor in American railroad construction. Many of these large firms operated on, what was for that day, a very large scale. They handled all the details of construction, arranging for subcontracting for parts of the road, providing construction equipment, labor, rails, bridges, and occasionally even supplying locomotives, rolling stock, and terminal equipment.[32] A single firm was often able to carry on the construction of not one but several railroads. One great contractor, Horatio C. Seymour, former New York State Engineer, had on hand at the time of his premature death in 1853 more than $30,000,000 worth of business.[33] As these firms were paid largely in the securities of the roads they built, they were playing by the mid-fifties a significant role in the financing as well as the building of new railroads. The securities which they normally received at a heavy discount were either exchanged for rails and equipment or sold through their New York offices to banking and brokerage firms or directly to the investor.

The gross contract was easily abused. Some contractors did only the barest minimum of the required work, turned in shoddy work, and cut every possible corner. As a result, railroad companies often had to continue to spend time and money on their roads long after they had taken them over from the contractors. More dangerous, from Poor's viewpoint, were the contractors who to assure work for their large staffs encouraged local promoters to build commercially unwarranted lines. Just as serious was the growing number of "contracting directors," particularly on the Western roads. Contractors who became directors or directors who invested heavily in the contracting firms building their railroads were, Poor feared, much more concerned with the profits of construction than those of future operations. Such men, the editor cautioned, would have few qualms about building unneeded roads and profiting at the expense of the ordinary stock and bondholders.

Although Poor had expressed skepticism about the gross contract in 1853, it was the Schuyler frauds in the summer of 1854 that first thoroughly aroused him to the abuses of contracting. Robert Schuyler, the president and one of the major contractors for the New York and New Haven, was heavily involved in Western railroad construction. Not only was he president of the Illinois Central, president and treasurer of the Sangamon and Morgan, but his firm, R. & G. L. Schuyler, was contractor for several Western railroads including the Great Western of Illinois, the Toledo and Cleveland, and the Chicago and Milwaukee. Unable to market the securities of these Western roads in which he had been paid, Schuyler, in order to pay his subcontractors, issued, as the New Haven's president and transfer agent, approximately 20,000 shares of spurious New Haven stock on which he borrowed cash.[34] When in the summer of 1854 Schuyler was unable to meet the demands of the subcontractors even by fraudulent devices, he declared his firm bankrupt and sailed for Europe.

Poor, who had been suspicious of Schuyler's widespread and complex operations, now launched an energetic editorial campaign against the exploiting contractors and contracting directors. He not only spelled out the abuses of contracting, but cited specific instances of chicanery and "sharp practices." The editor was especially angered by the sale of the Peoria Branch to the Rock Island at what he considered an excessive price.[35] The construction firm of Sheffield and Farnam which built the Peoria road also built the Rock Island,

and its partners, Joseph E. Sheffield and Henry W. Farnam, William Walcott and Thomas C. Durant, were all currently officers or directors of the Rock Island Company. What particularly annoyed Poor was that in the very report announcing the purchase of the Peoria Branch, the Rock Island's secretary, Azariah C. Flagg, one of the most respected financiers of his day, had made a lengthy plea for railroad reform.

Poor's favorite example, however, of a road exploited by both contractors and financiers was the Ohio and Mississippi.[36] The building of that broad gauged road between Cincinnati and St. Louis had been let in 1852 to H. C. Seymour and Company for $9,000,000 — $3,500,000 in cash, $2,750,000 in stock, and $2,750,000 in bonds. When the company brought an issue of second mortgage bonds to New York, Poor cautioned investors against the road, pointing out its high construction costs and its lack of bona fide capital. In 1855 his warnings were realized. The company, dissatisfied with the progress of construction, had earlier terminated its contract on terms very satisfactory to H. C. Seymour and Company. The banking firm of Page, Bacon and Company then took over the building of the road. The outlays for construction caused the bankers to overextend themselves and in early 1855 they were forced into bankruptcy. By then the road had a heavy debt with very little to show for it. Such an incubus, Poor maintained, must long continue to be an almost insuperable handicap to the road's financial success.

Although Poor performed a real service in pointing out the abuses of the gross contract, he failed to indicate its important uses. Abuses there certainly were. The contracting firm as a financial device to make possible speculative construction or the milking of railroads by their directors was soon to become, under the imaginative efforts of Thomas C. Durant and others, an exploitive technique surpassing Poor's direst warnings. Still the legitimate large-scale construction firm played an essential role in American railroad building. Such a firm had the experience and the equipment to build railroads more efficiently and more rapidly than local contractors. This was especially true in the West, where there were still only a few construction firms of any type. Moreover, contractors like Seymour and Sheffield enjoyed a high credit rating. They were, therefore, able to carry the financial risks of construction more cheaply than small firms and most new Western railroads. By the mid-fifties only the largest Western roads with the amplest of financial resources, like the Illinois Central, could afford to do without the services of the large contractor.[37]

The contractors' services, of course, came at a price. Even the most honest of them expected to be well paid for the work they did and the risk they took. This was in part the price that had to be paid if railroads were to be built by private enterprise in sparsely settled areas. It was, indeed, the price of pioneering. When Poor warned against investment in railroads organized and financed by only a few local promoters, or by outside railroad managers and contractors, he was protecting investors from the speculator and the exploiter. He was also advising them against the risks of a more socially accepted speculation, that of pioneering.

III

The investor, Poor frequently pointed out, might avoid such risks if he placed his funds in the bonds of railroads having strong local financial support. He repeated to American investors what he had already told foreigners, that, if a company had raised enough money to cover half its costs before coming to New York, "the public may be certain of two things: first, that a route upon which this amount of cash stock can be raised will probably furnish a profitable business; and, secondly, where its projectors have so large an interest at stake, its affairs will be carefully and prudently managed." [38] To examine the amount of local backing a road enjoyed, Poor considered one of his primary tasks in the evaluation of the prospects of new roads. And he regarded his analyses of the reports of new railroad companies seeking funds in New York as an even more effective method of carrying out a policy of retrenchment than writing about the general practices which were stimulating overconstruction.

Poor began his evaluations of the reports of specific roads at once. In the editorial of December 11, 1852, in which he announced his new policies, he cited two companies bringing out issues in New York — the Terre Haute and Alton and the Covington and Lexington — which, on the basis of their reports, were not entitled to borrow money. "We are more free to instance these from our friendly personal relations with those connected with them, and for the reason that in these cases," he added hopefully, "justice at least will be done to our motives." [39] Since Poor's analyses of these reports and the roads' responses to them were fairly characteristic of the many the editor made in the following years, the two will be considered here in some detail.

The Terre Haute and Alton Railroad Company, Poor reported, was planning to sell a $1,000,000 bond issue to help finance the construction of its 173-mile line across southern Illinois. According to its prospectus, the road was to be built for $3,000,000 or a little over $17,000 a mile. Of the sum, the company claimed that $1,525,000 had already been raised — $1,100,000 by stock subscriptions taken by individuals and the contractors, and $425,000 by county and municipal bonds. However, Poor pointed out, the company's exhibit failed to indicate what portion of the stock was taken by the contractors and "how much of it was *bona fide*." Nor did it show whether all the county and municipal bonds listed had actually been voted on. Furthermore, there was no engineer's report or other reliable source to show how the comparatively low estimated cost of construction had been reached. Even if this optimistic estimate was sound, a second mortgage would be necessary to meet the total cost of $3,000,000. And on what security was this second loan to be based? Finally, the prospectus gave no indication of how much work had actually been done on the road. For these reasons, Poor thought "the proposed loan would not only be unsafe, but its negotiation would establish a precedent tending to the most injurious results."

The defects of the report of the Covington and Lexington were less serious, for its bonds were guaranteed by the city of Covington. Nevertheless, like the Terre Haute and Alton, the Kentucky road had failed to give a breakdown of its stock subscriptions or to indicate how it had computed its total cost. The reported cost, Poor noted, "certainly falls below the estimate given us by the President of the Company." Also, the exhibit did not explain how the difference of $500,000 between the estimated cost and the money to be raised by current issues of stocks and bonds was to be met. This was especially important since the road had no authorization from the legislature permitting an increase of bonded debt. Finally, Poor told the company that it had erred in encumbering the road with two small mortgages, one to the city of Cincinnati for a tiny $100,000 loan, and another as security for bonds given for iron. Poor urged it to refund these two small issues and make a single large one secured by a single mortgage, an issue large enough to cover the whole cost of completing the road.

The two roads responded quickly, but very differently, to Poor's criticisms. The Covington and Lexington withdrew its bonds from the market. By the following March, when it again put the issue on sale, the company had printed a new prospectus which met nearly all Poor's criticisms.[40] The company this time set forth in more detail the stock subscribers and the bonds issued by counties and towns. It included a lengthy engineer's report describing carefully the road's route and its prospective business. Furthermore, the road reported that it had arranged for the removal of the Cincinnati loan, with its mortgage, and had received authorization from the Kentucky legislature to increase its bonded debt. Poor, satisfied with the new exhibit, recommended the road's securities to investors.[41]

The Terre Haute and Alton also took its bonds off the market.[42] But it answered Poor's criticisms by denouncing the *Journal* and questioning the motives of its editor. In a series of editorials in the Alton *Telegraph*, which were forwarded to the *Railway Times* in Boston and to one or two New York papers, Poor was accused of being the tool of John Brough and of Winslow, Lanier and Company, who were promoting a competing line from Terre Haute to St. Louis.[43] In the following spring the Terre Haute and Alton, like the Covington road, again tried to bring out its issue in New York, and again was censured by Poor.[44] This time Simeon Ryder, the road's president, gave up selling the issue in the open market and arranged for financial support from the powerful group of railroad promoters — including Edwin C. Litchfield, John B. Jervis, and Azariah C. Flagg — who were constructing and managing the Michigan Southern, the Rock Island, and other Western roads.[45]

Poor's charges, which Ryder never satisfactorily answered, proved in time to be correct.[46] Very little stock, the company's later reports indicate, was taken locally. Barnes, Phelps and Mattoon, the contractors who had agreed to build the road for $3,000,000 were paid for 7/18 of the cost in cash, and the rest equally in stock and bonds. They used the company's bonds to buy their iron from George Peabody in England, and their cash, which Litchfield and his associates had helped raise, to pay for labor and equipment. The stock issued to them was, as Poor suspected, a bonus for their work and in no way a bona fide subscription. Moreover, as Poor also had predicted, the estimated cost was much too low. By 1854, with the road still incomplete, its cost had reached $5,250,000, although some of this increase had resulted from the rising cost of railroad iron and equipment. The road, never a paying project, went into receivership before the end of the decade.

There was, on the other hand, some validity in Ryder's charge that Poor's criticism resulted primarily from his close connection with Winslow, Lanier and Company. That banking firm was, in December 1852, supporting John Brough, the president of the Madison and Indianapolis, in his attempt to build a rival road from Terre Haute to St. Louis. The construction of this road, as well as of other roads terminating in St. Louis, had been consistently blocked by the Illinois legislature, which refused to charter a railroad that might build up the Missouri city at the expense of the Illinois river ports. Poor, in answering Ryder's charges of favoritism, pointed out that, well before either Brough or Ryder had become interested in their rival projects, he had editorially opposed the policy by which Illinois "proposed to make all its railroads subservient to the building of *domestic* cities, instead of foreign." [47] Just as the state's attempt "to control the laws of trade by *legislation*" was in his opinion doomed to failure, so, he was certain, was "the attempt to constitute the Terre Haute and Alton railroad the only avenue for travel and commerce" across southern Illinois.

Nevertheless, Poor unquestionably favored Winslow, Lanier and Company, whose partners he knew well and whose business judgment he so thoroughly respected. This undoubtedly caused him to endorse too readily projects which they supported. Yet there is little reason to believe that he was, as the Terre Haute and Alton president intimated, the paid agent of Winslow, Lanier and Company — or, for that matter, of any other company or group of individuals. He did occasionally criticize companies, as for example the Covington and Lexington, for whom Winslow, Lanier and Company were agents. Besides, he had little to gain and much to lose by compromising his independence.[48] Moreover, Poor's views and those of the bankers coincided on general railroad policy. Both were troubled by overconstruction and both felt the need for railroad reform. For this reason, a respected conservative New York investment house like Winslow, Lanier and Company in most cases could be quite certain of Poor's support without having to buy it.

After December 1852, Poor continued to carry out his policy of evaluating the reports and exhibits of railroads seeking capital in New York. In his analyses the editor was particularly careful to examine the estimated costs. Poor no longer believed a Western road could be fully finished for $20,000 a mile. He now considered $35,000 a more accurate figure.[49] In the West land might be cheaper and terrain easier than in the East; but experience clearly showed that the cost of labor, rails, and equipment came higher. Poor now repeated regularly what he had before only occasionally suggested, that the cost of building a railroad was invariably underestimated. Although this was sometimes done intentionally to make the road a more attractive investment, it was far more often the honest failure of engineers and managers to appreciate the difficulty of its terrain, or the cost of terminals and other items. Moreover, during the 1850's many railroad men did not anticipate the rising costs of labor and equipment. Often, as was the case of several Western roads, they miscalculated the potential freight traffic and were forced to enlarge their plans to handle it. In any case, since the failure to prepare proper estimates injured the value of a railroad both as an investment and as a provider of transportation, Poor urged railroad managers to be more realistic in their initial appraisal of costs.

After checking a prospectus for reported costs, Poor looked to see if local stock subscriptions provided enough capital to finance half the required investment. He often refused to consider contractor's holdings as bona fide subscriptions. Nor would he accept stock based on land or farm mortgages. This type of stock subscription, he warned, could bring "a great deal of harm" to the local farmers as well as distant investors. In Poor's words:

> Designing men go about, and by drawing a brilliant picture of the advantage that a railroad would confer, or of the value of its stock, often induce people to put their farms or portions of them into the project; receiving stock therefor. The road is not built. The proceeds of the landed subscription are eaten up in expenses, or otherwise made away with, and the unlucky holder of the stock finds himself not only without his farm, but also without anything valuable to show for it.[50]

Poor was even becoming skeptical of county and municipal subscriptions. Yet after 1852 increasingly few roads in the West could meet Poor's test of having their stock raised locally. By 1854 even Poor agreed that 20 per cent of the total cost, 2/5 of the stock subscription, might legitimately go to the contractors for work performed.[51]

The editor of the *Journal* also reported unfavorably on a road whose reports or prospectuses were unclear, imprecise, or confused. Carefully drawn up reports, he pointed out, were necessary to win his confidence as well as that of most investors. As early as February 1852 he listed the following as the minimum of information which a report should include:

> 1st. A statement of the amount of capital stock subscribed. 2nd. Amount paid up and value unpaid. 3rd. Amount of debts, and for what purpose incurred. 4th. Estimated and actual amount expended, and for what objects; with explanations as to the cause of any discrepancy that may exist. 5th. Amount required to complete the road, and to make further improvements. 6th. The state and condition of road and equipment. 7th. Actual amount of receipts and expenditures, and for what purposes the latter were made. 8th. Number of miles run by trains. 9th. Amount received per passenger, and per ton of freight carried each mile. We give these as items which should always be found in every report, but by no means embracing *all* that should appear.[52]

After 1852 he wanted even more information. But, as was becoming so often the case, Poor expected too much. Although many reports did meet his standards, he continued to fume about the insufficiencies of the reports of both new and completed railroads as long as he remained editor of the *Journal.*

The basic information that Poor sought in all the reports he examined, however, was whether there was strong local financial support. The criterion that one half the necessary capital to build the road must be raised locally was not just an invention of Poor's. During the 1850's it was the test accepted by most conservative investors and investment bankers of a sound railroad investment. "It is a well-established commercial rule," one Western railroad president explained to his stockholders, "as unyielding as the laws of the Medes and the Persians — that any railroad company asking credit upon their own bonds, must show an amount, *actually expended in the road* EQUAL *to that which is asked* for. Any attempt to evade this rule must result in ruinous usury." [53]

Such a conservative test proved to be a sound one. The roads that raised at least half their capital locally were generally well managed, profitable companies enjoying a large local traffic. Such roads were the Galena and Chicago Union, the Cleveland, Painesville and Ashtabula, the Cleveland, Columbus and Cincinnati, the Columbus and Xenia, the Little Miami, the Cincinnati, Hamilton and Dayton, the Bellefontaine and Indiana, the Indianapolis and Bellefontaine, and the Terre Haute and Indianapolis. These companies, many of whose securities were marketed by Winslow, Lanier and Company and purchased by Continental investors, survived the financial storms following the crisis of 1857 with little difficulty.

On the other hand, during the 1850's the least successful of the larger roads were those financed principally by bonds. The Erie, the Ohio and Mississippi, the Marietta and Cincinnati, the Ohio Central, the Terre Haute and Alton, the Rock Island, the Michigan Southern, the Chicago, Alton and Mississippi, the Cleveland and Toledo, the Toledo, Wabash and Western were all encumbered by large bond issues. Often dominated by absentee managements, they were built at heavy costs, suffered from high operating expenses, and after 1857 all were unable to pay the interest on their bonds. Incidentally, they tended to be roads in which the British rather than the Germans and Swiss had invested most heavily.

There was little question about the soundness of the criteria Poor used in determining the value of specific railroad securities as investments. Nor was there much doubt as to the validity of his more general editorials warning against the dangers and describing the practices leading to overconstruction. The major complaint the reader of the *Journal* might have had was that Poor failed to carry out his policies rigorously enough. For one thing he too often would weaken the effect of his strong and sincere editorials on railroad reform by printing glowing descriptions of obviously speculative projects which had been sent to him by railroad promoters. Secondly and more serious, Poor failed to condemn and, in fact, actually approved of several roads that did not meet his criteria. His criticisms of the Terre Haute and Alton, the Rock Island, the Ohio and Mississippi, the Evansville, Indianapolis and Cleveland, and the Louisville and Nashville were absolutely sound.[54] The editor should have leveled many of the same strictures at the Marietta and Cincinnati, the Toledo, Wabash and Western, the Chicago, Alton and St. Louis, the Chicago, St. Paul and Fond du Lac, several of the Wisconsin roads and other companies. These roads, built by gross contract and financed largely by bonds, all defaulted on the bonds after 1857.

Still Poor never claimed infallibility. He stressed, "we may be mistaken as to facts and come to the wrong conclusion in a given case." [55] He urged those who disagreed with his statements concerning a specific company to express their opinions through the columns of the *Journal.* Moreover, he emphasized that there was no substitute for actually visiting the line of the road and coming to know its management personally. Finally, Poor pointed out that in occasionally printing articles sent to him by railroad promoters he was only doing what other railroad periodicals and daily newspapers regularly did. This was, however, a weak argument, for his policy, more than that of any other paper, was reform. The least he could have done was to insist that all contributors sign their articles.

Poor's mistakes appear to have resulted from honest errors in judgment rather than from any perversion of his editorial policies. A trip to Wisconsin in the spring of 1857 so convinced him of the value of the roads in that state that he enthusiastically recommended the purchase of the bonds of the Milwaukee and Mississippi and the Racine and Mississippi — two roads which were in serious financial difficulties before the end of the year.[56] Poor did not, however, give the same approval to Byron Kilborn's La Crosse and Milwaukee, but he failed to express his disapproval until well after he had returned to New York. Then he did urge the stockholders of that road to take up Kilborn's challenge for "a searching investigation." [57] Such an investigation, Poor maintained quite correctly, would prove Kilborn a swindler and his railroad "rotten to the core." In August, however, Poor was expressing his profound regret to the victimized investors for not making public long before his distrust of the "character of the men managing the company." [58]

Several of Poor's major errors came even more from misplaced confidence in leading railroad and financial entrepreneurs. He approved such financially unhappy projects as the Chicago, St. Paul and Fond du Lac because William B. Ogden was its president, and the Pittsburgh, Fort Wayne and Chicago because it had James F. D.

Lanier's support. His greatest mistake, however, came from his faith in that remarkable group of men who created the Michigan Southern.[59] Yet these men, including Edwin C. and Electus B. Litchfield, John B. Jervis, George Bliss, and John Wilkinson, forming an aggregate of the best railroading financial, engineering, administrative, and legal talents of the day, seemed to deserve confidence. When they took over the highly speculative company connecting Chicago and St. Louis, Poor gave it his approval. He also endorsed the Toledo and Cleveland and a road planned to connect Chicago and Indianapolis when they entered into the management of those roads. He even stopped his criticism of the Terre Haute and Alton when he found they had taken over its financing. Nor was his faith in them shaken by their close connection with the management of the Rock Island, which he increasingly came to distrust. Only after the railroad "empire" created by this group collapsed under the financial strains of 1857 did Poor decry the predilections of its managers for branch lines, through connections and gross contracts.

Although Poor made errors of judgment and at times failed to apply his policies forcibly enough, few of his more articulate contemporaries noticed these delinquencies. Rather they condemned him for applying his standards too often and too rigorously. The officers of the roads Poor criticized sometimes responded, as had the Covington and Lexington, by making the suggested changes in their exhibits and financial organization. More often, like Simeon Ryder of the Terre Haute and Alton, their officers replied with an emphatic attack on Poor and his *Journal.*

In these rebuttals they found strong support in the other railroad periodicals and the financial columns of the large Eastern urban newspapers.[60] In the West the *Railroad Record* of Cincinnati and, usually, the local press were the staunch defenders of the Ohio and Mississippi, the Evansville, Indianapolis and Cleveland, and other railroad companies whose securities Poor quite justly criticized. In the East such roads usually could count on the support of the New York *Tribune*, the *Railway Times* in Boston, and once in a while the *Railroad Register* in Philadelphia and even Colburn's *Railroad Advocate.* These papers all looked on Poor's critical analyses as unnecessary and ill-considered. "It is not part of the duty of a journalist," the editor of the *Railway Times* maintained, "in discussing questions pertinent to the general interests of railway property, to stir up the ill-feeling and bad blood of those engaged in the active management of railway property." [61] Other business periodicals, like *Hunt's* and the *Bankers' Magazine*, also disliked to comment on the merits of specific projects since it meant "making invidious distinctions." [62] Poor in making his critical analyses of railroad prospectuses and reports was obviously deviating from the accepted role of a business editor.

The other contemporary railroad and business papers not only failed to comment on speculative projects, but rarely made a sustained effort to point out abuses in railroad construction and administration. The *Railroad Record* for nearly three years after its founding in 1853 considered it one of its primary functions to protest against the *Railroad Journal's* call for slower and more careful expansion of the Western railroad network. During the spring of 1854 the *Record* and the *Journal* had a running debate in which the *Record's* editor, Mansfield, took Poor to task for maintaining that the cost of a Western road would be more than $20,000 a mile and that Ohio, at the present, would be unable to sustain as many roads as New England.[63] Mansfield cited Poor's earlier claims about the costs and earning potentials of Western railroads. Such inconsistencies indicated to the Cincinnati editor that the *Journal's* editorial policy was an attempt of the East to dictate to the West the conditions of her economic development. Poor readily admitted his earlier claims, replying that "experience has long since proven the inaccurateness of all such opinions." [64] The second part of the charge he thought too far-fetched to merit an answer. Within two years after the debate the *Record*, too, had changed its policies. In 1856 Mansfield was agreeing with Poor's views both on the cost of railroads and the dangers of overconstruction in the West.[65]

The *Railway Times*, although it claimed after the recession of 1854 to be a staunch advocate of retrenchment and reform, printed a number of editorials urging the construction of "air lines" and feeders, and favoring the use of farm mortgage bonds and generous land grants to finance Western roads.[66] It also ran many articles in 1853 and 1854 extolling the promise of projected railroad lines in the Mississippi Valley. At the same time it opened its columns to railroad promoters who were taking issue with the *Journal's* editorial policies. One such promoter, Oliver H. Smith, condemned the policies of that Wall Street "organ" which gave "the cold shoulder" to new Western roads as part of a sinister plot by "Eastern interests" to block the natural economic growth of the West.[67] Smith also helped sponsor a local railroad paper, the Indianapolis *Locomotive*, which voiced his protests against the *Journal's* editorial policies and promoted his own railroad, the Evansville, Indianapolis and Cleveland.

Among the commercial papers, the *United States Economist* remained sanguine about the construction of Western roads until the recession of 1854. *Hunt's Merchants' Magazine* and the *Bankers' Magazine* were more cautious. Although they were more outspoken about the need for retrenchment and reform, they rarely spelled out in detail the different abuses or suggested ways of remedying them. Unquestionably, despite his shortcomings, Poor was of the editors of his day the most outspoken advocate for railroad retrenchment and reform.

IV

One of the major answers of the Western promoters and editors to Poor's editorial policies of retrenchment was, when stripped of its conspiratorial implication, quite valid. A strict adherence to such policies would, as they contended, seriously retard the economic development of the West. Poor's insistence that one half of the cost of a road be raised locally, if rigorously applied, would prevent Eastern and European capital from financing railroads in sparsely settled areas. Moreover, Poor even refused to consider legitimate large-scale financing of railroads in new areas by such private concerns as contracting firms or railroad companies seeking feeders.

Yet the editor was the first to admit that railroads were essential for the economic growth of a new country. If the risks were too great for private capital, then railroads in new areas must rely on public support. Nevertheless, after 1852 Poor considered most of the current methods of public aid to railroads as powerful stimuli to overconstruction. After some uncertainty Poor answered this dilemma by advocating a plan of public aid by which the state government and the private individuals who were to benefit directly from the new transportation shared the initial risks of railroad financing.

Public aid should come, Poor urged, from the state, not from the federal or local governments. After 1852 he was never enthusiastic about federal aid to railroads.[68] Between 1852 and 1856 he emphatically opposed further land grants by the national government to the states for railroad building because, as he maintained, such land grants encouraged illegitimate construction. They caused roads to be built along routes determined by political considerations instead of business or "commercial" reasons. They gave aid and comfort to the speculator by supplying the means by which he could build roads without using his own funds. Moreover, Poor maintained, these speculative schemes were costly for the farmer and pioneer. In Illinois, he estimated, the price of land along the line of the Illinois Central had risen from $1.25 an acre to between ten and thirty dollars an acre even before the road was in operation. The real benefactors of the government's magnificent gift were the road's twenty-five stockholders, nearly all of whom lived in New York or Boston.[69]

During the period of hard times in the later 1850's, the editor acknowledged land grants to be an "efficient auxiliary" to the construction of railroads in the newer regions.[70] Nevertheless, such grants, he cautioned, "will prove a great misfortune instead of an advantage" if the settlers in these areas assume that the land alone will finance the new roads.[71] Poor insisted that:

In all cases this cardinal rule should never be lost sight of, — *that no road having a land grant should be built, unless it has a prospective business that justifies its construction.* The *lands* should never supply the inducement. They should be regarded simply as *aids* to not as *ends* of construction. . . . A *good* route is an insurance against all such mistakes.

From 1853 on Poor believed that local governmental support of new roads had as many disadvantages as federal aid.[72] During times of prosperity, such aid, he maintained, encouraged the building of roads that would not pay, while during the years of depression, municipal and county credit was of little benefit since, except for a few larger cities, it was rarely stronger than the credit of the roads themselves. Moreover, such aid normally gave the municipality control in the management of the road. When several communities backed a road, all had a say in its management. Confusion inevitably resulted. For these reasons he wrote in July, 1854:

We have been quite willing to see the practice of cities and counties subscribing to railroads fall gradually into disuse. In some parts of the country it is, we admit, impossible to construct them without the aid of municipal bodies, but this fact does not impeach the general correctness of our positions. . . . In the infancy of our railroads, and till confidence could be secured, both in their productiveness, and in the ability of private enterprise to successfully engage in their construction, it was frequently necessary for the community to aid them in its collective capacity. That period is now past, except, perhaps, in the more newly settled portions of the country.[73]

Where the sparseness of the population made the risk for private investment too great, the editor preferred state aid to municipal or federal assistance.[74] As Poor had written in his editorials on Southern railroad construction, the most satisfactory type of state aid was that exemplified by the Tennessee law of 1852. By this law the state lent to any railroad chartered in Tennessee $8,000, later $10,000, a mile in state bonds, provided that the railroad company had already prepared its road for rails. In return for the loan the state received from the road an equivalent amount in first mortgage bonds. Such a law gave new roads the advantage of state credit at comparatively little risk to the state. The railroad companies could avoid the heavy interest and discount charges incurred in marketing their own bonds or those of towns and counties issued in their favor, for throughout the fifties, new railroad companies could dispose of the state bonds at much higher rates than their own or municipal securities.

Poor came to prefer the Tennessee plan to the more common system of state aid as practiced by Virginia, of purchasing a third or a half of the stock in individual roads and electing a comparable number of directors. The provision in the Tennessee law that no aid could be granted until the road had been prepared for rails would, Poor believed, prevent the construction of unnecessary roads more effectively than the Virginia system. The Tennessee method had what to Poor was the further advantage of keeping the state out of railroad management. Finally, as a general law applying to all railroads in the state, the Tennessee statute prevented the political pressures that came into play in other Southern states where each road had to get specific approval by the legislature for state aid.

By and large Poor's preference for state aid seems to have been valid. During the 1850's state assistance helped provide much essential construction at little loss to the state governments. In that decade only Minnesota had unhappy results from her program of state support.[75] In the South where state aid was concentrated, it may have played a part in preventing the type of speculative construction which occurred in the West, both by providing funds from a source which was not available in most of the West and by allowing the state to have some control over railroad construction. State aid certainly helped keep the Southern roads locally owned and managed. Before the Civil War these roads, unlike those in the West, rarely had New York bankers and merchants on their boards of directors.

Poor's belief that federal land grants unnecessarily stimulated construction was probably true for Michigan, Wisconsin, and Minnesota, though less so for Iowa and the Southern states. As far as municipal aid was concerned, a comparison of railroad progress in Kentucky and Tennessee would indicate that the latter's dependence on state assistance was far more satisfactory than Kentucky's reliance on municipal support.[76] There seems, in fact, little question that municipal aid, which during the 1850's was used primarily in the Old Northwest, was responsible after 1852 for much of the overconstruction in that area. Possibly, as Poor often pointed out, since social and economic conditions in the Midwest in the fifties were entirely different from those in the thirties, a careful system of state credit similar to that in Tennessee might have been beneficial in the more sparsely settled states of Wisconsin, Michigan, and Iowa, and, if it had been realistically instituted and administered, even in Minnesota.

Even the most satisfactory type of public aid was, Poor repeatedly stressed, only a temporary expedient meant to cease "so soon as private capital shall be equal with the task of building our roads."[77] Thus, only in the states of the South and in the frontier West did public assistance to new railroads have real value.

In these, [wrote Poor in 1855] the population is not sufficiently dense, nor accumulated capital sufficiently abundant to provide the means for construction. The States must come to the aid of the roads, or remain without them. The necessity of the case, therefore, sanctions a policy objectionable under other circumstances. In the Northern States, where abundant capital exists for all legitimate enterprises, it would be very unwise and impolitic for States to interpose.[78]

Poor's view that government support, though necessary to bring essential transportation to undeveloped areas, should be dropped after the new roads could be adequately financed by private capital seems to have had widespread acceptance. Public aid — federal, state, and municipal — was for the most part discontinued once the projects assisted were able to stand alone.[79]

Although Poor appears to have been the only business editor to write in any great detail on the value of systematic state aid, his views seem to have been fairly close to those of his editorial colleagues as well as of a good number of American businessmen. At least De Bow, Kettell, Hunt, Homans and the railroad editors other than Poor did not protest against public aid; while Haven of the *Railway Times*, when he did discuss public support, called for much more generous financial assistance by the states and federal government than did Poor.[80] In the opinion of the editor of the *Railroad Journal*, then, the states, particularly those in the South and West, could play a proper and useful role by carrying some of the costs of pioneering. If they did, they could maintain the necessary supervision of the railroads projected and under construction, and at the same time keep down the costs of financing the new roads. On the other hand, if the risks of pioneering were carried wholly by private concerns and individuals, then high interest rates and heavy discounts had to be expected. The distant investor who in any case provided a large share of the funds would, or at least should, prefer the lower rates and more certain income from state bonds to the risky securities of new roads in sparsely settled areas. Thus Poor's advocacy of careful and systematic state aid and his warnings to investors against the purchase of bonds of railroads which had been unable to raise one half their capital locally were both part of his primary editorial objective to help prevent the overconstruction of American railroads.

The effectiveness of Poor's policy of retrenchment is difficult to evaluate. Only one state, Missouri, carried out any systematic plan of state support along the lines Poor had suggested. His warning against the practices which stimulated overconstruction probably had little if any lasting effect on railroad promoters. On the other hand, investors, bankers, and brokers appeared to have paid some attention to his warnings and his analyses of prospectuses and reports. Certainly the quick responses of most of the promoters of companies whose reports Poor criticized indicated that they thought attention was being paid to the editor's comments, while letters from investors and investment houses printed in the *Journal* indicate their confidence in his policies and specific analyses.

In any case, the money stringency and resulting economic recession in the summer and fall of 1854 gave pertinence to Poor's program. The heavy investment in railroad construction undoubtedly helped make capital difficult to obtain. The market, as Poor pointed out, had by the end of 1853 become "overstocked" with securities of new railroads.[81] The decline of security values was further intensified by the outbreak of the Crimean War. The financial demands of that war not only caused a further tightening of the money markets, but also led to the issuance of large amounts of bonds by the belligerents which many investors, particularly Europeans, found more attractive than American railroad securities. The resulting difficulty in obtaining funds, besides causing the failure of several financial houses, forced the fraudulent operations of Schuyler and others into the open. These events, by revealing weaknesses in the financial management of many American railroads, created a demand for reform in the financial and administrative management of these roads. In this way the recession of 1854 which made Poor's warnings against overconstruction less necessary led him to turn his attention next to financial and administrative reform.

⁎ 6 ⁎

Calling for Financial and Administrative Reform

AFTER 1854 Henry Poor's editorials concentrated more on railroads already in operation than on those under construction. Although he still continued to warn against the dangers of overbuilding, he turned most of his editorial attention to analyzing and advocating improvements in the internal management of the American railroads. From 1854 until the severe depression following the crisis of 1857 he emphasized the need for reform in financial management. When the depression years of the end of the decade indicated that financial reform was not enough, Poor's editorial analyses and suggestions became more concerned with administrative reform.

Poor's editorials on financial and administrative reform, like his earlier ones on retrenchment, won the emphatic approval of the investor. After the recession of 1854 cut his dividends and in some cases even threatened his interest payments, the investor began to show interest in the companies in which he had invested. He was soon demanding that they be operated in a more sound and efficient manner. During the 1850's, in fact, the investors were probably a stronger force for railroad reform than the shippers or farmers. Their influence is indicated by the composition of the New York railroad commission created in 1856 which had three members, one to represent the state, a second the railroads, and a third the stockholders.[1] Neither shippers, farmers, nor merchants were directly represented.

With its policies of reform and its growing number of subscribers among security holders, the *Journal* increasingly turned to serving the investor. By the mid-1850's it no longer carried engineering information. Its noneditorial pages during the middle of the decade began to provide more and more information which, like many of its editorials, were primarily of value to the investor. Before the end of the 1850's the *American Railroad Journal*, once one of the nation's leading technical papers, had become one of its foremost financial periodicals.

The other business and railroad papers were also becoming more specialized, and partly because of this specialization the other editors did not have the same interest as had Poor in railroad financial and administrative reform. Hunt, Homans, and Kettell, although they were often concerned with the effects of railroad construction and operation on the general business situation, had little time or inclination to examine the problems of the internal management of railroads. Zerah Colburn, Poor's former engineering editor, who started the *Railroad Advocate* for railroad engineers and mechanics, wrote on the problems of management. So too did George L. Vose when he became editor of the *Railway Times* in 1861. Their concern, however, was primarily with the improvement of operations rather than financial or general administration.

During the decade of the fifties, however, Boston's *Railway Times*, like the Cincinnati *Railroad Record*, the Philadelphia *Railroad Register*, the short-lived Indianapolis *Locomotive* and the Chicago *Western Railroad Gazette*, was a regional paper. These journals devoted most of their attention to local problems of industrial and transportation growth.[2] Although they discussed, particularly in times of depression, the need for reform, they tended to be skeptical of policies such as those advocated in the *American Railroad Journal* which had the approval of and were, in fact, often suggested by Wall Street banking houses. The editors of all the regional papers feared New York financial domination of their regions. Even the *Advocate* claimed as one reason for its founding the need to provide engineers and mechanics with an organ which did not merely "reflect the views of the money power."[3]

Although Poor specialized in serving the investor, he continued to think of the *Journal* as the one national railroad paper and of himself as the leading spokesman of the industry. He was convinced that his policies of reform were of even more value to the industry as a whole than to railroad investors. A program of reform was essential for the efficiency and the success of the individual companies. It was even more necessary if the American railroads were to continue to be supplied with funds essential for further growth. A reputation for inefficient and wasteful management was, Poor warned, certain to turn capital, particularly European capital, to other areas of investment. Poor believed that just because he had won the confidence of the investor who must supply the essential funds he had become an even more useful spokesman for his industry.

To help assure a steady flow of capital, Poor continued throughout the latter years of the 1850's to urge investors to purchase sound American railroad securities.[4] He maintained, as strongly as he had done before 1854, that the bonds of well managed, well located American railroads would, in a short time anyway, become one of the soundest and most profitable investments in the world. But he continued to warn against putting funds into speculative roads.

At the same time, he defended the railroad industry against the wholesale condemnations of some influential newspapers in New York, Britain, and Germany, particularly after the financial crisis of 1857. The construction of the American railroads, these papers charged, was, on the whole, a monstrous speculation in which millions of dollars had been and would continue to be lost.[5] On this speculation the newspapers placed the full blame for the crisis of 1857 and the following depression.

Poor made his defense on several grounds. In the first place, railroad earnings had until 1857 remained high. The drop after that year was confined largely to the roads in the West. There, Poor explained, bad harvests and low crop prices forced a reduction of freight traffic, while the decrease in large-scale emigration to the West reduced the number of passengers carried. During the depression following the crisis of 1857 comparatively few railroads failed to pay the interest on their debts and a number continued to pay dividends without interruption. The railroads' financial record during the late 1850's, he maintained, was as good as most other American industries.[6]

Poor further argued that the low prices of securities after 1854 was a reflection, as was the high interest rate, of the exceptionally heavy investment in other capital goods which railroad construction had stimulated rather than an indication of any intrinsic lessening of the value of railroad securities. Construction had been too rapid and it certainly helped bring on the crisis and depression of 1857. Nevertheless, the funds invested in railroads were by no means lost. They would soon prove to be productive investments. If this investment had placed a severe strain on available financial resources, its accomplishments, the editor reminded his readers, were impressive.[7] In three Western states alone, Ohio, Indiana and Illinois, as many miles of railroads were built between 1850 and 1857 as had been built in Britain in her great railroad boom of the 1840's. In five states of the Old Northwest the railroad mileage had risen during those seven years from an estimated 921 to 8,763 miles and the investment in railroads from $18,000,000 to over $250,000,000. And this was only a small part of the tremendous over-all investment brought about by railroad construction. Think of the money, Poor wrote, that had gone into the building of the great new cities of Chicago and Milwaukee, and into creating the hundreds of lesser towns and villages and the thousands of new farms that had sprung up along every new railroad in the West. The investment made in each new railroad had multiplied several fold the demand for capital.

Moreover, the editor maintained that the railroad expansion and its resulting strain on the American credit was only one cause for the nation's financial difficulties in the late 1850's. The slow return of European capital withdrawn during the Crimean War had unexpectedly intensified the pressures created by heavy railroad construction and the economic expansion of the West.[8] Even more to blame were the inadequacies of the country's banking system and the development of unfortunate banking practices.[9] Poor was particularly troubled by the rapidly growing call-loan market in Wall Street. Not only did he think the loaning of funds on call to stock market operators an illegitimate function of an incorporated bank but he blamed this practice for keeping the New York money market in "constant ferment." The banks were too willing to loan at call when they had funds and too anxious to call them in when the situation changed. "Excess is their rule both ways," complained the editor. A far more serious danger was the failure of the banks to control the issuing of bank notes. The New York safety-fund law, in the editor's opinion, actually encouraged rather than restrained overissuing. In order to prevent an unwarranted and unsound expansion of bank note credit, Poor urged New York and other areas to adopt the Massachusetts Suffolk Bank System, by which the New England country banks were kept in check by a weekly redemption of notes. Poor's real preference, however, was for a central bank which, like the Bank of England, would be "to the business community what the regulator is to the steam engine — controlling by its action whatever is disorderly or eccentric in the movement of the latter."

Finally the *Journal's* editor emphasized that many of the financial difficulties experienced by American railroads were the almost inevitable concomitant of sudden expansion. The railroads were suffering from growing pains.[10] With the experience of maturity these pains should lessen. The sudden expansion had, as Poor often warned, led to serious mistakes in estimating a railroad's cost and its traffic, in locating its routes, in judging its financial position, in evaluating its managerial ability, and in many other ways. Sudden expansion had also made the way easy for the exploiter. In 1853 Poor was already disturbed by the way directors like Daniel Drew and Nelson Robinson of the Erie were able to use their inside positions to manipulate, quite within the limits of the law, the road's stock on the New York exchange. The events of the summer of 1854 revealed how easily even fraudulent practices escaped notice.

Yet the real trouble, Poor told his readers, was not primarily bad faith. Rather it was poor management. There was less danger from deliberate exploitation than from a failure to understand and make use of current experience. Instead of condemning, the task was to investigate. If American railroads were to operate efficiently and be financially productive, all men interested in their success must apply their minds to thinking through better methods of managing railroad finance and operations.

II

In advocating financial reform Poor used the same techniques he employed in warning against overconstruction. He wrote editorials pointing out unsound practices and suggesting possible reforms. These general analyses he supplemented by examining the reports of individual companies for violations of sound financial usages. In 1854 Poor began his series of more general editorials on financial reform by urging that every possible step be taken to prevent a repetition of the frauds perpetrated by Schuyler on the New Haven, Alexander Kyle on the Harlem, and Edward Crane on the Vermont Central. In emphasizing the need for better management, the editor had no intention of belittling the dangers of bad faith.

As a means to prevent such frauds in the future, Poor wholeheartedly endorsed the plans devised independently by Winslow, Lanier and Company and the New York Central Railroad to prevent overissue or other fraudulent manipulation of stocks.[11] These companies recommended the creation of a new officer, the register, whose accounts should be distinct and separate from those of the road's transfer agent. Every transfer of stock would require the signatures of both the register and the transfer agent; and regular monthly reports from both offices would be forwarded to the railroad company's main office. With each transfer the old certificate would be destroyed and a new one issued. Though somewhat cumbersome, variations of this type of a cross check over the transfer of stock were quickly adopted by most railroads.

Poor also advocated a program to permit the stockholders and the public to keep a close watch on railroad directors and officers, and insisted that trustees of railroad bond issues take their duties more seriously. Trustees could have saved the railroads a large amount of money, Poor maintained, if they had considered their obligations as more than honorary, routine, or perfunctory tasks. "The trustee was," Poor pointed out, "duty bound, from the first, to see that the contract entered into between the railroad company and the purchasers of their bonds is strictly carried out . . . to watch, carefully, the application of all the money raised on the property he holds . . . [to] see that the proceeds of every bond to which he attaches his name, are religiously applied according to the understanding between . . . [the company and the bondholders]."[12] Very few trustees in the editor's opinion gave any thought at all either to the railroad or the bondholders until they were unexpectedly called on to administer a bankrupt property.

Yet even the most honest and conscientious directors and trustees needed a better understanding of railroad finance and administration. Basic to the understanding of financial management was an appreciation of the implications of heavy fixed assets. Few American businessmen had yet thought through the meaning of huge assets in the form of roadbed, equipment, buildings, real estate, and even the securities of other corporations, all totaling many millions of dollars. For one thing, Poor emphasized, such huge assets permitted a corporation to carry a much heavier bonded debt than had been up to then considered wise for transportation and industrial firms. Poor, applying his old criterion for roads under construction, concluded that the capital structure of a railroad was perfectly sound as long as its bonded debt did not exceed one half its total capitalization. To this generalization he made some very important qualifications. First, the company must make provision for eventually meeting its bonded debt; second, its stock capitalization must represent bona fide paid subscriptions; and finally, he urged the roads to keep their "floating" or unfunded, short-term loans at a minimum, advocating that any increases above a set limit require the stockholders' approval.

During 1854 one revelation which especially disturbed the editor of the *Railroad Journal* as well as many conservative investment bankers was the failure of the American railroads to make systematic provision for the redemption of their bond issues. Although mortgages on railroad property held by cities in return for municipal credit included provision for redemption, Poor on investigation found that only a handful of railroad companies had made similar provisions for paying off issues held by private individuals. In the fall of 1854 Winslow, Lanier and Company required the Ohio and Pennsylvania and probably other of the roads they financed to institute a program for systematic redemption of their bonded debt.[13] Pressure from the investment bankers caused the Erie to do the same. In their efforts the American firms were fully endorsed by their European correspondents. In a letter printed in the *Journal* in November 1854, Gogel, Koch and Company of Frankfort wrote Meyer and Stucken to urge "the leading Banking Houses in your city . . . to secure the creation of *sinking funds,* without which, you may be sure no further loans can be sold here." [14]

Poor, completely in accord with the bankers, pointed out editorially the advantage of sinking funds. To skeptical railroad officers and to stockholders reluctant to set money aside that otherwise could be used for dividends, he argued that a sinking fund, by making their securities more marketable, would make it less necessary for them to pay the almost ruinous discount rates on new issues. Furthermore, this sound financial practice was in the long run the cheapest. After all every bond issue "must be ultimately renewed, redeemed or foreclosed." [15] Foreclosure was generally disastrous to the stockholder, while renewal, in Poor's view, subjected "the debtor to a perpetual tribute more than sufficient in a few years to purchase the obligation."

The editor suggested two ways of systematically providing for the redemption of a railroad's debt. By one, that advocated by Winslow, Lanier and Company, the road placed every quarter a specified sum with a trustee or its New York fiscal agent for the purchase of its bonds on the open market. In the other, recommended by Lewis H. Meyer of Meyer and Stucken for the Erie, the principal was to be paid off at maturity from the proceeds of a fund to which the road would contribute regularly and which was to be administered by a responsible financier who had no connection with the company. Under pressure from the investment houses, a large number of American railroad companies adopted some type of sinking fund. By 1857 most mortgages, old and new, provided for a systematic redemption of the loan.[16]

As financially unhealthy as a failure to provide for the redemption of bonds, was, in Poor's opinion, the growing tendency to "water" or "inflate" stock capitalization. As early as May 1854 Poor wrote that he was "pained to see such enormous amounts of fictitious capital creeping into a great number of our railroads." [17] It already totaled, he estimated, more than $50,000,000. Although much of this fictitious capital represented stock bonuses paid to promoters and contractors of Western railroads, the oldest and most respected Eastern roads had added their share. Poor especially condemned the New York Central for creating $9,000,000 worth of stock at the time of its consolidation by issuing this amount in excess of the par value of the total amount of stock held by the individual consolidating roads.[18]

Poor agreed that this excellently managed and strategically located road was, from both the directors' and the stockholders' view, perfectly justified in issuing the extra stock. The Central could easily pay the dividends and meet the new interest charges. He protested, however, against "the excessive 'watering'" the road underwent in the process of consolidation on two counts.

First, it set "a pernicious precedent." The consolidation, as the largest business combination yet created in the United States, was being carefully watched by the whole business community. Other companies with lesser resources and less able management might well be tempted to inflate their total stock issues to the profit of their stockholders when they consolidated. Worse yet, the exploiter and the speculator would greet this new idea with special enthusiasm. "Where millions can be realized simply by giving a few slips of paper, which cost no more than the paper itself, the art being once discovered, there will not be wanting a plenty of imitators."

These objections, however, Poor considered "insignificant, in comparison with the wrong done to private right, to the commerce and to the general welfare of the country." Here was a private company placing a heavy tax on public commerce. Prior to the consolidation, Poor pointed out, "the aggregate cost of movement on the Central route required a capital of $24,000,000. The *same* movement (with such ordinary increases as is common to all roads) now involves an outlay of $33,000,000." The company had therefore, Poor contended, saddled the commerce between Buffalo and Albany with a perpetual tax of $550,000, "by which this commerce in return is not benefited a dollar." From 1854 on, until he wrote his last introduction to the *Manual of Railroads*, the editor continued to deplore the heavy tax placed on American trade by the ever growing amount of water in American railroad stocks.

In discussing the proper capital structure for a railroad, Poor's final point was that when the bonded debt did exceed the bona fide paid-in stock, it should be reduced at the first opportunity. That is, the primary aim of any financial reorganization should be to lower the interest charges by cutting down the debt. The plan Poor most favored was suggested by J. Edgar Thomson, president of the Pennsylvania Railroad, in a letter to the *Journal*. Thomson recommended that in a financial reorganization all a company's different bond issues be converted to one 6 per cent blanket mortgage with "the indebtedness exceeding the limit of one half of actual cost of the road and outfit, to be absorbed by a preferred 7 or 8 per cent stock, which shall be represented in the board of directors by one member." [19] If the road later failed to pay a dividend on its common stock, then Thomson proposed that the holders of preferred stock elect a new board which would have one member representing the owners of common stock.

Poor saw many advantages in this plan to convert bonds into preferred stock. It lowered the interest charges; it provided as certain an income as the bonds it replaced; and it gave the holders an immediate say in the affairs of the company in time of financial difficulties. In this way, Poor maintained, the preferred stock was actually more valuable than the lower classes of bonds for which it would be substituted. The investment bankers fully agreed. Lanier worked closely with Thomson to put his proposals into effect on the Pittsburgh, Fort Wayne and Chicago.[20] The important British house of Hessletine and Powell in letters to the *Journal* demanded that a similar plan be tried on the Erie. Although conflicts among the holders of the different classes of bonds and opposition of powerful stockholders prevented the adoption of Thomson's plan on the Erie and the Pittsburgh, Fort Wayne and Chicago, the use of preferred stock soon became the accepted way of reducing the top-heavy bonded capital structure of many American railroads. This was, in fact, the primary reason preferred stock first came into use in the United States as more than a temporary measure occasionally employed in financing construction. By the end of the century nearly all the preferred railroad stock traded on the New York Stock Exchange represented converted bonds.[21]

If heavy fixed assets required a new view of the structure of corporate finance, Poor emphasized that they demanded a revolution in accounting methods. In the calculation of its financial position, a railroad differed from a turnpike or a canal in that it had to consider operating as well as construction and maintenance costs. It differed from a textile mill or iron works in its very much heavier initial investment, the far greater extent of its physical plant, and the much wider diversity of its equipment. These differences made the determination of railroad costs an unprecedentedly difficult task. Yet, unless costs were determined, no road could be certain what its profits were or whether it was making any profits at all.

In keeping proper accounts, a railroad, Poor emphasized, must begin by differentiating between the costs of building the road and the expenses of running it. Even this was not easy. "One of the unsolved problems of railroad economy," wrote Poor in January 1855, "is the proper management of the *construction* account after a road is opened for business." [22] In most cases the American railroads began operation well before construction was fully finished. Moreover, as the traffic grew, the road often had to expand its facilities. Thus there were sound reasons for keeping the construction account open for a comparatively long period after a road began operation.

On the other hand, the abuse of the construction account was by the mid-1850's already proverbial. Its misuse had been, in Poor's words, "the great blight in the railway system" of old and New England.[23] "The construction account has come to be regarded an abyss," wrote John B. Jervis at the end of the decade, "never to be satisfied, constantly swelling the liabilities of the company."[24] Railroad managers, sometimes intentionally, but more often from a failure to appreciate the need and value of careful accounting, charged the costs of maintenance, repairs, and renewal of way and equipment to the construction account. Often too, and in this instance usually intentionally, they placed many of the actual running expenses in this account. In both cases the result was a false picture of earnings and with it the declaration of unwarrantedly high dividends.

To avoid the unintentional misuse of the construction account, Poor emphasized the importance of keeping the accounts of those divisions still under construction distinctly separate from those in operation. He also pointed to the need of accounting carefully for repairs and renewals, particularly of rails and equipment.[25] He stressed less than he had earlier, however, the value of a specific account for depreciation, for he apparently had accepted what was becoming the standard practice of charging replacements to the operating account. He did, however, urge railroad men to make as careful as possible estimates of the annual cost of maintaining rails and operating equipment in the best of condition. He also advocated a fund for unexpected contingencies.

At the same time the editor asked stockholders to check on intentional abuses by comparing, for any specific period of time, the amount of the increase in the construction account with an increase in gross receipts. Since a low rate of increase in gross receipts indicated that new construction was not yet required by expanding traffic, stockholders should demand an explanation of a disproportionate increase in the construction account. Finally, Poor suggested that the completed roads should pay for enlarging and improving its roadbed, equipment, and plant only with funds borrowed at a fair rate of interest or taken from bona fide earnings. In the latter case stock dividends might be issued to cover the amount of earnings so invested.[26]

Even where the cost of building was carefully separated from the cost of running a railroad, the determination of profit and loss remained exceedingly difficult. Any useful accounting procedures required, first, a breakdown of the different elements of total costs and operations and, then, the computation of each element into a useful, workable figure of measurement like a ton or passenger mile. Of the various cost components, the computation of fixed charges was the easiest. Of these, interest and tax charges were the simplest to determine; depreciation and renewals were much harder. The accountant must also consider the expense of obsolescence or, as the New York Railroad Commission in 1854 put it, "the necessary substitution of improvements in the way and works before the original ones have been worn out." [27] Still more difficult was an accurate computation of the operating costs. These covered such fairly constant charges as the repair and maintenance of roadbed, bridges, stations, shops, locomotives, rolling stock, and other equipment, as well as the administrative costs of salary and office expenses. They also included the more variable expenses of train operation, including labor and fuel, and of handling the freight and passenger traffic. Once computed, these costs — to have much meaning for the managers — had to be compared with train miles run, the number of passengers, and the amount and types of freight carried, both for through and for way traffic. Finally, to be of use the statistical data should be presented so that the costs and operations of each unit might be compared with those of the others as well as with its own record in previous years.

Such a breakdown of costs was, Poor stressed, not only essential for the railroad treasurer, but also for the operating superintendent and for the railroad investor.[28] Without it, the treasurer had almost no way of determining the financial position of his road or of knowing how much of the surplus of earnings over expenses was legitimately available for dividends. Without such a breakdown, the superintendent would have the greatest difficulty in differentiating between what equipment and what personnel were operating efficiently and what were not. Finally, with such information the investor had one of the best tools possible for determining the value of the railroad as an investment. By 1854 Poor was using the ratio of a road's net earnings or current operating expenses to gross receipts as a rough indicator of the efficiency of its management. Yet he realized the overall figures meant comparatively little until their component parts were known. Obtaining this information, Poor quickly came to realize, was an administrative rather than financial task. The essential requirement for the systematic collection of cost statistics was obviously a disciplined and carefully structured administrative organization. The need for accurate cost information, then, was one reason why Poor had by 1857 turned nearly all his attention to the problem of administration.

In his discussion of accounting, especially cost accounting, Poor did not try to devise careful formulas for determining costs as Charles Ellet had done before him and Albert Fink would do after him. Rather he aimed at pointing out the vital need for such information, and then, when the data had been collected, he tried to indicate how cost statistics might be profitably used. This he did most effectively in 1859, when, after he had been able to compile some fairly accurate figures, he printed a series of comparative statistical studies.[29] In these studies he compared the operations of ten representative roads — four Eastern and four Western roads and two trunk lines — for a period of years. For the Eastern roads Poor summarized his data in five tables. The first included cost of road, liabilities of the company, train miles run, number of passengers and number of tons of freight carried one mile, gross earnings for passengers and freight, cost of repairs and operating, net earnings, amount of earnings applied to interest and to dividends. In table 2 he broke down the cost of maintaining and operating the road under several subheadings, such as roadway, track and buildings; rolling stock, tools, and so on; operating engines and trains; administrative expenses, losses and damages, and so forth. All these headings in turn were broken into further categories. Table 3 showed the cost in cents per mile run by locomotives with trains for all the categories in table 2. Table 4 showed the receipts for each mile run and gave the ratio of various expenses to total expenses. Finally, table 5 indicated the cost, capital, receipts, expenditures, and so forth per mile of road. He had, in addition, a breakdown of the construction account in one case and an analysis of the "renewal fund" in another. For other roads, especially the Western roads where data were less available, his tables included less information.

While he was writing general editorials on the various financial reforms, Poor was also analyzing railroad reports to find signs of financial mismanagement. Between 1853 and 1860 Poor criticized many different American railroads for mishandling their financial affairs, or, at least, for giving the appearance of financial incompetency through the reports they made public.[30] For example, he censured the Michigan Central in 1854 and 1855 for its completely inadequate reports. The road, he pointed out, was paying high dividends. Yet, even though it had not added a single mile to its length, it had failed to explain why its construction account had recently increased more than $4,000,000. Moreover, the expansion was not accompanied by any comparable rise in gross receipts. Nor did its reports list the amount put aside for depreciation, renewals, and unexpected contingencies, nor show the stock held in other railroad corporations. Until these accounting deficiencies were clarified, Poor wrote that he had no alternative but to assume the dividends were being paid from capital rather than profits.

At different times Poor condemned the Michigan Southern, the Lafayette and Indianapolis, the Delaware, Lackawanna and Western, and the Panama Railroad for similar omissions and inadequate accounts. The Chicago and Rock Island, especially, received repeated censures for its expanding construction account, its garbled and inadequate reports, and in 1856 for what appeared to be a wholly unwarranted 12½ per cent dividend. Poor blasted the Camden and Amboy for its failure to make meaningful reports and questioned why, if not because of mismanagement, this road with its monopoly on the richest route in the United States found it necessary to raise money by making new bond issues. Poor was particularly dissatisfied with the financial management of the New York roads. The stockholders and the directors of the New York and Harlem and the New York and New Haven, he felt, had failed to take stringent enough measures for the weeding out of negligence and inefficiency that permitted Kyle and Schuyler to defraud their companies. The New York Central he condemned not only for watering its stock, but for its completely inadequate reports and its failure to explain its increasing ratio of expenses to receipts.

No road, however, received more notice in the pages of the *Journal* than did the Erie. In 1853 and 1854 Poor accused it of violating every canon of sound financial management.[31] It continued to borrow heavily, although its capital structure was already top-heavy with bonds. Until 1854 it failed to make any provision for the redemption of these huge issues. It suffered from officers and directors who speculated in its securities. Worst of all, the officers appeared to have no real understanding of the company's financial situation; or else they were manipulating its accounts to hide incompetence or worse.

The editor of the *Journal* was especially outraged by a 7 per cent dividend the Erie declared early in 1853. In issuing this dividend the company made no explanatory statement. Yet Poor, by comparing the annual report made to the state legislature in the fall of 1852 with the one issued in 1851, pointed out that in a period of nine months the capital account of the company had soared from $24,028,858 to $27,551,205, while its earnings for a year and nine months were reported at only $5,358,792. At the same time its total funded debt had been rising since 1849 at an average of $3,500,000 a year and a large part of the more recent issues were unsecured by any mortgage. Obviously, Poor insisted, the company was paying its dividends from borrowed funds. Moreover, he was convinced that the road's earnings were far below those reported to the legislature. The recently finished Erie could hardly operate as efficiently as the experienced and fully equipped Massachusetts roads. But assume that it did, and that its operating costs equaled the 1.445 cents a mile average freight and passenger costs of the Massachusetts roads, then, given the gross receipts reported by the Erie, its profit would have been .995 cents per passenger or one ton carried per mile, or less than half the net earnings actually claimed. Unquestionably, Poor contended, a large share of the running expenses was being put on the construction account.

Poor urged the company to answer these charges by making public a detailed statement of its construction account and running expenses, by explaining the phenomenal rise in the capital account and, finally, by describing just how it planned to use funds raised by current bond issues. "*Other* companies tell us what they have done, and are doing, and why should not the Erie?" Poor asked. After pointing to the careful report of the Baltimore and Ohio which explained a similar, though somewhat smaller, increase in its construction account, the editor concluded: "You have all these matters before you. A few dollars will copy and print all. Shall we have these data?" [32]

The directors of the Erie replied hotly that the *Journal's* attack was unwarranted and without any justification.[33] Since the Erie was one of New York's main commercial arteries to the West, they condemned him as practically a traitor to his community. Horace Greeley's *Tribune* and other civic-minded New York papers came quickly to the Erie's defense. Nevertheless, neither these papers nor the railroad supplied the requested information or effectively answered Poor's criticism, which time was to prove was, if anything, too mild. The editor continued to criticize the Erie until it received a new management in the spring of 1854. Then, impressed by the ability and honesty of the new officers, especially the new superintendent, Daniel C. McCallum, and by the reforms they instituted, he gave the road repeated commendations. After 1857, when the Erie again suffered financial difficulties, Poor, as he reëxamined the road's recurring difficulties, came to feel that it needed administrative rather than financial therapy.

Here, as in the case of his editorials on retrenchment it is difficult to assess the effect of Poor's efforts at financial reform. As the quick and sharp replies of the directors of the Erie indicated, they certainly carried some weight with investors. The response of John Murray Forbes to the editor's critical analysis of the Michigan Central's report is particularly revealing since of the Western railroads, the Central was one of the least dependent on the New York and European investment markets. A few days after the editorial appeared, Forbes wrote John W. Brooks:

> I don't want a controversial answer and you must avoid cutting into Poor's sensibilities as we want to make a friend of him. He tells Joy [the attorney for the Michigan Central] that he is not unfriendly to us, but we ignore

him and his publication and there is no doubt that he has cut our stock down 5 per cent by his confounded article.[34]

The Central had not ignored Poor's paper in placing its advertising, since only a few months previously Forbes and his colleagues had begun to advertise in the *Journal* for the Central and their other two roads, the Aurora and the Central Military Tract. But they had failed to answer Poor's request for information about the road. Apparently Brooks continued to withhold the desired information, for Poor persisted in his criticism of the Central's reports.

Brooks's failure to provide this information suggests that Poor's editorials, even when they had stockholders' support, had only a limited effect. Still many railroads did adopt specific reforms, such as instituting sinking funds, appointing registers for the transfer of stock, and somewhat later using preferred stock in financial reorganizations. Also the revolution in accounting methods caused by the needs of the new large railroads appears to have been well under way prior to 1860.[35] While the *Journal's* editorials on accounting probably caused few immediate changes, they undoubtedly made many railroad managers, especially those in the South and West, more aware of the difficulties involved in keeping accurate accounts and of the need for instituting more systematic procedures.

The significance of Poor's editorials, however, was not so much in how they affected railroad managers and promoters but rather what they reflected about the ideas and attitudes of railroad financiers. For Poor, in advocating these financial reforms, was usually expressing, often almost verbatim, the views of such leading New York and London financial men as James F. D. Lanier, Lewis H. Meyer, and Thomas W. Powell. Not only was the *Journal* the channel by which specific ideas of the bankers could reach the railroad managers, but the paper helped transmit their thoughts and attitudes on business practices and usages in general.

Poor was more closely associated than any railroad editor and as close as any other business editor to the group of Eastern financiers and merchants that Professor Thomas C. Cochran has identified as the men who set standards of business conduct and operation in the railroad world of the nineteenth century.[36] Poor, besides seeing these men in and around Wall Street during the day, met them socially in the evenings and at dinner at the Geographical Society and in later years at the Union League Club, an organization of which he was also an original member. The editor's attitudes quite naturally reflect those of the business leaders whom he respected and admired. It is not surprising, then, that the *Journal's* views on railroad expansion, on relations of directors to construction companies, on the use of the construction account, on the need for more accurate accounting, for more complete information, and more carefully defined responsibilities of managers to stockholders were similar to those held by the "general entrepreneurs" whom Cochran found to be defining the railroad leader's business role. Poor's paper, while less significant than personal contact and business letters, was still a noteworthy link by which the actions of Western and Southern railroad men were guided, from almost the very beginning of American railroad expansion, by the Eastern "prescribing group."

Yet the *Journal's* editorials were more than just a reflection of the ideas and attitudes of the conservative Eastern financiers. While Poor was close to this group, he was not really one of them. Few of these men came regularly to tea or dinner at the Poors' home on St. Mark's Place, where he and Mary entertained quite a different group. The friends who came frequently included prominent clergymen, intellectuals, and social reformers like Henry Hedge, Thomas Fox, James Freeman Clarke, Henry W. Bellows, Bronson Alcott, and Elizabeth Peabody.[37] Such visitors helped reinforce Poor's belief in the value of reform and his conviction that a rigorous and careful application of the mind to any man-made problems should produce the solutions so essential for man's progress. These beliefs probably made him more impatient than the Wall Street financiers with what appeared to be obvious blocks to necessary improvements and changes in the railroad industry. And though they may have caused him to advocate too sweeping and sometimes too simple answers to complex problems, such attitudes certainly made him more sympathetic to change and new ideas than many of his business colleagues. Besides, Poor's intellectual approach and his broader intellectual horizons may have helped him to perceive the more fundamental difficulties and issues.

Poor's larger views were more apparent in his analyses of railroad administrative problems than in his editorials on financial reform. He caught hold of and expanded the ideas of the professional railroad managers with greater enthusiasm and vision than did the financiers and investors. His editorials on managerial reform, therefore, reflect more of his own ideas and those of the railroad engineers and less of those of the Eastern financiers than do his comments on finance. Nevertheless, the suggestions Poor advocated for the improvement of railroad administration appear almost always to have had the backing of investors and Wall Street banking firms.[38]

III

Poor began to concentrate the major share of his editorial attention on administrative reform only after 1857. During the years between 1854 and the financial crisis of 1857, however, he wrote a considerable number of editorials on the problems of railroad administration and operations. It was during the mid-fifties that railroad men became aware of the difficulties raised by the operation of a large railroad. In those years the many roads which had been successfully financed in the first part of the decade began almost simultaneously to go into operation. By 1855 much of the basic network of railroads east of the Mississippi and north of the Ohio had been already laid down. Having built this network with amazing swiftness, the railroad men of the 1850's were now faced with the complex problem of operating it efficiently.[39]

By far the most serious and most novel of the problems of railroad operation resulted from the size and magnitude of the factors involved. The length of mileage operated, the amount of capital invested, the number of men employed, and the volume of traffic carried strikingly differentiated the new railroads from those that began operations before 1850. The increased magnitude of operations created even more difficulties in administration than in finance and accounting. In 1849 no company in the United States was operating as many as 250 miles of road and few more than a hundred miles. By 1855 close to twenty operating units were working more than 250 miles of road, and five of these were running lines at least twice the size of the largest road in the country in 1849.[40] In 1849 only two roads were capitalized at over ten million dollars; by the middle fifties at least ten companies had a greater capitalization, and five had issued well over $20,000,000 of stocks and bonds. The same pattern held for the number of workers employed and the amount of freight and passenger traffic carried.[41]

In meeting the problems created by the increased size of operations the railroad managers of the day had comparatively few precedents upon which they could rely. The transportation companies which had been organized earlier to build canals and turnpikes were not operating organizations. They merely constructed and maintained their roads or canals for the use of common carriers on payment of a toll. On the other hand, contemporary manufacturing companies, such as the Lowell or Pittsburgh mills, involved only a comparatively simple type of operation, usually with but a single plant that could be physically inspected in the space of half an hour. Even the experience of the earlier and smaller railroad companies could not offer much aid in solving the problems of large-scale administration. Daniel C. McCallum, superintendent of the Erie, pointed out that the management problems of such smaller roads were closer to the manufacturing firms of the day than to those of new roads of the fifties:

A Superintendent of a road fifty miles in length can give its business his personal attention and may be constantly on the line engaged in the direction of its details; each person is personally known to him, and all questions in relation to its business are at once presented and acted upon; and any system however imperfect may under such circumstances prove comparatively successful.

In the government of a road five hundred miles in length a very different state exists. Any system which might be applicable to the business and extent of a short road would be found entirely inadequate to the wants of a long one; and I am fully convinced that in the want of a system perfect in its details, properly adapted and vigilantly enforced, lies the true secret of their [the large roads'] failure; and that this disparity of cost per mile in operating long and short roads, is not produced by *a difference in length,* but is in proportion to the perfection of the system adopted.[42]

Poor quite agreed that system rather than size determined the efficiency of a road. His attention, like that of McCallum and the Erie's board of directors, had been turned to the problems of large-scale management by the realization that many small roads, old and new, were making better net returns than the large new ones.[43] In New England, where even the smaller roads were making relatively low profits, Poor felt that their financial difficulties resulted as much from the failure to systematize administration and operation as from an inadequate understanding of high fixed assets and heavy overhead costs.[44] As early as March 1854 he therefore announced his intention to study the problems of railroad management. "We believe that the science of *management* is the most important in its bearings upon the success of American Railroads," read the *Journal,* "that it includes facts and principles which are deserving of a full statement and of elaborate discussion." The editor then promised that "in this field the Journal will ever strive to be a faithful laborer." [45]

To the editor of the *Journal* the science of management fundamentally resolved itself into three principles — organization, communication, and information. Of these, organization was basic. Organization to Poor meant the careful division of labor from the president to the common laborer, so that each man had his own specified duties and responsibilities, and each was directly accountable to his immediate superior. The words "responsibility" and "accountability" appear constantly in Poor's discussions of management. By communication Poor meant primarily a method of reporting throughout the organization which would give the top management an accurate and continuous account of the progress of operations, and which in so doing would assure the necessary accountability all along the line. Information in an administrative sense was, to Poor, recorded communications — that is, a record of the operational reports systematically compiled and analyzed. Such information, the editor stressed, was not only essential for efficient operations but also necessary for a clear understanding of such financial matters as fixed costs, running expenses, operational performance, and rate making. It also provided very useful tools for more scientific experimentation to improve service.

In formulating his ideas, Poor learned much from reading the reports of and conversing with such leading operating managers as John Brough, Benjamin H. Latrobe, J. Edgar Thomson, George B. McClellan, and Daniel C. McCallum. Of these men he was closest to McCallum, and it is in his discussion of the work of the Erie's capable general superintendent that Poor's views on management are best revealed. "Mr. McCallum's strong point," wrote Poor, "lies in his power to arrange and systematize, and in his ambition to perfect his systems. To this end he has untiringly devoted his energies since he was appointed to the charge of this great work." [46]

In September 1854, not long after McCallum had become general superintendent, Poor, who had been so highly critical of the Erie since its completion in 1851, reported that thanks to the new superintendent the road was finally getting on its feet.[47] Already McCallum had reorganized the service so as to eliminate much duplication of work and thus had actually made the road more efficient by cutting down the number of paid hands. Further measures had been "taken to put every employee of the company at '*hard work*,'" if only by putting temporarily unoccupied workers to cleaning machinery and making minor repairs on the rolling stock and equipment. He had also systematized the methods of repairing locomotives so that more than forty engines which were normally lying idle waiting for the repair crews could be on the road. More important was McCallum's proficiency in adapting the telegraph to railroad operations.[48] Not only did he use the telegraph to make operations safer and far more efficient, but he also employed it extensively to facilitate over-all administration. Poor, concluding his remarks on McCallum's initial reforms, pointed out that:

> By an arrangement now perfected, the superintendent can tell at any hour in the day, the precise location of every car and engine on the line of the road, and the duty it is performing. Formerly, the utmost confusion prevailed in this department, so much so, that in the greatest press of business, cars in perfect order have stood for months upon switches without being put to the least service, and without its being known where they were. All these reforms are being steadily carried out as fast as the ground gained can be held.[49]

These first reforms were part of a larger and more fundamental reshaping of management along the lines of organization and communication that Poor favored. McCallum's careful "division of management" was best expressed in an organization chart of the Erie which he had drawn up for purposes of reference.[50] The design of the chart was a tree whose roots represented the president and the board of directors; the branches were the five operating divisions and the service departments, engine repairs, car, bridge, telegraph, printing, and the treasurer's and the secretary's offices; while the leaves indicated the various local ticket, freight, and forwarding agents, subordinate superintendents, train crews, foremen, and so forth. McCallum's subdivision went even further than was shown on the chart. The smaller units, such as the repair and machine shops, were "managed with the same careful system that characterises the general superintendence of the Company's affairs." [51] Within these subdivisions the duties of each grade in the hierarchy not only were carefully specified, but the grade of each individual in the organization was indicated on the prescribed uniform worn by all employees.[52]

The line of command within the organization followed closely the lines sketched on the organization chart. Orders must go from roots to the leaves via the proper branches. "All subordinates," McCallum insisted, "should be accountable to, and *be directed by their own immediate superior only;* as obedience cannot be enforced where the foreman in immediate charge is interfered with by a superior officer giving orders directly to his subordinates." [53] In the same way McCallum, discussing the powers of the more senior officials, emphasized that "their subordinates cannot communicate with higher officers, but through . . . [the senior officials] and can only be communicated with through the same means." [54]

McCallum was particularly concerned with communication from subordinate to superior; and on the Erie this communication was achieved by a thoroughgoing system of reports. Poor had only the strongest commendations for McCallum's system of providing communication and with it accountability. "This plan involves on the one hand a very considerable amount of extra trouble and expense," the *Journal* admitted, including "the maintenance of a large office with eight active clerks, but, on the other hand, it faithfully depicts in the general office every fact of practical importance to the management." [55] The plan included hourly, daily, and monthly reports. The hourly reports were primarily operational, giving by telegraph a train's location and the reasons for any delays or mishaps. Such "information being entered as fast as received, on a convenient tabular form, shows, at a glance, the position and progress of trains, in both directions, on every Division of the Road." [56] Just as important, the tabular forms were filed away to provide an excellent source of operational information which among other things proved especially useful in determining and eliminating "causes of delays."

Daily reports — the real basis of the system — were required from both conductors and station agents. They covered all important matters of train operation as well as the movement of freight and passenger traffic. Moreover, reports from two different sources on train movements, car loadings, damages, misdirected freight, and so forth acted as a reliable check on the efficiency and the honesty of both conductors and agents. Daily reports were also required from the engineers. These were compiled in a monthly statement giving for each engine the miles run, operating expenses, cost of repairs, and work done and were submitted as part of the monthly report required of each division superintendent. The superintendent's report on all operations of his division included cost, expenses, and work done for all types of equipment. Similar monthly reports were required from the heads of all the service departments. Like the hourly reports, wrote McCallum, "the information thus obtained is embodied in the statistical accounts kept in this office" to be used by the management as information essential for improving operations.[57]

To Poor the recording and filing of the operational and administrative information in statistical form was as important an aspect of McCallum's reporting plan as was the communication of data to the head office on the progress of operations. Poor, who had long considered operating statistics the basic tool for scientific management, believed McCallum's plan to be the most effective method yet devised to acquire such records.[58] Systematic reporting provided the necessary information on the expenses of a road and the performance of its equipment and personnel which was needed before intelligent action could be taken to reduce expenses and improve performance. Comparative studies of the monthly engine reports, for example, clearly showed what engines were best suited to the different tasks, which engineers operated their machines most efficiently, and where changes should be made.[59] The Erie and then other roads made public important operating data by printing engine reports, distributing them throughout their companies and publishing them in the *Journal* and other railroad periodicals.[60] Operational statistics, Poor further stressed, were necessary for intelligent rate making. Even more important such data were absolutely essential for accurate cost accounting, for the determination of a railroad's profit and loss.[61] All in all, Poor maintained, effective financial operation must at bottom rest upon a carefully conceived system of organization, communication, and recorded information.

Convinced of this view, the *Journal's* editor entered only occasionally into the widely argued, continuing debate over the merits of low *versus* high fares.[62] Although he recorded his opposition to the high fare point of view, he said little because he felt that neither he nor the major participants in the debate, William H. Swift, William Appleton, Elias H. Derby, James M. Whiton, and E. B. Grant, had sufficient information to prove the validity of their arguments. Instead of advocating, as did most of these men, that the railroads meet increased costs by increased fares, Poor urged railroad managers to use their ingenuity to reduce expenses through efficient administration. "The remedy is one we have always insisted upon — an economical administration of the roads. With such an administration we believe the usual rates can be rendered sufficiently remunerative." [63]

Economical and efficient operation was also Poor's answer to the problems of railroad competition. Before 1850 interfirm railroad competition was comparatively rare. This is attested to by the fact that Swift, Derby, and the others in their debates over low or high fares tended to assume that a road could set its rates unilaterally; that is, it could act with very little consideration of rates charged by roads on competing routes. Nevertheless, there was enough competition between railroads themselves and between railroads and waterways in the Middle Atlantic and New England states to indicate well before 1850 the costliness of competition. These early lessons were reinforced by the experience of the new Western roads. From the very first, parallel lines like the Michigan Central and the Michigan Southern and the roads on the two routes between Cleveland and Cincinnati began to compete aggressively among themselves for traffic.[64] They cut rates, granted discounts, openly and secretly, to large shippers, and solicited business through "runners," "drummers," and other agents paid by commission. By the fall of 1853 the Ohio roads had agreed to set rates and to divide traffic, 60 per cent of the through business to go by way of Columbus, 40 per cent to go via Dayton. In the following year, however, the Cincinnati, Hamilton, and Dayton broke the agreement and initiated an even more vigorous competitive war. The Michigan roads kept up an intermittent rate war throughout the 1850's.

Faced with these examples, the East-West trunk lines determined to act before rather than after competition had become too costly. In 1854, shortly after the Pennsylvania had opened its direct rail route to Pittsburgh, the presidents of the East-West trunk lines and their Western connections held a series of conferences. These meetings were called, J. Edgar Thomson informed the stockholders of the Pennsylvania, "with a view of agreeing upon the general principles which should govern railroad companies in competing for the same trade, and preventing ruinous competition."[65] The roads after much discussion decided to discontinue the use of commission agents and invidious advertising to solicit business, condemned the use of free passes, and agreed to set rates for through passenger and freight traffic between New York City and the West.[66] These freight classifications and rates were to be worked out by the superintendents of the different roads. Although no direct provision was made for enforcing these stipulations, the roads decided to form a "General Railroad Association of the Eastern, Middle and Central States" and endorsed a resolution urging all railroads to put all possible pressure on the legislatures of Maryland, Pennsylvania, New York, and Massachusetts to legalize the agreements reached in the present conventions and those to be decided upon in the future by the association.

Actually the 1854 agreements never really became effective.[67] The use of runners, the granting of rebates, and the cutting of rates continued with little abatement on competitive routes. Major conferences to regulate competition were held again in 1858 and 1860. In 1858 rates were set for both East and West through traffic between New York and Boston and various Western cities.[68] To enforce these agreements, the trunk lines appointed an umpire, Samuel L. M. Barlow, with the power to investigate complaints and fine offenders, while the Western roads appointed a commission of nine members with even broader powers. Yet even this was not enough. At first the New York Central balked at accepting the agreements, next the Erie began a rate war, and then the Michigan Southern refused to abide by the convention's rulings.[69] The 1860 agreement had a more lasting effect, but probably only because the coming of the Civil War, by permitting the roads to run at full capacity, temporarily solved the problems of competition.[70]

Like most railroad men, Poor watched the efforts of the railroads to control competition with keen interest. The more the editor observed, the more convinced he was of the futility of interfirm agreements. "Competition for business may be a very bad thing," he commented, "but it will always be found difficult to prevent by *compact* when a large number of roads compete."[71] Actually Poor considered competition a good thing. There was, he was certain, trade enough for all. Since there was, the best course, then, was to let

each company . . . follow out its own policy. None of them will, in the long run, do business at a loss. If they have sense enough to make contracts with [each] other, to keep rates at a living point, they will soon discover sense enough to act up to such a standard without such [a] contract. If managers can be trusted in one case, they can in the other. By leaving each company free, this will be the result in the end — fair rates of charges, founded on experience of what it should be, to be remunerative. This is the necessary standard to which all must come at last. It is the natural one.

Poor further stressed that the through traffic, the only traffic for which there was competition, was only a small part of any road's total business. The real answer, Poor maintained, was to compete with service rather than price. Efficient administration, by providing the shipper with good transportation service at a reasonable cost, would assure any road all the traffic it needed. It would give the company a profitable "natural monopoly."

Poor's answer appeared reasonable enough. Rate wars, as many investors agreed, were financially unfortunate for all concerned. Moreover, as other railroad editors also pointed out, the railroads were having real difficulty in enforcing price agreements.[72] Railroad managers, however, while concurring on the dangers of rate wars, still considered rate agreement as the most workable preventive to severe price competition. Yet by 1860 it was fairly apparent that neither formal contracts nor the setting of rates by common consent based on common experience would maintain the rate structure.

At that time neither railroad experts nor operators seemed to have fully appreciated the effect of heavy constant costs and unused capacity on price competition. There was not, contrary to Poor's assumption, enough traffic for all. Every road not running at full capacity — and this in the late 1850's included almost all the roads — was constantly tempted to increase its traffic by cutting rates or granting special rates to large shippers. Since the new traffic used available equipment, income increased far more rapidly than costs. Therefore it was possible to raise net income by lowering rates. The temptation to cut rates was even greater for the financially weak or less favorably situated roads like the Erie, for here the extra income often meant the difference between profit and loss or sometimes between solvency and bankruptcy. Yet a price cut on one road had to be followed by an even greater one by its competitors if they were to maintain their business. It was only in the 1870's that the railroads devised effective traffic or money pools managed by outside commissioners as a device to prevent the pressure of fixed costs and unused capacity from upsetting the established rates. After the rate structure was maintained by pooling and later by consolidation or government regulation, service did become an effective competitive weapon. Then, as Poor had argued, a carefully structured organization with effective channels for transmitting communications and methods for recording information was essential in maintaining a road's competitive position.

If the railroad managers paid little heed to Poor's suggestion to compete by service rather than rates, they probably gave more attention to his recommendations for the setting up of systematic administrative organizations. For one thing these proposals carried weight because they were sponsored by the best known professional railroad managers, particularly Daniel C. McCallum. For another, they were widely discussed in the railroad world. Douglas Galton, Britain's leading railroad specialist, described McCallum's work in a Parliamentary report printed in 1857. So too did the New York State Railroad Commissioners in their annual reports. Such expert railroad engineers as George Vose and John B. Jervis wrote much on the principles of systematic management which McCallum had first articulated and Poor had expanded upon. Even such a popular journal as the *Atlantic Monthly* carried an article in 1858 praising the new ideas on management.[73]

Yet just as McCallum's views were becoming widely known, Poor, their first popularizer, began to have doubts about them. He was growing increasingly uncertain whether or not systematic organization, communication, and information did meet many of the complex needs of large-scale management. In the months following the crisis of 1857 the editor turned a great deal of his attention to making further analyses and to suggesting further answers to the continuing problem of railroad management.

* 7 *

The Problem of Management

AFTER 1857 the topic which dominated Poor's editorials was the problem of management. The depression beginning in that year indicated that financial reform was only a partial answer, for even the roads with the soundest financial structures suffered. The depression also made clear that a careful and thorough "division of management" did not necessarily mean an increase in operating efficiency. Moreover, by cutting down trade and travel, the depression warned many a railroad manager, often for the first time, that he could no longer afford the luxury of slipshod and inefficient administrative methods. At the same time, railroad construction had slowed. In the Midwest, 9,595 of the 10,385 miles estimated to have been built between 1849 and 1861 were completed before the end of 1858. After 1857 many railroad men who had been preoccupied with construction had the opportunity and felt the need to examine the problems of management.

The analyses and suggestions concerning railroad administration which Poor made after 1857 were particularly his own. His program for financial reform had been largely that of the New York financiers, while in his writings on administrative reform before 1857 he was primarily making better known the ideas of Daniel C. McCallum and other professional railroad managers. This is not to say that all the analyses he made or the reforms he advocated after 1857 were completely his own creation. Other editors and writers, examining the same problems and situations, saw some of the same difficulties and came up with somewhat similar answers. Poor's chief contribution was the completeness of his analyses, his ability to see the problem as a whole, and his suggestions for over-all rather than piecemeal reforms. These later editorials reflect even more clearly than his earlier writings his basic economic and philosophical concepts.

In these later analyses of the problem of railroad management

Poor was especially influenced by what he learned during his trip to England in 1858. A careful examination of the more mature British system verified his suspicions concerning the effectiveness of the management of large railroad corporations. These observations did not change his belief that systematic organization, communication, and information were indispensable for large-scale railroad administration; but they did impress upon him the grave difficulties of adapting human capabilities and current business practices and institutions to the severe requirements demanded by the efficient operation of such large administrative units.

Of these difficulties the most obvious to the public eye was the problem of getting railroad employees to accept the strict discipline and rigid regulations that were an essential part of large-scale administration. The employees took no pains to hide their dislike of the new model management. In fact, some of the first strikes of skilled operatives on American railroads came in protest against administrative and operational regulations rather than over matters of wages and hours; and these strikes were most serious on the Erie where systematic organization had been most thoroughly established.[1] The tightening of control provided a significant motivation for the founding in 1855 of the National Protective Association of the Locomotive Engineers of the United States. The call for the association's first regular meeting registered a strong protest against "the blind system requiring implicit obedience" to all rules and regulations and asked: "Shall we longer submit to the tyrannical will of a few men who strive to aggrandize themselves and build themselves up the title of 'Napoleons' and 'Able Managers' by grinding down the pay and trying to suppress our rights as a free and independent class of men for the purpose of adding to their already enormous salaries for their '*Able Management*'?" [2]

To Poor such protests were rather extreme. The new rules and regulations must be faithfully followed. "We can see no other way," the editor wrote, "in which such a vast machine can be safely and successfully conducted." [3] Nevertheless, he stressed that the engineers had a valid point and urged that the regulations be given flexibility and that discretion within certain limits be allowed. He warned railroad managers of the danger of "regarding man as a mere machine, out of which all the qualities necessary to be a good servant can be enforced by the mere payment of wages. But duties cannot always be prescribed, and the most valuable are often voluntary ones." [4] On the dangers of overdiscipline there was a division of opinion among the other railroad papers. The *Railroad Record* had the same attitude as Poor, while the *Railway Times* strongly disagreed.[5]

Less obvious but far more dangerous than the reaction of the employee against the tightening of control was, in Poor's estimation, the deadening effect of fixed wages and prescribed duties on the initiative and interest of the men in the organization. Like many early commentators on corporation management Poor had found it difficult to believe that any man on a salary would do more work than was absolutely necessary to collect his regular wages. Incentive was even less when a man was in the pay of a large organization, for here "all of a similar grade receive very nearly the same rate of compensation, although some of the parties instead of being valuable officers, may possess no qualification whatsoever for their duties." [6] Thus, with salaries determined by grade rather than by ability shown or work accomplished, and with the functions of each grade specifically prescribed, Poor saw little reason for the railroad employee or official to exert himself to improve the company's service.

The inevitable tendency was for administration to bog down into mere routine. Railroad management, the editor feared, was following the pattern of military and governmental administration, with the same damaging effect on employees. Writing from London in 1858, he compared railroads to the English bureaucratic institutions. "Do the regular establishments in this country," he asked rhetorically, "the army, navy or church ever produce superior men?" [7] They seldom if ever did, even though they contained the nation's "best and most cultivated minds." This was because, Poor reasoned, "their duties being prescribed according to a given routine, they soon become little better than servile copyists or imitators, lose all desire and faculty to act up to their former ideals, and turn out to be little better than dead rubbish." The English army, the editor continued, was only roused from this condition by the Crimean War. At first individual heroes were sacrificed by an incompetency engendered by bureaucracy, but finally:

> The capacity for success grew out from the experience gained during the progress of the war, which forced the leaders to quit a routine which they had followed all their lives, to shape their actions to the exigencies of the moment, and the conditions in which they found themselves placed. Is there not some method by which railroads can be taken out of the category of red-tapeism, by which a living principle can be introduced to take the place of prescription or habit? There is one way in which it can, and that is to supply an adequate motive to good conduct, by rewarding merit at its worth. Till this is done, railroads, wherever they may be, will drag along in their beaten tracks and dullness and routine, and become worse managed and less productive year by year.[8]

Poor maintained, however, that the tendency toward routine and dullness was not inevitable if the top management provided real leadership. Leadership infused an *esprit de corps* into the organization that stirred the interest and initiative of subordinate officials and made strict regulation more acceptable to employees.[9] At the same time energetic leadership was essential to keep the organization operating as a single unit. The minds of the top management, stressed Poor, "must become the soul of the enterprise, reaching and infusing life, intelligence and obedience into every portion of it. This soul must not be a fragmentary nor disjointed one — giving one direction to the head, another to the hands, and another to the feet. Wherever there is a lack of unity there will be a lack of energy — of intelligence — of life — of accountability and subordination." [10]

Such leadership, Poor emphasized, demanded the highest talents. Not only must the top managers know how to handle men, but they must have expert knowledge and training in all aspects of railroad administration and operation. Yet, in far too many railroad companies, Poor pointed out, executives and superintendents, while understanding their own specific duties, were:

> unacquainted with those of every important department under them; there is, consequently, no connecting link between the different departments of service, and no intelligence to guide them to a common end. In such a case it will not be long before the *morale* necessary to a high state of discipline is completely broken. Instead of a unit, the different departments of service will often be arranged in hostile attitudes towards each other. Parties in influential positions, being left to themselves, soon come to regard their own interests as the chief objects of concern.

The lack of knowledge and training in the top management which hastened this type of organizational breakdown did so, Poor contended, because it disrupted the lines of accountability, communication, and information. A senior official could hardly be expected to exact accountability down the line if he did not comprehend the type of work being accounted for. Nor could he utilize a carefully systematized supply of hourly, daily, and monthly reports if he was not competent to interpret and understand properly the data he received. Subordinates finding it unnecessary, indeed often useless, to make reports and who rarely received explicit orders, were soon carrying out their own work without supervision from above. Ultimately, the railroad was being administered from the bottom rather than the top. "A sort of *imperium in imperio* grows up," Poor observed, "which really controls the conduct of all connected with the road." [11]

If the American railroads were, therefore, to operate efficiently, it was obvious that they must be managed by men of the highest ability and training in railroad management. Yet it was just as obvious that this was rarely the case. In trying to account for this deficiency,

Poor suggested that, in the first place, railroad companies do not provide incentives enough to attract and hold the most able men; and, secondly, they too often use other criteria than ability and training in the selection of men for the top managerial posts. Finally, the companies were frequently unable to detect the failure of leadership within their organizations. This blindness Poor blamed primarily on their inability to exact proper accountability and responsibility from their managers. The breakdown of managerial leadership in Poor's view was, thus, not so much the incapacity of human capabilities to meet the multitudinous responsibilities of top management. It was rather the failure of current business methods and organization to meet the requirements of large-scale administration.

These faults, in turn, rested on two major defects. Most important was the separation of ownership and control. Second was the inexperience of railroad presidents in the administrative and technical problems of railroad management. The largest number of presidents, Poor pointed out, were drawn from banking and trade. Yet a railroad, the editor complained in 1859, "cannot be managed in *Wall* Street, nor by bankers and brokers, nor by merchants devoting their whole time to their own affairs."[12] Stockholders and directors, he maintained, were overimpressed by "great names." They would too often entrust the affairs of their company to a man with a notable reputation in business but with little or no experience in running a railroad. What a railroad needed was a technically trained executive, not a successful merchant.

Poor's protests appear unrealistic. Knowledgeable as he was in things financial, he seems, in this case, to have underrated the paramount importance of finance to the new railroads. In the 1850's a railroad company might exist without good management; but it could hardly survive without an ample and steady supply of capital. Money was essential to finish construction, to expand facilities if traffic grew, to finance feeders and branches necessitated by competition, or even to survive sudden contractions of the money market. The primary task of a railroad president in the 1850's, especially in the South and West, was to raise and manage the company's funds. An executive who could command large sums of money was, therefore, an invaluable asset to any road. So long as the roads needed an immense amount of capital, the merchants and the bankers would continue to dominate railroad management. And for the same reason where there was a conflict between a technically trained and financially competent manager, as occurred between John B. Jervis and the Litchfields on the Michigan Southern and McCallum and Charles Moran on the Erie, the latter usually had his way. If pressed, Poor would have probably admitted all this; but he would have then insisted that it was the first duty of the financially oriented president to employ the best possible technically trained superintendent and to give him the widest latitude in the management of railroad operations.

The inadequacies of directors and stockholders raised still other problems of management. These deficiencies Poor in most cases traced to a relatively new business phenomenon which accompanied the rise of the large railroad corporation — the separation of ownership and control. By the end of the 1850's the editor of the *Railroad Journal* was tracing a great many of the railroads' difficulties to the basic fact that their managers did not own and owners did not manage. The complex requirements of large-scale railroad operation necessitating for almost the first time in American business the development of a technically proficient administrative hierarchy was creating a managerial class. The huge financial demands of railroad construction and operation, on the other hand, by requiring a vast amount of capital from private individuals, was creating an investor class and had spread ownership among a large number of persons many of whom lived at great distances from each other and from their property.

Poor was uncertain whether the resulting division of the business unit between management and ownership could be resolved within the accepted framework of the corporation. Writing from England in 1858 he noted that "another great obstacle to the success of railroads in both countries is the fact they are controlled by *joint-stock companies*." [13] "It is an axiom," he continued, "that corporations have no souls. They certainly have more soul than sense." In business, success must be earned. It must be, the editor was convinced, "the product of good sense united to steadiness of purpose, kept alive and active by a direct interest in the result of a person's labor and efforts." The managerial employees of railroad companies, Poor maintained, rarely have such qualities as these. "As I have before remarked," he wrote, "if we would reform our railroad management and bring it to a state of efficiency and economy, we must supply to every person employed, the motives and sanctions that are necessary to, and achieve success in the ordinary walks of life."

If the servants of a corporation did not have the incentives of ownership, the owners, Poor continued, had neither the good sense, interest, nor steadiness of purpose necessary for effective business management. Lacking the technical knowledge or the "sense" necessary to understand railroad management and usually lacking the time or interest to acquire it, the stockholders were unable to locate or remedy inefficiency, incompetence, or dishonesty on the part of management.[14] Nor were they able to suggest practical reforms or improvements. At first Poor, like other railroad editors after him, tended to take the stockholders seriously to task for not trying to understand more clearly the problems of management in general and the financial and administrative status of their own railroad properties in particular.[15] As the decade passed, however, he realized that this lack of knowledge and interest could hardly be avoided. The merchant, lawyer, manufacturer, and farmer who purchased stock were too busy with their own business to have time to investigate carefully and regularly the affairs of the companies of which they were part owners. It was quite natural that they took little positive interest in the way their roads were managed.[16] Besides a lack of time and inclination, the stockholder had difficulty in learning the facts of railroad management. There were few general works on the subject, and the reports of individual railroad companies were usually of little assistance.

Moreover, Poor pointed out, the rapid dispersion of railroad stock still further increased the difficulties of stockholder participation. When many of the roads were built, their stock was held in large part by the more prosperous farmers and merchants living along the line of the road. Because such stockholders, usually leaders in their communities, normally knew each other and the managers of the roads, they often, though certainly not always, exercised some control over the affairs of their companies. By the end of the fifties, however, stock was being purchased largely for investment or speculation by men living in distant cities.[17] As the stock of the larger companies became scattered and the stockholders no longer had personal contact with one another, concerted, vigorous, and intelligent action by a road's owners became almost impossible. When they did become concerned it was usually only because the dividends on their investment had greatly diminished or ceased altogether. Then, of course, it was too late for remedial action. At such a time, commented Poor, the "stockholders are loud and often violent in their denunciations, but they are entirely unintelligent and powerless, and would be no more successful were they placed in charge of their lines." [18]

If the managers lacked the incentive of ownership and the owners did not have the knowledge of management, Poor feared that the board of directors, the connecting link between ownership and management, had neither.[19] Directors, often owning but a few shares of stock and serving on a part-time, no-pay basis, tended either to give too little attention to the affairs of the company or to exploit their position for their personal benefit. When, as was often the case, a man was elected because he was a successful merchant, manufacturer, or banker, he was by the very reason of his success almost certain to be fully occupied with his own affairs. The negligence or indifference of such directors permitted a small clique to control the company and often to make large personal gains by contracting with themselves for construction or materials, by taking commissions for favors rendered, and by using their inside knowledge to manipulate the price of the company's securities on the stock exchange. Such exploitation meant a serious loss to the company both in the effectiveness of its management and in the return on its investment.

More common and thus more dangerous than dishonest or negligent directors were incompetent ones.[20] Too many directors lacked the knowledge or ability to perceive and rectify inefficient or inadequate performance on the part of management. Nor were they able to select capable superintendents and departments heads. A glib tongue rather than real ability too often proved the criterion for managerial selection and promotion. Furthermore, such directors, not understanding the problems of administration, tended to make sweeping changes in personnel for relatively minor reasons. The result was that:

> The great body of superintendents are *peripatetics*, wandering round from one road to another, without being allowed to remain in one place a sufficient time to get fairly warm in it, or to establish anything like a permanent system or policy, or to display the qualities they may really possess. Should one not prove acceptable to the president or directors who may be entirely unfit to form any opinion of his qualifications, he must go. This is one of the worst features about our roads. No sufficient encouragement is offered to young men to enter the service of companies, in the expectation that qualifications will regularly lead to preferment — thus offering the highest positions as the rewards of merit. As it is, merit and position have no necessary connection.[21]

Here then was one major reason for the failure of large-scale railroad administration. Competent and energetic leadership, so essential to such management, was often lacking because the board failed to recruit its managers properly, to supervise them efficiently, or to set stable policies for them to follow.

As serious in Poor's opinion was the board's inability to provide the owners of a road with adequate information about their property. Poor once wrote in exasperation that:

> Directors tell us nothing, for the best of reasons — that they generally know nothing about their roads. They are the medium of communication between the road and the force employed on it, and the stockholders. But a medium through which a correct idea of the condition of their road can reach the public, the necessary link — that of intelligence — is wanting. The public have gone on, — ignorant of the condition of their property, and of the manner in which it has been managed. All have suffered in a greater or less degree, while many have been totally ruined.[22]

Since the directors knew little about their road and the owners even less, management, Poor stressed, was often completely irresponsible.

Such irresponsibility was another basic cause for railroad mismanagement. Unless the managers, lacking as they did the incentives of ownership, were held to strict accountability for their performance by the directors and owners, Poor was certain that the highly structured administrative organization essential for the operation of a large railroad would break down. "The employees on a road," he warned, "must be responsible to an intelligent board of stockholders. If either link in the chain be wanting, the road will fail. No body can be trusted without exacting such accountabilities." [23]

Yet, as Poor, continuing along this pessimistic theme, pointed out, the difficulty of exacting such accountabilities was increased by the impersonal nature of the railroad corporation. Corporate organization made for a diffuseness and vagueness of responsibility which was not true of other business organizations and which not only made easy but actually encouraged the avoidance of responsibility and accountability. Poor maintained that when a man went to work for a corporation he tended to feel "absolved of those moral responsibilities" which he acknowledged in his own personal life.[24] This was because "a corporate body has no eye to detect the first departure from duty, and no indignant presence to rebuke and awe the offender." In managing his own affairs, Poor argued, "every person suffers from the penalty of his misconduct. . . . But as a servant of a corporation, the latter alone suffers for any wrong or mistakes he may commit." The impact of the manager's errors is so widely distributed and the loss to each stockholder so small that the manager "may be dishonest or incompetent without a sense of guilt or dread of loss, and without fear either of exposure or punishment." As a result "incompetency or dishonesty is usually only discovered from its effects, and then perhaps not till after a lapse of years."

Although he may have painted an exaggerated picture, Poor in analyzing the problems raised by the administration of a large railroad showed that he was far more aware than his colleagues of the close connection between the nature and structure of the corporation and the performance of its management. Other railroad editors and writers appreciated fully that the nature of the corporation made the control of a company by its stockholders difficult. They urged changes which would give the stockholders more effective control, which would assure the selection of competent managers and directors, and which would prevent the type of exploitation which men like Schuyler, Kyle, and Kilborn had made so notorious.[25] Yet these writers, including even John B. Jervis, the most experienced of the early railroad analysts, saw the problem primarily in moral terms.[26] Honest, moral, and good managers and directors watched by honorable, upright, and vigilant stockholders remained their primary answer to the problem of railroad management. Poor, much more than the rest, considered the problem one of organization rather than morality. To him the separation of ownership and control resulted in administrative disorganization largely because it often led to the breakdown of the lines of accountability, communication, and information between the managers, between the managers and the directors, and between the managers and directors and the stockholders.

Because Poor was searching for institutional rather than personal causes of the railroad trouble, the therapy he recommended was more far-reaching and penetrating than that of his contemporaries. Like them he suggested many technical changes to improve the calibre of and assure more certain accountability from the boards and managers. He urged, for example, that directors work on a full-time, full-pay basis; that more care be taken in the selection of competent and qualified executives and directors; and that most directors and the president be required to live along the line of the road rather than in Boston and New York. He advocated the creation of a stockholders' committee "to maintain a strict oversight over the action and policy of the directors and the condition of the road." [27] This committee, though having no authority in management, would have access to all essential information and would supervise, as was becoming the practice in Britain, an annual independent examination and audit of the company's books. Yet much more than his fellow editors and analysts, Poor concentrated his attention on solutions for the more deep-seated problems of railroad administration. His two major cures for the current railroad ills were publicity and the contract system.

II

Since, according to Poor's analysis, railroad mismanagement resulted fundamentally from the breakdown of the lines of accountability, communication, and information between the managers and the owners, Poor saw two antithetical though, in his opinion, quite logical courses of reform. On the one hand he proposed, by making public financial, administrative, and operational activities and results, a systematic strengthening of lines of accountability and information. On the other hand he suggested, in the contract system of management, a reorganization of the corporation which, by distinctly separating management from ownership, would remove the need for such strong lines of accountability and information. Both suggestions proved essentially unfruitful. Their failure, however, was not caused primarily by the inadequacy of Poor's analyses of the management of individual roads. It was rather because his preoccupation with internal organization and his basic economic and philosophical concepts prevented him from fully understanding the external business situation in which the individual railroad companies operated after the great expansion of the 1850's. In this failure to understand the full meaning of railroad competition, Poor was certainly not alone.

Through the contract system Poor hoped to separate ownership from management largely by replacing salaries with contracts or leases. Top management would lease a road from its owners or contract for its operation with them at a fixed rent or at a stipulated sum per mile operated. These managers, in turn, would let out contracts for the work on the lower levels, or if salaries were preferred, pay a premium or bonus according to the work accomplished. In December 1854, when Poor first proposed this plan, he told his readers to consider for the moment how such a scheme would improve the operation of even the best managed roads:

> Suppose the Erie Company were to lease their road for a period of five years, say, at 50 per cent of its receipts, to a private company composed of ten men, all of them as competent in their respective departments to be assigned them as is the present superintendent [McCallum]. To one, would be allotted the superintendence of repairs of track; to another, of machinery; to a third, the passenger traffic; to a fourth, the freight; to a fifth, the reception and disposition of freight, etc., etc.; each of the departments to be also subdivided, with a proper interest to various subordinates. Suppose for instance, that in addition to their ordinary salaries, a premium of $500 be offered to every engineer who should, during the year, run a given number of miles at a *minimum cost;* (taking fuel, wear and tear, and accidents, etc., into consideration); $400 to such as should come up to another limit; $300 to those that came within the *third,* etc., etc. Does any one doubt that a vast saving would be effected?[28]

By such a plan Poor hoped to restore incentive and initiative to management and at the same time to guarantee the security holders a more certain return on their investment. Since the management would receive all it made beyond the stipulated rent or contract price, there would be every incentive to increase the efficiency of operations. Besides bringing the roads out of "their beaten track of dullness and routine," this system, if widely adopted, should, Poor believed, create a professionalization of management that was badly needed in the railroad industry. Only qualified and competent men, he maintained, would take or be given such a lease or contract. They in turn would be careful to select the best men as their subordinates. Qualifications could be easily determined by a study of the record of the returns made by an employee or manager. Selection all along the line could be made on merit. Thus, Poor concluded, there would be a strong incentive to work up the ladder, for every skilled employee and managing official "would have his eye on the best roads in the country, and make the control of such roads the height of his ambition. Any person employed on a railroad would have a constant stimulus to improve himself, according to his capacity." [29] Thus the railroads would for the first time be assured of having trained and energetic younger men on hand to fill the higher posts.

Furthermore, Poor pointed out, by freeing the directors from the problems of management this plan would permit them to devote their full time to the financial affairs of the road — the only subject that they were normally competent to handle. In this way the security holders, with an assured rent and with directors to manage the sinking funds and other financial matters, could be as confident as anyone can be in business of a certain and steady return on their stocks and bonds. This was, after all, their primary interest in the company. By the contract plan, then, the owners would no longer need a knowledge of management and the managers would no longer lack the incentives of ownership.

Operation by contract was not an especially novel idea. In the years before the Civil War, American arms and locomotive and other specialized machine shops used the contract system as a standard operating technique.[30] There master workmen contracted with the shop owners to produce goods at an agreed-upon price. The management provided the tools, raw materials, equipment, and working space; the master workman hired the labor force at his own wage rates. States like Pennsylvania and New York began in the 1850's to contract out the repair and maintenance of their public works to private contractors. And, of course, American railroads had been from the beginning built by contract. From 1849 on Poor watched with interest the successful experiments abroad which led the London and Northwestern, the Eastern Counties, and other British as well as several Continental roads to operate their locomotives by contract.[31] Poor, however, was one of the very first to suggest that the contract and lease might be adopted as a management technique to restore incentive and with it efficiency to the American railroads.

Although the editor had proposed the contract plan late in 1854, he did not strongly advocate it until after the depression of 1857 and his trip to England in 1858.[32] By that time other railroad commentators had found merit in the suggestion.[33] Also one minor part of the plan, the payment of premiums to locomotive engineers for efficient operations, had been taken up by several companies including the Pennsylvania, the Reading, the Erie, and the Boston, Concord and Montreal. Of more importance, Poor in 1858 and 1859 could cite the example of at least one important American railroad which had made successful use of the contract system. That road, the Philadelphia, Wilmington and Baltimore, reported in 1858 that "nearly all the service excepting repairs of Bridges, that of Treasury Department and that of the Conductors and the Supervising offices, is performed by contract, instead of fixed salaries." [34] The operation of the trains, the handling of freight and repairs, the furnishing of fuel, and so forth were let out to different contractors at a fixed rate, usually on a per mile basis. Samuel M. Felton, president of the road and one of America's leading railroad engineers, reported uniform improvement of service since the adoption of the system. The ratio of net receipts to current expenses rose from 47 in 1856 to 58 in 1858 and the dividends remained steady despite the crisis of 1857. Felton's success and possibly Poor's advocacy of the reform led the Chicago, Burlington and Quincy as well as other roads to consider seriously adopting the contract system.[35]

Of all the roads, the Erie, Poor believed, could most benefit by adopting the contract method. Since the departure of McCallum in early 1857 that road, under the administration of financier Charles Moran, had been going from bad to worse; and by the summer of 1859 Poor maintained that only sweeping changes could revive it. He urged the security holders to lease the road to a competent operating company. That June the editor was authorized by a company of engineers headed by Charles Minot, a former superintendent on the Erie, to make an offer for the lease of the road for a period of ten years at the price of $18,500,000 to be paid in ten annual installments.[36] While the security holders and the management seemed to favor the plan, the board of directors headed by Daniel Drew appeared to have blocked action until the road went into bankruptcy that August.[37]

Poor blamed the rejection of his plan on the speculating directors who wished to continue their control of the company in order to carry on their stock market operations. While he was probably partially correct, the board had good business reasons for refusing to consider the contract idea. The Erie, unlike the Philadelphia, Wilmington, and Baltimore, was involved in a vigorous struggle for traffic, and the leasing of the road to an operating company of engineers might well have hampered its chances of success in this struggle. To survive in the trunk line rivalry which had begun for the trade of the West, the Erie had to be able to meet a rapidly changing competitive situation by adjusting rates, rescheduling trains, granting concessions to shippers, and so forth. At the same time it had to keep an alert watch on its feeder lines to the West and be ready to make new arrangements with them or even to purchase such lines in order to assure a continuance of traffic. Competition, therefore, made the complete separation of the policy-making board of directors and the operational management which Poor suggested somewhat hazardous. The managers of the operating company, who by Poor's definition would be the heads of operating and administrative departments, would have lacked the time, information, and experience to meet changing competitive conditions, while the directors who would be better situated to decide upon matters of competition would have been unable to put their decisions into effect. Here again Poor, partly because of his preoccupation with internal management reform, failed to take into consideration the new external problems of the American railroads created by competition among a few large business units which were saddled with heavy fixed costs.

Moreover Poor, probably because of his implicit faith in the ability and honesty of the engineer, did not take into account the possibility of incompetent or dishonest contractors. For his plan to be effective, the engineers taking the lease must not only be capable and well-trained in their respective departments, but must also be able to work closely with each other. In addition, such contractors must avoid the temptation of making a quick profit by exploiting the road and its equipment. Finally, there had to be a bond of good faith between the contractors and the company, for the terms of such a contract were far too complex in matters like repairs, replacements, depreciation, new equipment, and wage and rate policies to be fully and explicitly defined in legal terms.

Felton, having the advantage of practical experience in working out the contract plan, was more aware of its dangers than the *Journal's* editor. The president of the Philadelphia, Wilmington and Baltimore was especially concerned with the difficulty of coördinating the work of the different contractors — an obvious weakness in the plan which Poor failed to consider. In describing the operation of the plan Felton told his stockholders:

> Nothing can more effectively secure promptness, energy and thoroughness, than this system properly carried out in the hands of faithful contractors. Everything, however, depends upon the selection of capable, honest, and efficient men. A selection of incompetent and improper men would be fatal. Too great a subdivision of the work by contractors among too many discontented parties might also work to great disadvantage. If the party having the road way had no interest in the locomotive or car departments, he may suffer the Road to get out of repair, thus save money for himself at the expense of the Cars and Engines — but if he is also interested in the machinery as well as the Road, he cannot allow the road to depreciate without increasing his machinery expenses and vice versa. A community of interest to a considerable extent is, therefore, necessary. A want of this has to a considerable extent led to the abandonment of the contract system

in some parts of Europe as a failure, where had it been fully and properly tried, it would have resulted in entire success.[38]

Poor, even though he failed to point them out in the *Journal*, may have understood the limitations of the contract plan. He advocated the plan seriously for only a few months in 1858 and 1859; and this was just after his most ambitious program of reform through publicity had been rejected. Publicity was, throughout his writings on management, Poor's primary answer to the problems of railroad administration and operation.

III

As editor of the *Journal*, Poor had been advocating publicity long before he began the study of management. Publicity exercised by state railroad commissions and an association of railroads had been Poor's answer in 1849 to New England's railroad difficulties. In 1851 and 1852 he had recommended complete publicity in the sale of Western railroad securities in the New York bond market as the most certain way to assure the roads a fair price on their bonds. After 1852 he stressed that if a speculative boom was to be avoided only those roads presenting complete and detailed accounts of their affairs in their prospectuses and exhibits should be given funds for construction. By the mid-fifties he was urging the publication of reports and accounts as one of the most effective methods of bringing about much needed financial reform. Quite naturally, then, when Poor began to look for an answer to the problems of large-scale railroad management, he turned to his favorite technique for reform, that of publicity.

Poor advocated a system of published reports by which "every important act of the managers of a railroad be laid before the public." [39] "Full and complete statements of every act [must] be required," he repeatedly stressed. "Daylight should be let into every department of service." [40] Poor's aim basically was to enlarge and extend McCallum's system of internal reports. Such a reporting system should be instituted on all railroads and should be extended beyond the superintendent to the directors and then to the stockholders. The information recorded in the internal reports should be carefully compiled and synthesized by the department and division heads. From this information each official, at specified intervals, preferably semi-annually, should make a complete report to the president who in turn would include them in the annual report to the stockholders. To be of real value for comparative study and analysis, the methods and forms of reporting should be uniform for all the roads and should be submitted by them on approximately the same date.

Only such a system, Poor insisted, could assure the flow of accountability and information from management to ownership that he deemed so necessary to large-scale administration. The managers and the directors, knowing that all their important acts were to be made public, would do their best to fulfill their prescribed duties and responsibilities. "No man would enter or continue in the service of the company, without determining to qualify himself for the discharge of his duties in a creditable manner, well knowing that exposure and censure would await him, were he to be negligent or incapable." [41] Besides, Poor continued, such publicity might well provide a real incentive to management; for each man, realizing that the result of his work would appear in print and would be compared to that of similar officials all over the United States, would strive to make the best showing possible.

Almost more important than providing incentive and accountability, such publicity could give directors and stockholders accurate information about railroad management. Full, accurate, and regular reports, Poor maintained, would permit directors, untrained in railroad management, to get a complete and sound over-all picture of their roads, would provide them with instruction on the technicalities of railroad operation, and would make possible the rapid detection of incompetency or dishonesty. Such reports would in fact "furnish a sort of platform in which they [the directors] can meet and mingle with the force employed in conducting the operations of our roads." [42] This would in turn restore the rapport between the directors and employees that was so necessary for good morale in a large organization.

The stockholders, too, would gain. They would now have available the information necessary for taking a discerning interest in the affairs of their company, for evaluating the work of the directors and managers, and for making intelligent suggestions and decisions at its annual meetings. Moreover, with such information readily at hand security holders might even develop an inclination and find the time to study railroad affairs; for complete reports "would lay the foundation of a proper conception of what a road is, and what it should be, and inspire an interest which would render the study of the economy of railroad management as attractive and agreeable as it is now repulsive and disgusting." [43]

Finally publicity, in Poor's opinion, would make the railroad corporation official once again responsible to public opinion and public criticism. No longer would the impersonal structure of the corporation allow a double standard of business ethics that permitted the railroad director to be during office hours "absolved from those moral responsibilities which he acknowledges and respects in his private or personal relations." Besides restoring personal responsibility, the criticism of an informed public might well provide constructive suggestions for the improvement of railroad management. Thus Poor observed that:

> Were directors obliged every six months to publish what they had done, and what they proposed to do, they would have the benefit of a constant public criticism; and as men so situated are predisposed to make their statement as favorable as possible, they would be forced to act with a good degree of honesty and discretion, to save their *reputation,* about which most men are much more concerned, than about integrity of character. The only way to render wholesome a noxious hole, is to let in the sunlight. — So the only way to introduce honesty into the management of railroads, is to expose every thing in or about it, to the public gaze. Concealment in either case is certain to breed disease. Instances are very rare in which integrity is preserved unless strict accountability is exacted.[44]

There was no question in Poor's mind of the real need for publicity; the great problem was how to attain it. One way was by government regulation. From 1849 on Poor had urged the state and national governments to require railroad companies to make full and accurate reports at least annually to the state or national legislature.[45] By the late fifties, however, Poor had begun to lose hope of getting effective action by legislation. In the first place few states seemed interested in requiring satisfactory reports from railroads. During the 1850's not a single state in the Old Northwest made adequate provision for the publication of railroad reports even though the general railroad incorporation laws of Ohio, Michigan, Illinois, and Iowa all required such reports. In the East and South where more interest was shown in compilation and publication of required railroad reports, state regulations were, in Poor's opinion, too often like those of New Jersey and Maine. "Merely a mockery" were the words he used to describe the requirements of those two states.[46] By 1860, however, Massachusetts, New Hampshire, Vermont, Connecticut, Pennsylvania, Missouri, Tennessee, and Virginia required reports and provided for the publication of reports which Poor considered "commendable, if not complete." [47] Still, this incompleteness greatly reduced their value as instruments for financial and administrative railroad reform.

In Poor's opinion the requirements of these states were inadequate not only because they failed to call for enough data but also because the data asked for were usually not detailed enough. Nor was the information required standardized enough to be useful for comparative analyses. These publicity laws, which tended to follow the pattern set by the Massachusetts law of 1846, called for general financial, operational, and technical information listed under six or seven broad categories.[48] Far more complete and to Poor much more satisfactory than the Massachusetts requirements were those of the New York laws of 1850 and 1855.[49] Under these laws the state engineer and between 1855 and 1858 the state railroad commission sent to the railroad companies questionnaires which broke down the general information required by the Massachusetts laws into more detailed and meaningful parts. Thus concerning a road's financial structure the New York questionnaire asked for data on the different classes of stocks and bonds, divisions of the floating debt, and the provisions for sinking funds. It required that cost be given in enough detail to permit a fairly accurate estimated valuation of the physical properties of the road. It divided the freight business of the road into several classifications and also required that both freight and passenger traffic be separated into way and through business with the through traffic divided into traffic moved towards and away from tide water. The operating costs instead of being lumped under one heading, as they were in the reports of Massachusetts and other states, were divided into three main categories, the maintenance of roadway and real estate, the repair of machinery, and the day-by-day operations of the road. Under each category there were several headings and for each heading the roads were to indicate the amount charged to passenger and to freight traffic. While passenger and freight rates were not asked for, the roads were required to report monthly earnings, gross and net, for both way and through traffic of passenger, freight, express freight, and mails. They were also asked to show payments received for rents, storage, use of engines and rolling stock, and so forth. The state engineer and later the railroad commissioners who compiled these reports made valuable comparative and analytical studies of the data received. Poor found such information extremely useful during the 1850's for his investment analysis work and for his more general studies of the effect of the railroad on the American economy. In addition, he considered the New York provisions for detailed and uniform reporting an important advance in the systematizing of accounting procedures because they were detailed enough to give directors, stockholders, and managers a clear picture of the financial situation of their roads.

Nevertheless, even the New York railroad reports, Poor maintained, had many limitations. In the first place they were still not yet detailed enough. To be of real value for an understanding of the finances and operations of a road the categories should be broken down into the actual component parts of the costs, expenses, traffic, income, and so forth. Secondly, the New York questionnaire asked nothing about administrative organization, methods, and practices.

The most obvious limitations of the New York and all state-required reports were, however, the deficiencies in the data submitted. Although at first the roads did not disregard the law completely, they often failed to return full reports; and even where the returns were complete the state had no practical way of checking their accuracy. As the decade of the 1850's passed, as competition between the roads grew, the difficulties of obtaining useful information increased materially. Thus Poor noted in March, 1858, that for the year ending September 30, 1855, thirty-eight railroad companies submitted their reports at the proper time; but by March 15, 1858, only twenty-seven reports for the year ending September 30, 1857, had yet been received. Moreover, only ten of these reports "were returned in so correct a form to be of substantial value." [50] Since there was but a trifling fine of $250 for failure to comply with the law, many companies were beginning to ignore it. Finally Poor pointed out that even the most accurately answered reports told little or nothing of the roads' operational or financial policies and progress and gave no details of the operations of the different departments and divisions of the service. "Legislative reports," he pointed out, "merely give *results*. What we want are the *processes* by which they were reached. These must be given voluntarily, and with a desire to *communicate* information, instead of *suppressing* it." [51]

For a time Poor had hopes of getting such voluntary action from the railroads themselves. He constantly pointed out that the railroads had everything to gain from making full and complete reports. Such reports, by giving the investing and general public confidence in the roads and in their management, would assist the roads in raising money and in avoiding hostile and discriminatory legislation. Moreover, important roads like the Baltimore and Ohio, the Pennsylvania, the Philadelphia, Wilmington, and Baltimore, the Illinois Central and a few of the Southern roads made excellent reports to their stockholders — reports which not only included most of the results asked for by the New York laws but which also indicated how the different departments achieved such results.[52] Why, asked Poor, could not other companies follow the example set by these roads? Admitting that competitive considerations — "secret diplomacy," he called it — might be a factor, he laid the blame primarily on the indifference, incompetence, and occasional dishonesty of the railroad directors.[53]

By the end of the 1850's Poor thus found himself facing a dilemma. He acknowledged that the best systems of accountability and information through publicity were to be found in the government-owned roads in Europe, especially in Prussia.[54] Yet the rigid government control that was exercised on those roads was patently impossible in

America. On the other hand, it had become obvious that the detailed publicity Poor desired was not to be had from the great majority of railroads without outside pressure.[55]

As a possible solution to this dilemma, Poor, backed by several of the leading investment houses in New York, offered a publicity plan of his own in February 1858. By this scheme Poor planned to send out annually to all the roads in the United States a uniform questionnaire of some six hundred questions covering all aspects of railroading. "These interrogatories," he wrote, "call for no information that should not be reported annually to the stockholders, and that is not of the highest value to both them and to directors of roads." [56] The questionnaire was basically an enlargement of the form which railroads in New York state were required to submit annually. Poor asked for much more detailed financial and technical information; for example, he had ninety-four questions on locomotives alone. He also asked nearly a hundred questions on administrative, financial, and operational methods and practices which were not included in the New York laws. To verify the information submitted, Poor's plan called for an annual inspection of each road by a commission of competent engineers. He intended to collect and publish the engineers' reports and the answers of the railroad companies in quarto-sized volumes which would include maps and plans of the different railroads. Poor then planned to add "a sketch of the history of each road reported upon, showing the annual increase of its construction account since it went into operation, its earnings and expenses, with such other information as may be necessary to a correct idea of its value." [57]

The cost of this scheme was to be covered by the investment houses backing the plan. The sponsors included such influential names as Winslow, Lanier and Company; Duncan, Sherman and Company; De Coppet and Company; Marie and Kanz; Herman Gelpcke; Joseph W. Alsop; John Ferguson; and Robert Benson and Company of London. These bankers and banking houses, all leaders in the marketing of American railroad securities abroad, had obviously become disturbed by the deficiencies in managerial competency and financial honesty revealed during and after the crisis of 1857. As they had long been sympathetic to Poor's demands for better information, now they apparently hoped the editor's ambitious plans might bring railroad reform and at the same time provide them with useful investment data.

Poor counted on the financial pressure from these investment houses to bring recalcitrant roads into line. He hoped, however, that when the roads realized the advantages of such a plan, they would cooperate voluntarily. Most railroads, especially those in the West, undoubtedly would have benefited by filling out Poor's questionnaire. By answering the very detailed questions on grading, alignment, trackage, bridging, ballasting, depots, terminal facilities, locomotives, rolling stock, repair shops, and so forth, many companies would have probably obtained their first accurate inventory. In the same way, by being forced to break down assets, liabilities, receipts, costs, and expenses into their component parts and to consider allocations of funds for depreciation, renewals, and obsolescence, such roads would have not only a more accurate picture of their over-all financial situation but also more uniformly itemized information on which to compute costs and rates scientifically. Again, a mere reading of the queries on management might have helped many managers and directors to define more clearly and explicitly their notions of organization, communication, and recorded information. Certainly, with an accurately answered questionnaire before them, their directors and stockholders could be assured of greater accountability from the management and with it gain the necessary responsibility. Finally, by comparing the answers of their officials to those of equivalent officers on other roads they could quickly see where administrative, operational, and financial improvements should be made.

The plan, Poor believed, would prove even more valuable to the industry as a whole than to the individual roads. He expected that the compiled and edited reports would become "a manual covering the whole of railroad economy" and through such a compilation "the experience of the best managed roads may thus become the common property of all." [58] This manual, he hoped, would serve as the primary source of data for the scientific study of finance, administration, operation, and engineering which would bring the efficiency of American railroads to their maximum peak.

There was little active response to Poor's proposals. Except for the *Railroad Register*, the other railroad papers took almost no notice. T. S. Fernon of the *Register* feared it as part of a scheme either to strengthen the money power of Wall Street or the antitariff interest in Washington.[59] More valid were Fernon's criticisms of the futility of expecting "authentic" answers to some of the questions asked. Although the questionnaire may not have asked for anything that should not be reported to the stockholders, Fernon might have further pointed out, it did ask for data which most railroad companies preferred to keep from competitors, shippers, and the general public. Poor and his sponsors did not fully understand the nature of railroad competition if they really expected the railroad managers and directors to make public the information on rebates granted and discriminatory rates charged. Poor was even more naïve if he counted on accurate answers to the questions about the speculative activities of the directors, the participation of directors in other railroad companies and related enterprises, or on all the many aspects of a road's financial position.

In any case, the railroads appear to have paid little attention to Poor's scheme, and the financial houses, although they were beginning to exert their influence on the management of individual roads, were not yet unified, interested, or powerful enough to reform the industry as a whole. However, as their strength and interest increased, Wall Street did help bring about real improvement in the financial and operational management of many railroads. An analogy between what Poor attempted to do through institutional means and what J. Pierpont Morgan did a generation later by personal action may not be too far-fetched. Through their concentrated financial power, Morgan and his associates, as representatives for the security holders, particularly foreign ones, forced the directors and managers of a good number of American railroads to be more accountable and responsible and to provide the security holders with more accurate information.[60] Before reorganizing or refinancing a road, Morgan's experts like Samuel Spencer made reports on the road's plant and equipment, its financial situation, and its administrative organization and personnel which were along the lines of the questionnaire Poor had advocated in 1858.

Since in the 1850's the banking houses did not have the power Morgan's later acquired and since the railroads seemed to ignore his proposals, Poor dropped his questionnaire plan. He returned, as the next best thing, to his old campaign to improve state legislative requirements for the collection, compilation, and publication of full and accurate information. In fact, he began to advocate compulsory annual reports from all incorporated companies.[61] At the same time Poor concentrated on his own compilation and analyses of railroad information. In 1859 he published his series of comparative statistical studies of the finances and operations of the dozen roads mentioned in the preceding chapter; while the need for information necessary for reform was one reason Poor compiled in the following year his *History of the Railroads and the Canals of the United States,* which will be described in a following chapter.[62]

In later years as editor of the *Manual of the Railroads of the United States,* Poor continued to carry on his campaign for publicity. Testifying before the Cullom committee in 1885, he urged the creation of a National Railroad Bureau to which all railroads should make full financial and operational returns.[63] Poor's recommendations were carried out in the Interstate Commerce Act of 1887 which incorporated such an office into the Interstate Commerce Commission as its Bureau of Statistics. The work of this national commission, especially after the Hepburn Act of 1906, and that of some of the state commissions carried forward Poor's efforts towards effective publicity.

IV

The fact that publicity continued to be proposed for well over half a century after Poor stopped editing the *Journal* as a basic method for securing business reform stresses the vitality of Poor's suggestions. On the other hand, the failure of publicity to accomplish all that he and its later advocates expected of it indicates its limitations as a technique of reform. Since publicity was Poor's primary solution to the railroad problems of his day, its lack of success suggests that his basic intellectual and economic concepts were inadequate for a realistic understanding of the new business problems created by the great railroad expansion of the 1850's.

Publicity as a reform closely reflects Poor's fundamental beliefs. Believing in the perfectibility of man and the ability of man to attain perfection by his own rational efforts, Poor also considered that man was essentially good and would naturally wish to use his reason to improve himself. Therefore, given accurate information, investors, managers, and directors would inevitably act rationally upon it; and the more information they received, the more intelligent would be their decisions and courses of action. The most rational course would be one which would benefit the individual and in turn would benefit society.

The ideas of classical economics, which Poor had learned from Samuel Newman at Bowdoin, helped to define his philosophical views. He fully agreed with the economists of the Manchester school that men in business should be freed from artificial restrictions on their action and should be able to compete with each other on equal terms. Competition between well-informed rational men working to improve their own positions by improving their services or products would in his opinion constitute the most efficient of economic systems. It is not surprising, therefore, that concomitantly with his campaign for publicity, Poor was also strongly championing general incorporation laws for railroads. If railroad managers had a complete freedom of choice in locating their roads, Poor optimistically assured his readers, they would select the most commercially productive routes and thus benefit everyone since "the greatest good of the greatest number in every State, is promoted by the most perfect transit of both travelers and merchandise." [64] At the same time, if the investor had full and accurate information he, acting rationally for his own self-interest, would provide funds for only those roads that were commercially needed.[65] By providing the maximum of information either through voluntary means, financial pressure, or state legislation, Poor hoped to make economic self-interest and competition a force for social progress.

A primary function of the state was, then, in Poor's opinion, to permit rational men to compete in the most effective manner. Thus while the state should never play an active decision-making role in any purely "commercial enterprise," it should, through legislation and through railroad commissions, help provide private individuals and companies with the information necessary to make intelligent business decisions.[66] The existence of such laws and commissions Poor believed would also prevent those few individuals who preferred to obtain rewards through illegitimate methods from achieving success. To Poor, therefore, the proper role of the state was, like that of publicity, essentially negative. Both were to aid the individual in taking positive action, while both acted as policemen to inhibit deviation from morally approved goals of achievement. In fact, Poor looked upon a fully informed public opinion as an even stronger agent than the police power of the state for enforcing proper conduct.

Such concepts as the rationality of man, the efficacy of competition, and the negative function of the state hampered Poor's understanding of the new railroad problems and limited the usefulness of his suggestions for reform. Thus, although Poor saw clearly the problems raised by heavy and continuing fixed costs for the financial organization of the individual roads, he did not appreciate the implications of high constant costs for competition between units, especially when the roads began competing for traffic which fluctuated widely and rarely totaled the full capacity of the competing roads. He failed to see that such fixed costs and unused capacity rendered his ideas of competition obsolete and his favorite reform of publicity insufficient.

Poor had urged, it will be recalled, the railroads to compete for traffic by improving service rather than by cutting rates. The more efficient a road's administration, the more certain were its profits. A well-managed road, he maintained, would soon have a "natural monopoly" of all traffic necessary for business success. Actually, if a railroad manager confined himself to improving the efficiency of his road rather than aggressively working for new traffic or at least a fair share of the existing traffic, he invited bankruptcy. More certain ways of obtaining immediate traffic than the improvement of service were to build or purchase feeder lines; to undercut competitors by offering special rates to shippers, cutting all rates on routes where competition existed and raising them where it did not; and, when competition had brought rates too low, to make treaties with competitors dividing the traffic and maintaining rate schedules. Often, too, the desire for extra profit or the pressure of costs caused the roads to deviate secretly from these agreements. To survive in the competitive conditions that came into existence during the 1850's, the roads resorted to competitive methods which from their point of view made any very detailed presentation of their accounts or activities almost an impossibility. And if a road was determined not to give information, it was extremely difficult for any outside agency to get accurate data about that road no matter what laws were passed. These were the same conditions, requiring as they did a flexibility in management, which made impractical Poor's plan to have the policy-making board of directors contract out the day-to-day operation of a road to a separate company of railroad managers.

Poor was not the only railroad reformer to be limited by such an intellectual background. Few, if any, of Poor's contemporaries in America suggested in print more realistic solutions to the railroad problems of the 1850's. On the other hand, although none wrote as much as Poor did about it, nearly all other railroad editors and writers agreed on the value of publicity as a way to improve railroad operation and management.[67] George Vose, when he made the *Railway Times* in 1861 an organ for the railroad engineer, became a particularly enthusiastic advocate of obtaining more complete, detailed, and accurate railroad reports.[68] Publicity, supported as it was by the railroad press, investors, investment bankers, railroad engineers, commissioners, and state legislators and popularized by the leading railroad editor of the day, was undoubtedly during the 1850's one of the most widely accepted methods of railroad reform.

Even after the Civil War business reformers, who by then had much experience with the facts of railroad competition and Wall Street speculation and manipulation, appeared to be unaware of the limitations of publicity as a business reform. Thus, Charles Francis Adams, who was among the first to understand that heavy fixed costs invalidated the old idea of price competition as a motivator and regulator of economic enterprise, still expected publicity to create a rational well-informed public opinion which would control malpractices of railroad managers and financiers.[69] On the other hand, the Western shippers and legislators who formulated the Granger laws of the 1870's, who believed that positive government control over rates was necessary, and who regarded competition as the only satisfactory business relationship between the railroads, still maintained their faith in publicity as the most certain way to prevent most railroad evils.[70] The failure of the state commissions to achieve extensive practical results from publicity did not, however, affect its popularity as a way of reforming business. As late as the first decade of the twentieth century such a reformer of business as Woodrow Wilson was still convinced that unregulated competition combined with "pitiless publicity" was the most satisfactory method of regulating American business.[71] It was only after the reduction of price competition by the consolidations of the 1890's and by the Hepburn Act and its later modifications that publicity, the provisions for which were an important part of these Congressional acts, began to fulfill the expectations of its earlier advocates.

In writing on railroad reform, Poor was seeking to systematize and improve the new administrative and financial structures created to manage America's first great business units. At the same time he was trying to define in this new business situation the role and functions of the different groups involved in operating these structures — the executives, the directors, the professional managers, and the stockholders. To the laboring force Poor, like most of his business and editorial contemporaries, paid little attention. Some of his proposals, such as the contract system, met with little lasting success. Others, including the institution of a sinking fund, the use of preferred stock in financial reorganizations, better accounting procedures, better administrative organization, appear to have been quickly accepted. Still other reforms, as the more precise definition of the obligations of the managers to the stockholders and the use of publicity, came to be accepted only after construction had slowed and large-scale consolidation was well under way. In advocating these proposals the editor, even though he had his strongest support from railroad financiers and investors, was convinced that he was working for the best interests of the great majority of American railroads. In outlining his program for reform, as in most of his other editorial writing, Poor thought of himself as the spokesman for the industry as a whole rather than as the representative of one special group.

* 8 *

Spokesman for the Industry

THROUGHOUT HIS EDITORSHIP Poor always kept in mind his role as spokesman for the industry. Like Minor before him and most business and trade journalists after him, he defined this as a twofold task. One aspect of this role was to point out and extol the industry's achievements. The second, and probably to his readers the more important, was to present the railroads' position on the broader political and economic issues affecting their interests. In carrying out the first of these tasks Poor's editorials provide useful information about the impact of the railroad expansion of the 1850's on the economy of the nation, much in the same way as his editorials on promotion, finance, operation, and administration reveal a good deal about the effect of the railroads on the development of American business structures. In fulfilling the second function, Poor's writings indicate something of the nature of the relationship between business and government in the years just before the Civil War.

The issues on which most nineteenth-century industries and their spokesmen took strong stands were almost always those involving specific legislation. Such legislation fell into three categories. There were those national and state measures aimed at aiding or subsidizing an industry. Secondly, there were those which by giving aid and comfort to one industry or economic interest led to discrimination against others. A third type, resulting from the federal nature of the United States, was legislation passed by one state for the benefit of its citizens at the expense of those of other states. The railroads were concerned with all three types, and on all three Henry Poor wrote a good deal. Because the railroad industry was even in the 1850's large and complex, Poor, in presenting the railroad's stand on these legislative issues, often found railroad men opposing his views. Yet on most of the positions he took he appears to have had the support of the majority of the industry. In any case, in nearly every instance the editor was firmly convinced that he was speaking for the best interests of the railroad industry as a whole.

Poor's stand against discriminatory legislation was probably more popular than his position on government aid. As has been already pointed out, the editor's rather careful and cautious view of government aid to railroads reflected his own personal convictions and those of many Eastern investors and businessmen. Undoubtedly many promoters in the South and West were annoyed by the *Journal's* conservative attitude. Yet since Poor did not argue against the use of government aid in the more sparsely settled areas, but rather for its systematic and rational employment, his policies were probably accepted by the more conservative of the railroad men in the newer regions. On nearly all other issues of a political or legislative nature on which Poor spoke, the editor had his strongest backing in the South and West. This was particularly true of his stand on the tariff.

On the national level, no nineteenth-century legislative issue concerning American industries received more attention from their spokesmen than the tariff.[1] More than land subsidies or financial aid, tariff protection favoring one group often meant obvious discrimination against another. This was very clear in the case of duties laid on rails and railroad iron; and here the resulting conflict was particularly interesting because it was an interindustrial one rather than a clash between the industrial and agricultural sectors of the economy. Because American manufacturers were unable to supply the railroads' needs for rails and some other types of equipment, a large number of railroads carried on a continuing, if intermittent, battle against the iron and steel tariff for more than a generation. For almost thirty years, Poor, as representative for the railroads, played an important part in the fight for tariff reduction.

When Poor first became editor of the *American Railroad Journal*, however, he saw little harm in the tariff. As a Maine Whig he had accepted easily enough the arguments spelled out in Henry Clay's "American System." Moreover, during his first year or so as editor, he looked on his paper as a spokesman for the iron as well as the railroad industry. In 1849 the iron industry was suffering severely from ruinous British competition. The British manufacturers, after the collapse of the railroad boom of the 1840's, had, by dumping their products on the American market, pushed the price of rails down from between seventy and eighty dollars a ton in 1847 to less than fifty dollars in 1849. At that price very few American manufacturers could produce rails at a profit. Therefore, Poor and his assistant editor for mining and metallurgy, James T. Hodge, gave their editorial approval to the iron makers' demand to replace the *ad valorem* duty of 30 per cent set by the Tariff of 1846 by a fixed rate which would assure satisfactory protection. Hodge worked closely with Abram S. Hewitt and John F. Winslow in conventions held in the fall and winter of 1849 to unify the industry in its demands on Congress.[2] During the following session of Congress Hodge traveled occasionally to Washington to present the iron industry's case.

In speaking for the iron industry, Poor and Hodge gave the standard home market arguments for a protective tariff.[3] By building up local industry, the tariff would help provide the American farmer a near-by market and therefore higher prices for his products. In time, too, he might enjoy cheaper manufactured goods. Poor, more than most writers, stressed the relation of transportation costs to the need for protection. Not only did the creation of local industry lower the costs of transporting agricultural crops to market, but also the tariff was necessary to equalize the difference in transportation costs involved in the production of iron in Britain and the United States. The British coal and iron deposits, Poor pointed out, were contiguous and on or close to tide water, while in the United States coal and iron were widely separated and rarely near cheap water transportation. This differential in transportation costs, even more than the difference in labor costs, gave the British iron manufacturer an advantage that could only be met by tariff protection.

In 1850 Poor found it increasingly difficult to speak for both the railroads and the iron industry. As railroad construction began to expand rapidly, railroad men began to look askance at any legislation that would increase the cost of construction. During the year, therefore, Poor changed his arguments for a tariff, and in the following year he dropped the Mining Department and its editor, Hodge, from the *Journal*. Poor no longer spoke of a tariff as necessary to protect the iron industry. Instead he began to write about it as a device to prevent the growing unfavorable balance of trade from creating a stringency on the money market. After 1849 imports rose phenomenally and none more quickly than British rails. Rail imports had jumped from 13,537 tons in 1847 to 61,753 in 1849 and now rose to 142,037 in 1850 and 188,626 in 1851.[4] To pay for these imports a great deal of specie had to be shipped to Europe; and Poor, it will be recalled, was afraid that this export of specie could lead to a dangerous tightening of credit. As bank notes were based on specie reserves, Poor maintained that any reduction of specie "necessarily contracts the circulation of paper five times that amount."[5] One way to prevent a credit stringency was, he reasoned, "to impose a rate of duties which shall always leave a small balance of trade in our favor."[6] The tariff had, then, become for Poor "a question of *finance* rather than *protection*."[7]

In the fall of 1852 Poor, speaking for a large segment of the railroad industry, came out strongly for reduction or even repeal of the tariff on rails and other railroad equipment. For one thing New York's rapid recovery from the sharp economic recession of 1851 had convinced him that California gold was abundant enough to permit heavy exports of specie without causing a serious contraction of bank note issues. Far more important, the price of iron rails began to rise sharply in the summer of 1852. In addition to the huge American demand for rails — imports in 1853 reached 298,995 tons — the British home market had revived. At the same time the call for iron and rails on the Continent reached a new high. As a result the price of rails rose from a little over forty dollars a ton early in 1852 to over seventy before the year's end. Since the duty was an *ad valorem* one, it rose proportionately. The increase in six months of the duty alone, Poor pointed out, had added from $1,500 to $1,700 a mile to the cost of building new railroads.[8] It was not surprising, therefore, that in the session of Congress beginning in December 1852 several proposals were made to permit railroad companies to postpone payment of duties on imported rails or to reduce, suspend, or repeal the tariff on rails.[9]

Poor began his long campaign for the reduction of the duties on railroad iron in the weeks before Congress met in late 1852. In his editorials he emphasized that he still approved of a tariff for other iron products. The repeal or the reduction of the duties on rails, he maintained, would result in expanding rather than depressing the iron industry, for, ran his basic argument, the growth of a healthy American iron industry depended primarily on the healthy expansion of the railroad network. Every ton of rails laid down created a demand for two or three more tons of iron. "The amount of iron used in the construction of a fully equipped railroad is estimated to be equal to the quantity required for rails," the editor argued, "and there can be no doubt that the demand created for this article in all forms by the various enterprises to which railroads give birth, by the towns and manufacturing establishments which spring up on its line, and the general stimulus imparted to every kind of business is at least equal to the one-half the aggregate of what is used for the road and its equipment."[10] The railroads rather than the tariff were, Poor insisted with much justification, responsible for the recent price rise. Since only a few iron works manufactured rails, Poor thought it was only good business sense to encourage railroad construction by the lowering of the tariff on rails. Furthermore, he added, the Treasury had a surplus and would not feel the loss of revenue involved. Although these arguments found their way into the congressional debates and some of the daily papers, they seem to have had little effect. In any case, no action was taken during the 1852–1853 session of Congress on proposals to change the tariff on rails.

During the next session the railroads made a more determined bid for tariff reduction. The price of rails continued high, while the increasing tightness of the money market made payment of duties for the new roads still more painful, especially as the duty had to be paid in cash and in one lump sum. In February 1854, the representatives of more than thirty railroad companies, taking a leaf from the iron makers' book, met in New York to consider ways and means to obtain a repeal of the tariff on rails. The meeting first elected officers, including Poor as secretary; then after much discussion it appointed a permanent committee of five to take such measures for achieving the repeal, reduction, or suspension of duties "as they may deem expedient and proper." [11] The committee, a strong one, included Samuel F. Vinton, president of the Toledo and Cleveland and for many years an Ohio congressman, George Ashmun of Springfield, Massachusetts, who had also spent more than a dozen years in Congress, John Stryker, director in the Michigan Southern, Noah L. Wilson, vice-president of the Marietta and Cincinnati and, as its secretary, Henry V. Poor.

Most of the committee's initial work fell to Poor. He began by sending out circulars to all the railroads explaining the committee's purpose. From those interested he asked for information about the amount and type of rails used and for other pertinent data. The circular further asked each company to contribute a hundred dollars to cover the committee's costs. To this the road was to add later 5 per cent of any sum saved by a change in the tariff schedule. Enough railroads signified their cordial approval of the committee's proposition to justify continued action by Poor and his colleagues.[12]

During the rest of 1854 and the first part of 1855 Poor compiled information, wrote editorials, and occasionally discussed with congressmen the tariff on rails. In his arguments for repeal he developed and refined points he had made in 1852. He marshaled statistics to demonstrate his basic argument that the railroads, not the tariff, provided the greatest stimulus to the growth of the iron industry.[13] He added that the railroads by reducing the cost of transporting both raw materials and finished goods had cheapened the manufacturers' costs. A third and probably much less valid argument was that at this time the differential between the labor expenses in the British and American iron industry had been further reduced by the heavy emigration from the British Isles and by even heavier immigration into the United States.

Poor also answered the charges of the protariff press. Their accusations that the committee represented a conspiracy of greedy American capitalists and the minions of the British iron industry to defraud the government and ruin American industry were of course, Poor wrote, absurd. There was nothing conspiratorial about the New York railroad meeting. It was open to the public and its proceedings reported in the daily newspapers. The committee was strictly accountable for all its expenditures to the railroads it represented. Moreover, Poor continued, it was the Western and Southern farmer and merchant rather than the Eastern capitalist who suffered most from the duty on rails. The local shareowners had to meet the unanticipated high extra cost of more expensive rails and a proportionally higher duty to be paid in cash; and to raise money to pay these new expenses they had to pay the costs of borrowing at a very heavy discount. Finally Poor asked why the $500,000,000 railroad industry should be asked to make heavy sacrifices for the sake of a few rail mills whose total capitalization was a little more than $3,000,000.

Yet despite the efforts of Poor's committee and some strong support in Congress, particularly from the representatives of the Southern and Western states, little was achieved in 1854 and 1855.[14] A bill introduced in April 1854 by Senator George E. Badger of North Carolina and amended by Stephen A. Douglas of Illinois to suspend duties on rails until 1857 failed to pass the Senate; nor was a similar bill more successful in the House. In the next year a bill introduced by James C. Jones of Tennessee to allow railroad companies three years to pay their duties did pass the Senate but was defeated in the House. On the other hand, the railroads' strong demands for tariff reduction had blunted completely the iron industry's efforts to increase the tariff. This, in turn, had helped prepare Congress to accept a general reduction of duties.

In the 1856 session Poor and his committee, despite claims of the opponents to the contrary, did little.[15] In the first place, the price of rails had dropped after the end of the Crimean War from over eighty to close to fifty dollars a ton; secondly, a general tariff reduction now appeared to have a good chance of being adopted. The tariff bill passed in the following session, that of 1857, lowered the duty on all types of iron from 30 per cent to 24 per cent.[16] After 1857 Poor and the railroads were little concerned about the tariff until the great increase in duties made during the Civil War. Then Poor once again acted as the representative of the railroads in working for tariff reduction.

The controversy over the tariff divided the railroad press, with the *Railway Times* coming to take the position opposite to that of the *Journal.* At first the *Times* was somewhat ambivalent as to where it stood on the tariff.[17] In 1852 it thought the iron industry needed protection but agreed that the price of rails was excessively high. In 1853 its editor turned toward the protectionist position. Finally in 1854, particularly after the organization of the railroads' committee in New York City, he came out strongly against the reduction of the tariff on rails. Haven's major arguments were that a reduction would injure the vitally important American iron industry and in so doing would result in making American railroads completely dependent on the British manufacturers. He fully accepted the charge that Poor and his committee were part of a conspiracy of the British iron makers to dominate the American economy. Because the New England railroads had completed construction and, therefore, had little to gain from the reduction and because the region was strongly protariff, Haven's stand was undoubtedly supported by a good number of his New England readers. Possibly he may have taken this stand just because his major competitor, the *Journal,* took the other position.

The *Railway Times,* quite naturally, was supported by the *Railroad Register* of Philadelphia, since the latter's editor considered himself as much the spokesman for Pennsylvania's iron as its railroad interests.[18] The *Railroad Record* of Cincinnati, on the other hand, strongly backed the efforts of the *Journal's* editor to reduce the tariff on rails.[19] This division reflected both the regional nature of the tariff controversy and the regional character of the railroad press. It also indicated that Poor, both as editor of the *Journal* and secretary of the railroads' association, was speaking for the nation's industry as a whole rather than for any one group or area. The fact that Poor, as spokesman for the country's largest industry, was working for a reduction of tariff duties emphasizes the fact that the tariff controversy then, as almost always, was as much a conflict between business groups as one between businessmen on the one side and farmers and planters on the other.

II

During the 1850's the railroads were concerned with many types of state legislation as well as the national tariff. Aside from financial aid, the railroads took the most interest in legislation which, like the tariff, discriminated against them to benefit other economic interests. Many of the roads were also disturbed by taxes and other charges levied by some state legislatures on the traffic and business units of other states. The business enterprise which suffered the most from railroad construction was, of course, the canals. Unfortunately for the railroads, they were in many cases state owned and operated. These canals were, then, even more certain of state protection than most entrenched private interests. Both Pennsylvania and New York, for example, required the railroads competing with state-owned canals to pay tolls equivalent to those charged by the canals on all freight carried. In Pennsylvania this payment was required until 1861 when the last of the state transportation works was sold to the Pennsylvania Railroad. The tolls on the central New York lines were repealed after a prolonged and determined legislative battle in 1851.[20] Yet the flour mill operators, bargemen, and freight-forwarders along the Erie Canal did not consider the repeal to have ended the fight. All during the decade of the 1850's they agitated to reimpose tolls on freight carried on the New York Central, the Erie, and the Northern railroads. After 1855 when the Erie Canal showed an operating deficit, they were joined in force by state officials and taxpayers' associations.

In presenting the railroads' case against the payment of tolls Poor had economic logic on his side. There was nothing more unreasonable, his editorials repeatedly pointed out, than to increase the cost of railroad transportation and so to hinder the economic growth of the states and the nation in order to preserve a weaker, less efficient form of carrying commerce.[21] In arguing against the reimposition of tolls in New York, Poor mentioned that they would increase the cost of living in New York City and the other towns in the state and add to the cost of products shipped west by New Yorkers. Such added transportation costs would place New York at a disadvantage in competition with other seaports for the trade of the West, just as, in his opinion, the similar tax in Pennsylvania had long handicapped Philadelphia. If, as some supporters of the toll bill argued, the state needed income, then, Poor contended, it was "better to tax the results of commerce rather than the process." [22] Finally Poor maintained that the actual competition between the railroads and the canal in New York was exaggerated. Even if the railroads carried passengers, finished goods, and such semimanufactured agricultural products as flour and processed meats, the Erie Canal would for many years to come be able to carry such bulky goods as wheat, corn, lumber, and so forth, much more cheaply than the railroad.

In the spring of 1860 the demand to reimpose tolls reached a climax. In that year in New York the toll bill was coupled with a "Pro-Rata Bill," an act requiring the railroads to charge the same rate on local as on through traffic. Similar bills against the differential in rates charged on the long and short hauls were also at that time being considered by the Pennsylvania and the Virginia legislatures. In all three states they had powerful agrarian support. The Eastern farmers expected the pro-rata and toll laws to raise the transportation cost of Western products and thus provide an effective means to combat competition from the rich Western lands. Trunk line competition, by forcing the lowering of through rates with resulting comparable increases in local rates, had placed the Eastern producers in an especially disadvantageous position.

Poor urged the merchants and traders of New York City to join the railroads in combating this threat to their business from the rural agrarian areas.[23] He was pleased when the city's chamber of commerce on this issue gave, for almost the first time, its support to the railroads. In April 1860 Poor was happy to report that the agrarians had been blocked. The railroad's victory, however, was a narrow one. Fortunately for them the Secession crisis, then the Civil War and wartime prosperity turned the attention of legislatures in New York and other states to other problems and issues.

Poor's protests against the levying of tolls on railroads for the benefit of canals and of the business interests which had grown up around the canals were mild compared to those he made against taxes and discriminatory legislation passed by one state against the railroads and the commerce of others. To the editor these parochial "state policies" were more than just economically unsound and constitutionally invalid. Since they violated his basic economic and philosophical attitudes by creating "artificial" barriers to the development of an efficient transportation system and so retarded the progress of the man and the nation, they were positively immoral. In these protests against state discriminations, Poor had strong support from nearly all railroad men except those whose roads directly benefited from such legislation. The other railroad papers, particularly the *Railway Times*, therefore joined in many of Poor's criticisms against "state policies" though none took as strong and vehement a stand as did the *Journal*.[24]

When Poor became editor of the *Journal*, economic particularism was still strong. Some states, like Illinois, refused to charter a railroad terminating in any town outside of the state. New York, for a time, obstructed Boston's trade with the West by not permitting the construction of a bridge at Rouse's Point at the northern tip of Lake Champlain. Virginia tried to block the construction across her territory of, first, the Baltimore and Ohio, and then a western extension of the Pennsylvania. Mississippi refused to allow the Memphis and

Charleston to cross her boundaries unless the line was lengthened by many miles so as to include one or two Mississippi towns. Maryland and New Jersey made the most of their position on one of the nation's most traveled routes by placing a heavy transit tax on all passengers and freight passing through their territories.[25]

In New Jersey Poor found the situation particularly frustrating. There the Camden and Amboy enjoyed a monopoly across the state, and the state profited substantially from this monopoly not only from the transit tax but also because it was a stockholder in the road. Poor considered Congress the only force powerful enough to break this lucrative partnership. "It is from *national* action that we must look for immediate redress," he wrote. "The General Government can authorize the construction of a *Post* road between the above cities."[26] Only by the competition of a government-sponsored railroad, Poor believed, would efficient transportation be provided at fair rates on one of the country's most important commercial routes. Here, where an unholy combination of powerful private and public interests was successfully exploiting American railroad commerce, Poor would make an exception to his position against permitting the government to take a positive role in American railroading.

Few states exploited their geographical position more vigorously than Pennsylvania; and Poor's attacks on Pennsylvania's policy best illustrate his stand on this type of economic discrimination.[27] In the 1840's Pennsylvania had for some time prevented the building of the New York's Erie Railroad along the most practical route which carried it for some miles into Pennsylvania. It finally permitted the road to follow this route on payment of annual "tribute" of $10,000 over and above the regular taxes. In 1852 Pennsylvania had passed a law prohibiting the use of the 6-foot gauge in the state explicitly to prevent extension of the Erie or its feeders into and across her territory. In the 1850's too it denied a branch of the Baltimore and Ohio the right to extend its line to Pittsburgh.

Pennsylvania's policy received nation-wide attention late in 1853, when the state supported the city of Erie in its refusal to allow the standardizing of the gauge of the line running along the shore of Lake Erie.[28] In November 1853 the Buffalo and State line and the Erie and North East, companies in which the recently formed New York Central had a large stock interest, contracted to change their tracks so as to permit the running of a single gauge from Buffalo to Cleveland. Up to this time the break in the gauge had required a transfer of all goods and passengers at Erie. The citizens of Erie met this threat to their prosperity by tearing up seven miles of the new track as soon as it had been laid down. Then the railroad company defying a municipal ordinance began to relay the rails. In the resulting armed clashes which successfully blocked any further work on the road, two townspeople were wounded and much railroad property was damaged. During these "Erie riots" the town received the full support of the Pennsylvania newspapers, the state legislature, and its governor, William Bigler. The governor not only condoned the violence but recommended that the legislature annul the charter of the road which was to connect the Ohio roads with the Erie and North East at Erie — a recommendation which the legislature immediately approved. Bigler in his special message to the legislature justified the position of the state, first, by pointing out:

> It so happens that Pennsylvania holds the key to the important link of connection between the East and the West, and it must unhesitatingly say, that where no principle of amity or commerce is to be violated, it is the right and duty of the State to turn her natural advantages to the promotion and welfare of her own people.[29]

He then insisted that the state must protect itself from the ambitious schemes of New York State and New York City and of those "great over-grown and grasping monopolies," the New York Central and the Erie.

The editor of the *Railroad Journal,* incensed by the actions of the town of Erie and the state of Pennsylvania, was even more outraged by the arguments used to vindicate their positions.[30] It was absurd to think that New York had carefully devised designs for capturing Pennsylvania's trade. After all, Poor reminded Pennsylvanians, nearly all of Philadelphia's and Pittsburgh's connections with the West had been financed with the assistance of New Yorkers. Moreover, New York would suffer less than other parts of the nation from Pennsylvania's restrictive measures. As the center of American commerce New York City would continue to get the lion's share of the trade of the West. The Erie Canal was still the largest carrier of bulky products and much of the Western trade that traveled east by railroad would still come to New York even if it was sent via Philadelphia rather than Buffalo and Dunkirk. Instead, Pennsylvania's policies injured the Western farmer who had to pay an increased cost on the eastward transportation of his agricultural products and on the westward shipment of finished goods. They hurt even more the investor in the railroads whose property was damaged or whose traffic was delayed or diverted.

For these reasons Poor maintained that Pennsylvania was the real victim of her restrictive policies. The Baltimore and Ohio and the city of Baltimore were sure now to obtain a larger share of the Western trade. Once lost, this business would be hard to regain. Of more significance, the state's support of wreckers of railroad property and her cancellation of a corporation's charter would injure the credit of the state and her railroads. Pennsylvania, Poor reminded her legislators, already had an unsavory reputation with investors because of the mismanagement of her state debt in the 1840's. "A war of *aggression* upon the property of distant creditors," the editor warned, "would cause investors to refuse to take the loans necessary for the completion of many railroads in Pennsylvania.[31] They will say: 'Gentlemen, experience has shown that railroad property in your State in unsafe.'"

This seems to have been an effective argument. In the first weeks of 1854 Pennsylvania municipal and railroad bonds dropped several points, with the result that in February, J. Edgar Thomson, president of the Pennsylvania Railroad, condemned the *Railroad Journal* in the strongest language for "endeavoring . . . to destroy the credit of Pennsylvania, to depreciate her bonds, and the bonds of her cities and railroads." [32] The quickness and intensity of Thomson's response reflects, like the reactions of Ryder, Forbes, and other railroad promoters, the power of Poor's pen.

Not only did Pennsylvania's restrictive measures violate the tenets of sound economy — as did those of other states — but, as Poor maintained, they contravened the principles of the American Constitution. In 1849 the editor, referring to an earlier example of Pennsylvania's economic provincialism, wrote:

> The very object of the union was to protect the several States from the partial legislation of any of their members for the purpose of benefiting themselves at the expense of others; and we deny the right of any to impose either directly or indirectly, any burdens upon the citizens of any other States, as a tax for the privilege of passing through it. The exercise of such a power would . . . array the several States of the Union in hostile attitude to each other, and would be equivalent to disunion itself.[33]

In his reply to Governor Bigler in 1854 Poor enlarged on this view. Pennsylvania, by insisting on a break in through traffic at Erie, had, in his opinion, placed an unconstitutional tax on the movement of interstate commerce, and it was, in fact, on constitutional grounds that the railroads were finally permitted to lay down the single-gauge track through Erie. The courts agreed that the actions of the city and the state interfered with the movement of interstate mail and violated the contract clause of the Constitution.

To Poor the surest antidote to restrictive measures by the states on railroad transportation was a general incorporation law for railroads.[34] He urged other states to copy the "general railroad law," passed by the New York legislature in 1850. This law permitted any company which paid a registration fee of $1,000, raised stock subscriptions of at least $100 a mile, and met requirements for safety and for the publicity of accounts to receive a charter without specific legislative sanction. Such laws, by permitting anyone with the necessary capital to start a railroad company, would, in the editor's opinion, allow the construction of railroads to follow the demands of commerce rather than the whims of special interests and local politicians. Furthermore, this type of "general" or "free" railroad law would help to bring to an end corporate monopoly and special privilege. In New Jersey, Pennsylvania, and other states, roads with legislative influence would no longer be able to prevent the incorporation of potential competitors. Also such legislation would eliminate the need for railroad managers to become involved in expensive lobbying and in log-rolling and other political deals. In this way the general incorporation laws would divorce railroads from politics, reduce the initial cost of railroad construction, and prevent a charter from becoming, as it already had become in England and several American states, a prize in itself — a piece of goods to be sold to the highest bidder. In his vigorous espousal of the general railroad laws, Poor, believing as he did in the negative functions of the state, failed to see that complete freedom of incorporation might be as easily abused as too much political interference. Yet the laws he advocated were largely responsible for breaking down the barriers to the freedom of interstate commerce, in the years just before and after the Civil War.

In the 1850's the shift away from economic particularism and localism had already begun. States like New York and Illinois soon dropped their policies of hampering the trade of other states in order to build up their own. In the first half of the decade several states passed general railroad laws. By 1855 Ohio, Indiana, Illinois, Michigan, Wisconsin, Arkansas, and Louisiana had adopted versions of New York's 1850 law. The Tennessee and Missouri laws providing for state aid to railroads were in fact general incorporation laws. In the East, however, no state besides New York adopted such a law before 1860. There such laws were resisted until well after the Civil War, while Maryland, New Jersey, and Pennsylvania continued to tax national commerce for their own particular benefit. It was in the West, then, the area where localism had never been strong, where in the years following the Mexican War the spirit of "Manifest Destiny" ran the highest, and where the large majority of producers depended on a national or international rather than a local market — it was there in the West that Poor's views had their best reception. Nor is it surprising, in view of Poor's upbringing on the New England frontier, that his views on these legislative matters were more often closer to those of the Westerner than of the Easterner.

III

One reason why Poor proved an effective spokesman of the industry was that in writing against taxation, tolls, and other discriminatory legislation against railroads and railroad traffic, he was expressing his own strong convictions. This was also true of his editorials describing the railroads' achievements and comparing the virtues and advantages of the railroad with other forms of transportation. Poor had no doubts whatsoever that the railroads were transforming the economic structure of the nation, and that this transformation, in spite of the temporary problems and difficulties it raised, would benefit every American. In fact, the railroads were, in the editor's opinion, providing an essential impetus to political and social as well as economic progress.

By breaking down economic localism and by making the nation an integrated economic whole, the railroads, Poor maintained, were making possible the success of democracy in the United States. For one thing, without the rapid expansion of the railroad system, it would be extremely difficult for a democratic people to govern so vast a territory — the size of which had recently been greatly increased by the successful war with Mexico.[35] In the past, history demonstrated, size and liberty were incompatible. The administration of widespread areas had almost invariably, Poor maintained, required a centralized autocratic rule. But the railroad, which had brought New Orleans, Kansas, and Lake Superior closer to Washington than Berwick and Land's End were to London at the time of the signing of the Declaration of Independence, now provided Americans with the means for retaining both their liberties and their extended territory.

The railroad was also breaking down the barriers between the country and the city. By placing the amenities of urban life within the reach of the rural farmer, it helped make his life less narrow, limited, and barren. At the same time, it gave the city man access to the relaxations and pleasures of country life. "This we consider the highest type of civilization. It is not the migratory life of the barbarian; it is not the life of the *city*-zen of the ancient republics and those of the middle ages. It is a combination of the two. It contains the excellencies of both." [36] Of more importance was the effect that Poor believed the railroad was having in helping to reconcile local and sectional ideological and political differences, particularly those between the North and the South. Developing the ideas expressed in his early editorials, Poor maintained that improved communication and increasing social and business association would soon make clear the foolishness of mutual suspicions and mutual misunderstandings, while the expanding railroad network would help create a unified national economy in place of the conflicting sectional economies.

In speaking for the industry Poor concentrated on the economic rather than the political or social impact of the railroads. The impact of the railroad expansion was certainly as profound as Poor made it out to be. In the 1850's the rapid growth of the railroad was making possible the swift spread of commercial agriculture in the South and West. It was laying the essential transportation foundation for the industrialization of the East. And, most obvious to the men of the day, new railroads were reorienting the course of American commerce.

Well before 1850 the Erie Canal had begun to turn the trade of the West from the South to the East. By the 1840's the Great Lakes and Erie Canal route was, with the aid of a few canals in the West, challenging the Mississippi River–New Orleans and New York coastal shipping route as the nation's basic trade artery. In 1851 and 1852 Henry Poor predicted that the new railroads in the West, by feeding and by supplementing the Northern water route, would complete the revolution the canals had begun.[37] New York, Poor contended, would soon surpass New Orleans as the major market and port of export for Western products, and that the "artificial" means of commerce would replace the "natural" ones. He further forecast that in the coming decade those cities at the transshipment point between the railroads and lake shipping, such as Chicago, Detroit, Toledo, Sandusky, and Cleveland, would all have a much larger relative growth than the river ports of Cincinnati, Louisville, and St. Louis.

These predictions were eminently sound. Where in 1849 there had been only a handful of canals and a very few railroads, there were by the end of the 1850's dozens of railroads pouring grain and other agricultural products into the lake ports or bringing them directly to the Eastern seaboard. Chicago, which in 1850 sent eastward only 1,388,000 bushels of flour and grain, in 1861 shipped 50,510,000 bushels, and the bushels of grain and flour received at Buffalo soared from 12,105,559 in 1850 to 61,460,601 in 1861.[38]

By that time even the Southern staples were moving north instead of going to the East and Europe via New Orleans. In 1852 Poor published letters he received from planters and merchants in Kentucky and Tennessee pointing out that it was cheaper to send tobacco destined for Europe north via railroad and canal to New York than by river to New Orleans.[39] As soon as the trunk lines were finished, they began to carry a large portion of the crop. According to annual reports which Poor read and excerpted in the *Journal,* tobacco shipments eastward on the main stem of the Baltimore and Ohio rose from 3,487 hogsheads in 1852 to 27,839 in 1853, and to 45,881 in 1858, while those on the Pennsylvania grew from over 1,000,000 pounds in 1857 to a little more than 8,250,000 in 1860. With the completion of some of the Southern lines late in the decade cotton shipments north by rail rose even more strikingly. The Pennsylvania carried 733,651 pounds from Pittsburgh to Philadelphia in 1857, 5,680,365 in 1858, 17,897,569 in 1859, and 28,673,305 in 1860. The Little Miami, which in 1857 carried only 459 pounds of cotton destined for points east of Columbus, in 1860 shipped 154,505 pounds plus 30,901 bales. By then cotton was almost as important as wheat and flour in bringing revenue to the road.[40]

The Northern railroad and canal route, Poor pointed out, had many advantages for the eastward movement of crops and agricultural products over the river and coastal shipping route via New Orleans.[41] It was shorter and quicker. Transportation on canal and railroad was more certain and regular than on river and coastal shipping. Deforestation of the upper reaches of the Mississippi Valley had, the editor noted, made the soil less absorbent and so tended to cause severe floods in the spring followed by extreme low water in the fall just when the crops had to be sent to market. Moreover, the Northern route was healthier, especially since yellow fever remained in New Orleans long after the coming of frost had ended it in New York. More important, the markets in the Eastern ports were usually more steady and "much more uniform" than in New Orleans. Finally, New Orleans suffered from extremely high freight handling charges.

Although Poor wrote less about it, the railroad during the 1850's was diverting from the Southern route even more of the westbound traffic of manufactured goods than the eastbound agricultural products. The shipment of railroad equipment is a typical example. As late as 1851 roads in southern Ohio, Indiana, and Illinois received their rails, locomotives, and other equipment by way of New Orleans.[42] By the middle of the decade nearly all railroad equipment went West by railroad and canal and usually it went the whole way by rail. The annual reports already cited indicate a rapid growth in the westward traffic of finished goods which was achieved primarily at the expense of the canals.[43]

Toward the end of the decade the editor began to point out the rapid shift of traffic along the Northern route from the canals to the railroads, particularly in eastbound agricultural freight. By 1858, the reports of the New York Canal Commission, which Poor printed in the *Journal,* indicated that the New York railroads carried more pork, beef, butter, wool, and cattle, as well as more merchandise and manufactured goods than the canals.[44] Of the seven categories given in the New York canal commissioners' reports the canal tonnage only surpassed railroads in two, vegetable foods and the products of the forest. In 1860 Poor used the canal commission's information to compile statistics demonstrating the rapidity of the shift of traffic to the railroad.[45] In 1853, the editor noted, the New York canals moved 700,-389,932 tons one mile, while the Central and Erie railroads together operated 156,327,872 ton miles. Six years later the ton-mile operated by canals dropped to 544,309,072, while those of the two roads rose to 304,263,639. For the same period receipts of the railroads for through traffic rose from $4,346,044 to $6,533,018 while those from through canal shipments declined from approximately $6,400,000 to $3,470,000. It is little wonder, then, that the New York state officials were in the late 1850's so troubled by the state's heavy investment in canals. Nevertheless Poor maintained, as he had done earlier, that since the cost of canal shipping remained lower than the railroad rates throughout these years, the canal must for a long time to come carry the lion's share of such heavy bulky products as wheat, lumber, and potash.

Besides turning the trade of the West to the East, the railroads during the 1850's were opening large new areas in the West and to a lesser degree in the South to commercial agriculture. As Poor stressed in his articles promoting Western railroads, much rich farming land in the West had in 1850 little or no "commercial value" because of the prohibitive cost of transporting its crops to market. The railroads by bringing this essential transportation to large areas in the Northwest made that section during the following decade the breadbox of the nation. Between 1850 and 1860, the census of 1860 reported, the production of wheat in the five states of the Old Northwest increased 100 per cent, corn 58 per cent, oats 50 per cent, potatoes 100 per cent, and cattle 59 per cent. "So great are their benefits," continued the census, "that, if the entire cost of railroads between the Atlantic and western States had been levied on the farmers of the central west, their proprietors could have paid it and been immensely the gainers." [46]

The railroad, in fact, carried commercial agriculture almost to the frontier line. In 1854 Poor, impressed by the heavy freight traffic on the newly opened roads west of Chicago, told an audience at a meeting of the American Geographical Society:

> The pioneer, as he moves forward over the prairie of the west carries with him the railway — as necessary to his life as are the axe and the plough. The railway keeps pace with the frontier line of settlement; so that

the crop this year of a frontier farm, in the great march of civilization, has only to be held to the next, to be sent whizzing to the Eastern market at a speed of thirty miles to the hour.[47]

In nearly all his writings about railroads Poor talked almost wholly about freight traffic, thus emphasizing the fact that in most of the United States railroads were built, unlike those of Britain, to carry freight rather than passengers. The first Southern roads, the South Carolina and the two Georgia lines, were primarily cotton carriers. Even the North-South lines from Wilmington, North Carolina, to the Potomac were by the 1850's depending heavily on freight for revenue.[48] In the West almost all the early railroads, excepting those on main East-West passenger routes from New York to Chicago, received the greatest portion of their income from moving wheat, flour, cattle, and other agricultural products. After 1855 the only major roads in the West earning more revenue from passengers than freight were the Michigan Central, the Michigan Southern, the Cleveland and Toledo, and the lines that in the following year formed the Pittsburgh, Fort Wayne and Chicago.[49] By 1859 all these roads, except the Cleveland and Toledo, were relying on freight traffic for most of their gross income. In fact many of the early roads in the South and West found their freight traffic so unexpectedly heavy that they had to expand their facilities greatly a short time after they had gone into operation.

Even in the East many roads like the Reading and the Boston and Lowell had been built primarily as freight carriers. Except for the New York Central, the other East-West trunk lines (the Baltimore and Ohio, the Pennsylvania, the Erie, and the Atlantic and St. Lawrence) were earning, as soon as they were completed, a good deal more from freight than from passengers.[50] Moreover, during the 1850's the freight traffic increased much more rapidly than passenger on nearly every Eastern road. By 1859 Poor's statistics showed that passenger traffic accounted for a major portion of railroad revenue only in the small, comparatively densely populated states of Rhode Island, Connecticut, Delaware, New Jersey, and Massachusetts.[51] In Massachusetts, Poor reported, gross earnings from freight were almost equivalent to those from passengers, $4,291,599 to $4,627,315, while in New Jersey freight receipts totaled $2,033,282 and passenger $2,379,364. By that time, too, such roads as the New York Central, the Harlem, the Hudson River, and several Massachusetts roads which had been built to carry passengers were depending on freight for 40 per cent or more of their revenues.[52]

Although Poor realized the significant changes that the railroads were making in American industry during the 1850's, he wrote less about this matter than about the railroads' effect on commerce and agriculture. The reason may have been that the industrial changes were less apparent and dramatic, though in the long run more important, than those in commerce and agriculture. Poor did, however, stress that each mile of railroad laid down increased the demands on American industry. Not only did the new farms, towns, and cities need machinery, tools, coal, iron, and lumber, but the railroads as freight carriers enlarged the markets for manufactured goods in the older as well as newer regions of the nation.[53] Such a nationalizing of the markets stimulated industrial growth by encouraging large-scale production and marketing.

Finally, Poor was quite aware that the railroads themselves had become the market for a major portion of the products of many American industries.[54] In his editorials on the tariff Poor had emphasized that the railroads had become the largest consumer of the goods of the iron industry. On the other hand, Poor did not fully realize how this new demand was creating a revolution in blast furnace and rolling mill practices. As Louis C. Hunter has shown, the change in demand from the quality production of iron for the blacksmith to the quantity production for the railroads made possible the replacement of charcoal by coke and so brought the blast furnace back into the plant.[55] Poor did note, however, the demand that the railroads had created for products of other industries besides iron. In the 1850's the railroads quickly became a major market for such bulk materials as lumber and coal and for more specialized goods like copper for engine parts, felt and textiles for car seats, India rubber for car springs, animal, whale, and after 1859 mineral oil for lighting and lubrication.

Poor wrote little about the effect of the railroad expansion on the American machinery and machine tool industry, though he certainly understood its importance. During the 1850's the nation's foundries, forges, and machine shops turned an increasingly large share of their attention to making products to be used by the railroads. At the same time these shops, like the railroad maintenance and repair works, moved westward with the railroads. In many cities in the South and West the earliest and largest industrial plants were the railroad shops and those plants making equipment for railroads. There is, for example, no evidence of important car works operating west of the Alleghenies before 1849. Less than ten years later there were large car manufacturing shops in Cleveland, Cincinnati, Columbus, Dayton, Louisville, Maysville, Indianapolis, St. Louis, and Chicago.[56] The locomotive works, requiring as they did highly skilled labor and the highest grade metals, moved West much more slowly than the car and machine shops. Yet the shops of A. Harkness and Sons in Cincinnati were by 1850 beginning to build locomotives for the Ohio and Indiana roads.

Poor, on the other hand, had a good bit to say on how the railroad helped make possible the urban concentrations so necessary for large-scale industrial growth.[57] Not only did the new transportation assure the big cities a heavy and steady supply of staple foodstuffs, but it also increased by several hundred miles the radius from which the city might draw its highly perishable foods. Poor watched with particular interest the role of the railroads in expanding the dairy and truck-garden industries. He urged the roads to supply special milk trains and to make provision for moving fresh fruits and vegetables to the city. Besides food, the editor pointed out, railroads like the Reading, the Delaware and Lackawanna, the Erie, and the New Jersey Central were bringing to the urban centers in increasingly large amount the coal so necessary to heat the city homes and supply the power for city shops and mills.

In describing the impact of the railroads on the nation's economy Poor wrote on more different aspects than did the editors of other railroad papers. This was partly because of his personal interests and convictions and partly because of the regional nature of the other journals. Mansfield of the *Record* wrote a good deal about the influence of the railroads on the economy of the Old Northwest, Haven wrote a moderate amount on the railroads and New England, and Fernon gave some description of the railroads and the development of Pennsylvania's economy. More local in their outlook, the other editors may have been less sensitive than Poor to the basic changes the railroads were making in the over-all economy of the United States during the decade of the 1850's.

IV

When the nation's most serious political crisis occurred in December 1860 with the secession of South Carolina from the Union, Poor had an opportunity to use his knowledge of the railroad revolution of the 1850's in the cause of unity and the Union. From early December 1860, to early February 1861, Poor wrote, apparently at the request of the paper's editor-in-chief, Henry J. Raymond, a series of editorials in the New York *Times* on the subject of "the effects of secession on the commercial relations of the North and South and upon each other."[58]

Poor appears to have had two major reasons for writing this series in the *Times*. One arose from his conviction that the severing of the Union was complete and senseless folly. Although a Republican and strong antislavery man, the Union always meant more to him than slavery, and he thought the same was true of most Southerners. He was thus determined to demonstrate to his Southern readers the economic unreasonableness of secession. Surely most Southerners, he felt, were unwilling to sacrifice economic and political well-being "for the gratification of an excited temper, much less for the indulgence of political theories or abstractions."[59] Many but needed to be informed of their economic self-interest.

Poor also wanted to answer specifically the arguments made by some Southerners about the economic advantages which would result from secession. These arguments were being used in New York and London almost as much as in the South: in New York by such editors as James Gordon Bennett and Thomas Prentiss Kettell, and in London by *The Times* and one or two other papers. Such arguments, Poor feared, had become as discouraging to Northerners as they were encouraging to Southerners. In his first editorial Poor remarked that:

> Our people have been told so often by the Herald, and other political or professional calamitists, that our *commerce*, which is our life, will be utterly destroyed by disunion — that our Shipping, with all its incidental branches of employment, will be instantly transferred to Southern ports, and that property of all kinds will fall to *one-fourth* of its present value, that they have come to believe it.[60]

What may have been even more serious from Poor's point of view was that a large number of European investors also appeared to accept this argument. The threat of secession had indeed caused a sharp break in the security markets, and much of the decline was attributed to the heavy selling of railroad and government bonds held abroad.[61]

Poor therefore began his series by answering the proposition that secession would be economically advantageous to the South. He then went on to show that the North, largely because of the railroad expansion of the past decade, was far and away the economically stronger of the two sections. The South, Poor first warned, would find it next to impossible to replace Northern shipping, credit, and commercial services on which she was wholly dependent for marketing her crops.[62] Direct trade to Europe, to take one example, could not be decreed by mere legislation. No shipmaster would go regularly to Southern ports where cargoes were found only in the fall months when the crops were harvested and where there was rarely a large market for goods carried from Europe. The Southern states, Poor pointed out, "do not consume foreign but *domestic* merchandise. They import from the North ten dollars in domestics for every one imported, directly or indirectly, from Europe. If they opened a *direct* trade, they would not have returned to their port more than a tenth, in value, of their exports."[63] Since transatlantic shipping must go to New York and Northern ports for assured markets and return cargoes the North must continue for economic reasons alone to finance American trade movements and to provide commercial insurance as well as short- and long-term credit.

Nor would secession, Poor continued, solve the South's basic economic problem. She would still have the greatest difficulty in using her unskilled but expensive Negro labor for any purpose other than growing her staple crops. Political action could not insure a diversification of crops or the promotion of industry. "The South must continue to produce cotton," Poor contended, "not only as a means of existence, but because they can put their labor to no other use."[64]

Poor then went on to analyze the effects of the railroad expansion of the previous decade on the relative economic power of the North and South. The railroad had, the editor began, encouraged the rapid growth of the Northern population and, even more significant, had helped to fill the Northwest with free, nonslaveowning farmers. In the ten years between 1850 and 1860, the population of the free states had increased 5,611,974, of which more than 2,400,000 had been in the five states of the Old Northwest plus Iowa. The increase in the six Western states alone was, Poor emphasized, more than that of the total population growth, 2,022,415, of all the slave states.[65]

Besides stimulating the rapid growth of free population in the Northwest, the railroad had tied that area economically to the Northeast. With the aid of numerous statistics Poor showed how his earlier prediction had been fulfilled. New York, he demonstrated, had completely triumphed over New Orleans. In 1850, 773,858 tons of Western produce had reached tidewater via the Erie Canal and less than 40,000 tons more on the central New York railroads; in 1858 the Erie Canal carried 1,273,099 tons of through eastbound freight and the four trunk lines — the New York Central, the Erie, the Pennsylvania, and the Baltimore and Ohio — carried 766,312 tons more, making a total of 2,039,611 tons brought East on the northern routes. "The number of tons of Western Produce delivered annually at tide-water over these routes," Poor noted, "exceed twice the number of tons of all kinds of produce delivered at New Orleans, and considerably exceed the same in value."[66] The value of agricultural shipments from the West to tidewater in New York State, according to the most recent official reports, totaled over $160,000,000. On the other hand, the statistics of exports from New Orleans showed that the value of the products of the Mississippi Valley sent to the Eastern states and to Great Britain did not exceed $1,200,000 and most of this came from south of the Ohio and Missouri rivers. Such facts documented how the railroad and canal had broken the South's hold on the trade of the West. "The free navigation of the Mississippi which only a few years ago was considered so indispensable, is for the Northwestern states an imaginary rather than [a] real necessity," Poor warned the South. "The peaceable effect of Secession may be to close its mouth, in which event the entire trade of the Valley could be easily, and in the end to the convenience of all, sent over the Northern and Eastern routes." [67]

Finally Poor emphasized how the railroad had increased the industrial strength of the North. He took as a point of comparison the value of South Carolina's agricultural and Massachusetts' industrial production.[68] The value of South Carolina's exports of cotton, rice, lumber, and naval stores in both the coastwise and foreign trade totaled $28,-088,587. The worth of articles manufactured in Massachusetts in 1855 was, according to the state census of that year, placed at $175,384,523. Assuming that 15 per cent of this production was used within the state, the value of goods shipped away was $139,000,000, or almost five times that of South Carolina. Indeed, Poor maintained with only a little exaggeration: "By virtue of her skill and industry, assisted by her capital, which is their product, *the State of Massachusetts annually sends into the commerce of the country, value greater than the entire cotton crop of the South!*" [69] The editor then examined the amount of merchandise carried by the railroad as one excellent index of industrial productivity. The freight carried annually by the Massachusetts roads was, after making deduction for duplication of items, at least 3,000,000 tons. "This amount for a single state [in the] North is greater than the total tonnage of the Railroads of all the Southern States. At the low estimate of one hundred dollars per ton the aggregate value would be $300,000,000, a sum considerably greater than the exports of all the Southern States, both Foreign and Domestic." [70] Although the other Northern states were less industrialized than Massachusetts, they were rapidly following Massachusetts' example. The Southern states, on the other hand, had been making much less industrial progress. Given the North's preponderance of population and industrial power, it meant that even if the South seceded peaceably, it would remain economically dependent on the North. If war came, the hope that the rural and agrarian South could be victorious in a prolonged military struggle was, Poor insisted, completely chimerical.

Poor's arguments reached an even wider circulation than he had anticipated. In the spring of 1861 shortly after the firing on Fort Sumter, Raymond had his series of editorials reprinted in a small booklet. Its first edition was taken wholly by the State Department for distribution at home and still more widely abroad.[71] The department, considering it an effective presentation of the economic power of the North and the probability of an ultimate Northern victory and a restoration of the Union, apparently hoped that it might help to keep foreigners from returning United States government bonds during the current crisis and encourage them to buy war loans in the future.

Although he occasionally rigged his statistics to make his views more convincing, Poor's arguments were essentially correct. The South might have in time and by tariff or other subsidies made itself more economically independent, but once war came only a swift Southern military or diplomatic victory could have prevented Northern economic strength from bringing on its defeat. And unquestionably the great railroad expansion of the 1850's, more than any other single feature, was responsible for the North's dominant economic power. The railroads had, as Poor pointed out, opened the granaries of the Northwest, bound the Northwest to the Northeast, and stimulated the rapid industrial expansion in the Northeast. In fact a strong argument can be made for the thesis that the amazingly swift railroad expansion of the 1850's was much more responsible than the Civil War for initiating large-scale industrial development in the United States. The railroads in the fifties created as great a demand for the products of American industry as did the war in the sixties. But where the railroad used these goods in the creation and operation of a transportation network essential to the nation's continuing economic growth, those used for military purposes were from an economic view almost completely wasted.

Railroad construction dropped off sharply with the outbreak of hostilities; a brief examination of the evidence indicates that the war was a long time in taking up the demand for industrial equipment which railroad construction had required. The Northern powder and heavy ordnance plants, for example, expanded very little during the whole war period. Munitions were made in factories and shops that had been recently enlarged to meet the rapidly growing demands of railroad building in the previous decade.[72] For these and other war industries the problem was one of conversion, not expansion. Since conversion to war manufacturing and then back to peacetime products was a prolonged task, the growth of the basic industries of the United States appears to have been retarded rather than stimulated by the Civil War. In any case, significant indices of industrial growth such as the value added to goods by manufacturing, the production of pig iron, coal, copper, and lead all show a slower rate of growth during the war years than in the period before and after the war.[73] The pattern also holds true for the production of corn, wheat, number of milk cows, value of farm machinery, and other indices of agricultural development.[74]

Poor's editorials on the economic effects of secession summarized his analyses of the impact of the railroads on the American economy during the 1850's. After the winter of 1860–1861 Poor occasionally extolled the railroads' achievements in articles and pamphlets and even more regularly represented both in writing and in person the railroads on legislative issues. But he never did this again as the editor of the *American Railroad Journal.* In the spring of 1861 Raymond asked Poor to write editorials for the *Times* on what amounted to a full-time basis. Poor accepted the offer and during 1861 he concentrated his editorial attention on his articles for the *Times,* writing about secession and the war, particularly about war finance. He wrote less and less about railroads and spent increasingly less time in the *Journal's* office. Finally in July 1862 he resigned as editor of the *Journal.* Although Poor wrote comparatively little about railroads after 1861, he continued, as editor of the *Manual of the Railroads of the United States,* to carry on in the years after the Civil War one of the most important types of work he had learned as editor of the *Journal* — the collection, compilation, and dissemination of reliable business information.

★ 9 ★

Providing Business Information

TO MAINTAIN the *Journal's* position as the nation's leading railroad periodical and in fact to stay in business at all Poor had to supply information useful to his readers. Neither his writings as spokesman of the industry nor his editorials on railroad reform were enough in themselves to assure him of a profitable subscription list. During the early years of his editorship, his analyses of the developing bond market in New York contained much of value to the railroad managers, especially those in the South and West; later his evaluation of prospectuses and reports of individual companies as well as of the changing conditions in the industry were particularly useful to investors both at home and abroad; and finally, many of his writings on administration and management included information which railroad managers and directors could use. But the editorials which contained this material took up only a small portion of each issue; the other pages of the *Journal* provided as much as and often more railroad and business information than did its editorial columns.

During the 1850's those noneditorial pages of the *Journal* not devoted to advertising contained much the same type of material as they had when Minor and Schaeffer were editors. Under Poor, however, the content changed and new features were added, the most important of which included a section devoted to reports of judicial decisions and other legal matters concerning railroads, a share and bond list, and individual histories of nearly all sizable American railroads. Poor continued Minor's and Schaeffer's practice of printing annual and other railroad reports, statements, and prospectuses and state and national government documents concerning railroading or almost any other business or economic matter. Following the earlier editors, he extracted items from newspaper exchanges and other railroad and commercial papers which he thought might be of use to his readers, and printed letters from subscribers and others dealing with railroad matters. Poor, however, edited these materials more than his predecessors had done, compiling much of the data from the reports, documents, exchanges, and letters and rendering them into more usable and often statistical form.

In editing and compiling the copy for his noneditorial pages Poor's emphasis shifted during the 1850's. The changes reflected both the new developments in the industry and Poor's own shifts in editorial policies which often, in turn, were a response to the changing railroad situation. When Poor first became editor, he revived, it will be recalled, the *Journal's* technical and engineering content. In his first years he also printed much promotional material for individual companies. By the mid-fifties he had dropped his engineering department, and by then he was placing much less emphasis on promotion. From 1853 on, as he continued to warn against overconstruction, his noneditorial pages began increasingly to be oriented toward the investor.[1] In editing reports and other documents, Poor extracted matters of financial interest rather than those concerned with engineering or promotion, choosing his compilations and statistical summaries primarily for investors and financiers. In the mid-1850's, the letters which Poor printed were no longer those written by engineers but by men interested in railroad finance and to a lesser extent in administration. Although promotional articles and letters, both signed and unsigned, still appeared in the papers, they were much fewer in number than they had been before 1853. This change in content, like the similar change in editorial policy, was undoubtedly an important reason for the quadrupling of the *Journal's* subscriptions, for most of the new subscribers were investors.

As the *Journal* became more an investors' paper, it began to supply specialized services to its new readers. Most important of all, of course, were the analyses made of the reports and prospectuses of individual companies. Although Poor used these evaluations to reinforce his proposals for retrenchment and reform, he also was well aware, once the investor came to make up a large share of his reading public, of their value in keeping up his subscription list. In addition to giving investment advice and analyses in his paper, Poor corresponded with and talked to investors and bankers about railroad and government securities. The editor also served the investors by presenting their position on legislative matters affecting their interests, much as he did for the railroads on other issues. Particularly strong were the editorials he penned in 1853 against the efforts in the Ohio legislature to invalidate certain city and county bonds and later against the attempts made in New Hampshire and apparently one or two other states to invalidate the issues of several railroad companies on the ground that by selling at discount these companies had violated the usury laws.[2] In other columns addressed to railroad security holders, particularly those living abroad, Poor explained their legal rights, privileges, and responsibilities, pointing out how these differed in different states.[3]

Poor's efforts to define the investor's legal position developed into a special section in the *Journal* devoted to the legal aspects of railroad business. "The Journal of Railroad Law," as Poor entitled this section, started in 1853, soon became a regular and for a short time a unique feature of his paper. At first the editor, relying on his own legal training, compiled and condensed the law reports. But as the number of cases increased he appears to have turned the editing of the column over to a practicing lawyer.[4] The digests which Poor printed of the great majority of the significant cases on railroad law decided in the state and federal courts were valuable to railroad and businessmen other than investors. Their publication must have added at least a few lawyers and law firms to the *Journal's* subscribers. In any case, the other railroad editors apparently considered the innovation worthwhile, for by 1860 nearly all of them had incorporated a column devoted to railroad law in their own papers.

Poor's compilations of railroad and financial information, though intended primarily for investors, were, like his law digests, of use to other readers as well. In order to give investors a better picture of how the individual railroads fitted into the larger pattern of American railroading, Poor often printed summaries and descriptions of the railroads of different states and occasionally of the different regions. Also when the editor thought the investors might be particularly interested in a railroad, as, for example, when its securities were first listed on the New York exchange, he would write summaries of its past and present operations. Another useful source of information was in his columns listing monthly earnings and data upon freight and passengers carried by various roads. In the latter part of his editorship Poor ran columns enumerating names and addresses of railroad officers and directors, thus providing a sort of rudimentary directory of directors. These last two features often appeared in railroad papers other than the *Journal.*

Of Poor's compilations the one which was most valuable to his readers was his stock and bond list. This list pulled together and summarized concisely much of the information the editor had collected in the office of the *Journal.* Its publication helped bring Poor to devise more satisfactory ways of collecting information from the railroads. It also turned him to printing financial and statistical "histories" of individual roads. This in time led to the publication in 1860 of his *History of the Railroads and Canals of the United States* and in the years after he left the *Journal* to the publication of the *Manual of the Railroads of the United States.* Because of such compilations Poor had become even before he left the *Journal* the leading railroad statistician in the country.

The stock and bond list, which gave considerably more information than the daily prices of securities, had become a regular feature in the British railroad papers during the 1840's. Prior to 1853 both Minor and Poor had attempted to run a similar column in the *Journal.* They were unsuccessful: first, because until the investment market became centralized and systematized in New York City, there was little demand for this type of information in the United States, and second, because the information was difficult to obtain. Thus Minor, when he began his share list in 1845, was unable to find much information for the eighty-four railroads listed, except those of Massachusetts and New York where the state legislatures required the submission of annual reports.[5]

Poor, when he started his share and bond list in June 1849, was able to obtain more information. He had the advantage of being able to use a careful compilation of American railroad statistics made by Schaeffer, the former editor of the *Journal* in 1847.[6] He was also able to get more data from annual and other reports than Minor had been. Still there were many blank spaces in the columns of the list which was designed to give for some hundred and fifty railroads, or nearly every railroad then in operation or under construction in the United States, the following information: the length of the main line and of its branches, miles finished, cost per mile, capital stock paid in, debts over surplus, ruling grade, the previous year's gross earnings, expenses, net earnings, dividends declared, and the current price of its securities. Since the data were hard to come by and since there appeared little demand for such information, Poor after only a few months dropped this list.

The *Journal's* share list became a regular and successful feature only when it was instituted to meet a real need and not merely in imitation of the British periodicals. In 1851 when Poor began to report on the New York security market for the Southern and Western railroads, he included at the end of the reports a list of prices paid for securities.[7] This list soon came to include twenty-five bonds and close to seventy-five stocks. The latter were largely shares of New England roads traded on the Boston exchange. In this list he also included the price of the bonds of the federal and state governments as well as those of the larger municipalities. In 1853 as he began to write for the investor, the editor enlarged the list to include for each railroad with securities listed information on its mileage, funded debt, capital paid in, total cost, and the previous year's gross and net earnings.[8] By indicating the ratio of stocks to bonds, of capitalization to cost, and of gross to net earnings, these figures provided the investor and financier with a rough approximation of a railroad's financial picture and one which he could compare at a glance with those of other roads.

The problem now became primarily one of obtaining information. Even though more states had begun to require reports and many roads were printing fairly complete annual reports, the information Poor was able to find in printed sources was far from satisfactory. Nor did his repeated pleas for fuller, more accurate, and more systematically recorded information have much effect. To obtain more complete data for his share and bond list was one reason why Poor sent a detailed questionnaire in the summer of 1854 to all the railroad companies in the United States.[9] One result of the questionnaire was a revised and improved share list.[10] Brought up to date the list provided some information on close to one hundred and seventy railroads, of which about forty-five were still being constructed. Poor now added a separate bond list which gave a brief description of each issue, where and when the interest and principal were payable, and the price asked and bid. Significantly enough, of the seventy-six issues listed, sixty-eight were payable in New York City. The list carried similar information for federal, state, and municipal bonds. At this time, too, Poor began to print with his share and bond list the weekly circulars which such investment houses as De Coppet and Company, Marie and Kanz, and Cammann and Company mailed to their foreign customers on the condition of the New York security market, as well as those of British firms like Robert Benson, E. W. Satterwaite, and the Barings, which described the prices and the market for American securities in London.[11] Thus by 1855 the investor in American securities, both here and abroad, could find on three pages in the *Journal* a fairly complete picture of the weekly changes in American security prices and a concise summary of the financial condition of the American railroads.

In 1859 Poor again revised and expanded his share and bond list. Although he apparently did not send out another questionnaire, both he and the printer, Schultz, spent much time writing and visiting railroad offices to fill the gaps in their information. When the list was completed copies were sent to the railroads asking them to make the necessary corrections. The finished product was an impressive piece of work.[12] Here were listed over 750 securities of more than 350 companies. More information was given for each company than in the earlier lists. The first series of columns listed the road's physical assets including mileage owned (broken down into the main line, branches, second track and sidings, miles under construction) and the number of engines, passenger, and freight cars owned by the road. A second series of columns under the heading "Abstract of balance sheet" covered, first, the value of the property and assets of the company, broken down into the value of the "railroad and appurtenances," the rolling stock, the amount invested in "foreign" companies, and, then, the liabilities — share capital paid in, bonded and mortgage debt, floating debt — and, finally, total capitalization including all other assets and liabilities. Next came two columns, one giving the mileage operated, including roads leased, and then the train mileage run. This was followed by the gross and net earnings and finally the dividends issued and the current price of shares. At the beginning of each entry Poor indicated the date ending the fiscal year for which the information was given. This was followed by a bond list which was similar to the previous one. Shortly after he put out the new list, the editor replaced the circulars of De Coppet, Benson and others by his own table of daily sales during the preceding week on the New York stock exchange as well as the closing prices of American securities on the London exchange as received by the latest ship.[13]

The new share and bond list, then, provided more information on capital structure and physical assets than the old; and, by including train miles run as well as the mileage figure, it enabled the reader to break cost, earnings, and other data down to the per-mile and per-mile-run figures necessary to make useful comparison between one road's financial capabilities and another's. Since information on traffic moved was not listed, significant ton-mile figures could not be obtained from this tabulation. Nor was there any breakdown of revenues and expenses into freight and passenger categories. Moreover, as Poor was well aware, there was no certain way of assuring the accuracy of the figures. Nevertheless, the list provided more information on American railroads than any other single source.

After 1855 other railroad papers printed stock and bond lists. But none, not even those in the British railroad periodicals, contained the detail of the *Journal's,* nor were they complied from more reliable sources of information. Like the *Journal,* the other American papers were by 1860 reporting daily stock prices. The *Railway Times,* the *Railroad Register* and the *Railroad Record,* as regional business papers, recorded the local prices of goods and commodities as well as securities. They likewise carried occasionally the weekly circulars of the London firms of Benson and Satterwaite and, less often, those of New York houses. Nevertheless, the major source of information for American businessmen on the daily security prices and the analyses concerned with day-to-day changes in values was still, as it had been since the 1830's, the financial columns of the daily press, particularly the New York papers. By studying his daily newspaper in addition to the share list in his weekly *Railroad Journal,* the investor, the banker, and the speculator had readily available information to help him decide what securities to buy or sell. After 1860 he could obtain additional assistance from the more detailed information published in Poor's *History of the Railroads and Canals of the United States.*

II

Poor's *History of the Railroads and Canals* was his most ambitious effort at compiling railroad financial and operating statistics. The book was essentially the result of the editor's firm conviction about the value of publishing reliable and detailed information on the past performance as well as the present operation of American railroads. Only by examining long-term trends could the investor and financier be sure of the road's worth as an investment. "The aggregate results for 10, 15 or 20 years" were essential, Poor had often maintained, for determining "the value of the route, and the character of its management." [14] Such a length of time permitted mistakes, errors, and mismanagement to come to light and allowed for reforms to be introduced. It also provided a check on the reliability of the information submitted annually by the road. An even more important incentive for completing his history was the editor's often repeated belief that any effective railroad reform must be based on accurate information. Not only was "one of the surest tests of the present value of a road its past history," but a compilation of the past story of all the American roads was essential, in Poor's opinion, "to study the philosophy of Railroads. When we have their history, we shall begin to understand their significance, and the causes upon which their success or failure depends." [15] Though the grandiose plan he devised in 1858 for obtaining such information had failed, a less ambitious compilation might still lead to some of the same results.

Another reason why Poor undertook the task of collecting in one work the financial and operating statistics of American railroads was because no one else would. In Europe where most governments particularly those of Britain and Prussia showed an active interest in the collection of economic statistics, public officials were gathering useful information on railroads. In the United States, however, only a few states were trying to collect data, and the national government was doing almost nothing at all.[16] One of the functions of the early trade and business journals in this country was to collect and publish the type of economic statistics which government bureaus compiled abroad. Israel D. Andrews, when he made one of the very first detailed reports on American commerce and transportation, emphasized this role. "In the absence of statistical statements published by national authority," Andrews commended as a major source "of valuable information in making this report, the publications called 'Hunt's Merchants' Magazine,' 'De Bow's Review,' the 'Bankers' Magazine,' and the 'American Railroad Journal,' as the most valuable in this country." [17] The superintendents of both the census of 1850 and that of 1860 relied heavily on these same sources.[18]

It was at the request of Andrews, in fact, that Poor wrote his first general over-all study of the American railroad system. Andrews had been asked in 1851 by the Secretary of the Treasury, in response to a Senate resolution, to make a report on the commerce and trade of the British North American colonies with the United States, with particular reference to the commerce of the Great Lakes and the Western rivers. Andrews, interpreting his task broadly, began by making an analysis of the trade and transportation of most of North America, and requested Poor to write a section on the railroads and canals of the United States and Canada. Poor's article included over a hundred pages of text in which he described, state by state, nearly every railroad and canal in the country, indicating how each fitted into the local and the expanding national transportation pattern.[19] Since he supplied few statistics, he provided a geography of American railroads rather than a picture of their finances and operations. Nevertheless, it was certainly the most complete report on American railroads since von Gerstner's *Die Innern Communicationen der Vereingten Staaten von Nordamerica* had been published some twenty years earlier. Poor did devote several pages to rather general remarks on the cost, construction, and income of American railroads. These included many of his arguments, which already have been mentioned, on how the railroads were altering the flow of American commerce and beginning to transform the American economy. Poor concluded his section of the report with a list by states of the railroads of the country, giving for each road the miles it had in operation and under construction. The mileage figures were totaled at the end by states and the nation. This total, 12,808 miles, was higher than Poor's later estimates for the year 1851, which suggests that occasionally the same mileage was counted twice and that the sources of Poor's information were optimistic.[20] Finally, Poor rounded out his work by submitting a large 34¾ x 39 inch map indicating the railroads and canals of the United States then in operation or under construction. This seems to have been the first of the large-scale railroad maps that after 1853 Poor published and mailed to subscribers annually as a supplement to the *Journal*.[21] These carefully prepared maps did much to make Poor the foremost railroad cartographer of his day.

His work on the Andrews report like his compilation in the following year of the share and bond list helped convince the editor of the need for more accurate information about American railroads and reinforced his belief that this information could only be obtained by going directly to the railroads themselves. Not only were public records inadequate, but the reports issued by the railroad companies were both incomplete and varied in content and form from company to company and from state to state. Even the form of the reports of a single company often varied from year to year. To compile from such data any kind of useful information for comparative analyses was close to impossible.

Almost all this Poor pointed out in the questionnaire he sent in the summer of 1854 to the president of every railroad which he knew to be operating in the United States. The editor had in preparation, the questionnaire began, "a work upon the Railroads and Canals of the United States." [22] He was "forced to make a direct appeal to Railroad Companies as the only sources in many cases, of information." He urged them, therefore, even if they had already sent him their reports, to answer the questions and send a balance sheet. He requested them to follow the form used by the Boston and Worcester Railroad Company which he enclosed "to serve as a sort of *model* of what I wish to obtain from every Company in the United States." Poor concluded the questionnaire by saying that he was "aware that furnishing the information requested will impose a serious burden," but that he hoped "it may be some compensation for your trouble that it will be the means of presenting before the public a correct and satisfactory statement of the affairs of the Company with which you are connected." In an editorial following up the questionnaire, he reminded the railroad companies that few were "in that position which would lead them to desire to conceal the condition of their affairs, and even such should, we presume, knowing the impossibility of such concealment, make a public exhibition of their affairs a matter of policy." [23]

The information which Poor requested was, for its day, quite detailed. Although not as much was asked by the reports as required by New York State, it included data on the road's charter, its construction (cost, estimated and actual, date of completion of the different divisions and of the finished road), and its physical features such as gradient and alignment, gauge, pattern and weight of rail, double track, sidings, and amount and value of equipment and rolling stock. Poor, of course, wanted information on capital structure, earnings and dividends for each year since the road began operations. He indicated his interest in financial reform by asking about sinking funds, about the provisions for financing repairs, new equipment, and emergencies, and about the details of the construction account. For the preceding year only he requested a breakdown of expenses, earnings, and traffic moved according to the freight and passenger business and to the through and way traffic. For that year he also wanted the total miles run by passenger, freight, and repair trains. For railroads still under construction the questionnaire asked for data on their routes, finances, construction contracts, the current condition of construction, estimated freight and passenger traffic, and so on.

Many of Poor's questionnaires were returned quite promptly and filled out with surprising completeness; others came in after a follow-up letter or two and then only partially answered; still others, though fewer than might be expected, were not returned at all.[24] On the basis of his returns Poor revised and enlarged his stock and bond list. Of more importance, he printed in the *Journal,* beginning in the fall of 1854 and continuing until the spring of 1856, histories of a large number of the railroads then in operation in the United States. In printing these descriptions of more than one hundred and twenty American railroads, usually one to three in an issue, the editor supplemented the data he received from the questionnaire with information derived from reports, newspaper exchanges, and other sources filed in the *Journal's* office. Besides operating and financial statistics which he usually presented in tabular form, Poor gave the factual details of the road's charter, its developing organization, its initial and later financing, its important early officers, the growth of its physical plant including mergers, subsidiaries purchased, and other roads it financed, and the character and amount of its business. Poor rarely said anything about a road's financial, administrative, or operational policies. Nor did he, as in the editorial columns of the paper, comment on the road's management or its present and continuing value as an investment.

Although he planned at first to have the reports compiled in book form by 1855, he did not get the first volume published until 1860.[25] No doubt the task was more difficult than he anticipated, for in 1855 and 1856 he was still putting together and printing the data on the individual roads. The ensuing depression and his trip to Europe may also have altered his plans. Possibly, too, he hoped that the publicity plan he had devised in 1858 might make the less comprehensive project unnecessary. He did, however, keep his histories up to date, and in 1859 he began to work in earnest on what he planned to be a three-volume study of American railroads and canals.

In preparing this work he had the assistance of Dr. Richard S. Fisher, editor of *Dinsmore's Railway Guide,* one of the standard compilations of railroad routes and timetables. Fisher, a fellow member of the American Geographical Society, an editor of a number of atlases, gazetteers, and statistical digests, was probably one of the few men in the United States who then made his living as a professional statistician.[26] Poor and Fisher used the individual histories based on the 1854 questionnaire as the basis for their compilations. They may have sent out another questionnaire. If so, its form was, judging from the information published in the *History,* close to that of the 1854 questionnaire. Poor apparently had come to believe that a very detailed report like the one he drew up in 1858 as one of his proposals to improve railroad management or the one required by New York State required too much of the railroads. Moreover, it would call for more work in compiling on his part than was needed for the type of study he had in mind. In any case, he and his assistants appear to have used reports and possibly letters written to railroad companies to complete the statistics already in hand.

The first volume of the *History of Railroads and Canals of the United States,* which included the states north of Virginia and east of Ohio, was published in the fall of 1860. The second and third volumes were never published, even though Poor had completed his work on them before the secession crisis and war turned his attention to other matters.[27] Before Poor left the *Journal* in 1862 he printed in its pages all the data for Virginia and her railroads plus the compilations of a few roads in the South and of many important roads in the West. The information on each individual road in the *History* was more statistical, less chronological, and had fewer factual details than the longer sketches which had previously appeared in the *Journal.* In the sketches of the individual roads in the *History,* as Poor said in his introduction, there were "no explanations of its acts or policy, or speculation as to the cause of its success or want of success." [28]

The descriptions of individual roads in the *History* began by listing the officers and directors of the company and the address of its main offices. This was followed by a tabulation of the length of the road, including the double track, sidings, and the numbers of each different type of rolling stock. There was a brief summary of each history, giving facts about the charter, dates of completion of construction of various sections of the road, comments on extensions built and subsidiaries purchased, and information on connections and traffic agreements with connecting roads. There was, of course, much on the cost and financing of construction, followed by comments on the share capital and a complete description of the bond issues including the details of sinking funds created for these issues. The sketch ended, as had the earlier ones in the *Journal,* with an abstract of the balance sheet, the income account, the construction account, and a statistical statement, usually in tabular form, of the costs of railroad equipment, earnings for freight, passenger and mails (and — where the data were available — for through and way traffic), operating expenses, net earnings and dividends paid for each year since the road began operation. For some of the more important roads Poor broke these data down into per-mile-run and per-mile-operated figures. The *History* included similar information on the canals then in operation, both private and public; and for Massachusetts and Pennsylvania there was a section on street railways.

Besides the individual sketches Poor included some general information. He listed by states the act of incorporation and any other legislative acts affecting the individual companies, giving for each act the citation to year and page of the law in the state statute books. He also listed general laws relating to railroads and printed New York's general incorporation law in full as "the model upon which in other States all similar laws have been passed." [29] Poor, careful geographer that he was, included in this first volume two sizable railroad maps executed for him by his good friend G. Woolworth Colton, having a scale of 20 miles to the inch, which was large enough to include "each station on every road" and, in the manner of present-day road maps, to indicate the mileage between each station.[30]

Of particular value were Poor's summaries of railroad construction and operation of each state. Here he began by describing, year by year, the construction completed within the state, naming the companies and the amount of mileage each built in that year. With the first mention of each railroad Poor stated briefly whether the company still existed, had merged with another, or had been discontinued. If it was still in operation, he commented briefly on its financial record. At the end of this chronological story of each state's railroad construction, Poor inserted a table which estimated how much of the share capital and debt for each of the state's railroads was no longer "productive." By this he meant funds on which neither interest nor dividends were still paid. Finally and most valuable to railroad historians and statisticians were Poor's tables which summarized for each state the total figures on capitalization, costs, earnings, expenses, and mileage for each year since the first railroad in that state went into operation.

How accurate and reliable were these figures? Any evaluation of the reliability of such statistics depends, first, on the accuracy of the information supplied by the individual roads and, secondly, on the care used in the compilation of the data supplied. The accuracy of the information, in turn, depends upon the willingness of the companies to supply it and their ability to do so with care and accuracy. In general, the majority of the railroads seemed willing enough to give information if not too much labor was required in recording it and if it was not detailed enough to affect competitive considerations, that is, as long as details of rates and amounts of specific classification of freight carried were not requested. The railroads from the beginning had been used to giving information. Unlike manufacturing and shipping firms they had been considered "public works" and as utilities were expected to give some account of their activities. This was particularly true of roads which states or municipalities had helped finance. Moreover, unlike family owned and operated industrial firms, these companies had a large number of stockholders who expected to be told something of the business in which they were part owners. Railroad managers in raising capital for their roads had become used to having investors, bankers, and even the editor of the *American Railroad Journal* investigate their financial and operating statistics. It may be significant that the roads which tended to ignore Poor's requests for information, like the Camden and Amboy, the New York Central, the Michigan Central and the Ohio roads which had been first financed in Boston, were among the American railroads least dependent on the New York investment market. The roads who were willing to give information, however, often did so in a hurried and careless way. The clerk or secretary who was given the task of completing the questionnaire was often unable to obtain the information requested, and what he did get he was likely to record with little thought for accuracy.

The accurate handling of the information after it had been received caused the editor, like every other statistician, a great deal of trouble. Poor was satisfied that the transcribing, the arithmetic, and the proof reading had been done with all possible care — which was not always true in the compilation of some of the *Manuals* in later years. That errors crept in was inevitable. To catch errors, both intentional and unintentional, was one major reason why Poor insisted on having comparable figures for each road over a period of several years. "A single statement," he reminded his readers in the *History's* introduction, "as experience has shown, is a very unsafe ground upon which to base an opinion." [31]

In any case, the *History* was well received upon its publication, especially by other railroad and business editors, who appreciated its obvious value to investors and businessmen. They stressed its significance in providing information useful for improving railroad transportation. "Indeed," wrote the editor of the *Railway Times*, "no one who wishes a large mass of substantial facts upon which to base his railroad moralizing can be without it." [32] Homans of the *Bankers' Magazine*, after pointing to Poor's qualifications for his task and to the broad value of such a compilation, stressed the need for the national government to create a "Statistical Bureau or Central Office" for the collection and publication of essential railroad, banking, commercial, and other economic statistics to supplement and assist the work Poor and other business journalists and statisticians were doing.[33]

No one was more certain that the *History* had a significance broader than the usual investor's manual or railroad manager's handbook than its author. He believed that it would provide a basis of solid information essential to railroad reform and progress. In the summer of 1860, shortly before the book went to press, Poor in a letter to his wife expressed this faith in his work:

> To tell you what I am doing would be to show you columns of figures to be added, divided, or subtracted, or the memoir of some rr. or canal, which is little less than a record of names, & dates, & distances — all this is the most prosaic business possible. It may lay the foundation by and by, for something better. First comes the form — then the soul, the natural sequence must be respected. . . . I am getting along well though slowly. The work I am doing will never be done again. So I am making it as valuable and complete as possible. It will be the record of a great achievement — of the greatest material development the world has yet seen.[34]

If Poor's faith in the power of reason, substantiated by a firm foundation of accurate information, seems oversanguine, it nevertheless helps to account for the quality of his work both as a statistician and an editor. Because he was recording, analyzing, and taking a part in the building of the American railroad system, to him the greatest material accomplishment the world had yet seen, his years as editor of the *American Railroad Journal* were the fullest and most satisfying years of his life.

III

In making a final evaluation of Poor's eminently successful work as editor of the *American Railroad Journal* one must begin by reviewing his own contributions and those of his competitors to the development of business journalism and the systematic providing of business information in the United States. Poor took over a paper which was losing money and made it financially profitable. Moreover, he did this in a field noted for its high business mortality, in the face of rapidly growing competition. His paper was the only railroad paper in the spring of 1849. There were published within a decade five weeklies and two monthly periodicals devoted to railroads. Yet during this period Poor rapidly increased his circulation and enlarged his advertising patronage without lowering his relatively high subscription rate and by actually increasing rather than lowering his advertising rates.

One obvious reason for Poor's success was that his paper, the first and oldest, was the best known of American railroad papers. Therefore, to get a share of the rapidly growing market for railroad journals his competitors had to win subscribers from railroad and business men who would have normally taken the *Journal* or who were already among its readers. The only way they could accomplish this was by specializing on the regional or technical aspects of railroading. Thus the *Railroad Record,* the *Railroad Register,* the *Western Railroad Gazette,* a monthly founded in Chicago in 1857, and before 1860 the *Railway Times* were regional papers; the *Railroad Advocate* and the *Railway Times* after 1860 were primarily engineering journals. Two short-lived papers founded at the end of the decade in New York, *Hillyer's Railroad Magazine* and the *American Railway Review,* though interested at first in the broader topics of railroad development, soon became primarily concerned with the more technical aspects of the industry.

Such specialization by his competitors actually strengthened Poor's position because his remained the one paper concerned with railroads in all parts of the country and was therefore not only assured a broader circulation base both here and abroad, but also attracted advertisers who wanted a nation-wide coverage for their products. Moreover, specialization by his competitors meant that Poor too could concentrate on railroad finance, and still be considered, more than any other editor, by the railroad and the general public as the industry's spokesman and advocate.

Yet being a first comer in no way guarantees primacy. Minor with the field to himself failed to make the *Railroad Journal* pay. Poor succeeded where Minor failed because he carried out more effectively the major functions of a business journalist. In the first place, his close contact with the men and problems of the industry and his firm grasp of the facts and figures made Poor a most effective spokesman for the railroads. Second, and much more important, he provided reliable business information in a more useful and compact form than did Minor or most of his competitors. He was particularly successful in supplying information for the investor, probably the most rapidly growing group of businessmen interested in railroads during the 1850's. He thus increased his subscription list, even though after he began printing financial information he ceased to provide technical and engineering data. And finally, the *Journal* was successful because its editor pioneered in developing a new role for an industrial and trade paper. He was one of the first American business editors to consider as one of his most important functions the analysis of the problems currently giving most concern to the men in the industry and the proposal of improvements and reforms to help solve these problems.

Poor's achievements in providing information, in fact, developed in large part from his work as an analyst and reformer. His editorials on railroad building and finance and his warnings against overconstruction which led him to analyze the reports and prospectuses of new companies filled a real need for the growing number of investors purchasing American railroad securities. Once the investor was attracted to the paper by his editorial policies, Poor changed the orientation of his noneditorial pages to provide primarily financial rather than technical and promotional news and information. In providing statistics and other data on railroad finance and operations Poor far outdistanced his competitors.

The dominance of the *Journal* in providing information on railroad finance is well illustrated by the experience in the late 1850's of both the *Railway Times* and the *American Railway Review,* founded in 1859. The *Times* in the mid-1850's had, more than any other regional paper, tried to challenge the *Journal's* position as a financial paper and as the spokesman of the industry. But in December 1859, it gave up the race and became an engineer's paper. The *Review* was started in 1859 by a group, including a railroad supplier, financier, and three engineers and contractors, which called itself the American Railway Bureau. The bureau's stated aim was to supply information to "Stock Brokers, Bankers, Engineers, Contractors and Superintendents" about stocks, bonds, capital structure, legal obligations, physical plant, current business, and future prospects of individual American railroads.[35] Although the *Review* began by concentrating on information for railroad investors and financiers, it had within a year or so changed its emphasis to the publication of technical and engineering data.

The daily press, the circulars written by the investment banking houses, and, to a lesser degree, other business periodicals, provided more information on railroad finance and therefore offered more competition to the *Journal* in this field than did the other railroad papers. *Hunt's Merchants' Magazine* and the *Bankers' Magazine* printed, or rather reprinted, from reports, documents, other periodicals, and newspaper exchanges many facts and statistics on railroad finance and operation. They carried stock and bond price listings and included excellent summaries of the condition of the New York money markets. But because they were monthlies their information was of less immediate relevance, and because they rarely made specific analyses of the railroad industry and never of individual railroad companies, they were probably less useful to railroad and business men concerned with railroad finance than the *Journal.* A more serious competitor was Kettell's *United States Economist,* since that paper was a weekly, had competent reports on the financial markets, and included a good bit about railroads. Kettell's articles, however, described by one banker as "too sweeping and hasty to be always accurate but . . . always suggestive and clever," were much more concerned with trade and commerce than with railroad development, and he did not enjoy the close contact which Poor maintained with the railroad industry.[36]

Poor expected his paper to supplement rather than compete with the information on railroads and finance provided in the bankers' and brokers' circulars and in the daily press. These weekly circulars, which gave current prices of railroad and government securities both in the New York and London money markets and occasionally had some brief interpretive remarks on market conditions, were sent by the investment houses to customers, particularly those who lived abroad. The daily papers in New York had since the mid-1830's carried special financial sections which gave stock market listings and brief analyses of the doings on the exchange. Kettell himself had begun his journalistic career by writing the financial column in the 1830's for James Gordon Bennett's New York *Herald.*[37] In the 1850's, when railroad securities began to dominate the security markets, the *Tribune* and the *Herald* devoted a great deal of attention to railroad finance. The *Journal of Commerce,* the *Commercial Advertiser,* and the *Courier and Enquirer* tended to stick to commercial news, while the *Post* and *Sun* and the recently founded *Times,* though they had their stock and money columns, had less concern than the other New York papers for financial and business information.[38] The financial columns of the New York papers had little of the detailed information on specific roads which Poor supplied and their analyses were usually short-term in view and rarely considered such railroad problems as administration and operation. A reader would therefore find little duplication in the pages of the *Journal* and those of his daily newspaper. Moreover, in Poor's opinion, neither the *Tribune* nor the *Herald* gave a satisfactory picture of the industry or of individual roads, the first being almost always too sanguine in its outlook, the second much too pessimistic.[39]

Poor, then, while maintaining the *Journal* as a national railroad paper was able to provide information on railroad operations and especially finance which could not be obtained elsewhere. One reason for this accomplishment was that his editorial policies of analysis and reform were based on his awareness of the need for information and the type of information that was most wanted.[40] In the United States in the early 1850's the editors of trade and business periodicals rarely analyzed business developments except those directly concerned with the stock and commodity markets and even here they seldom proposed reforms. The *Railway Times* and the *Railroad Record,* directly, and *Hunt's Merchants' Magazine,* indirectly, at first took Poor to task for his critical analyses of developments in the industry and of the activities of individual companies. Before the end of the decade, however, the *Railroad Record* indicated a change in attitude by insisting that "it is our duty as journalist to discuss all questions of policy in the management and operation of railroads."[41] Poor, therefore, played an influential role in making the analyses of an industry's problems and the proposing of reforms an accepted function of American trade and industrial journals.

This function remained an important one for the business editor. In fact, the most successful business editors of the nineteenth century appear to be those who concerned themselves most seriously with the major problems facing their industry. This seems to be true for the mining, iron and steel, and insurance journals. It is certainly the case for the railroad papers published after the Civil War in the United States. It is also true that John Herapath had made his journal the leading British railroad paper in the 1840's because of his analyses of railroad problems in general and comments on individual roads in particular. Possibly Poor developed his ideas of the function of a railroad editor as an analyst and reformer from reading some of Herapath's editorials.

It might be well to mention here, parenthetically, two major differences in the development of the early American and British railroad press. In the first place, fewer technical and no regional papers of any consequence were published in Britain. The railroad papers, printed in London, concerned themselves almost wholly with promotion and finance. This may account for the second difference. In Britain railroad papers apparently were subsidized to help promote private ventures more than in the United States. Herapath, in fact, ran on his masthead: "The ONLY Railway Journal neither *the property of an Engineer* nor *under* the CONTROL of a COMPANY."[42] Although the *Journal* and the other American papers may have been paid to publish promotional articles, they were not paid very much. The evidence points to the fact that when they were encouraging railroad promotion they gladly printed articles without expecting any payment for the service. In any case, there is little evidence that any American railroad paper of lasting significance depended on the subsidy of any man or company or single group of promoters or companies for its livelihood.[43]

In the United States after the Civil War the older railroad papers had difficulty in holding their own against the newer ones that developed more pertinent and more meaningful editorial policies and programs. The *American Railway Review* and *Hillyer's Railroad Magazine* failed to survive the war. In 1872 Boston's *Railway Times* and Cincinnati's *Railroad Record* both stopped publication. Three years later Philadelphia's *Register* became the *Railway World* and took on a more national outlook. The *Journal*, after Poor's departure in 1862, quickly lost its dominant position.[44] Schultz, who took over its editing, carried on the share list and other financial features, but did little analysis of railroad problems or editorial writing of any kind. Succeeding editors were unable to revise the paper's reputation until 1886 when Matthias N. Forney, a trained engineer and former editor of the *Railroad Gazette*, purchased it. Forney, who merged the paper with *Van Nostrand's Engineering News* and called it the *Railroad and Engineering Journal*, made the paper into a highly specialized technical periodical.

After the war the three leading railroad papers, all of which were founded in Chicago, by then the nation's foremost railroad center, were the *Railroad Review* started in 1868, the *Railroad Age* founded in 1876 and, most influential of all, the *Railroad Gazette*, the successor to the monthly *Western Railroad Gazette* first published in 1857. The *Gazette* became the leading paper only when it had been moved to New York after the great Chicago fire of 1872 and was purchased by Silas W. Dunning and Matthias N. Forney. The new editors were soon providing accurate information about railroad operations and engineering and carrying out a strong editorial policy advocating changes and reforms in the industry. Forney, a forceful writer knowledgeable in things technical, urged improvements in locomotive power, inquired into the poor quality of American steel rails, and turned his attention to the increasingly complex techniques of railroad operation. Dunning, a Civil War veteran with a training in journalism, compiled very complete listings of monthly returns of traffic carried, earnings, and receipts. He also made analyses of railroad reports which were similar to Poor's, though rarely as critical. Although, like Poor, Dunning showed an interest in the internal problems of railroad administration, he concentrated his editorial attention on the primary problems of his day — those raised by competition, rate making, and state and federal regulation. In the *Gazette* in these years appeared some of the most informed and intelligent commentaries written on the problems of competition between large units saddled with heavy fixed cost and excess capacity. In fact, Arthur T. Hadley, as Dunning's assistant editor in the years after Forney left it to edit the *Railroad and Engineering Journal*, wrote many of his pioneering analyses of imperfect competition and government regulation in the editorial offices of the *Gazette*.[45] Dunning's biographer summarized that editor's concept of the role of a business editor in words that might well have been said of Henry Poor: "His ambition was to make a journal which should have a positive influence on railroad practices and legislation, by supplying accurate information and explaining the principles of railway management in a way to promote their adoption by the companies and the country." [46]

Neither Dunning nor Forney attempted to provide the type of information Poor had supplied on railroad investments and finance. Poor's successor in this field was the *Commercial and Financial Chronicle*. The *Chronicle*, founded in 1865 by William B. Dana, the editor of *Hunt's Merchants' Magazine*, as a weekly to supplement that paper, soon supplanted the older journal.[47] It carried, besides reports of the stock and money markets, detailed summaries and analyses of annual and other reports of railroad corporations. During the 1870's and 1880's these analyses were often quite critical of the roads' managements and finances, while the general editorial policies protested against speculative railroad finance and unnecessary construction.[48] It also provided much of the same type of information Poor had given his readers on railroad and government securities, although not in the detail that Poor again began to supply after 1868 in his *Manual of the Railroads of the United States*.

In accounting for the success of an editor, or of any man for that matter, it is difficult to assign one or even a few reasons. It is equally dangerous to list the reasons by importance, since the attributes making for achievement usually reinforce one another. So in the case of Henry Poor, his way of thinking, his experience in frontier law and railroading, his intellectual development in Andover, Bowdoin, and Bangor, his membership in the Geographical and Statistical Society, his close connections with the prominent intellectual and literary men and with railroad and financial leaders all helped make his writing and compilations significant and useful. So too did the situation in which he found himself in the 1850's as editor of the leading journal of the nation's first big business during its first great expansion. His work, in turn, convinced him still more of the validity of his intellectual premises, the meaningfulness of his broader education and training, and the importance of his noneditorial activities. By challenging his analytical talents and giving purpose to the enjoyment he took in the collection of geographical and economic facts, his activities gave him a sense of usefulness and fulfillment. The end result was a good journal written by a well-balanced and mature man.

⁎ 10 ⁎

Wall Street and Washington

ALTHOUGH HENRY POOR IN 1860 was enjoying a full and rewarding career, he radically altered his occupation and way of life in the following years. The change essentially resulted from events set off by the Civil War which turned Poor from business journalism to a life of business on Wall Street and of lobbying in Washington. He continued to use his pen, though much less than he had during the 1850's, and the most significant aspects of his later career remain his writings and the compilations of business information. In 1861 and 1862 and in the 1870's and 1880's he wrote much about money, banking, and public financial and economic policy; during the 1860's and early 1870's he wrote about and lobbied against the tariff on rails; and for close to two decades after 1868 he edited and published the *Manual of the Railroads of the United States*. As its editor he provided, as he had done in the *Journal*, reliable business information; and in the introductions to his annual volume he compiled and often analyzed the meaning of a large mass of statistics on railroad development.

Poor's later writings have less significance than those he penned as editor of the *Journal*. This was partly because he only wrote intermittently after he left the *Journal*. His new activities and interests now kept him from being fully informed about the rapidly changing developments in the railroad industry. In writing on the tariff and governmental financial policy he had, on the other hand, a more intimate awareness of the current situation. He played a small, but meaningful part in the shaping of tariff and financial legislation. Nevertheless, Poor's writings on these subjects were less unique than his earlier work on railroads because the tariff, Civil War finance, resumption of specie payments, and the currency questions were the major political as well as economic issues of their day. Much more was said about them at the time and by later historians than has been written about the impact of the first great expansion of the railroad network on the American business world. But Poor's later writings do contribute something to the understanding of America's economic past, particularly since many of his views on the major issues of the day were representative of that key group of Eastern financiers who did so much to prescribe the attitudes and opinions for the American business community.

Since these later writings were so closely related to Poor's work in Washington and Wall Street an evaluation of them must be prefaced by a brief summary of his career after 1860. The change in Poor's way of life first began with the invitation from Raymond early in 1861 to become an editorial writer for the New York *Times.* The *Journal's* editor found this request difficult to refuse, for in 1861 the recording and analyzing of the nation's greatest political crisis had more immediate meaning and importance than analyzing developments in the railroad industry.[1] Moreover, in 1861 there was less to write about on railroads. The crisis of secession and the coming of the war had all but stopped railroad construction; while before the end of the year a war-engendered prosperity was temporarily allaying the problems which had so disturbed railroad men during the depression of the late 1850's.

In July 1861, after he had been writing several months for Raymond, Poor sold his share in the *Journal* to Schultz, the printer and publisher.[2] He agreed, however, to stay on as coeditor with Schultz and until the summer of 1862 continued to write an occasional editorial for the *Journal.* In the following month Samuel Hallett, an internationally known railroad promoter, offered Poor a salary of $300 a month to edit a biweekly paper to be called *Samuel Hallett's North American Financial Circular.*[3] He accepted the offer even though he had earlier and apparently still considered Hallett an erratic financial adventurer. In this circular, which concerned itself with reporting on and analyzing primarily for foreigners the New York security markets, he rarely said anything about Hallett's promotional schemes or about those of anyone else for that matter.

Poor continued to write for the *Times, Hallett's Circular,* and the *Railroad Journal* until, late in the summer of 1862, he began to devote all his energies to the Union Pacific Railroad. Almost immediately after the road was chartered in June 1862, Poor was appointed one of its five government commissioners.[4] This appointment resulted partly from his editorial writings of the previous year and a half. Poor's comments in the *Times* and *Hallett's Circular* about war finance had helped to give him a reputation as an expert in government as well as railroad finance. This reputation had been increased when he took part during January 1862 in an attempt to revise the Legal Tender Act along lines more acceptable to the New York financial community. In the committee hearings and in private conferences on this bill many powerful Republican politicians came to know Poor personally. Such personal contacts, as well as Poor's close association with Hiram Barney and Lewis Tappan, both important figures in the New York State Republican party, undoubtedly carried weight in his selection as a commissioner.[5]

More important for Poor's appointment was, most certainly, the prestige of his articles in the *Journal* on railroads in general and the Pacific railroad in particular for investors both in the United States and in Europe. The administration's awareness of the confidence of the investor in Poor's judgment is made clear in a letter the Secretary of the Interior, Cabel B. Smith, wrote Poor on July 4, 1862, immediately after the news of McClellan's defeat before Richmond reached Washington. In this letter Smith urged the editor to use his pen to reassure the public here and especially abroad that the disaster did not threaten the ultimate success of the Union cause.[6]

At a meeting held in September 1862 to draw up the Union Pacific's preliminary organization, Poor was elected provisional secretary.[7] On his return to New York he found himself the company's only full-time officer. For more than a year he shouldered not only the routine work of organizing such a venture, but also the responsibility of raising the capital to meet the requirements of the charter. Actually, Poor wrote comparatively few articles in his efforts to encourage stock subscriptions. He relied instead on correspondence and personal calls upon leading financiers and merchants in the Eastern cities.[8] In this canvassing he had a good bit of assistance from William B. Ogden, the company's provisional president, but little from the other officials. Poor and Ogden had difficulty in persuading the men they called upon to put funds into such a risky investment as a first transcontinental railroad during a period when dividends were high and government securities could be had at bargain prices. Nevertheless, by the end of the summer they had sold enough shares to permit the formal organization of the company.[9] At the meeting during which this organization was formed Poor was again elected secretary.[10]

Yet within only a few months he had left the company. The reasons for Poor's resignation from the Union Pacific are not clear. Possibly the previous year's work had convinced him of the immense problems which had to be met if the road was to be financed and built before the war came to an end. He may have been disturbed, as were a number of the railroad and financial men most interested in the project, by the aggressive tactics of the new vice-president,

Thomas C. Durant; for at this time nearly all the men Poor knew and trusted, such as Ogden, Lanier, and J. Edgar Thomson, had resigned as directors or refused to take an active part in Union Pacific affairs.[11]

Moreover, Poor had been planning in the fall of 1863 a permanent retirement from business activities. During the previous years he had used his knowledge of railroad finance in order to make some excellent investments. Then, succumbing to the get-rich atmosphere of wartime New York, he joined many of his Wall Street friends in speculation, particularly in gold. Poor's speculations were at first most successful. "I suddenly find myself in possession of means which a year ago would have been up to my ideas of an ample competency, moderate to be sure but enough to live on in Brookline," he wrote his wife in June of 1862. "I am in with a money making set — excellent people too, and have been eminently successful — all *inter nos.*" [12] Poor became increasingly sure that he could before too long carry out the vaguely formed plans he and Mary had of moving to Massachusetts. Ever since Henry Hedge had accepted late in 1857 the call to John Pierce's former church in Brookline, Mary had been more and more taken with the idea of returning to her old home and living near her favorite sister. Poor, though fully enjoying New York, was attracted by the thought of a life of writing on economic and historical matters without the pressures of deadlines or outside business activities. In January 1864 he purchased a house next to the First Parish Church in Brookline. May first was then set as the date the family would move from New York.

The financial panic of mid-April 1864 forced a major change in these plans.[13] Poor, who had been giving more thought to the move to Brookline than to the financial markets, was caught unawares by a sharp break in security prices. To meet his obligations he was forced to sell many of his long-term investments. For a moment he thought he would have to sell the new house. Then as his financial position became more clear, he found he could afford to keep the house and still have an income of about $5,000 a year. This was enough to permit the family to carry out the move to Brookline, but not enough to allow him to leave the office for the library and the study.

Because Poor was so close to retiring from business life, he did not, as he otherwise might have done, attempt to return to editing the *Railroad Journal* or another business paper. He expected to recoup his losses quickly and soon join his family permanently. He would undoubtedly have been better off if he had decided to return to business journalism, for the next few years were the most trying and frustrating of his whole life. Within a few weeks after his financial disaster he had set a new pattern of work. In May 1864 he joined an old friend, Henry Fitch, to form the brokerage firm of Henry Fitch and Company.[14] In June he traveled to Washington as a representative for the railroads to try to prevent Congress from raising the duties on rails. He carried out the task satisfactorily, for which he was well paid; in the following years he spent much time each spring in Washington lobbying with a good deal of success against the tariff on rails. His market speculations and his brokerage activities with Henry Fitch were, however, less financially rewarding than Poor had hoped.

To earn the additional money he needed for retirement, Poor, therefore, took on in these years a variety of tasks. He made occasional trips to examine railroad properties for New York financiers. Early in 1866 he spent several weeks making a detailed appraisal of the accounts and the physical plant at the Pittsburgh, Fort Wayne and Chicago and allied lines for James F. D. Lanier and other of its New York directors.[15] In the following year he made an even longer trip to report for Frederick A. Delano and Uriel A. Murdock on the proposed extension of the Selma, Rome and Dalton.[16] Poor traveled to Alabama, examined the proposed line of road, reported favorably of its cost and future profits and advised the New Yorkers to carry out their plans for financing this road.

While he was in Washington on tariff business, Poor accepted other lobbying commissions. In 1866, for example, he helped the Erie collect claims from the War Department and obtained a tax adjustment for a car spring company.[17] In that year and the next he spent even more time in working for the passage of a bill which would provide funds for the construction of the European and North American Railroad.[18] During the war John Alfred Poor had revived his scheme for building a road from Bangor to St. John. In 1865 and in 1866 he and his brother had been successful in getting the legislatures of Maine and Massachusetts to turn over claims which the two states had against the federal government to the European and North American Railroad. Henry Poor's lobbying in Washington in behalf of this road had some effect, for in 1868 Congress appropriated funds to meet part of these claims. However, the most significant piece of legislation besides the tariff acts for which Poor lobbied at this time was the Gold Contract Bill. He worked hard though with comparatively little success for the congressional approval of this bill which he and a number of New York and Boston bankers considered would provide an essential first step toward the resumption of specie payments.[19]

Poor cared little for his work in Washington and Wall Street. He particularly disliked having to spend long periods of time away from his family. He accepted this distasteful way of life only because it was providing him with the capital he needed to retire from the business world. He was, therefore, stunned when the sharp monetary stringency of November 1867 forced the firm of Fitch and Company into bankruptcy. His prospects for a life of leisure and study now seemed even further from realization than they had in the spring of 1864.

Poor was aroused from a state of extreme despondency by a suggestion from his son.[20] Henry William proposed that he and his father form a railroad commission house which would specialize in railroad insurance and the provision of railroad and business information. Young William, who had graduated from Harvard in 1865, had already proved himself a businessman of ability and charm. After graduation he became agent for a number of insurance firms to sell different types of policies to railroad companies. Very soon he was making an excellent living from this relatively new branch of the insurance business.[21] After the formation of H. V. and H. W. Poor he continued to carry out this specialty; while his father in the spring of 1868 began work on compiling his first *Manual of the Railroads of the United States*. It was an immediate success, and from 1868 on Poor's *Manual* has appeared annually to provide businessmen with information on American railroads and, in later years, on industrial and other corporations.

In the first years of editing the *Manual* Poor would have liked to spend more time than he did on its compilation and publication. He was, however, being constantly drawn into his son's side of the business. In 1869 William, in addition to his insurance work, had begun to concentrate on the importation of steel rails for there was a heavy demand for this superior type of rail as soon as it appeared at a reasonable price. As an ally of Henry Clews, a well-known New York broker, and C. Edward Habicht, for a long time the Swedish consul in New York City, and as the American agent for at least two British steel manufacturers, William enjoyed several years of profitable trade in steel rails.[22]

The elder Poor because of his British connections helped his son obtain contracts in Britain. He became involved in trying to collect for rails sold to the Selma and Gulf Railroad. For a time, because the firm held a large block of securities given in payment for the rails, he served on its board of directors.[23] He became even more involved with Ezra Cornell and the railroads the telegraph magnate was building in and about Ithaca. In fact the Poor firm contracted in 1870 to build as well as to supply rails and iron for the Utica,

Ithaca and Elmira Railroad.[24] This road, which was to be seventy-six miles in length on completion, was to connect Ithaca with Courtland on the east and Elmira on the west. During 1871 and 1872 Poor found the building of this road was taking more and more of his personal attention.[25]

Then early in 1873 he decided the time had come to cut himself loose from these business activities and carry out his long-held plans to retire to Brookline. During the prosperous years since 1867, the firm of H. V. and H. W. Poor had done well. The senior partner now had the capital he had been trying to accumulate since 1864. Moreover, Poor was disturbed by the unhealthy inflationary condition of the country's business. In the winter of 1873 the Poors stopped importing rails. In April they severed all connections with the Selma and Gulf by making arrangements in England, as Poor wrote his wife, "for the construction of the road by parties who are to take up our bonds and pay us." [26]

Throughout the year Henry Poor negotiated with Cornell about the Utica, Ithaca and Elmira. In January Cornell agreed to buy back the Poors' construction contract. Payment came slowly, but by April the firm had received all but $65,000.[27] That September Poor wrote his wife that the final settlement had at last been completed with Cornell. In the same letter, dated September 19, he told of the chaos created in Wall Street by the failure of Jay Cooke and Company. "It has been a terrible day in New York," he wrote Mary, "but fortunately we have not been affected by the disasters. It is another stock speculation, but we have not had anything to do with speculation for years." [28]

The crisis and following depression, however, affected the Poors' relations with Ithaca's railroads. Neither Cornell nor his heirs were able to make good the settlement agreed to in September 1873, and the Poors remained in the management of the road for almost a decade.[29] But Henry Poor turned over almost all the work and responsibility connected with the road to William, who for a time became its president.

After 1873 Henry Poor rarely left Brookline on any business matters except those of the *Manual,* and for a period of several years after he retired he paid comparatively little attention to its publication. In 1878 he helped his son organize a brokerage and banking firm which became in time, under the name of Poor and Greenough and still later Poor and Company, one of the leading Wall Street houses. Poor, who remained a partner until 1888, helped his son's new venture in several ways.[30] As the nominal head of the firm's Boston office on Devonshire Street, he occasionally handled negotiations for the firm.

He also seems to have been responsible for turning his son's attention to the Southwest; for beginning in 1871 he and his close friend, George S. Coe, president of the American Exchange Bank, had been interested in promoting at least one Texas railroad. Because of a continuing interest in the Southwest, the firm had by the early 1890's become the fiscal agent for the Missouri, Kansas and Texas, and the younger Poor had become a director of that road and others in that area. The older Poor also proved of real assistance in obtaining for the firm in 1885 the contract which made it the agent in the United States for the English Association of American Stock and Bond Holders of London; in the 1880's Poor's name still had influence among foreign investors. Yet these activities took comparatively little time and rarely interfered with Poor's researches and writings on money, banking, currency, and public finance to which he devoted much time after his retirement to Brookline, nor did they interfere with his continuing commitments to the editing and publishing of the *Manual.*

II

As this brief sketch of his later career indicates, Poor used his pen only intermittently during the years after he left the *American Railroad Journal.* His later writings were concentrated on four major topics. Two of these, Civil War finance and the tariff, provided the most significant contributions from his pen before his retirement from active business. A third — money, banking, and currency — was what he concentrated on after he settled down in Brookline. The *Manual,* especially the writing of its introductions about the annual growth and development of the American railroad system, remained a continuing interest both before and after retirement.

In these later writings Poor remained an analyst of the current economic scene, and, as he had done earlier, he used his analyses to suggest improvements. Yet in these later years he was a business reformer in rather a different sense than he had been as the *Journal's* editor. Like many of his and Mary's friends, Poor during and after the Civil War seems to have lost his strong concern for perfecting man by improving social and economic conditions. He now called for improvement and reform in the name of economic and business efficiency and equity rather than as part of a program for the advancement of the social, political, and economic well-being of mankind.

The Civil War, which seems to have changed his attitude towards reform, also turned Poor's interest away from railroading to matters of public finance including money and banking. His writings on Civil War finance were, in turn, preceded by a more general economic analysis of the secession crisis and the war. When Poor first began writing regularly for Raymond's New York *Times*, he began by enlarging on the themes he had developed in his initial series on the effect of secession on the commercial relations of the North and the South.[31] His analyses in the early months of 1861 concentrated particularly on the thesis that the South's fundamental weakness arose from the concentration of her wealth in land and slaves. One result of this concentration, Poor pointed out, was to give the North control of Southern commerce.[32] This control would not be altered despite the claims of the Confederacy that its free trade policy would bring great benefits to the American planters and the British manufacturers. Poor did, however, condemn the Northern congressmen for giving force to Southern arguments in the critical border states and in Britain and France by passing a high tariff in February 1861. This action, he insisted, was as serious a political as it was an economic blunder.

A second crucial result of the South's overconcentration on agriculture, Poor's editorials emphasized, was that she did not have available nor would she be able to develop the industrial facilities to fight a large-scale war. A final and much more immediate effect of the South's lack of economic diversity was, in Poor's opinion, the difficulty she would have in raising funds.[33] The taxable value of Southern wealth was, the editor showed, much less than that of the North. Nor would the South find it easy to supplement taxes by borrowing. The attempt to market the first issues of Confederate bonds demonstrated clearly how little surplus the Southern planter had available and what little confidence the foreign investor had in the new government. Not only had this first issue of $75,000,000 found an unresponsive market, Poor wrote, but the current market value of the bonds of the most financially sound of the Southern states had declined steadily after they joined the Confederacy.

The analysis was certainly accurate, although Poor apparently discounted, as did nearly all Northerners, the time it would take to transform the relative strengths and weaknesses of the North and South into military effectiveness. Yet Poor would probably not have stressed this point even if it had occurred to him. He hoped, as did Raymond, that his analytical editorials might possibly help to strengthen the resolution of the North to stand up to the South; to keep the wavering border states from joining the Confederacy; and to obtain stronger support for the North from the merchants, manufacturers, and investors of Great Britain and France. Actually, Poor's editorials could hardly have had much effect, for in periods of high crisis rational economic analysis has less appeal or influence than the little it has in normal times.

After the firing on Fort Sumter, Poor concerned himself with the economic aspects of military and diplomatic policy. He urged and then supported the placing of a blockade which would "close every Southern port as effectively as if an impassable barrier were constructed across its mouth."[34] The blockade led Poor, like most Northerners, to examine their government's relations with Great Britain.[35] Since Britain had such a large economic stake in the cause of the North, she should, Poor reasoned editorially, accept the blockade. Because the South lacked any shipping of its own, because its ports would before long be effectively blockaded, any cotton England received she had to obtain through Northern ports. Moreover, the states of the North and West still comprised one of Britain's largest markets, while the West was rapidly becoming one of her major sources of foodstuffs. The sooner the war was over, the sooner Britain would once again be sure of her cotton supply and of enjoying her large American market. The British decision to recognize the South as a belligerent was, then, to Poor a blind misreading of economic self-interest; while her later acceptance of the Union blockade indicated to the editor that she was beginning to see the light.

As 1861 passed, Poor became both in the *Times*' editorials and *Hallett's Circular* concerned with the government's policies for financing the war.[36] He, like nearly all those connected with the problem, realized that each of the three alternatives for paying for the war — increased taxation, borrowing large sums, and the issuing of paper money — had its difficulties. To meet effectively a large share of the costs, taxation would be so severe as to be politically impossible. As for the second method, the Federal government was having almost as much difficulty as the Confederacy in borrowing money. The first war bond issues, short-term notes carrying a high interest, over 7 per cent, had been sold largely through an organization of the banks belonging to the clearing house associations of New York, Boston, and Philadelphia. Yet their sale had been disappointingly slow and what had been marketed had been disposed of only at a heavy discount. The great danger of the third alternative, that of issuing money, was that irredeemable paper currency would, as it had done in the past, depreciate rapidly, creating disastrous inflation.

These questions of war finance which troubled the Treasury Department and Northern financial circles during most of 1861 came to a head that December when a money stringency precipitated by the Trent affair forced most of the Northern banks to suspend payments. This crisis made the sale of Federal securities almost impossible. The Secretary of Treasury, Salmon P. Chase, who disliked to recommend the levying of heavy taxes, had already started to issue demand notes from the Treasury. As 1862 opened, a large segment of the public and an increasing number of congressmen and other public officials began to consider irredeemable paper money as the only way to meet the financial demands of the war.[37]

Poor in his editorials, agreeing with most Northern bankers and financiers, refused to admit the necessity of issuing legal tender notes. But unlike many bankers and brokers he thought the issuing of some type of noninterest-bearing Treasury note essential. The plan he advocated in his writings was briefly as follows.[38] Let the Treasury issue $250,000,000 demand notes bearing no interest and convertible into 6 per cent long-term bonds. In order to prevent their depreciation, these notes would be backed by revenues from new heavy taxes. "Treasury notes," Poor repeatedly emphasized, "can only be relied on so far as the means are, and are known by the general public to be, provided for the redemption of the entire issue." [39] To raise $250,000,000 a year Poor advocated the levying of a 3 per cent income tax, new excise taxes on liquor, tobacco, sugar, and cotton, stamp taxes on contracts, agreements, notes, bills of exchange, loans, mortgages, debentures, conveyances, leases, wills, and so forth, and the issuing of costly licenses to firms dealing in and manufacturing wines, beers, spirits, tobacco, and to innkeepers, cab and livery firms, and so forth.

Assuming as did most Northerners that the war would be over by the end of 1862, the editor thought that the rest of its cost could be met by long-term loans. Poor believed that long-term 6 per cent loans, backed by adequate sinking funds, would find a wide market if they were issued in small denominations and marketed energetically to all classes of the population in every part of the Union. He was certain that "among the widespread population of our country the small bonds would be taken at par, even when the stocks, in large sums, were less readily negotiated." [40] Poor stressed that this plan for tax-supported revenue notes was only a temporary war measure; but he believed it should permit the government to meet the financial crisis without resorting to irredeemable legal tender notes or even, as Chase had advocated, bank note expansion based on the sale of government bonds to private and state banks.

Late in January 1862 Poor had a chance to put his ideas into action. On January 11, a delegation representing the Associated Banks of New York, Philadelphia, and Boston and headed by James Gallatin of New York, conferred with Secretary Chase and the financial committees of both houses of Congress for the purpose of working out a plan by which the banks could assist the government and so avoid the printing of legal tender notes. The delegation urged the treasury department to stop issuing demand notes and to meet the crisis by printing $100,000,000 worth of interest-bearing two-year treasury notes and by making a large issue of 6 per cent long-term bonds to be sold by the associated bankers without any limitations on price. On the fifteenth Chase and the bankers accepted a somewhat modified version of this plan; but both House and Senate committees refused to go along with it. A week later, on January 22, Chase agreed reluctantly in a letter to the House Ways and Means Committee to support a bill authorizing paper currency as legal tender which Representative Elbridge G. Spaulding of New York had proposed. Two days afterwards Henry Poor left New York at the behest of a group of the city's financiers to help work out some compromise with the congressional committees which might still prevent the issuance of irredeemable paper currency.

On arriving in Washington, Poor went right to work.That evening, the twenty-fourth, he dined and spent several hours discussing the currency problem with three congressmen, Roscoe Conkling, Charles B. Sedgwick, Valentine B. Horton, and with Governor William Sprague of Rhode Island, and an old family friend, Governor John A. Andrew of Massachusetts.[41] All these men, including Horton, an influential member of the House Ways and Means Committee, were determined opponents of the legal tender bill. During the next week Poor was constantly conferring with them and with other congressmen and politicians. On the twenty-eighth, the day the debate on the Spaulding Bill began in the House, Poor spent many hours with members of Congress "drawing up a bill for Congress on finances." [42] The following day he spent almost entirely with the Ways and Means Committee discussing his and other proposals.

The "bill" Poor helped prepare was undoubtedly the amendment to the legal tender bill offered by Roscoe Conkling on February 3. Conkling's proposal incorporated some of the views Poor had been editorially advocating.[43] It called for the issuing of $500,000,000 worth of 6 per cent twenty-year bonds in small denominations, with a minimum legal discount and, of more importance, the printing, at the discretion of the Secretary of the Treasury, of $200,000,000 worth of one-year treasury notes in place of an equivalent amount of bonds. These notes, again at the discretion of the secretary, could bear interest or not. In any case they would not be legal tender. Poor remained in Washington until February 6, when the amendment was defeated along with a second proposed by Horton. Spaulding's legal tender bill then passed by the sizable majority of 93 to 59.[44] The majority, convinced that noninterest-bearing Treasury notes were not enough to meet the financial needs of the Federal government, had accepted greenbacks as the best possible alternative. Even though the battle had been lost, Poor was not too distressed when he returned to New York. He had liked playing a part in the law-making process and had especially enjoyed becoming acquainted with some of the most influential law makers of the day.

III

Poor's trip to Washington, by making him personally known to many leading politicians, undoubtedly helped bring about his appointment as a government commissioner of the Union Pacific. The appointment and his later election as the road's secretary, in turn, took him away from writing, except for doing an occasional promotional piece for the road, for close to two years. Then after his financial difficulties in the spring of 1864, Poor returned to Washington once more to try to affect legislation by personal contacts and the use of his pen. This time his task was one for which he had been well trained as editor of the *American Railroad Journal*—the lobbying for the railroads against the tariff on rails and railroad equipment.

Since the passage of the tariff act of February 1861, which Poor in his *Times* editorials had condemned as an economic and political blunder, the country's manufacturing interests had obtained progressively higher rates from Congress. In 1862 the iron industry, for example, had won an increase on rails from $12.00 to $13.50 a ton. By 1864 most American industrialists were confident that under the need for war revenue they would obtain much higher tariff protection. The iron industry was, in fact, asking for a tariff rate of $22.50 a ton on rails with comparable rises in the rates on other railroad products.[45]

Railroad managers, taking alarm at last, decided on counteraction. In late spring of 1864 the presidents of a number of major roads asked Poor to organize resistance to the proposed rate increase. As the secretary of the organization formed in 1854 to fight similar increases, Poor was a logical candidate for this task. The former editor, being in no position to turn down the $2000 the roads were offering, accepted their invitation without hesitation.

He began his new task first by drawing up and mailing to congressmen and other important politicians a carefully prepared, statistically documented circular which pointed out the unfortunate effects the proposed rates would have on railroad industry and on the American economy as a whole. He then went to Washington where he attended congressional committee hearings and talked with numerous representatives and senators. His mission was successful.[46] In the tariff bill passed June 30 nearly all rates on important commodities were raised, except for those on rails, boiler plates, rods, and so forth.

In 1865 the iron industry made no real attempt to raise the rates. In the following year, however, working largely through the American Iron and Steel Association, the industry made a determined effort to obtain the rates proposed in 1864. By the late spring of 1866 the association had succeeded in getting a rate of $22.50 written into the new tariff bill. The managers of the leading roads, once more alarmed, called a meeting in New York and again hired Poor to organize the campaign against the proposed rates.[47] Besides paying him an excellent commission they gave him enough funds to hire some assistants. Poor worked hard that June in Washington.[48] In early July he helped organize a large railroad convention in Philadelphia to protest against the proposed tariff changes. Again the line was successfully held.

At the opening of the next session, both the lobbyists for the iron industry and Poor were on hand. This time Poor was aided by an enlarged staff which included William Dennison, former governor of Ohio. He also had the support from the Johnson administration, for the Secretary of Treasury, Hugh McCulloch, had strongly endorsed the report of his Special Commissioner of Revenue, David A. Wells, who emphatically advocated tariff reduction. Yet even with this opposition the Iron and Steel Association's staff was able to get both the House and Senate committees to increase the rates on all types of iron. But once more Poor's work showed results. For when the final bill was passed in February these increases had been deleted. The pattern of 1867 was repeated in 1868. Again the administration urged a lower tariff. Again the majority of congressional committees wanted to raise rather than lower the rates on iron duties and again Poor helped prevent the proposed increases from becoming law.

In 1869 and 1870 Poor concentrated primarily on steel rates. The successful introduction of the Bessemer process in the United States in 1867 and 1868 had made possible the large-scale production of steel rails and other steel railroad products. Immediately steel manufacturers demanded extremely high tariff rates on steel products. Representatives of the Iron and Steel Association proposed, as Congress opened in December 1868, to replace the 45 per cent *ad valorem* tax on steel products by fixed duties. They asked that the duty on Bessemer, blister, shear, and cast steel ingots be placed at 3½ cents a pound; at 4 cents a pound on rails and other products which had been "cut, rolled or hammered into a pattern"; and 8 cents a pound if made into carriage, car, or locomotive springs.[49] Similar increases were asked for rolled, hammered, shaped, and finished iron goods.

In most cases these demands were equivalent to an *ad valorem* tax of 100 per cent or more.

By February 1869 Poor could report to the railroads that the *ad valorem* tax would remain unchanged during the current session of Congress. In 1870, however, the real showdown came. The struggle kept Poor in Washington all spring. He was unable to prevent a change from an *ad valorem* to a fixed rate. Yet he was able to get the rate set on steel ingots and on rails and other shaped steel at 1¼ cents a pound or 28 dollars a gross ton instead of the 3½ cents to 4 cents a pound demanded by the iron industry. He was also able to slice down comparably the rates on railroad springs.

After 1870 the railroads had less need of Poor's services in Washington, for tariff reduction was becoming something of a popular crusade. In 1871, the danger of increased rates on railroad iron and steel was so slight that Poor did not bother to go to Washington. In 1872 a bill for a general 10 per cent reduction on iron and steel and nearly all other rates had such strong congressional support that Poor again felt it unnecessary to spend time in Washington. He did, however, arrange with his close friend and neighbor, Edward Atkinson, an ardent tariff reformer, to keep him informed of developments in Congress.[50]

After 1870 Poor only went once again to the capital about the tariff and this was not until 1880. During the depression years after 1873 the railroads temporarily slowed construction and the demand for rails declined rapidly. At the same time manufacturers in both the United States and Britain, anxious to keep operating as long as possible, cut their prices. So tariff rates became much less important to the railroads. By 1879, however, conditions were again changing. The railroads, especially those in the West, were beginning large construction programs. This and the revived demand for iron and steel elsewhere had driven up the price of American rails from 40 dollars a ton at the beginning of 1879 to 65 dollars at its close.[51] In the meantime the British price remained close to 24 dollars a ton. In hopes of cutting costs several major Western roads including the Illinois Central, the Chicago, Burlington and Quincy, the Mobile and Ohio, and several Texas roads paid Poor to go to Washington to work for reduction of the 28 dollar tariff which with the drop in the price of British rails gave the steel industry the 100 per cent tariff it had demanded in the late 1860's. Poor was in Washington in January and February and again in June seeing congressmen and testifying before congressional committees. No reduction was made that year, but Poor's work may have helped pave the way for the reduction of steel rail rates to 17 dollars a ton which was incorporated into the tariff of 1883.

In carrying out his work as the railroads' "specialist" on the tariff, Poor used both written and oral persuasion.[52] He talked constantly to congressmen in their offices, their homes, and even on the floor of Congress. He attended the meetings of the Senate Committee on Finances and the House Ways and Means Committee whenever any aspect of the tariff on railroad products was being considered. He also prepared circulars explaining the railroads' position and attacking the iron and steel industry's demands. Occasionally he helped antitariff congressmen draw up bills or amendments and occasionally even wrote speeches for them to deliver on the floor of Congress. In reaching congressmen Poor had the help of those senators and representatives who because of their own political and economic interests, were particularly anxious to keep down the rates. Most useful in this respect was Ginery Twichell, a Brookline neighbor who had been president of the Boston and Worcester and who was at the time president of the Atchison, Topeka and Santa Fe, as well as a member of Congress. As an influential member of the House Ways and Means Committee Twichell kept Poor informed about the latest developments on the tariff and arranged, whenever necessary, for his admission to the committee meetings or to the floor of the House. As a close friend and a man of some learning and of catholic tastes, Twichell also became Poor's closest companion during his leisure hours in Washington.

Poor's work for the railroads had other aspects besides personally persuading congressmen. He wrote articles condemning the tariff on rails for newspapers like the New York *Times,* the New York *Post,* and the Boston *Transcript.* He helped organize antitariff conventions like the one that met in Philadelphia in July 1866. Also he mailed out printed circulars to railroad men all over the country asking them to send the enclosed protests against proposed rate increases back to their congressmen in Washington. This seems to be the extent of his efforts. There is no indication that the railroads through Poor or the iron industry through its association offered special favors to congressmen who voted their way. Nevertheless, congressmen could hardly forget, and Poor was certain to remind them, that the railroad managers, promoters, investors, and shippers whose protests Poor voiced could influence more votes in more areas of the country than the men who worked in and with the iron industry.

In writing and speaking against the increased rates on railroad iron Poor used much the same arguments he had used for the same purpose in the 1850's.[53] Briefly, his major argument began by stressing that railroads were absolutely essential to the further growth of the economy of the United States. To increase the cost of new railroad construction and the cost of transportation on the completed roads by raising the price of rails, equipment, and machinery was not only to discriminate against the nation's largest and most essential industry but to retard the nation's economic progress. For to inhibit railroad construction meant slowing down the agricultural advance in the trans-Mississippi area, delaying the recovery of the agrarian South, as well as holding back the industrial development of the East. If the iron and steel industry had the capacity to meet the demands of the railroads, there might possibly be, Poor's argument continued, some justification for a high tariff. But in the sixties and early seventies demand far exceeded supply. No matter what the customs rates were, the railroads must import some iron and steel from Britain. With such a huge market for their products, the demand of the iron and steel industry for increased rates, he insisted, was particularly unreasonable. "The steel makers tell us," Poor wrote in 1870, "that unless the duties are increased, as demanded, they will be compelled to close their works. They told us [this] in 1866. . . . They have repeated the same ever since, yet they have not closed their works, but have gone on increasing them and the make of steel in a wonderful degree." [54] The aim of the steel manufacturers who had already formed a tightly knit patent pool was, Poor repeatedly insisted, not protection but monopoly. In presenting these arguments and in answering those of his opponents Poor relied on a large amount of factual information which he liked to give in statistical form. After 1868 much of this information came from his own *Manual of the Railroads of the United States.*

Although Poor worked hard in Washington, he never really enjoyed the business of lobbying. Had it not been for the substantial salary the railroads paid him, he would have given it up. For one thing he had little use for the mind and motives of the ordinary congressman.[55] For another, the iron and steel industry proved a formidable antagonist. It had an impressive arsenal of appealing arguments and, more important, a tight, tested, and most effective organization. The arguments made by the representatives of the iron and steel industry in presenting their case and in countering that of the railroads followed the standard protariff line.[56] Protection, they claimed, was essential to foster this basic American industry, to protect the laboring men in the mills from the competition of cheap foreign labor, and to provide a home market for American agricultural products. In their arguments they did not hesitate to stigmatize Poor or any other proponent of tariff reduction as paid emissaries of sinister British interests who aimed at wrecking the American economy.[57] Except for the last point, the iron lobbyists were undoubtedly as sincere in their arguments about the benefits of the tariff as Poor was in his belief in its detrimental effect on American economy. Yet of the two, Poor's arguments were certainly the more valid. Until the steel industry's capacity was great enough to meet all the demands on it, the nation's economy would have gained more than the iron and steel industry would have lost from a reduction in the tariff on rails and railroad iron. Nevertheless, in a country full of infant industries, the iron makers' arguments found strong support.

Yet it was his opponents' organization rather than their arguments that gave Poor the most difficulty. Here the iron industry had a real advantage. For one thing all the iron and steel companies were united in their efforts to increase the tariff rates, while there were many railroads that saw no reason to oppose the increase. This was especially true of the smaller eastern roads which were already completely built and well equipped. Some railroads with interests in iron production like the Pennsylvania and the Reading were, in fact, actively hostile to Poor's activities.[58] Moreover, in the American Iron and Steel Association the industry had a powerful instrument to help achieve its goals.

The association, founded in the 1850's, was revived in 1864 in large part to win tariff concessions from Congress. By 1868 it was claiming that it was "the most powerful organized body of manufacturers that exists in our country." [59] The association's tariff committee with its permanent staff in Washington operated in much the same fashion as did Poor. Its members buttonholed congressmen; prepared statements presenting their arguments and countering Poor's; sent copy to newspapers; forwarded printed circulars for the different railroad officials to mail to the congressmen. As Poor had Twichell's aid, so they had William "Pig Iron" Kelley and other congressmen from manufacturing districts to get them on the floor of Congress and to support their arguments at committee hearings. The association made clear the effectiveness of its committee in its annual report published in 1868.[60] The report described in detail the way the administration's bill for tariff reduction was handled and how it came out of committee a bill to increase not to reduce the rates. Except for the well-conceived delaying tactics of its opponents, the report read, the increases would have passed during that session of Congress. They will be passed, the association promised, at the next session.

This report suggests the significance of Poor's work. Against such an organization those newspaper editors, college professors, and civic-minded lawyers dedicated to tariff reform had really little chance of carrying out their proposals. Even the administration, when it responded in part to an increasing public demand for tariff reduction, could at first do little to get its program through Congress. Until the tariff became a major political issue in 1872, one of the most effective counterbalances to the demands of business interests for the tariff increases was other business interests like the railroads, the shipbuilders, and several different mercantile groups whose profits would be adversely affected by such increases. Of these groups, the railroads represented by Henry Poor were certainly among the most active.

Besides the tariff, Poor occasionally found himself lobbying during the postwar years for currency legislation. His experience in Washington and his reputation as a financial expert made his services as useful to bankers as to railroad managers. His first chance after 1862 to influence currency legislation came in the fall of 1865 when he accompanied the banker, James F. D. Lanier, to Washington to report on the market for American government securities abroad.[61] The end of the war in April 1865 had made necessary a reorganization of government finances. Most bankers and other financial men wholeheartedly agreed with the Secretary of Treasury on the need both to refund the debt and to retire the paper currency from circulation as soon as possible. Both refunding and the resumption of specie payments called for the marketing of large amounts of American government securities abroad. For if either of these financial operations was to be successful, European investors must purchase the new securities issued to refund the war bonds and to help provide the gold necessary to make possible the withdrawal of greenbacks from circulation. Hugh McCulloch, the Secretary of Treasury, therefore asked Lanier, who was planning a trip abroad in June 1865, to report on the current European attitude toward United States bonds. Lanier, after spending some time in Frankfort and London, became convinced that the market for American securities would remain strong only if the government made absolutely clear its intention to remove the unbacked legal tender notes from circulation. On his return Lanier asked Poor to help him write his report. Poor then accompanied the banker to Washington where they both talked with Secretary McCulloch and President Andrew Johnson. McCulloch probably used the information submitted by Lanier and Poor to reinforce the strong recommendation he soon made to Congress for the passage of an act to retire the legal tender notes. The bill Congress passed in March 1866, while only partially carrying out McCulloch's recommendations, did provide for the retirement of $10,000,000 in the following six months and $4,000,000 each succeeding month.

A little more than two years later Poor was again involved in currency matters. This time he represented a large group of financiers headed by George S. Coe, president of the American Exchange Bank in New York, and by John Murray Forbes in Boston. These men were disturbed by Congress's reversal on the retirement of greenbacks. The recession precipitated by the Overend-Gurney failure in London in May 1866 created a demand for an expansion rather than a contraction of circulating media. During the latter part of 1866 and most of 1867 farmers' organizations, labor associations, and different types of businessmen put increasing pressure on Congress to abandon the policy of contraction. As a result the House in December 1867, and the Senate on January 22, 1868, passed resolutions revoking the power of the Secretary of Treasury to withdraw greenbacks from circulation.[62]

New York and Boston bankers, hoping to salvage something for their basic policy from Congress, turned to Poor. The former editor had written an article in December in which he suggested a general course of action.[63] He then helped George S. Coe to work out, partly on the basis of this article, a more specific plan which was incorporated into two legislative proposals. The first, the Gold Contract Bill, would legalize all contracts which specified payment in gold.[64] This act should, its authors believed, bring gold back into circulation. Therefore their second bill called for the retirement of legal tender notes as the use of metal currency increased. These bills would provide, Coe and Poor believed, "the natural road to resumption."

Late in January 1868, Coe and Poor left for Washington. Coe soon returned, but Poor remained and concentrated on obtaining the passage of the Gold Contract Bill.[65] It was reported out of committee on February 10; but, then, the impeachment of President Johnson stopped all legislative action until late spring. In June, Poor who, following the advice of John Murray Forbes, had continued to put all his efforts on the Gold Contract Bill, was delighted to report that it had passed the Senate.[66] He was optimistic about its passage by the House; but despite all his efforts it was tabled by the House on July 17, shortly before adjournment.

Poor, however, did help win influential support for the Gold Contract Bill.[67] Special Commissioner of Revenue David A. Wells, recommended it in his report to the Secretary of Treasury written that fall. Early in the following session Senator John Sherman included a provision for legalizing gold contracts into a general bill for gradual resumption. In February a gold contract bill similar to the one Poor had lobbied for in the previous session passed both houses of Congress, only to receive a pocket veto from President Johnson. Although the Gold Contract Bill failed to become a law, the proposal, as much Coe's as Poor's, was a sensible one, given a belief in the dangers of irredeemable currency, for it did provide for a gradual contraction of paper money and a return to a specie standard in a fairly painless way.

After 1868, Poor did not return to writing about or lobbying for currency legislation until well after he had retired to Brookline. Nor did he after 1870 spend much time in Washington on the tariff. This was not only because there was less need for his services. It was also because after 1868 Poor was devoting more of the time he spent with his pen to editing and publishing the *Manual.* After his retirement, however, Poor made use of his experiences in Wall Street and Washington both in his historical and theoretical analyses of financial and economic matters and in his tracts on more current issues of public economic policy.

✶ 11 ✶

The Manual

IN HIS LATER YEARS Henry Poor's two continuing interests were the editing and publishing of the *Manual of the Railroads of the United States* and the writing of books and articles on money, banking, currency, and national economic policy. Although his writings on these broader economic and financial matters were quite widely read in their day, it is his work on the *Manual* that has had a lasting significance. In printing his annual volumes Poor continued to play a major role in the development of one of modern business's most important ancillary services, the provision of reliable information. The organization he created to supply such information is today, still operating under the name of Poor, a leader in this specialized field. In writing the introductions to the *Manual* Poor continued and extended his former functions of reporting on and collecting statistics about the performance of the American railroad system. The statistics he collected remain the most useful single source of information available on the railroads of the United States before 1888, the year when the Interstate Commerce Commission's Bureau of Statistics first began collecting and publishing data on railroads.

It was young William who suggested that his father publish a *Manual of Railroads of the United States* when they formed the firm of H. V. and H. W. Poor late in 1867.[1] William, probably because of his efforts to sell insurance to a large number of railroads, saw the need for a single volume which included essential information about the many different railroad companies. In 1867 the only available handbooks of this type were directories of railroad officials.[2] These books, published in New York since the mid-1850's, gave very little information beyond the names and addresses of railroad officers and directors. What William apparently had in mind was a volume similar to *Bradshaw's Shareholders' Railway Manual and Directory* which had been since the late 1840's the standard British railroad manual. The British book included, besides names of the officers and directors, some information about each road's finances and operations.[3]

Poor, delighted by his son's suggestion, immediately envisaged the proposed work as more than just an American version of a *Bradshaw's Manual.* He looked upon it as a revision and expansion of his *History of the Railroads and Canals of the United States.*[4] It would include much more information on construction, finances, and operation than did *Bradshaw's* and, unlike the British volume, would have operational and financial statistics for each major road for a period of several years in order to make comparative analysis possible. Poor planned to write a long introduction, beginning with an historical sketch of the development of the railroads in the United States. This sketch would be illustrated by stastics including total figures for mileage constructed and for the operational and financial performances of the railroads of each state, region, and the nation during the immediately preceding and earlier years. It would also include a brief analysis of the recent developments in the industry, particularly in railroad finance, with suggestions for improvements and reforms. In writing the introductions to the *Manuals,* Poor would, in fact, carry out on a much smaller scale many of the same functions he had earlier performed as editor of the *American Railroad Journal.*

When he began compiling the first volume of the *Manual* early in 1868, Poor was fortunate to obtain the services of Dr. Richard S. Fisher, the statistician who had helped him with the *History.*[5] The two, with William's help, drew up a printed questionnaire which Poor mailed in February 1868 to the presidents of over four hundred companies. In his hand-written covering letter he first pointed out the value to the individual firm as well as to the industry as a whole of the compilation he was planning. Then, stressing the need for presenting "the accounts of the operations of the leading Roads for *several years,*" he asked for copies of the company's annual reports for the preceding years.[6]

During the spring Poor and Fisher worked hard on the *Manual.* They checked the forms as they came in and sent out follow-up letters to those roads which had failed to send back the questionnaire. In April, Poor began to write his introduction — the first of several "Sketch[es] of the Rise, Progress, Costs, Earnings, Etc. of the Railroads of the United States." During the spring both Poors were busy getting advertisements for the *Manual* and were successful in obtaining almost enough to cover the costs of printing. By the middle of May the data had been compiled, the introduction finished, and the manuscript sent to the printer. At the very end of that month railroad and financial men were buying the first Poor's *Manual of the Railroads of the United States.*[7]

The *Manual* was an immediate success. The press and the business and trade journals gave it enthusiastic notices.[8] By the beginning of July over 1500 copies had been sold at five dollars a copy, and before the end of the summer most of the 2500 copies printed had been sold. This sale gave the Poors close to the estimated five-thousand-dollar profit they hoped to make from the book.[9] The *Manual* was a financial success undoubtedly because it did provide railroad managers, investors, and other businessmen with information unavailable in any other single source.

The type of information given on the individual roads in the later volumes followed closely that provided in the first *Manual;* and the data there were, in turn, patterned on those given in Poor's earlier *History of the Railroads and Canals of the United States.* In the *Manual* the information was presented in more compact form than in the *History;* more was given on operations and somewhat less on the historical and legal background of each road. The data in the 1868 and later *Manuals* were listed under four major headings: "line of road," "rolling stock," "operations and general balances," and "officers and directors." Three of the categories carried almost the same type of information which had been carried under similar headings in the *History,* but added "gauge" and "weight of rail" under "line of road" and listed the different types of freight cars under "rolling stock." In the remaining category, "operations and general balances," the *Manual* often had more detailed information under the "general balances" which, as in the *History,* gave full descriptions of each bond issue as well as the balance sheet for the previous fiscal year. It further listed miles run by passenger, freight, and service trains; the totals of passengers and tons of freight carried, as well as gross earnings from passengers, freight, mails, express, and other sources. The expenditures, broken down into more details than in most of the individual sketches in the *History,* included the cost of the maintenance of the way and rolling stock, of the moving of trains, the handling of freight and passengers, and miscellaneous expenses. This was followed by a listing of total operating costs and net earnings. For the larger roads Poor computed the operating statistics in total-miles-run-by-trains and per-mile-of-track-operated, and for some gave the operating ratio. Where he had the data available Poor provided, usually in tabular form as he had done in the *History,* an individual road's record of construction and equipment costs, maintenance and operating expenses, passengers and freight carried, and earnings over a period of years. This new information helped give railroad investors, bankers, and managers a fairly clear picture of the current operations and past performances of a large number of American railroads. This was information which would have been difficult, if not impossible, for most individuals to obtain anywhere except in the pages of Poor's *Manual.*

Other information was supplied. The major corporate changes in a road's history were listed. For the larger companies details of the stocks and bonds held in other companies were given. So too was information on land grants, including the amounts authorized, taken up, and sold. In order to make the *Manual* more useful to the financial world Poor provided data on government securities which he expanded in his later volumes. In describing the issues of the national and state governments he mentioned the laws authorizing the issue, its type, the interest and principal, and where and when each was payable. In the 1869 and later volumes Poor listed for the issues of the national government the monthly prices paid since 1865. He also gave gold prices for the same period and included a statistical summary of the revenues and disbursements of the United States for the preceding decade.

Because the quantity and quality of his information were superior to that in any other type of railroad or investors' manual or directory published, Poor soon had a virtual monopoly of the field. The two annual railroad directories being published in 1867, one by A. H. King and the other by John Ashcroft, went out of business shortly after Poor's book appeared. King published his last volume in 1868 and Ashcroft his last in 1871. Poor's success, however, attracted imitators.[10] Two other *Manuals of Railroads* appeared; but both were short-lived. One edited by James H. Lyles was published only in 1869 and 1870, and the other, put out by James Vernon, appeared only once, in 1873. These two told more than did the *Manual* about the history of the individual roads and the areas through which they passed; but they had nothing like the detailed information on operation and finance that Poor included. Thus from 1873 until 1900 when John Moody published his manual of corporation securities, Henry Poor had the field almost to himself. Nor was he troubled by competition from *Bradshaw's* and other European manuals which carried information on American railroads, for they included little more data than had Lyles or Vernon. In fact, Poor's *Manual* enjoyed a good market in Europe, particularly in Britain.[11]

From 1868 on the *Manual* prospered steadily. The number of copies published annually increased regularly. So, too, did the income from sales. The exact circulation of the book is uncertain; but it rose from somewhat over 2000 in 1868 to over 5000 by the beginning of the 1880's.[12] The demand for the *Manual* permitted Poor to raise the price in the 1880's from five to six dollars without affecting its sales. From the first the cost of printing and later other expenses were covered by advertising. The income from advertising seems to have been around $8,000 in the 1870's and, if the rates remained the same, must have been considerably more in the 1880's. Increasing income from sales and advertising meant that the profits rose from in the neighborhood of $5,000 on the first volume to at least $8,000 by 1878, in spite of the current severe depression, and close to $15,000 on some of those published in the 1880's.

Although the content of the *Manual* remained much the same after 1868, its size grew as the number of the railroads increased and the staff became more expert in obtaining information.[13] In the 1870's, besides Fisher, this staff included Henry Stone, Poor's nephew who had before the war worked on the *Journal* and L. S. Hand, who helped handle the advertising and sales in addition to assisting in the compilation of data.[14] As the staff became more efficient, Poor added new information on state and national securities, on land grants made to the railroads by the national government as well as on the railroads themselves. In 1876 the questionnaire was enlarged.[15] The new one reflected the growth of railroad consolidations by asking for more data on corporate history, foreclosures, sales, leases, subsidiary corporations, and so forth. It also had new headings for income from rentals and leased lines and requested more detailed information on payments of bond interest and sinking fund installments. One other addition, which asked for the type and amount of steel rails, may have been suggested in part at least by Poor's lobbying activities in Washington.

In compiling his information for the *Manual* Poor relied as heavily on his own questionnaire as he had done for his earlier compilations in the *Journal* and for the *History*. The data submitted by the roads were checked against their annual reports and the railroad reports printed by a number of state railroad bureaus or commissions. "As a rule," Poor noted, "the reports of the companies are to be accepted as trustworthy, although often meagre and incomplete." [16] In obtaining information for the individual roads, but more especially for the general statistical summaries which appeared in his introductions, Poor made good use of the reports on railroad companies issued by Massachusetts, Connecticut, Pennsylvania, Ohio, and Minnesota. These he found "full and explicit." On the other hand, the printed summaries of the other states requiring reports — Maine, New Hampshire, Vermont, New Jersey, Michigan, and Wisconsin — were much too incomplete to be of value.

As had been the case in the 1850's, Poor was comparatively successful in getting the railroad companies to supply the information he wanted. Some of the more powerful companies which, as Poor pointed out, "have often but a small number of stockholders, treat their road as private property, and give as little information as possible." [17] Financially embarrassed companies were also chary of giving data; many of the recently opened railroads or those still under construction were by necessity unable to return a completed form. Nevertheless, even though "in some cases, information has been refused; [and] in others, grudgingly and scantily given," the majority of roads returned completed questionnaires. In 1872, the first year Poor summarized the information for the individual roads in his introduction, 352 roads were listed. On twenty-two no information was given and for twelve of these Poor wrote "information refused." [18] About 125 more failed to make full returns, but included most of the essential data. Many of these were roads still under construction or just opened for operation.

Again, as was the case in the 1850's, most railroad officials, accustomed to issuing information to stockholders, investment bankers, and state officials, were willing enough to send information which was not detailed or specific enough on rates and on freight carried to affect competitive considerations. Moreover, in the 1870's and 1880's railroad managers may have been more willing to give information to Poor whom they knew and whose work they made use of than to state officials whom during that period of agrarian unrest they distrusted. Finally, no more than in the 1850's could many railroads afford the bad publicity of not complying with Poor's requests. The public, Poor emphasized, "has the right to infer that full statements are not given because they would show something wrong or unfavorable in the affairs of the delinquent company." [19] Since most roads still needed funds for construction and expansion and were usually interested in maintaining the current value of their securities, they disliked to have the confidence of investors, bankers, brokers, and their own stockholders thus shaken. Even William K. Vanderbilt sent Poor full data on the New York Central, although the editor had in his introductions to the *Manual* and in his correspondence with officials of the road vigorously condemned the Vanderbilt roads for stock watering.[20] Of course, there was, Poor was quite aware, no certain way of knowing whether the information sent by the roads was doctored to present an overfavorable picture or was in any other way inaccurate. On this matter he pointed to the value of his comparative statements, as he had done earlier, for not only was it difficult for a road to doctor its statements repeatedly, but, added the editor, "time is certain to disclose, speedily, incompetency or misconduct in financial matters." [21]

Although the information submitted by the railroads was probably as correct as could be expected, the compilation and transcription of this data were not always as accurate as they might have been. The *Manual's* accuracy, in fact, varied quite closely with the attention Poor gave to its publication. At first, in spite of his other activities, he devoted a good bit of time to the *Manual.*[22] In addition to writing the introductions, he wrote most of the letters asking for information and helped sell the volume after its publication. But after the printing of the first couple of issues he left nearly all the routine work of compilation to Fisher and Stone, although he did make an effort to check carefully the copy before it was sent to press.

From 1873, the year he retired to Brookline, until 1881 Poor paid little attention to the *Manual.* He continued to write the introductions, which during these years were little more than statistical compilations, but left young William with the responsibility of getting out the annual volume. In 1878 when Poor left Brookline for a short period to help organize his son's brokerage firm, he temporarily gave the *Manual* more attention.[23] At that time the Poor's Railroad Manual Company was formed. In this new firm Henry Poor held most of the stock and received most of the profits although the older firm of H. V. and H. W. Poor continued to publish the annual volume. While in New York, he improved the format of the *Manual* by placing the sketches of the individual roads, as they had been in the *History,* in alphabetical order by states. Before this the roads were entered only in the order in which the data on each road was completed and the reader had to rely wholly on the index to find the entry he wanted. In this same year Poor also began his useful list of "former names of Companies whose title has been changed or whose lines have been acquired by others." [24]

In 1881 Poor once again took an active part in the editing of his already famous publication. William, who never had much time for or any real interest in the *Manual,* had, with the return of prosperity, become completely involved in matters of railroad finance. Stone rarely bothered to take the necessary care in compiling the data; while old Dr. Fisher, although careful and accurate, was rapidly becoming a chronic alcoholic. Poor was shocked at the condition of his book when he returned to the New York office, apparently at his son's request, in the spring of 1881. "For want of *painstaking* care," he reported to his wife, "the Manual had run pretty wild." [25]

For three years Poor left Brookline for extended periods of time to work wholly on the *Manual.* First of all he concentrated on improving the accuracy of the printed data both in the body of the book and in the introductions.[26] He added little new information but did increase the number of sketches which included comparative data covering a period of years. For the larger roads he put the abstracts of the "general balances," or the "financial statement" in a clearer, more usable tabular form. Also in these years he expanded and improved the information given in the statistical tables in his introductions and began printing more concise tabular statements for each state at the beginning of the section for the railroads of that state.

As important as improving the quality of his book was, in Poor's mind, the creation of an expert staff. He felt strongly that he must continue to give the publication his closest attention until he had trained a staff in which he had complete confidence. As a man of seventy he found little enjoyment in these lengthy sojourns away from home. In December 1882 Fisher, whom prolonged drinking bouts had made almost useless, died. "He was the most perfect workman in his art that I ever knew," Poor wrote Mary, "and had many great qualities subject to one fault only. Poor fellow — he had little to live for." [27] In the same year Stone left the *Manual.* Poor, however, had already begun to recruit the new staff. Of the new young men, John P. Meany quickly proved the most capable, although Poor reported that all were bright and enthusiastic. Meany soon headed the staff, with Hand staying on as his chief assistant. Another man, Ropes, took over Hand's task of traveling through the Northeast and Midwest, getting data and soliciting advertising and subscriptions. After the completion of the 1883 *Manual,* Poor was highly pleased with the work of his new force. "The more I see of my *staff* here," he wrote Mary, "the more I am impressed with its ability. We are the most perfect organization yet gotten together." [28] Poor, therefore, decided to give Meany a free hand with the 1884 volume, promising to come to New York to help only if Meany clearly needed him.[29]

Poor was a little too optimistic. The 1884 *Manual* went off well enough with only a little help from the senior editor.[30] But in the next year Meany let the publication fall way behind schedule.[31] With the older man's aid, Meany finally had the *Manual* out by late July, but there were a great many careless errors in the transcribing and proofreading which neither he nor Poor caught. They were, however, spotted by the editor of the *Railroad Gazette* and other railroad experts who had enthusiastically praised the improvement in the *Manual* since 1880.[32] Although he had to admit that Meany had proved himself "this year hardly competent," Poor once again gave him full responsibility for the next number.[33] This time Meany did a creditable job. Not only did he put out the *Manual* almost on schedule with practically no help from Poor, but he also compiled the first new annual supplementary volume, *Poor's Directory of*

Railway Officials and Railway Directors.[34] After 1885, Poor's staff, having successfully mastered the techniques of compiling the *Manual,* continued to do a creditable job with little assistance from their mentor. They had, in fact, been so well trained that they, in turn, became the teachers for a whole generation of business statisticians in the country.[35]

After 1886, when he retired as a partner of his son's firm and when he turned the publication of the *Manual* even more completely over to Meany, Poor concerned himself less and less with the *Manual.* He appears to have written the introduction to the work until 1889. He may have even written some later ones; but from 1890 until 1900 when Meany wrote his impressive "A Study of Railway Statistics," the introductions were little more than brief statistical compilations. Poor may also have had some say in the decision to publish in 1890 a supplementary volume, *Poor's Handbook of Investment Securities,* which contained information on industrials and other firms not included in the *Manual,* just as he most certainly had in the decision to issue a supplementary directory of directors in 1886.[36] The *Manual* of 1893 was the last on which Henry Poor's name appears as author. But after 1890 its policies, contents, and most probably even the introductions of the *Manual* were those of John P. Meany rather than of Henry V. Poor, although throughout the 1890's the yearly *Manual* could not go to press until it had been sent to Brookline to pass "the old man's" inspection.[37]

Before examining in detail the introductions which Poor wrote fairly regularly from 1868 until 1889, it might be well to watch the editor and his staff go through one of their annual performances.[38] In order to get the information from those roads whose fiscal year was the calendar year, the yearly questionnaires were sent out in December. Because many roads used a fiscal year ending June 30 for their accounts, this timing hurt the value of the *Manual,* since the information on these roads was a year old when it was published. One reform, therefore, that Poor heartily favored was the instituting of the same fiscal year for all railroads.[39] As each questionnaire was returned, it was filed with the previous forms and reports of that road. The new data were compared with the older forms, and with recent annual reports and state reports in order to catch any errors or obvious discrepancies. They were then copied upon two forms — one of which would go to the printer, while the other Poor would use in making up the statistics for his introduction.

In March, Poor or Meany would begin to send letters to the companies which had failed to return the questionnaire or had made what appeared to be an error in the information submitted. In April and

May these letters would be followed, if necessary, by telegrams. Besides sending letters and telegrams, one or two of the staff went personally to railroads with offices in the Eastern cities when it was necessary to get or check on information. Poor himself occasionally made such a trip, which he rather enjoyed, for his reputation as editor of the *Manual,* his long years in the industry, and his impressive face framed in snow white hair and trim beard made him in the 1880's one of the respected old men of the railroad world. After the copy for a road's sketch was completed, it would be returned to the company for correction. This often was a cause of delay in the publication of the *Manual,* but Poor apparently thought it worthwhile, as it both helped to assure the accuracy of the returns and to keep the goodwill of the railroads.[40]

June was always the busiest month for the *Manual's* staff. The mass of copy had to be given a final check, telegrams sent to roads which had failed to return their copy or were tardy in turning in their original data, and final corrections put in. Even more difficult was the final compilation of data for the statistical summaries in the introduction. Once these were compiled, Poor revised and completed his introduction which went at the end of the month to the printer with the last pages of the text. The end-of-June deadline was often missed; but by mid-July at the latest the newest volume of *Manual of the Railroads of the United States* would be on sale. Poor usually stayed on in New York a week or so after publication to write forwarding letters, to oversee the mailing and the initial sales, and to give the man currently in charge of sales a few words of advice before the latter left for his annual trip to the South and West. Then Poor was off for a well-earned vacation with his family at Andover, Maine, where in 1877 he had purchased as a summer home the large house that his grandfather Merrill had built long before.

II

Poor's primary continuing concern with the *Manual* was with the introductions which he wrote for each annual volume. Like the *Manual's* text, the content and the caliber of the introductions reflected closely the amount of attention Poor gave to the volume. Thus the first few introductions and several of those which were written in the 1880's were full of detailed and accurate information; while those during most of the 1870's, like those of the 1890's after the *Manual* was left to Meany's charge, were merely statistical summaries. This is not to say that these statistical summaries were of little value, for they were always the most significant part of any of the introductions; but once they were initially compiled, it took little effort to keep them up to date.

Those introductions which included more than statistics were concerned both with the present and the past of American railroading. Several had a long historical sketch of the American railroad system describing its growth and its impact on the American economy. Nearly all provided a brief analysis of the recent railroad developments which often included suggestions for improvements and reform. These sketches were, to a large degree, extensions of Poor's earlier writings in the *Journal.* In writing them he not only carried out several of the services he had rendered earlier as editor of the *Journal;* but also the ideas and attitudes he expressed were pretty much those he had developed during and even before the 1850's.

In his historical descriptions and analyses, which made up the larger part of the early introductions and those written for the 1876, 1881, and 1889 volumes, he carried out his old role of spokesman for the industry.[41] In the early introductions he stressed the railroads' achievements and their tremendous impact on the American economy. In the later ones he helped defend the railroads against what to him and to them appeared to be discriminatory legislation. Most of the historically oriented introductions began with a brief description of the beginnings of canal construction in this country, with emphasis on the experience of the Erie Canal. This was followed by a description of the laying down of the early railroad system. Here Poor carried the story in some detail to the 1850's and gave in some volumes the dates of the opening of most of the major roads east of the Mississippi. Besides recording the progress of construction, the editor also documented the rapid increase in freight transported, particularly in the post-Civil War years, and the simultaneous drop in freight rates.

In so doing Poor emphasized the immense influence railroad construction was continuing to have on American agriculture and industry.[42] He pointed out, much as he had done in the *Journal's* editorials, how the railroad gave commercial value to much of the already settled lands of the South and West, opened large new areas for commercial agriculture and permitted the American farmer in all parts of the country access to the world markets. He also showed the importance of the railroad as a market for iron and steel and many other industrial products, as the creator of a national market for the output of all types of mills and factories, and as a stimulus to industrial production in new areas. Since a railroad opens up new demands and new resources, and since "the value of the tonnage traffic of our railroads exceeds, each year, six times their cost," Poor stressed, as he had done earlier, that the value of the commerce and wealth which the railroads created far surpassed the value of the capital invested in their construction.[43] By helping to expand the national wealth, the railroads had aided the country, Poor suggested in the late 1860's, to overcome easily the burdens created by the heavy costs and the economic dislocations of the Civil War. At the end of the 1880's he was writing that the railroads had come to play such a dominant role that the health of the nation's economy depended largely on their financial and economic position. "In this respect the railroad system may be regarded as the barometer of the entire industrial system." [44]

In the historical sections and also in other parts of his introductions Poor often commented on the cyclical or wavelike growth of the railroad system and its effects on the economy.[45] The great "waves" of construction were periods of high business prosperity; when the wave receded, economic depression came. These great waves of construction, he pointed out in 1889, "were checked only by extraordinary financial revulsions." [46] The first great construction boom beginning in 1849 had ended with the crisis of 1857, the second beginning after the war closed with the crisis of 1873, while the third, started in 1879, was slowed by the financial crisis in 1884 and after a couple of "years of hesitancy" had again surged forward.

The basic cause of the cyclical downturns, Poor reminded his readers, was building beyond current needs. This, in turn, resulted from overoptimism about the potentials of freight traffic. There were, in Poor's opinion, three other significant causes of too rapid construction. One was government subsidies, especially land grants; for in the years before the 1873 crisis a great deal of building had been done primarily to prevent the grants from lapsing.[47] Competitive construction was an even more serious cause. Poor in 1873 and again in 1883 urged stockholders of the great roads, particularly in the West, to protest against their companies' "suicidal" construction policies which resulted from competitive building.[48] The third cause was speculation on Wall Street.[49] Speculators there encouraged unnecessary construction in order to profit from the watering of stock, the manipulations of securities of new companies, construction contracts, and the sale of materials to the new roads. In the years after the Civil War Poor failed to warn against the breaking of the wave as quickly as he had done in the 1850's. He, too, was overoptimistic in the first years of the 1870's and the 1880's.[50] But in both 1873 and 1883, well before the major financial panics occurred, he warned that railroad construction and speculation were going too far.[51]

If overbuilding caused railroad construction to slacken, the long-term needs of the country for railroad transportation, particularly in the South and West, assured its revival. The rapidly growing population and continuing movement westward would in a comparatively short time provide, Poor maintained in depression years, traffic for those roads which had been built too far ahead of a settled population.[52] Meanwhile, under pressures of reduced gross earnings, many railroads were doing more to increase their efficiency and lower their costs. Other more provident roads took advantage of low prices to replace rails and equipment. Still other railroad companies, by suffering through the purges of financial and legal reorganization, had their financial structures placed in a much more healthy position. As a result, the roads after a few years of depression were well prepared to meet once again the demand for transportation by beginning new construction.[53] In all his writings Poor never really envisaged a limit to the long-term growth of the country or its railroad system. He was always completely certain that the nation and railroads would quickly pull out of any economic depression.

While Poor described the railroads' position in the nation's economy, he also spoke out for them against the growing demand for regulatory legislation. This was especially true in the 1880's when the protest of farmers and shippers against the railroads was reaching a crescendo.[54] Here Poor's main argument was that, because the railroad had provided essential transportation at decreasing cost, it was the farmer's best friend, not his enemy. The editor used his statistics to show how sharply transportation costs of agricultural products had dropped in the past two decades. At the same time he defended the differences in the per-mile rates charged for long and short hauls with the legitimate argument that, once the cars were loaded, the cost of transporting a shipment of freight a hundred miles was only a little less than carrying it several times that far. He further argued that if long-distance traffic had to be carried at the same rates as short-haul loads, many bulky products like corn and wheat could not pay the freight.

Poor's protests were directed primarily at legislation calling for positive control, especially rate-setting. He still favored legislation which by publicity and other means would prevent "illegitimate" and exploitive practices and would help honest rational men make sound business decisions. In his defense of the railroads against government rate-setting Poor used many of the arguments he had used in the 1850's. In fact, in the introduction to the 1881 volume he made a long comparison between the attempts of the New York legislature in the 1850's to re-impose tolls on the railroads and the current attempts in New York and elsewhere to regulate railroad rates.

In his later arguments, however, he made more explicit use of his basic economic and philosophical concepts than he had done earlier.

The rapid construction of the American railroad system was, he insisted, proof that reliance on the self-interest of individuals operating under conditions of unrestricted competition resulted in the greatest good for the greatest number. In the creation of this vast railroad network, "the only *role* of government has been that of a *police officer*." [55] The position of government had, in Poor's opinion, been most perfectly defined in the general railroad law of the state of New York which since the war most states had wisely imitated.[56] To change the role of government from this properly negative one to a more positive one could only lead to disaster. If the government rather than the railroad made decisions on business matters like rates, the decisions would be on political rather than economic or commercial grounds and, since such decisions would surely violate the natural laws of trade, government control could end only in chaos.

Such arguments were familiar enough in the 1880's, as were most of the rebuttals. True, rates had on the average dropped, but on the noncompetitive sections of railroads they had if anything increased. The railroads had, indeed, opened for the farmers the world markets. But that was just the trouble. Although neither the agrarians nor the railroad men appeared to have fully realized it, the farmers now had to meet the depressed prices of an overproduced world market. Competition, as Poor himself said often on other pages, was, by stimulating overconstruction and fierce rate wars, causing as much economic harm as good. This was because the railroads were not mere individuals competing with many individuals for the favor of other individuals, but a few great agglomerations of men, money, and material controlling vast economic power. Or, to use Poor's words in 1889, "the very mightiness of the contestants and the magnitude of the interests involved" constituted perhaps the "most potent cause of all" for the current demoralization of business.[57] Still, Poor could hardly have been expected to give up his long and firmly held faith in the positive good of competition and the negative role of government when this same faith was still held by so many and much younger businessmen, reformers, and even agrarians.

If Poor used the introductions to his *Manuals* as a platform to protest against government rate regulation and control, he also used them to urge railroad reform. Except for his support of the steel rail, the changes or reforms he favored were very much like those he had advocated in the pages of the *American Railroad Journal.* In his earlier introductions Poor pointed to the high operating costs of American railroads as compared to those in Britain or on the Continent.[58] To cut costs the editor advocated such technical improvements as the adoption of the steel rail and the substitution of coal or coke for wood fuel by Western as well as Eastern roads. Wood, he stressed, was the most expensive of fuels. The editor also pointed out, as he had done twenty years before, the costs of running at high speed. He urged the roads to concentrate on handling slow moving freight traffic. Passenger business, he reminded his readers, was, as it had been for a long time, little more than a public service. "There is no doubt," he wrote in 1869, "that some of our most important lines lose largely on their passengers, at the same time that this service seriously interferes with their goods traffic." [59]

More detailed were Poor's demands for financial reform. In words that had a familiar ring, the editor pointed out that the construction account was still used "to charge to construction what should go to the working account. By such means an extravagant show of net earnings is sometimes made, which suddenly disappears when the *working* account can no longer borrow from construction." [60] Even more distressing was the steady growth of fictitious capital.[61] Increases in stock capitalization made without any commensurate addition to the total plant meant that savings made in the costs of moving traffic were not reflected in lower rates but went to pay the dividends on the watered stock. In his first introductions Poor listed some of the worst offenders. In 1868 the Lake Shore whose construction and equipment had cost $4,868,428 had a capital account of $11,250,000; the ratio between cost and capitalization was about the same on the Hudson River; while the New York Central, which at the time of its consolidation in 1853 had issued $9,000,000 worth of new stock, distributed in 1869 a stock dividend of 84 per cent, amounting to some $24,000,000 in water.

During the 1880's Henry Poor condemned the continued watering of stock as one of the worst blights within the railroad industry and one which was a significant cause for the depression of 1884.[62] In the three-year period ending December 1882, Poor estimated that almost $975,000,000 worth of fictitious capital had been created by American railroad companies. The state laws forbidding the issuance of stock "unless its full equivalent is paid" were easily circumvented by the making of contracts under which construction was paid for in stocks and bonds which could be sold in the open market at any price.[63] Since the state laws were unable to prevent this evil, Poor insisted that the investor had a real responsibility. By refusing to purchase the securities of a railroad which watered its capital the investor would not only protect himself but also help assure a healthier growth of the American railroad system.

Poor also repeated his old fears about the difficulties of large-scale administration. Disturbed during the late 1860's by the tendency towards consolidation, the editor asked where the enlarged companies expected to recruit executives competent and experienced enough to manage their vast properties. Furthermore, he continued to be uncertain whether initiative and incentive, "activity and enterprise," could be instilled into the ever-expanding bureaucratic structures.[64] "Just in proportion as the mileage of a railroad is increased, will the sense of responsibility be weakened on the part of those entrusted with its management."[65] This dictum Poor felt was proved valid by the fact that in the United States the ratio of net to gross earnings tended to decrease as the average size of the American railroad increased.

For many reasons then the editor protested against the continuing railroad consolidations. They added to the cost of transportation by making management less effective. They provided an excellent opportunity for roads to increase capitalization without enlarging their plant. They removed the stimulus of competition which Poor considered essential to a healthy railroad system as well as a healthy economy. Yet by the mid-1880's the disastrous effect of competitive construction and the bitter rate wars finally began to convince even Henry Poor of the necessity for railroad consolidation.[66]

Poor's major answer to the problems of railroad administration and finance was much the same as it had been in the 1850's. More detailed, uniform, and regular publication of railroad financial and operating accounts, he remained persuaded, would help lower costs, improve administration and operation, and prevent financial exploitation and mismanagement. Therefore Poor continued to urge the states to expand the data required from the railroads and to better the quality of the compilations they published. He praised such state commissioners as Charles Francis Adams of Massachusetts and George B. Wright of Ohio for their achievements in improving and standardizing reports in their states.[67] In 1885, when testifying before the congressional committee chaired by Senator Shelby M. Cullom which was studying the problems of the regulation of interstate railroads, Poor advocated the creation of a national railroad bureau "to which all railroads should make full returns of their financial condition and the results of their operation."[68] If uncertain about the other provisions of the Interstate Commerce Act of 1887, the editor was pleased by its section 20 which authorized the new Interstate Commerce Commission to call for annual reports from the railroads and to prescribe a uniform system of accounts.

In the last years of his career Poor was able to see the reform he had so long advocated becoming a reality. The introductions to the *Manual* not only lauded the work of the national Interstate Commerce Commission, but praised even more that done by the different state commissions to improve railroad reporting. "Each year helps to bring about a better system and greater uniformity in their [railroad] reports, due very largely to the requisitions of Boards of Railroad Commissioners now appointed for nearly every state," the *Manual's* introductions noted. "The United States Interstate [Commerce] Commission has also rendered a valuable service in this connection." [69] The railroads themselves, especially through the agency of the recently formed Association of American Railway Accounting Officers, were likewise doing their share to assure more complete and accurate reporting.

In the 1890's the national commission's bureau of statistics, headed by Henry C. Adams, as ardent a believer as Poor in the value and power of publicity, accomplished a great deal. By working closely with the state commissions and the Association of American Railway Accounting Officers, Adams succeeded in bringing much new uniformity and system to railroad reporting.[70] His aim from the first was to have full, detailed, uniform reports for each railroad which would be checked and supplemented by a board of expert examiners who would personally examine the road's books and property.[71] This plan, which was not very different from the one Poor had proposed in 1858 to be carried out by the New York banking houses, was finally achieved through two acts of Congress. In 1906 the Hepburn Act gave the commission the necessary power to obtain from any recalcitrant roads the required reports, while an act passed in 1913 provided for examination of a road's books and properties.[72]

The statistical information Poor provided in the introductions to the *Manual* probably had more lasting value than his analyses and his suggestions for reform. These statistics not only provided the real meat of each annual introduction, but they also assured Poor's reputation as the leading American railroad statistician of his day. In compiling his data on the performance of the railroads of the United States, Poor relied at first on information from state documents and the scattered reports of important railroad companies. After obtaining over-all totals of miles constructed, construction costs, capitalization, traffic moved, earnings, expenses, and profits, he computed useful averages and ratios for each state, the different groups of states, and the nation as a whole. These included figures on cost per mile, earnings per mile, ratio of stock to bonds, ratio of net earnings to costs and net to gross earnings, average tonnage carried, ratio of freight to passenger earnings, and so forth. With such averages and ratios he compared the activities of the railroads of one group of states with those of another and the record of the current year with those of past years.

From 1872 on, Poor relied largely on data compiled from his own files; and until 1878 this information was condensed into three tables.[73]

Of these the most important summarized the information he had obtained about the individual companies. In this table the roads then in operation were listed alphabetically by states, and for each the following data were given: mileage, including one entry for main and branch lines and one for all other track; locomotive engines, passenger and freight cars; "general liabilities" including capital stock, funded debt, floating debt, and total cost of the road and equipment; train miles run, passengers carried, and freight moved; gross earnings from passengers, from freight, from all other sources, and total gross earnings; earnings less operating expenses; and dividends. The different columns were totaled for each state. The information in this table followed closely that which Poor had included in the *Journal's* stock and bond list during the late 1850's, except that it broke down traffic between freight and passenger.

The second table included totals and ratios of the primary table's data by states, groups of states, and the nation. After listing its population and area, it gave for each state and each group of states the inhabitants per mile of railroad, the number of square miles for each mile of railroad, cost per mile of road and equipment, the percentage of total receipts coming from passenger and that coming from freight traffic; the percentage of receipts to cost, the cost of construction and equipment, receipts per mile of railroad, receipts per inhabitant, the percentage of operating expenses to receipts, per cent of net earnings to receipts and to cost, and finally per cent of dividends to capital stock. In the body of the introduction Poor compared, on the basis of these two tables, the current year's performance with the past one. Occasionally he added briefer tables to illustrate these comparative studies. The most important historical statistics, however, were probably those included in the third major table, which was the one table Poor had included in his earliest introductions. This was a statement of mileage built in each state for the preceding thirty or more years.

The accuracy of these statistical tables was limited by the same considerations that affected the reliability of the information on the individual roads, that is, the correctness of the data submitted and the care taken in its transcription, compilation, and computation. The over-all compilations raised more problems than the editing of the text. First of all, Poor had to determine just what was a railroad. The editor decided not to include roads laid down for temporary use such as logging, coal, and other mining roads.[74] He did include those permanent roads used primarily in the operation of industrial concerns, especially if they had separate corporate identities. He also counted city transit lines if they were powered by steam locomotives. Next there was the problem of duplication; for often larger roads would include the operations of a subsidiary in reporting on their total figures, while the subsidiary would also report its annual financial and operating data.[75] Then came the difficulties raised by the different fiscal years the roads used. As Poor gave his information for the calendar year, this often meant computing the data from two different reports covering two different fiscal years. In getting accurate total figures Poor was also harassed by the failure of some roads to complete fully their questionnaires. In 1873, for example, there were no operating returns for 9,781 of a total 67,104 miles of road. On the 9,781, Poor noted, 6,427 were roads which were under construction or had just gone into operation and so had as yet no annual operations to report. This left three thousand miles of road, or a little under 5 per cent, on which traffic and earnings were not, or were only sketchily, given. "In such cases," Poor wrote, "we have made an estimate of these items based on the actual returns received from roads situated in the same group and transacting similar business." [76]

Finally there was the problem of allocating the data of interstate roads to the states through which they ran. Except for the mileage figures, however, Poor solved this by merely allotting the information to the state in which the road was domiciled. Thus, Poor pointed out, "The State of Iowa shows only $8,968,646 of earnings, and only $6.82 to an inhabitant, while the actual earnings of all the roads in operation in that State were undoubtedly twice that sum; but they are embraced in the statement of other roads which have portions of their lines in other states." [77] The editor felt this was not necessarily a handicap to the value of his table, for useful comparisons could best be made between regions rather than states. For this reason he grouped the states into five areas and gave totals for these areas, each of which he felt expressed "not only the natural divisions of the country, but [which] all differ greatly in the industrial pursuits of their people." [78]

The editor did his best, however, to allocate properly to each state the figures in his table of miles constructed annually in the United States. Here he used the data from state reports where he considered them reliable. Where no accurate figures were available from public documents, he worked out an allotment by comparing the information in his annual reports and questionnaires against the best available maps of the different areas. In computing mileage data Poor included just the main line and branches, not second track, sidings, and other mileage. He also corrected data given for preceding years whenever he received new information.

The mileage figures before 1868 presented Poor with a slightly different problem. Here he and Fisher in compiling their first mileage table in 1868 appear to have used the information from the old volumes of the *Journal* and from the *History,* although the figures in the *Manual* do not agree exactly with either those given in the *History* nor with those mileage figures Poor used to print in the *Journal* in the first issue of each year. The compilers probably made corrections in the earlier data for duplications and adjusted the figures by the use of more recent information put out by state reports.

The reliability of the *Manual's* mileage figures may be tested by comparing them to similar data from the Census of 1880 and from a study made by Frederick L. Paxson of railroad construction in the Old Northwest between 1847 and 1860.[79] The data in the Census of 1880's volume on transportation were compiled from a questionnaire sent to the roads asking them to report the amount of mileage constructed on their lines for each year since they began operations. Its accuracy then depended on the data available in each company's files and the care taken by the clerk assigned to fill out the form. Paxson's figures on railroad mileage constructed in the Old Northwest before the Civil War were based on a study of local newspapers and annual reports published during the 1850's. All three sets of figures are comparatively close. The total mileage reported by the census is fairly close to, though a little less than, that given in the *Manual* for the years up to 1851 (see Table I). From 1851 to 1853 the census reports about 10 per cent less mileage, for 1854 and 1855 about 10 per cent more, and after 1858 consistently about 5 per cent less. Paxson's and Poor's figures for the five states of the Old Northwest for the 1850's start and end fairly close to each other, but from 1852 until 1859 Poor's run consistently behind Paxson's (see Table II). All this suggests, as does a comparison of the mileage data in the *Manual* to the earlier tables in the *Journal,* that in compiling his information Poor did not count the mileage of a road until it was fully open for operation. He did not, for example, include, as did both Paxson and the census, the mileage for the Illinois Central and one or two other large Illinois roads until 1856 when they were almost completely open for traffic. Also he did not list most of the mileage of the Michigan Central until 1849. Again, the New England mileage shows a large jump in 1849 when several of the northern New England roads came into operation. In any case, this comparison with two other sources indicates that Poor's data, the most convenient to use and most readily available of the three, provide fairly reliable, if somewhat rough, figures of the annual growth, state by state, of the American railroad system.

Since Poor's concern with the *Manual* waned in the years after his retirement, his statistics were less complete and accurate after 1873.

TABLE I

Comparison of Poor's Mileage Figures
to Those of the Census of 1880

Date	Poor	Census	Difference
1832	229	329.80	101
1833	380	445.71	66
1834	633	659.63	27
1835	1,098	797.45	—301
1836	1,273	1,077.53	—195
1837	1,507	1,425.91	—71
1838	1,913	1,878.79	—34
1839	2,302	2,264.67	—37
1840	2,818	2,755.18	—63
1841	3,535	3,361.06	—174
1842	4,026	3,865.74	—160
1843	4,185	4,153.55	—41
1844	4,377	4,333.51	—43
1845	4,633	4,610.42	—23
1846	4,930	4,943.19	13
1847	5,598	5,205.70	—392
1848	5,996	6,262.16	266
1849	7,365	7,310.44	—55
1850	9,012	8,571.48	—450
1851	10,982	9,845.94	—1,136
1852	12,908	12,134.38	—774
1853	15,360	14,304.00	—1,056
1854	16,720	17,746.16	1,026
1855	18,374	20,198.99	1,825
1856	22,017	21,669.86	—346
1857	24,503	23,746.90	—756
1858	26,968	25,712.95	—1,255
1859	28,789	27,420.07	—1,369
1860	30,635	28,919.79	—1,715
1861	31,256	29,935.64	—1,320
1862	32,120	30,655.64	—1,464
1863	33,170	31,229.54	—1,940
1864	33,908	32,176.94	—1,731
1865	35,085	32,995.66	—2,089
1866	36,827	34,399.24	—2,428
1867	39,276	36,939.92	—2,336
1868	42,255	39,407.78	—2,847

In 1878 the basic table giving a summary of the operations of each road was dropped and in its place only a little more was added to the table summarizing the record of the past year's railroad performance by states and groups of states. When he first returned to the *Manual* office in 1881, Poor was too concerned with improving the accuracy of the information in the main body of the volume to think much about the statistical summaries in the introduction. But in 1883 he turned almost his whole attention to them. First of all he brought back the basic table to which he added a column for baggage, mail, and express cars; one for the length of line operated, and one, in addi-

TABLE II

Comparison of Poor's and Paxson's
Railroad Mileage Figures 1847–1860,
for Ohio, Indiana, Illinois, Wisconsin, and Michigan

Date	Poor	Paxson	Difference
1847	608	660	52
1848	679	750	71
1849	727	798	71
1850	1,276	1,105	−171
1851	1,846	1,691	−155
1852	2,426	2,545	119
1853	3,670	3,832	162
1854	3,963	5,628	1,665
1855	4,360	6,943	2,583
1856	6,626	7,872	1,246
1857	7,524	8,535	1,011
1858	8,669	8,915	246
1859	9,170	9,413	243
1860	9,592	9,514	−78

tion to net earnings, to show total revenue available. In his second table which provided statistics on performances by states and groups of states, he dropped the useful ratios and percentages. He added a new table which showed for each road for the previous five years the liabilities (value of stocks and of bonds outstanding) and earnings, both gross and net, as well as miles of road owned and miles worked. This, then, provided a quick reference for comparative study of a road's record over time as well as with the performance of other roads. He also included a fourth table which gave for the past year the location and mileage constructed by roads with totals for each state.

In 1883 Poor spent much time in training his staff to compile the statistical tables. He worked hard on this introduction because, as he wrote his wife, "I want for once a perfect example, then it can be followed." [80] He found creating such an example a burdensome task indeed.

> To give you some idea of its magnitude, [he wrote Mary], I would state that there are two tables of roads in which are entered 1600 different lines, each line calling for twenty-five different entries; so that for the 32,000 lines there are 80,000 different entries. *"Hic labor: hic opus est!"* If I had not the best lieutenants in the world the thing would be impossible — my foil is a little Shakespeare daily.[81]

In compiling his data Poor had the advantage of being able to compare them to the advance sheets of the Census of 1880's volume on transportation. This first thorough report of American railroads to be made by the census had been compiled by Arnin E. Shuman with the assistance of S. Wright Dunning, the editor of the *Railroad Gazette.*

In fact, when Poor found that discrepancies existed between his figures on current mileage and those of the census revised for the additions since 1880, he sent out a second questionnaire to get a new set of mileage statistics.[82]

The response to Poor's work repaid him in good part for the effort he had made. The *Manual's* editor must have been especially pleased by Dunning's long editorial in the *Railroad Gazette* praising "the careful, intelligent and conscientious work in the introduction which must have cost great labor (and all done after the rest of the work was completed)."[83] Dunning added that no one, perhaps, knew better than he "the extraordinary difficulty of securing and compiling, in anything like uniform shape, the statistics of *all* the railroads of the United States," even when he had the legal authority of the United States Census Office behind him. The *Gazette's* editor particularly approved of the comparative data provided in the introduction and in the sketches of the individual roads. The new introduction made possible, he pointed out, almost instant comparisons on a per-mile-operated basis of stocks, debts, interest charges, earnings, and dividends, as well as traffic carried, maintenance and operating expenses, and costs of construction and equipment. This statistical introduction, Dunning concluded, made this volume of the *Manual* the most satisfactory ever published and its compilation provided far and away the best set of statistics available on American railroads.

After Poor left the supervision of the *Manual* to Meany, the calibre of the statistics again fell off. Dunning and other railroad editors complained that too many typographical errors had gotten past the proofreaders.[84] Dunning was especially critical when the basic table summarizing the activities of each road was again dropped. He and other commentators, however, did praise the new tables Meany incorporated into the *Manual's* introduction, especially one which showed the dividend records of all roads for the preceding five years and another which listed railroads sold under foreclosure and included receivers appointed during the past year.

From 1889 on the United States government through the Bureau of Statistics of the Interstate Commerce Commission began to provide statistics similar to those which Poor had been compiling since the 1850's. Henry C. Adams followed fairly closely the procedures Poor had used. He presented his data by territorial areas rather than states, pointing out, as Poor had done, that comparative figures are most meaningful for areas with homogeneous economies.[85] He defined a railroad more rigidly than Poor, excluding elevated and street lines powered by steam locomotive and roads used primarily in connection with the operations of industrial enterprises. Also his official figures did not include a number of intrastate lines over which the commission had no jurisdiction. However, when Meany excluded a number of railroads "consisting chiefly of switching roads and roads operated in connection with other industries," and when Adams listed unofficial figures with his official ones, that is, data estimated on lines not submitting data, the mileage reported in Poor's *Manual* was very close to that listed by the Interstate Commerce Commission.[86]

Adams encountered many of the same difficulties Poor had in the compilation and publication of his information.[87] Serious complaints were made about the accuracy of transcribing and computing the data. The bureau's volumes required more time for publication than did the *Manual*. Adams had difficulty in getting complete information from some roads until his powers were strengthened by the Hepburn Act. The questionnaire sent out by the bureau was fuller and more detailed than Poor's. This made the final results more useful to the scholar and government official. But the investor, businessman, and often railroad manager continued to prefer the much more compact form in which the *Manual's* information was presented and the useful comparative data it included. At first even an economist like Arthur T. Hadley found the statistics in Poor's annual volume more useful than those published by the Interstate Commerce Commission.[88]

Editing the *Manual* and compiling its introductions gave Poor the most useful and satisfying occupation he had undertaken since he left the *Journal*. But here his accomplishments were in the collection and compilation of information rather than in its interpretation and analysis. This was largely, of course, because he devoted much less time and space to writing the introductions to the *Manual* than he had in penning his weekly editorials for the *Journal*. Moreover, because the work on the *Manual* did not require him, except for the years between 1881 and 1885, to leave Brookline often, Poor never regained the close contact he had enjoyed with the railroad world as editor of the *Journal*. This distance from railroad men and problems made it easier for the editor to retain a firm faith in the value of his earlier ideas and proposals and more difficult for him to understand and find new answers to the industry's changing problems and needs.

III

Except in the introductions of the *Manual* Poor wrote little about railroads in his later years. Save for a few articles dealing with the Pacific railroads, he concentrated his writing, as has already been pointed out, on broad problems of finance and public policy. These works on money, banking, currency, and national financial policy suffered from somewhat the same defects as the *Manual's* introductions,

They did not express the ideas of a man intimately concerned with the changing scene. Rather they were the views of a man who, no longer really active in day-to-day work, was thinking through his economic ideas and was seeking for generalizations which conformed to the realities of his own past experience and ideas.

Poor, like many journalists and businessmen who have retired from an active life, hoped to use his knowledge and experience to add something to the sum total of human knowledge by writing a broad synthesis about the field of learning in which he had become most interested. As in the case of most such ventures, Poor's writings contributed little that was new, even to his special field of economics and finance. They did, however, appeal to other businessmen with similar general experiences and ideas, and so they helped make Poor a spokesman of the Eastern financiers and bankers on the foremost economic and political issues of the last decades of the nineteenth century.

Of his later writings only those on the Pacific railroads were narrow in their scope. In penning these articles he was hardly acting as the spokesman of the railroad industry alone. Here he was little more than a paid publicist. The first of these articles, *The Influence of the Railroads of the United States in the Creation of Its Commerce and Wealth,* written in 1869, was intended to make a case for the giving of a land grant to the Northern Pacific.[89] Actually in the pamphlet Poor said little about either land grants or the Northern Pacific. Instead he used the statistics taken from the current volume of the *Manual* to develop one of his favorite themes. After indicating how the railroads were energizing the growth of American industry and the expansion of its agriculture, he pointed out that land grants would help assure the continuing rapid growth in the West. Nowhere, Poor added, would they be more valuable than along the Northern, the least arid and most fertile transcontinental route.

In 1871 and again in 1879 and 1880 Poor wrote articles defining the legal relations of the Union Pacific and the Central Pacific with the government. In 1871 the government and the railroads were disagreeing on the terms of the charter which called for the repayment of the government loan in thirty years with interest computed semiannually. Attorney General Amos T. Akerman insisted that this meant payment of the interest semiannually and threatened to stop payment on services rendered by the roads to the government if the roads failed to meet the interest charge. The railroads claimed it could be paid at the end of the thirty-year period. Poor in his pamphlet, *The Pacific Railroad: The Relations Existing Between It and the Government of the United States,* gave a lawyer's brief of the railroads' case.[90] The wording of the congressional act authorizing the road and the arguments used in the congressional debates over two Pacific railroad bills, he maintained, indicated that when the road was chartered nearly everyone realized that it could not be built without a government subsidy. If the interest were paid semiannually, he maintained, the subsidy would be less than Congress had intended it to be during the critical first years of construction and operation. He also stressed that the government and the nation had gained immeasurably from the building of this first transcontinental.

In 1879 Congress passed the Thurman Act which required the Union Pacific and the Central Pacific to pay 25 per cent of their net earnings into a sinking fund for the retirement of the debt. Again the roads, who felt the act placed an unwarranted and unconstitutional financial burden upon them, called on Poor to explain their position. In the first of three articles, one of which carried almost the same title as the 1871 article, he gave a factual interpretation of the various conflicts between the government and the roads.[91] He pointed out that in all cases the Supreme Court had supported the roads and would most certainly continue to do so by annulling the Thurman Act which violated legal principles and simple justice. Poor repeated his arguments in more readable, and less legalistic form in an article published in the spring in the *North American Review*.[92] When the Court upheld the Thurman Act, Poor registered a strong protest in a third article which he had published as an introduction to the *Manual* entitled "Review of the Decision of the Supreme Court of the United States in the Sinking Fund Cases."[93] In this lawyer's analysis Poor quite naturally followed the dissenting opinions of Justices William Strong, Joseph P. Bradley, and Stephen J. Field, who argued that the act was a violation of contract, injured public credit, created insecurity to all corporate property and took away property without due process of law. Poor undoubtedly was quite convinced of the correctness of all that he wrote for the roads, but he probably would not have bothered to write these articles if he had not been fairly well paid for them.

He does not seem to have been paid for one final article he wrote on the Pacific railroads in 1880. In *Land Grants to Railroad Companies to be Recalled Where No Rights Have Been Vested* he strongly protested against the attempt of the transcontinentals, especially the Northern Pacific, to obtain from Congress an authorization to extend the time allowed for the building of line in order to obtain the land grant.[94] Here Poor stressed, as he did in the *Manual* after 1873, that land grants stimulated both overconstruction and speculation.

Much more significant than his writing on the Pacific railroads were the books and articles Poor wrote about money and banking, since they provide a clear expression of the concepts of money and banking held by a number of late nineteenth-century businessmen. Poor's ideas developed not only from his own observations of the operations of American banking and currency during the 1850's and 1860's but also from long conversations on the subject with leading American financiers, particularly George S. Coe, president of the American Exchange Bank, chairman of the New York Clearing House Association and one of the most influential American businessmen of the day.[95]

Poor, who had written scattered articles on banking and money during the 1850's in the *Railroad Journal* and in the early 1860's in the New York *Times,* first tried to synthesize his ideas in an article written for the *Bankers' Magazine* in 1868. It was this article, "On Sound Principles of Banking" which led to his going to Washington to lobby with Coe for the Gold Contract Bill.[96] Although because of this essay he began to consider making a study of the financial history of the United States, he was too busy to begin such a scholarly task until he retired from his business activities in 1873. Then he went right to work writing "The Currency and Finances of the United States," which was published in the *North American Review* in January 1874.[97] The purpose of the article was, he said, "to demonstrate the principles that lie at the foundation of all convertible currency," rather than to suggest any detailed plans of currency reform.

For three years after the publication of this article Poor devoted most of his time to doing the research for and writing his magnum opus, *Money and Its Laws.*[98] This study he divided into two parts. In the first he compared the monetary "principles" he had established with those developed in the past by economists and other writers; in the second part he recounted the history of the financial policies and programs of the United States, indicating when and how the Americans applied or failed to apply what he considered the proper policies.

The generalizations which Poor first made in his articles for the *Bankers' Magazine* and the *North American Review* and then developed and defined in great detail in *Money and Its Laws* can be briefly summarized in the following way. Gold and silver are the natural mediums of exchange because they have in themselves real, intrinsic worth. Yet because modern business is carried on by accounting transactions and bills of exchange drawn on goods in transit, gold and silver are used only to balance the accounts of individuals and nations. Currency is needed to facilitate further business and commerce by supplementing the work done by the exchanges and the clearing houses. If this currency is to meet the needs of modern business it must be convertible; that is, it must be based on items having intrinsic value, which are gold and silver and commercial paper drawn against actual goods. A currency based on items like public securities or land mortgages which cannot be converted at once into items with real value will tend to lead to inflation and in time of economic and business difficulties may create financial distress by becoming worthless. Such "principles" made Poor a constant advocate of a single specie standard and a central bank. Currency should be based only on reserves of specie and self-liquidating business paper. The proper issuers of currency were banks which knew best how to meet local conditions. The issuance of local bank notes, however, should be controlled by a central bank which, as was done under the old Suffolk System in New England and by the former Bank of the United States, could at any time call for the immediate redemption of such notes at face value in specie or bills of exchange.

These generalizations guided Poor's analyses of all monetary theory, practice, and legislation, past and present. Because Poor, like most of his contemporaries, believed all economic action followed natural laws, his generalizations became for him laws applicable to all places and times. Thus in the first part of his book, where he gave the history of monetary theory, he found that few economic theorists had discovered the same natural laws of money. To Poor the writings and generalizations of nearly all these theorists from Aristotle to Adam Smith, David Ricardo, John Stuart Mill, and on to W. Stanley Jevons and William Graham Sumner were, therefore, absurd, foolish, and, occasionally, dishonest and immoral. That everyone else was wrong and only he right did not seem to disturb Poor in the least. The basic fault of his book is therefore not so much in the weaknesses of his generalizations but that he looked upon a generalization as a "law," a truth. This made it unnecessary, even if he had thought of it, to examine his own basic assumptions and values and to appreciate how really very limited were the experience and knowledge from which he derived his generalizations. But such intellectual sophistication is asking a little too much from a nineteenth-century retired business journalist.

The second part of *Money and Its Laws* which records the development of banking and monetary policy in the United States is more useful than the first. Poor does go to the sources, and his clear bias makes his analyses, if anything, more clear. Here, as might be expected, Alexander Hamilton is the major hero and Andrew Jackson the chief villain. Poor spells out fairly accurately the essential role the Bank of the United States played in developing the economic structure of the country and the real loss that was felt when its charter was not renewed. Civil War finance also receives much attention and here Salmon P. Chase runs a close second to Jackson as an irresponsible politician, illiterate in financial and commercial matters. For Chase was not only responsible for creating the worst kinds of "nonconvertible currency," both irredeemable paper money and bank notes based on public securities; but he also failed to make use of available banking facilities and existing "convertible currency."

The last chapters of the book are devoted to proposals for a program which will undo the damage Chase's mistaken policies caused. The first step must be to demonetize as well as to resume specie payments on the greenbacks. The currency necessary to take the place of the old legal tender notes should be provided by state and national banks which would issue notes based on gold and self-liquidating commercial paper. To do this the law placing a 10 per cent tax on state notes must be repealed; while the national banks should be allowed to return their bonds to the Treasury for an equivalent value of specie. Yet such reforms could only be successful if a central bank were created.[99] This new Bank of the United States with branches in every major city in the nation would act as a depository for government funds and a clearing house for state and national banks. These functions would permit it to call at any time for the redemption of local bank notes and so permit it to maintain, much as once had the Bank of the United States and the Suffolk Bank in Boston, a sound, flexible, and "convertible" currency. Such a plan would have undoubtedly improved the American banking system which certainly needed some type of central bank. But it would have hardly done, as the experience of the Federal Reserve in later years has shown, all that Poor expected. Nor did such a plan have any real chance of obtaining congressional approval in the late 1870's and 1880's. Yet in this case Poor's proposed therapy for the nation's banking and monetary troubles was probably sounder than his analyses of the disease.

In writing *Money and Its Laws* Poor received much help and criticism from George Coe. Coe, in turn, shortly after the book was published, called on Poor for assistance.[100] In 1877 the Eastern financial community was becoming disturbed by what it considered a new threat to the nation's financial and economic stability. The South and the West, the debtor section of the country, thwarted by the act of December 1874 which called for resumption of specie payments, saw in the unexpected decline of the price of silver a chance to return to cheap money. In November 1877 the bill proposed by Congressman Richard P. Bland for the remonetizing of silver which had been demonetized in 1873 and providing for its unlimited coinage at a ratio of sixteen to one passed the House for the second time. In early January 1878 Coe began to unite the financial community against the bill. He organized a committee of prominent bank officers, merchants, and representatives of insurance and trust companies from Boston, New York, Philadelphia, and Baltimore who were to petition Congress against the Bland proposal and were to communicate with the clearing house associations in other parts of the country urging them to make similar joint protests. Coe then asked Henry Poor to write the committee's memorial to Congress.

The memorial, a long one, was divided into three parts and filled with many tables of statistics.[101] First, by reviewing the history of coinage in the United States and Europe, Poor indicated why silver had been demonetized in Great Britain and most of the countries of Europe as well as the United States. This was because the difficulty of maintaining by law the proper ratio between the two metals had meant that the undervalued one was almost always driven out of circulation. Poor next answered in detail the charge that the bill demonetizing silver in 1873 had been secretly or underhandedly passed. He pointed out that in the three years from the time the proposal was made until it was passed in Congress ample publicity had been given to the bill which had been many times fully debated in Congress.

The memorial then goes on to describe the dangers which would result from the remonetizing of silver. If coined at sixteen to one, as Bland proposed, it would drive out gold coinage. However, since gold would remain the standard abroad, the use of a silver currency would interfere with our foreign exchange and foreign trade. Worse still, a depreciated currency whose basic value depended on the price of silver in the world markets would lead to inflation. At the same time, its fluctuations of price would put a premium on speculation. Dislocation of trade and a reduction in real wages and in the value of accumulated savings, the memorial concluded, would be the result of the Bland Bill. Poor finished his writing on January 29, and the next day he informed Mary, "a copy has gone to the President with as strong a letter as Coe could write."[102] President Harrison may have paid more attention to the financier's protest than did Congress, for he vetoed the compromise Bland-Allison Bill, which limited the amount coined at sixteen to one, after it passed the Senate on February 27, only to have it passed over his veto. Poor's and Coe's analysis seems sound enough. A silver standard at sixteen to one would have certainly resulted in inflation and encouraged speculation. Still, like most of their business colleagues, they failed to appreciate the inequities created by a gold standard, particularly in this period of deflation. Nor did they make any attempt to understand the real economic and financial needs of the South and West.

Poor used the arguments he had developed in the memorial in other writings. That spring he represented the East in a debate with Bland, the spokesman of the West, in an article which appeared in the pages of the *North American Review* under the title of "Debtor and Creditor." [103] Here he devoted most of his allotted space to answering the charges made by Bland that the demonetization of silver in 1873 was a subtle trick perpetrated by Eastern and European capital with "no other object than wholesale robbery of debtors." [104] Later in the year Poor finished a much longer study, *Resumption and the Silver Question*.[105] This book included a great deal more historical and comparative information on coinage and monetary policies here and abroad than did the earlier memorial, but its main arguments were the same. Poor also repeated his conviction that the most satisfactory answer to the currency question was the issuance of notes by local banks controlled by a central bank. In the 1890's, when the silver issue came to a political climax, Poor again took up his pen to call for the gold standard and an improved banking system. *The Money Question,* subtitled, like his earlier book on the silver question, "A Handbook for the Times," added little new in the way of ideas or interpretations but did fill in the details of the story of government financial policy from 1878 until 1896.[106] Written as a document for the 1896 campaign rather than as a serious analysis of recent currency problems, it was reprinted and used again for the elections of 1898 and 1900.

Poor also wrote campaign documents for the elections of 1888 and 1892. They ostensibly dealt with the tariff, but actually were concerned almost wholly with currency, banking, and the growth of the American railroad system. Possibly this was because Poor had difficulty in bringing himself to advocate the protariff arguments he had spent so many years countering. The first of these books, *Twenty-Two Years of Protection,* which Poor hastily threw together in the late summer of 1888, was historically oriented.[107] In it Poor divided the history of the nation into three periods: that of construction, that of "attempted destruction of the work of the fathers," which was, of course, a period of Democratic domination, and the period since 1860 of Republican rebuilding.[108] In discussing the later period Poor, again playing a favorite theme, pointed to the tremendous expansion of the railroad system and with it the growth of the nation. Since this growth took place for the most part in a period of high tariff, he added, as sort of an afterthought, that high tariff was responsible for it. The book was so poorly organized and carelessly written that it is difficult to believe it influenced a single voter. Still the Republican National Committee appears to have mailed it out in large numbers to all parts of the country, and four years later they apparently urged Poor to revise and republish it.[109] The new version, entitled, *The Tariff: Its Bearing Upon the Industries and Politics of the United States,* was much improved by Poor's revision.[110] The only section of real value, however, remained the one in which Poor used a large number of statistics from the *Manual* and elsewhere to show the influence of the railroads in creating the nation's wealth and increasing its national income.

If Poor's writings on the tariff, currency, money, and banking have comparatively little lasting value or interest, they did at least help make their author's life an active one. Writing on the paramount political and economic issues of the day kept him alert and well informed. It also helped him to feel that he was still playing a necessary and useful role. And so the long years of retirement were happy ones. During the winter and spring he spent his time reading and writing in the comfortable, well-stocked library of his home on Walnut Street in Brookline. There his days were enlivened by the numerous grandchildren growing up about him, and his work was stimulated by conversations with his many close friends. These friends, who included men of such diverse talents as Henry Hedge, Frederick Law Olmstead, Edward Atkinson, John D. Long, Ginery Twichell, and Moses Williams met weekly at each other's homes. The "Whist Club," as the group called itself, played cards, talked over the day's events and current issues and trends or discussed history, economics, philosophy, and religion. The Poors spent the summer and early fall in Andover, where Henry Poor always delighted in the beauty of the mountains, woods, and village of his birthplace. Here, too, grandchildren and old friends filled the house and leisurely recreation and pleasant conversation were the order of the day. Such was the life Henry Poor continued to enjoy until January 1905; and until the very end he watched with a keen and lively interest the continuing development and changes in the American economy which he had observed, recorded, and analyzed for well over half a century.

Appendix

Appendix: The 1854 Questionnaire

New York, August 21st, 1854.

Dear Sir: —

I have in preparation a work upon the Railroads and Canals of the United States, and I take the liberty of applying to you for information in reference to the road with which you are connected.

I beg leave to refer you to a succeeding page, upon which you will find a brief history of the Boston and Worcester Railroad Company, with a statement showing its financial condition at the present time. I desire a statement in reference to your road, similar to the above, varied of course to meet what is peculiar in its Charter, history, or condition.

I am forced to make a direct appeal to Railroad Companies, as the only sources, in many cases, of information. In few of the States only, are Railroad Companies required by law to make public reports of the condition of their affairs, and the results of the operation of their roads. It would be impossible therefore to secure that degree of accuracy, desirable in a work like the one proposed, without having the several statements corrected and verified by persons whose positions give them access to all the sources of information, and whose identity with their respective roads have made them familiar with their history. Even where I have the reports published by Railroad Companies, I prefer such Companies should furnish, in the manner requested, the data to form a basis for a Statement of their affairs, especially as it may be desirable to state facts which do not appear in any *published* report.

The annexed Statement of the Boston and Worcester Railroad is designed to serve as a sort of *model* of what I wish to obtain from every Company in the United States. The following recapitulation will show what that Statement contains, and what I wish to procure in each case.

1st. The *title* of your Company, its directors and officers, the location of its principal office, of its transfer offices, and the date of the annual meeting, or the close of its *financial* year.

2nd. Its chartered privileges, whether contained in the original act of incorporation, or in amendments thereto.

3rd. The first estimated cost of the road, with the estimated amount of its income.

4th. The date of commencement of work of construction; also of the completion of the several divisions, or sections, and of the whole road.

5th. A Statement showing the physical features of the route of your road, with its alignment and grades. Also a Statement showing the length of line, maximum and total gradients in either direction, with the length and inclination of the several planes, without going into too great detail. Also a

Statement showing the minimum and total curvature; also the gauge of the road.

6th. The pattern and weight of rail used.

7th. The total cost of road when opened for business; and for each succeeding year; also total amount of *stock;* the yearly mileage; cost per mile; gross receipts; current expenses; net receipts; dividends; receipts from passengers; do. from freight; do. miscellaneous; yearly earnings per mile, and annual per centage of gross and net receipts on the cost of the road.

8th. The total amount of capital authorized by charter, with the amount of paid up capital for each year. Also the amount of stock taken by corporate, or municipal bodies, and how paid; also the amount and nature of the indebtedness of the Company, and how secured; the amount of the funded debt, when contracted and when and where payable, and whether convertible into the stock of the Company; the rate of interest payable on funded and floating debt, and how and, where payable; also the contingent debt of the Company, if any.

9th. The rate and amount of dividend paid since the road went into operation; whether the same was paid in *cash* or *stock;* also the amount of earnings expended in *construction;* also whether any portion of the stock, and what amount, has *preference* in *dividends* over other, or *common,* stock.

10th. The length of *double* track; also of sidings; also the plans or measures in progress for the improvement of the road, and whether the same be in good or bad condition, and whether well or poorly equipped; the amount of equipment, or rolling stock on the road, and its value.

11th. What policy or measures have been adopted, if any, to provide a sinking fund for the payment of the indebtedness as it may fall due; also the present amount of sinking fund; also the amount reserved for repairs or equipment, whether of an ordinary or extraordinary character.

12th. The items that make up the construction account, classified under appropriate heads.

13th. A synopsis of the last annual report, with a Statement showing the character of the business, or traffic for the past year, the amount received from passengers; do. from freight; also the number, and receipts from *through* passenger and freight business, as distinguished from *local* or *way* business; also the expenses on account of *each;* also the different items that make up the expense account.

14th. The total number of miles run by the trains the past year, classified as *freight, passenger,* and *repair* trains; also total number of passengers and tons of freight, distinguishing the *through,* from *way,* or *local* passengers and freight, carried one mile.

15th. A copy of the balance sheet of your Ledger at the date of your last report.

In addition to the above, please add whatever in the case of your own Company may be important or desirable to be known.

I shall feel obliged by the communication of any facts illustrating the history, value, position and progress of Railroads other than those with which you may be connected.

Where a Railroad is in progress, please describe the route, the means at the command of the Company, the estimated cost of the road, the character of the work, the probable time required for its completion, contracts for construction, with such other information as may be necessary to a distinct idea of the object and condition of the Company.

In all cases I desire if possible to obtain *full sets of Reports* issued by the several companies: especially copies of their Charters.

I am aware that furnishing the information requested will impose a serious burden upon you. I would not trouble you were it not absolutely necessary to do so to accomplish the object I have in view, which is to present a full, concise, and correct history of the public works of the United States. I wish each Company to furnish the data as materials for its history. I hope it may be some compensation for your trouble that it will be the means of presenting before the public a correct and satisfactory statement of the affairs of the Company with which you are connected.

The progress of Railroads in the United States, and with these, of the country, in intelligence, in wealth, and in social comfort is without a parallel. A history of these works is a most interesting chapter in the history of the country, and better than anything else illustrates the force and practical character of our people.

Respectfully soliciting your aid and coöperation, I am, very truly.

HENRY V. POOR
Editor of the American Railroad Journal

Bibliographical Note

THIS STUDY is based largely upon a collection of Poor papers and the resources of the Baker Library at the Harvard Business School in Cambridge, Massachusetts. The Poor collection, which my uncle, Henry Poor Chandler of Washington, D. C., kindly put at my disposal, might best be called the Mary Poor collection. Mary Poor, like many nineteenth-century New England ladies, saved nearly all the correspondence she received from her family and close friends and also collected a large number of letters that she had written to the various members of her family. The collection includes the correspondence between Mary and her husband from 1838 until the late 1890's. Poor, in his letters to his wife, said much about his business as well as social activities. As a result the correspondence includes a good deal about Poor's work during the summer months, about his business trips, and about the years between 1864 and 1873 when the family lived in Brookline and he carried on most of his business in Wall Street and Washington, but it shows very little of what he did at other periods. However, some of the gaps can be filled in from the clippings, diaries, personal account books, and some unpublished documents which Mary Poor also saved concerning chiefly the early days in Andover. Very useful, too, was a much smaller collection of Poor papers belonging to Charles Lyon Chandler, professor emeritus, Ursinus College, which include business rather than personal correspondence. Standard and Poor's Corporation of New York City also has a few items concerning its founder.

In the Poor collection are most of Henry Poor's published books, pamphlets, and articles, which can also be found in the Baker and Widener libraries of Harvard University. A list of the titles of Poor's published works, all of which have been described in the text, has been compiled by the Library of the Bureau of Railway Economics of the Association of American Railways in Washington, D. C., in a mimeographed bibliography last revised in 1942, entitled "Henry Varnum Poor, 1812–1905 —— List of His Writings and Maps." The only important omissions are *The Effect of Secession on the Commercial Relations of the North and South* (New York, 1861), "The Proposed 'Pacific' Railroad; Features, Traffic and Provisions by Congress," *Proceedings of the American Geographical Society* 2:3–40 (1863–1864). *Three Secession Movements in the United States* (Boston, 1876) and Richard P. Bland and Henry V. Poor, "Debtor vs. Creditors," *North American Review* 127:117–131 (July–August 1878). The list also includes two works for which John P. Meany rather than Poor was responsible, "A Study of Railway Statistics" which was the introduction to the 1900 *Manual* and *Poor's Ready Reference Bond List,* first published in 1905.

Aside from the Poor papers belonging to Charles Lyon and Henry Poor Chandler, the most useful letter collection for this study was the

John A. Poor collection in the Library of the Maine Historical Society in Portland. This collection includes correspondence, reports, pamphlets, clippings, and so forth dealing with John Alfred Poor's work in the promotion and operation of the Atlantic and St. Lawrence and other Maine railroads. It was collected by his daughter, Laura Poor, when she wrote *The First International Railway and the Colonization of New England: Life and Writings of John Alfred Poor* (New York, 1890). The John Mussey papers, also in the Library of the Maine Historical Society, help round out the story of the part the Poors played in Maine railroading.

Of the other letter collections examined, only the William Reynolds collection in the Allegheny College Library in Meadville, Pennsylvania, and the Archives of the Burlington Railroad in the Newberry Library in Chicago, Illinois, include any significant correspondence of Henry Poor. An examination of the Thomas Wren Ward papers in the Massachusetts Historical Society, the John P. Cushing, the Bryant and Sturgis papers, and the records of the Northern Railroad in Baker Library revealed little directly about Poor but did provide useful background material. A detailed examination of similar records did not, then, appear to be worth the time, labor, and expense involved. I am, therefore, grateful to Professor Thomas C. Cochran for showing me his notes on the few letters that he found concerning Henry Poor in the papers of the railroad archives he had examined in preparation for his *Railroad Leaders, 1843–1890* (Cambridge, Mass., 1953). I am also indebted to Professor Leland A. Jenks for permitting me to use his excellent notes on British railroad investment in the United States.

More important than letter collections in a study of railroad and business journalism were, of course, the *American Railroad Journal,* the other railroad papers, and the leading business and commercial journals of the day. There is a complete file of the *Railroad Journal* in the Baker Library; and between Baker Library and the Library of the Bureau of Railway Economics can be found an almost complete file of the *Railway Times,* the *Railroad Record,* the *Railroad Register,* the *Railway Advocate,* the *American Railroad Review,* and *Hillyer's Railroad Magazine.* The only railroad papers published during the time Poor edited the *Journal* of which I was unable to obtain copies were the *Western Railroad Gazette* and the *Indianapolis Locomotive.* The latter is not listed in the *Union List of Serials.* Enough reprints of the former were printed in the *Journal* and the other railroad papers to give a fair picture of the *Gazette's* contents and policies. Besides examining the available American pre-Civil War railroad papers, I looked at those volumes of the *Herapath's Railroad and Commercial Journal* and the *London Railway Times* which are in Baker Library. I also went through the *Railroad Gazette* and *Railroad Age* for the post-Civil War years. In either Baker or Widener Library I was able to find almost all the volumes of such early commercial, technical, regional, and business papers as *Hunt's Merchants' Magazine, Bankers' Magazine, Commercial and Financial Chronicle, De Bow's Review, Western Journal and Civilian,* and the *Journal of the Franklin Institute.* The only important pre-Civil War business periodical whose files are incomplete in the Harvard libraries is the *United States Economist* whose volumes for the years of 1854 through 1858 are missing. Nearly all these journals have lengthy subtitles, but I have cited only the primary title by which each is referred to either in the *Union List of Serials* or in the other papers of the day. As all these journals are described in the text of this study it seems unnecessary to do more than list them here. Nearly all the railroad manuals and directories mentioned in the preceding chapters can be found in Baker Library, and the few which are not there are available in the Library of the Bureau of Railway Economics. Newspapers, which were used in this study only to supplement information found in periodicals and letter collections, included the *Eastern Argus* and the *Advertiser,* both of Portland, Maine; the New York *Times, Tribune,* and *Herald* and the London *Times.*

As useful as the railroad periodicals for filling out the story of American railroading during the 1850's, and particularly the story of railroad finance, is the superb collection of railroad reports in the Corporate Division of the Baker Library. Any important gaps in these reports, as in the case of periodicals, usually can be filled in at the Library of the Bureau of Railway Economics. These prospectuses, exhibits, surveys, reports, records of stockholders' investigations and regular annual reports are one of the most valuable and least used sources of information on early American railroad and business history. Not only do they give information, often in a surprising amount of detail, on the prospects, problems, operations, and finances of the companies, but they also provide data on the nature of the traffic moved and work done by the company. Another valuable source was the reports on railroad companies published by several states, particularly Massachusetts and New York. Probably the most informative of the pre-Civil War state reports was that made by the New York Railroad Commission for the year 1855.

Since there are many bibliographical compilations of printed materials on the railroad industry (see "Railroad Bibliographies: A Trail Check-List, August, 1938" mimeographed at Washington, D. C., by the Library of the Bureau of Railway Economics), it seems unnecessary to list here the large number of contemporary works and more recent books written on railroading during the period covered by this study. Far and away the most useful bibliographies for my purposes were those given in Frederick A. Cleveland and Fred W. Powell, *Railroad Promotion and Capitalization* (New York, 1909) and *Railroad Finance* (New York, 1912). These two books and Ray Morris, *Railroad Administration* (New York, 1910) remain the best available works on their specific subjects. Of the more recent broader studies of railroading Edward C. Kirkland, *Men, Cities and Transportation* (Cambridge, Mass., 1948, 2 vols.) and Thomas C. Cochran, *Railroad Leaders, 1843–1890* (Cambridge, Mass., 1953) are invaluable.

Notes

Chapter 1: The Editor

1. Mary Poor to Henry William Poor, January 14, 1873, in the Henry V. Poor Collection. Hereafter all letters cited unless otherwise indicated will be from this collection. The papers which belong to Henry Poor Chandler of Washington, D. C., are described in the bibliographical note.

2. The story of Poor's boyhood is based almost entirely on materials in the Poor collection. Especially useful for Poor's earliest years were two manuscripts written by Henry's brother, Silvanus, Jr., giving the history of the town and of many of its families; two typewritten essays on early Andover by Henry's oldest daughter, Agnes; and Henry Poor's own *History of Andover, Maine* (printed as a supplement to the Rumford Falls *Times,* August 13, 1904). The story is given in more detail in Alfred D. Chandler, Jr., "The Pen in Business — A Biography of Henry Varnum Poor," a doctoral dissertation submitted at Harvard University in 1951, ch. 1.

3. Laura Poor, *The First International Railway and the Colonization of New England* (New York, 1890), p. 13. There is some information on Henry Poor's early life in the first few pages of this book.

4. Leonora C. Scott, *The Life and Letters of Christopher Pearse Cranch* (Boston, 1917), pp. 23–24.

5. Stone's career is described in Nicholas P. Gilman, "Thomas Treadwell Stone," Samuel A. Eliot, ed., *Heralds of a Liberal Faith* (Boston, 1910), III, 358–361.

6. Scott, *Cranch,* p. 69, from a letter dated Bangor, Feb. 12, 1841. For Stone's views while he was at Andover, see Thomas T. Stone, *Sketches of Oxford County* (Portland, 1830), especially pp. 71–78. The ideas expressed here are more systematically developed in Stone, *Sermons* (1854) and "Man in the Ages," *Dial,* 1:175–182 (Jan. 1841). Both Henry and Mary have good comments on Stone's thought, especially in Henry Poor to Mary Pierce, Nov. 3, 1839, and Mary Poor to Feroline Fox, July 26, 1842.

7. Poor's introspectiveness as a boy and young man is apparent in Henry Poor to Mary Pierce, June 2, 1839; June 6, 20, 1840.

8. This pamphlet was published in Paris, Maine, in 1831.

9. For example, Henry Poor to Mary Poor, Aug. 30, 1863; and Henry Poor to the editor of the Brunswick *Telegraph,* July 12, 1886.

10. The courses required at Bowdoin at this time are outlined in Lewis C. Hatch, *History of Bowdoin College* (Portland, 1927), pp. 49–63, 75.

11. Samuel P. Newman, *Elements of Political Economy* (New York, 1835), *passim,* but especially preface and chapters 5, 7; also Joseph Dorfman, *The Economic Mind in American Civilization, 1606–1865* (New York, 1946), II, 743–745; and Dumas Malone, ed., *Dictionary of American Biography* (New York, 1946), XIII, 466–467.

12. Hatch, *History of Bowdoin,* p. 309; *Catalogue of the Peucinian Society, Bowdoin College* (Brunswick, 1838), p. 28.

13. Richard G. Wood, *A History of Lumbering in Maine, 1820–1861* (Orono, Me., 1935), pp. 74–82.

14. Henry Poor to Mary Pierce, Nov. 3, 14, 1839.

15. The quotation, by Thomas W. Higginson, is given in O. W. Long, *Frederic Henry Hedge, A Cosmopolitan Scholar* (Portland, 1940), p. 21. Long gives the best summary of Hedge's career; while Ronald V. Wells, *Three Christian Transcendentalists* (New York, 1943), ch. 4, has the most careful analysis of his thought. Nearly all of Hedge's ideas can be found in two collections of his essays: *Ways of the Spirit and Other Essays* (Boston, 1877) and *Martin Luther and Other Essays* (Boston, 1888). Henry Poor's correspondence shows that Hedge and Stone were close friends who often carried on long discussions in the Poor's home.

16. These views are expressed rather crudely in Henry Poor to Mary Pierce, Nov. 3, 1839; June 7, 1840; Feb. 5, July 7, 1841; and far more explicitly in Henry Poor to Mary Poor, June 20, July 15, Aug. 12, 18, 23, 26, 1858.

17. See especially *American Railroad Journal,* 22:136, 152–153 (March 3, 10, 1849); 23:520–521, 585, 694 (Aug. 17, Sept. 14, Nov. 2, 1850); 24:8, 33–34 (Jan. 4, 18, 1851). Hereafter the *American Railroad Journal* will be cited as *ARJ*.

18. Mary describes her participation in the intellectual renaissance of Boston in Mary Pierce to Henry Poor, May 21, June 7, July 4, 27, 1839; June 13, 1840; July 11, 1841.

19. The best of several summaries of John Pierce's life is William B. Trask, "Memoir of John Pierce," New England Historic Genealogical Society, *Memorial Biographies, 1845–1852* (1880), pp. 213–226.

20. For example, *ARJ*, 22:152–153, 313 (March 10, May 19, 1849); 23:328, 520–521 (May 25, Aug. 17, 1850).

21. Poor expresses his dislike of the law in letters to Mary Poor of Sept. 22, 1839; Dec. 20, 1840; and Sept. 7, 1863.

22. *ARJ*, 23:616 (Sept. 28, 1850).

23. Henry Poor to Mary Poor, Oct. 14, 1846; June 2, 13, 20, 1847; May 28, June 5, July 4, 1848; William Pierce to Mary Poor, Dec. 27, 1847, all touch on Poor's lumbering business.

24. John Alfred Poor's earlier views and enthusiasms are best expressed in his *Plan for Shortening the Time of Passage between New York and London . . .* (Portland, 1850); *Commercial Importance of Portland* (Portland, 1855); and for his later views on the same lines his *The Railway. Remarks at Belfast, Maine, July 4, 1867* (Boston, 1867); *Trans-continental Railway. Remarks at Rutland, Vermont, June 24, 1869* (Portland, 1869).

25. In her *The First International Railway,* Laura Poor tells the story of her father's railroad work in a discursive and laudatory manner. Far more satisfactory is the excellent account in Edward C. Kirkland, *Men, Cities and Transportation* (Cambridge, Mass., 1948), I, chs. 7, 14; also for a more detailed story see Chandler, "The Pen in Business," ch. 2.

26. Henry Poor, *History of Andover,* pp. 8–10; Laura Poor, *The First International Railway,* p. 29.

27. A petition of the citizens of Andover to the Maine Legislature, dated June 30, 1835, is in the possession of Silvanus Poor of Andover, Maine. The town raised two hundred dollars to finance Silvanus' trip to the legislature and also to neighboring villages to obtain local support.

28. There is a copy of this petition in the John A. Poor Collection in the Library of the Maine Historical Society in Portland, Maine.

29. Portland *Advertiser,* Sept. 23, 1844; a clipping from the Sherbrooke *Gazette,* Sept. 5, 1844 in the John A. Poor Collection. Clippings from this scrapbook will be indicated by JAPS; also Oscar D. Skelton, *The Life and Times of Sir Alexander Tilloch Galt* (Toronto, 1920), pp. 59–63.

30. Portland *Advertiser,* Sept. 14, 23, 1844; John A. Poor to Henry Poor, Sept. 10, 20, 1844. Both letters are in the John Alfred Poor Collection. Letters from this collection will be indicated by JAP.

31. The meeting and subsequent events are described in the Portland *Eastern Argus,* Sept. 25, 28, Oct. 21, Dec. 3, 10, 18, 21, 26, 1844; Jan. 1, 11,

13, 1845; *Advertiser*, Jan. 31, Feb. 27, 1845 and supplemented by data from JAPS.

32. Boston's efforts to win Montreal's favor are told in *ARJ*, 17:319, 321–323 (Oct., Nov. 1844); 18:156–157 (March 6, 1845); also in *Eastern Argus*, Jan. 4, 11, 22, Feb. 19, 1845; and *Advertiser*, Jan. 20, 1845. Poor's description of his celebrated dash to Montreal is given in Laura Poor, *The First International Railway*, pp. 34–41.

33. John A. Poor to Henry Poor, Feb. 17, March 21, 1845 (JAP); *Advertiser*, March 24, 1845; and several clippings from Montreal newspapers in JAPS.

34. Kirkland, *Men, Cities and Transportation*, I, 215–219, summarizes the story of these roads, and also, p. 210, describes the gauge controversy. There is much material on both these matters in the John A. Poor Collection. Henry was given the task of promoting the Androscoggin and Kennebec road, John A. Poor to Henry Poor, Aug. 29, 1846 (JAP).

35. John A. Poor to Henry Poor, Oct. 1, 1847 (JAP). Poor describes his scheme fully in articles published in the Bangor *Whig*, Nov. 4, 13, 23, 1847 (JAPS).

36. John A. Poor to Henry Poor, Dec. 7, 1847 (JAP); and an extract of a letter from John A. Poor to Henry Poor, Dec. 1, 1847, printed in Laura Poor, *The First International Railway*, p. 60.

37. Kirkland, *Men, Cities and Transportation*, I, 218–222, has the best summary of this plan, about which there is a mass of material in the John A. Poor Collection. Poor himself described it in detail in his pamphlet, *Plan for Shortening the Time of Passage between New York and London. . . .*

38. William P. Preble to John Mussey, Dec. 30, 1845; Alexander T. Galt to William P. Preble, July 3, 1845, a copy; John A. Poor to John Mussey, July 10, 25, 1845; all four letters are in the John Mussey Collection in the Library of the Maine Historical Society. John Alfred, while in Boston attempting to raise money, was stricken by an almost fatal illness, a direct result of his trip through the blizzard to Montreal. Henry hurried to Boston, remaining there for two months before he was able to bring his brother back to Maine. In several letters to his wife during April and May 1845, Henry describes nursing his brother.

39. The promotional campaign was closely followed by the Portland papers; especially good are *Eastern Argus* (Democratic), May 9, 14, June 9, 30, July 16, 1845; *Advertiser* (Whig), May 14, 16, 27, July 4, 23, Aug. 26, 1845; also *ARJ*, 18:156, 347–348, 602 (March 6, May 29, Sept. 18, 1845). There is much material on the organization of the campaign in both the Mussey and John A. Poor collections.

40. Henry Poor to John Mussey, Aug. 23, 25, 1845, Mussey Collection; clippings from Bangor papers in JAPS. Several letters in the John A. Poor and the John Mussey collections described the promotional campaign the Poors carried on in Bangor.

41. *Advertiser*, Sept. 26, 29, 1845; *Eastern Argus*, Aug. 12, 1845. For an indication of Henry's work after John Alfred's move to Portland, see John A. Poor to Henry Poor, Aug. 29, 1846 (JAP).

42. The work of and problems involved in selecting a route are told in John A. Poor to Samuel Poor, Oct. 8, 1845 (JAP); "Report of the President and Directors to the Stockholders of the Atlantic and St. Lawrence Rail Road Company, August 4, 1846," an unpaged manuscript in the John A. Poor Collection; *Report of the President and Directors to the Stockholders of the Atlantic & St. Lawrence R.R. Co., August 3, 1847* (Portland, 1847), pp. 3, 5–7. The annual reports will be cited as *Report of At. & St. L.* and date. All but the first of the annual reports were printed in Portland. The surveys were made by the consultant engineer, Alvin C. Morton, previously with the Erie Railroad, and James Hall, the local resident engineer. John Alfred was an active member of the board's Committee on Surveys.

43. John A. Poor to Josiah S. Little, Nov. 6, 1848 (JAP); *Report of At. & St. L., July 22, 1848*, p. 5; Laura Poor, *The First International Railway*, p. 58.

44. *St. Lawrence and Atlantic Railroad — Proceedings of a Special General Meeting of the St. Lawrence Railroad Company Held at Montreal on 30th of July 1846 and the Report of A. C. Morton, Esquire, Chief Engineer* (Montreal, 1846), *passim.*

45. Copies of Poor's correspondence as chairman of the construction committee are in one letterbook in the John A. Poor Collection, as is Poor's report to the committee.

46. The story of the formation of the Portland Company can be found in a circular published by Septimus Norris entitled, "To the Citizen of Portland," dated Jan. 12, 1847, in the Mussey Collection; and in a letter of Norris in *ARJ,* 20:25–26 (Jan. 9, 1847). *ARJ,* 22:521–522 (Aug. 18, 1849) gives a detailed account of the company's plant.

47. *Report of At. & St. L., July 22, 1848,* pp. 3–6.

48. John A. Poor to Josiah S. Little, Nov. 6, 1848 (JAP).

49. *Report of At. & St. L., July 22, 1848,* pp. 6–7.

50. *Eastern Argus,* Feb. 7, 16, 1848; *Advertiser,* April 19, 1848; Portland *Transcript,* April 22, May 13, and one undated. All these articles are in JAPS.

51. *Report of At. & St. L., July 22, 1849,* pp. 4–5.

52. "Fifth Annual Report of the St. Lawrence and Atlantic Railroad Company," printed in *ARJ,* 23:113–114 (Feb. 23, 1850); Skelton, *Galt,* pp. 71–72.

53. John M. Wood to John A. Poor, June 24, 1849 (JAP).

54. The terms of the contract are given in *Report of At. & St. L., Aug. 6, 1850,* pp. 6–7. Henry Poor, who was in Portland with his brother when the contract was finally signed, discussed it in *ARJ,* 22:567 (Sept. 8, 1849).

55. The details of the Canadian company's contract are given in *ARJ,* 23:113–114 (Feb. 23, 1850).

56. *Report of At. & St. L., Aug. 5, 1851,* pp. 5–6; *Report of At. & St. L., Aug. 3, 1852,* pp. 6–8. For completion of road and branch lines, see Henry V. Poor, *History of the Railroads and Canals in the United States* (New York, 1860), pp. 9–10.

57. Henry Poor to Mary Poor, May 14, 28, June 3, 1848, and Mary Poor to Henry Poor, May 18, 1848, indicate how well established the Poors felt. Hard times and departing friends are described in Henry Poor to Mary Poor, March 5, 1849, and Mary Poor to her parents, Jan. 21, Feb. 6, 1849. In the latter letter Mary tells of their decision to move.

58. *ARJ,* 21:675, 689, 725 (Oct. 21, 28, Nov. 11, 1848); Portland *Transcript,* Nov. 25, 1848 (JAPS). For Minor's difficulties in making the *Journal* pay, see *ARJ,* 19:753 (Nov. 28, 1846), 21:401, 593 (June 24, Sept. 16, 1848). For Poor's articles, see *ARJ,* 21:689, 690–691, 737–738 (Oct. 28, Nov. 17, 1848).

59. The terms of the purchase, including the sale of a third interest to Schultz, are given in a letter from John Alfred to Henry Poor, of which only the bottom half remains. This fragment is in the possession of Charles L. Chandler. For the sale see also *ARJ,* 21:801, 817 (Dec. 16, 23, 1848). The Poors showed good sense in having the *Journal* moved to New York. That city, already the publishing center of the United States, was in 1849 showing much more interest in railroad development than Philadelphia.

60. Henry Poor to Mary Poor, June 7, 1861. His salary is given in the letter on the sale cited above. By the late 1850's Poor's salary had been increased to two thousand a year, an excellent salary for an editor in that period.

61. Henry Poor to Mary Poor, Feb. 12, 1849.

62. Henry Poor to Mary Poor, March 5, 1849.

63. Poor indicates his policy on unsigned articles in *ARJ,* 22:280 (May 5, 1849). When he was to be out of town on short trips, Poor prepared editorials in advance, Henry Poor to Mary Poor, Sept. 2, 1859.

64. The nephews were Frederic Hedge, Henry Stone, and Walter Fox. Mary tells of her work on the paper in a letter to Feroline Fox, June 28, 1849.

65. Henry Poor to Mary Poor, Sept. 6, 1851; *ARJ,* 27:652 (Oct. 13, 1855). While persons in the book trade sold subscriptions and advertisements on com-

mission, the *Journal* had no regular authorized agents in the United States, *ARJ*, 26:408 (July 1, 1854). In Europe Alger and Street of London handled the *Journal's* foreign business, *ARJ*, 27:57 (Jan. 27, 1855).

66. Henry Poor to Mary Poor, April 26, 1849; for connection with Nova Scotia stone company, see *ARJ*, 31:381 (June 12, 1858). His work in railroad promotion will be mentioned in following chapters.

67. Mary Poor to Lucy Hedge, March 23, 1850.

68. Mary Poor to Lucy Hedge, Jan. 27, 1850. Mary describes Harris's congregation in letters to Lucy Hedge, March 23, April 23, 1850. Harris's career in New York is described in Herbert W. Schneider and George Lawton, *A Prophet and A Pilgrim* (New York, 1942), ch. 1, *passim*.

69. Mary gives her views and Henry's of Osgood and Bellows in letters to Lucy Hedge of Oct. 1, 1854; Jan. 19, 1855; and June 12, 1856, and their opinions of Frothingham in letters to Lucy Hedge of Feb. 14, March 13, 1859.

70. This quotation and those on Harris's congregation are from Mary Poor to Lucy Hedge, Jan. 27, 1850.

71. Mary's activities in these organizations fill her letters; especially good are the letters from Mary Poor to Feroline Fox, June 12, 1856; March 26, 1859; and to Lucy Hedge, Nov. 20, 1854; March 3, 1859. The reforms of the Misses Peabody, Blackwell, and Sedgwick are given in their biographical sketches in Dumas Malone, ed., *Dictionary of American Biography* (New York, 1946). Elizabeth Blackwell was Mary's obstetrician and pediatrician.

72. Mary gives good examples of the Poors' activities in these reform movements in Mary Poor to Feroline Fox, Oct. 26, 1851, and Mary Poor to Lucy Hedge, May 12, 1859.

73. Mary Poor to Feroline Fox, Oct. 26, 1851; Mary Poor to Lucy Hedge, March 4, 1852, March 13, 1857; Lucy Hedge to Mary Poor, Aug. 20, 1856.

74. These visitors are mentioned in Mary Poor's diary and letters. For the influence of Hedge as editor and Fox as owner and later editor of the *Christian Examiner*, see Frank L. Mott, *A History of American Magazines* (New York, 1930), I, 289.

75. Poor's active and influential role in the society's affairs is mentioned in the excellent history of the society — James K. Wright, *Geography in the Making* (New York, 1952), pp. 8–9, 17, 25–27, 32, 52–53, 398.

76. Many of these men who served on committees with Poor are mentioned in Mary Poor's diary and letters.

77. Poor's cartographical and geographical work is described in Wright, *Geography in the Making*, p. 27; *Annual Report of the American Geographical Society, 1857* (New York, 1858), p. 49; *ARJ*, 27:46 (Jan. 21, 1854), 28:254 (April 21, 1855), 29:408 (June 28, 1856).

78. Poor tells of some of the arrangements for his trip in letters to Mary Poor of May 12, 13, 15, 1858.

79. The financial history of the Mississippi Central is outlined in its published annual reports from 1853 to 1859; for its more general history, see Carlton J. Corliss, *Main Line of Mid-America; the Story of the Illinois Central* (New York, 1950), pp. 184–195. Murdock was a member of the firm of Chouteau, Merle and Sanford and had close business connections with the London banker, George Peabody. Muriel E. Hidy, "George Peabody, Merchant and Financier, 1829–1854," unpublished Ph.D. thesis submitted at Radcliffe College, 1939, pp. 332–333, 341.

80. Henry Poor to Mary Poor, July 11, 1858.

81. *Annual Report of the President and Directors of the Mississippi Central Railroad to the Stockholders, May 1, 1859* (Memphis, 1859), pp. 5–6. Poor wrote Goodman on July 16 that he had completed the negotiations. Goodman arrived in London to sign the contracts on August 18. While in England Poor spent a little of his time, he wrote his wife, "assisting Mr. Morton with his business" (Henry Poor to Mary Poor, Aug. 31, Sept. 5, 16, 24, 1858). Alvin C. Morton, the former chief engineer of the Atlantic and St. Lawrence, had during the 1850's become a prominent railroad contractor. In 1858 he had, among other jobs, con-

tracts to build a large portion of the Atlantic and Great Western Railroad, the broad gauge railroad which was to be the Erie's primary Western feeder. Early in 1858 some of Morton's contracts had been abruptly cancelled; consequently the engineer was in London trying to get the road's British financial backers to restore the contracts. This complex story is outlined in Paul Felton, "The History of the Atlantic and Great Western Railroad Company," an unpublished doctoral dissertation submitted at the University of Pittsburgh in 1943, and given in detail in letters from A. C. Morton to William Reynolds, Feb. 9, 1858, and to the president and directors of the Meadville Railroad (the Pennsylvania section of the Atlantic and Great Western), Feb. 25, 1858, which are in the William Reynolds Collection, Allegheny College Library, Meadville, Pa.

82. The interview with Stephenson is described in a letter to Mary Poor dated June 10, 1858. The following paragraphs are based almost completely on the long letters Poor wrote his wife in which he gave a day-to-day account of his activities.

83. Late in July Poor, apparently at the request of Benson and Fisher, answered statements undoubtedly made by Sampson in the financial pages of the London *Times* questioning the financial soundness of the Illinois Central in particular and American railroads in general. Poor maintained that a number of American roads had continued to pay dividends during the depression, that the Illinois Central was not a typical American railroad, and that, while, as he had always argued the Illinois railroad was a speculation, it should under the present efficient management become a highly successful speculation, London *Times,* July 23, 28, 31, 1858, New York *Times,* Aug. 13, 1858, and reprint of article in New York *Evening Post* in *ARJ,* 31:539–540 (Aug. 21, 1858).

84. Poor's paper and Murchison's explanation about Kane are given in the *Proceedings of the Royal Geographical Society,* 2:336–342 (Oct. 1858).

85. Henry Poor to Mary Poor, June 13, 1858.

86. Poor gave the printed materials he had collected to the Geographical Society, *Journal of the American Geographical and Statistical Society,* 1:95–96, 126–127 (1859).

87. Henry Poor to Mary Poor, Aug. 12, 1858.

88. The information in this paragraph is based on a brief examination of the careers of eight railroad editors and seven editors of other service journals. The railroad editors included D. Kimball Minor and John H. Schultz, Poor's predecessor and successor on the *Journal;* the editors of four of the *Journal's* major competitors, Edward D. Mansfield of the *Railroad Record,* Zerah Colburn of the *Railroad Advocate,* George L. Vose of the *Railway Times,* and Thomas S. Fernon of the *Railroad Register;* and the two most prominent post-Civil War railroad editors, Silas W. Dunning of the *Railroad Gazette* and Matthias N. Forney of the *Railroad Gazette* and the *Railroad Journal.* The editors of the service or trade papers include Hezekiah Niles of *Niles's Weekly Register,* John S. Skinner of the *American Farmer,* Freeman Hunt of the *Hunt's Merchants' Magazine,* I. Smith Homans of the *Bankers' Magazine,* James D. B. De Bow of *De Bow's Commercial Review of the South and West,* Thomas Prentiss Kettell of the *United States Economist,* and Alfred A. Beach of the *Scientific American.* Biographical data on Mansfield, Vose, Forney, Hunt, De Bow, and Beach can be found in the *Dictionary of American Biography;* on Colburn in *Appleton's Cyclopedia of American Biography* (New York, 1887–1890), I, 682–683; on Dunning in *National Cyclopaedia of American Biography* (New York, 1892–1938), XX, 129; on Skinner in Albert L. Demaree, *The American Agricultural Press* (New York, 1941), pp. 23–25, 89; on Kettell, *De Bow's Review,* 8:86 (Jan. 1850). Some information on Schultz, Kettell, and Homans can be found in Mott, *A History of American Magazines,* I, 681–682, 696, II, 94, 299. The best source for data on most of these men is their own papers. Of the important railroad editors only John Haven of the *Railway Times* says nothing about himself. Demaree, *American Agricultural Press,* p. 69, points out that the great majority of farm editors were journalists before they began editing their agricultural papers.

89. The background and interests of the mid-nineteenth-century railroad entrepreneurs are given in Francis W. Gregory and Irene D. Neu, "The American Industrial Elite in the 1870's — Their Social Origins," in William Miller, ed., *Men in Business* (Cambridge, Mass., 1952), pp. 197–203 and Thomas C. Cochran, *Railroad Leaders, 1845–1890* (Cambridge, Mass., 1953), pp. 220, 223.

Chapter 2: The American Railroad Journal

1. Two other types of periodicals supplying information useful to business professions were the journals of medicine and law. The first of these carried little information that might be classed as business or economic information. The latter did, but in the first half of the nineteenth century the legal journals did little more than report cases, Frank L. Mott, *A History of American Magazines,* I (New York, 1930), 451–452, II (Cambridge, Mass., 1938), 93.

2. Frank L. Mott, *American Journalism* (New York, 1941), pp. 49–52, 181–182, 187, 260; also Robert G. Albion, *The Rise of the New York Port, 1815–1860* (New York, 1939), 281, 329, 331.

3. Norval N. Luxon, *Niles' Weekly Register* (Baton Rouge, 1947), *passim; Fisher's National Magazine,* published for a few years in the 1840's, carried, like *De Bow's* and the *Western Journal,* some commercial and financial information. For brief comments on *De Bow's Review* and the *Western Journal,* see Mott, *History of American Magazines,* II, 116, 338–348. Some information on Hazard's publication, like those of Hunt and De Bow, can be found in their biographical sketches in Dumas Malone, ed., *Dictionary of American Biography* (New York, 1946).

4. The nature of these two, like *Hunt's Merchants' Magazine,* will be made clear in the following chapters. For publications of Gouge and Raguet, see their biographical sketches in Dumas Malone, ed., *Dictionary of American Biography.*

5. The story of the farm journals is well told in Albert L. Demaree, *The American Agricultural Press, 1819–1860* (New York, 1941); for their major function in providing information see chs. 2, 3, 10; for sources of information, ch. 3; for advertising, ch. 6; for number of periodicals, p. 17; for Skinner, ch. 2.

6. Skinner's *American Farmer* was preceded only by the *Agricultural Museum,* which was published for less than a year in 1810 in Georgetown, D. C. For brief comments on the early scientific journals and the mechanics magazines, see Mott, *History of American Magazines,* I, 151–152, 302–305, 445–446, 556–558; II, 78–79, 316–319.

7. The names of the majority of industrial journals published in the 1850's are in Mott, *History of American Magazines,* II, 92. Before 1849 there were two local papers in the mining regions which concentrated on providing mining information. They were the Pottsville (Pa.) *Mining Journal,* founded in the 1820's, and the Marquette (Mich.) *Mining Journal,* started in 1845. Another, *The Mining Journal,* began publication in New York in 1847 and carried on a feeble existence until Poor purchased it in 1849.

8. *ARJ,* 2:79 (Feb. 2, 1833) gives a good description of Minor's publications.

9. Henry Poor to Mary Poor, March 5, 1849. John Alfred estimated an income of $7,500 from 1,500 subscriptions and $1,000 from advertising; see fragment of letter from John Alfred Poor to Henry Poor belonging to Charles L. Chandler.

10. The subscription price of the *Journal* was $3.00 from 1832 through 1834, $5.00 from 1835 through 1842, $3.00 from 1843 through 1845, and $5.00 after 1846. Throughout Poor's editorship it remained at $5.00 a year.

11. Minor's *Railroad Journal* was not the first railroad paper in the country. Six months before Minor began publishing the *Journal,* the *Railroad Advocate* of Rogersville, Tennessee, was started. Minor was unaware of its existence when he first put out the *Journal.* The *Advocate* was published for less than a year, in-

cluded much more than railroad news, and had no noticeable effect on the *Journal* or on American business, trade, and technical journalism in general.

12. *ARJ*, 1:68 (Jan. 28, 1832). Minor printed similar letters from William G. McNeil, Benjamin Wright, Jonathan Knight, James P. Stabler, and Casper Weaver in the issue of Sept. 1, 1832, pp. 562, 563, 569.

13. The many prominent engineers contributing articles to the *Journal* included: Benjamin Wright, James Knight, Ephraim Beach, Robert Mills, William Gibbs, Alexander Twining, John M. Fessenden, John C. Trautwine, John E. Jervis, J. Edgar Thomson, Benjamin H. Latrobe, William R. Casey, Herman Haupt, Edwin F. Johnson, Ellwood Morris, B. Aycrigg, Charles B. Stuart, Benjamin F. Isherwood, Charles L. Schlatter, J. S. Van de Graff, Uriah A. Boyden, Squire Whipple, John A. Roebling, William H. Talcott, Christian E. Detmold, and Charles Ellet.

14. *ARJ*, 5:417 (July 9, 1836); for sale to Hedge, see *ARJ*, 8:352 (June 1, 1839). In September 1837 the *Journal* was temporarily forced to suspend publication. The remaining 1837 issues were printed in the spring of 1838. When regular publication was resumed in July 1838, the number of pages was reduced and the paper was printed twice a month instead of weekly. In 1843 and 1844 it was published only monthly.

15. Printed in *ARJ*, 16:336 (Nov. 1843). A more detailed analysis of the *Journal* as an engineers' paper is given in Alfred D. Chandler, Jr., "The Pen in Business — A Biography of Henry Varnum Poor," ch. 3.

16. Ellet's numerous articles were probably the first significant contributions to railroad economics in this country. Particularly interesting are his suggestions for cutting later operating costs by laying out and constructing new roads more exactly to meet the requirements of anticipated traffic. His articles include *ARJ*, 10:122–127, 145–151 (Feb. 15, March 1, 1840); 11:227–229, 293–296, 323–325, 355–357 (Oct. 15, Nov. 15, Dec. 1, 15, 1840); 12:16–28 (Jan. 1, 1841); 14:65–66, 78–84, 131–133 (Feb. 1, March 1, 1842); 15:70–71, 130–135 (Aug. 1, Sept. 1, 1842); 16:21–26, 341–349, 353–362 (Jan., Nov., Dec., 1843); 17:1–8, 97–106 (Jan., April, 1844). The controversy raised by Ellet's views was carried on in the pages of the *Journal* from 1840 until 1845.

17. The variety of the contributions can be seen by listing the articles submitted by John A. Roebling, a German born and trained engineer who became America's most famous bridge builder. Roebling's first article, published in March 1838, the year he began his engineering career in the United States, dealt with the "Relative Value of the Different Kinds of Steam, from Different Liquids as a Moving Power." This was followed in December 1838 by "An Essay on the Obstruction of Streams by Dams; with Formulae for Ascertaining the Rise of Water Caused by Their Construction," and "A Treatise on Reservoir Locks." In 1840 an article he sent Schaeffer on the "Theory of the Crank, with Reference to De Pambour's Mode of Calculating the Propelling Power of a Locomotive Engine," stirred up a professional controversy that filled the pages of the *Journal* for more than a year. In 1841 Roebling's contributions included "Plan for Constructing Railroads," "The Motion of Bodies on Curved Inclined Planes, and the Controversy, Pending on the 'Theory of the Crank,' Settled," and his classic article, "Some Remarks on Suspension Bridges, and on the Comparative Merits of Cable and Chain Bridges." Two years later he described the result of his initial efforts at making rope wire in "American Manufacture of Wire Ropes for Inclined Planes, Standing Rigging, Mines, Tillers, etc." After Roebling began to manufacture wire rope on a large scale, first in western Pennsylvania and then at Trenton, New Jersey, he contributed less frequently to the *Journal,* although two of his best-known essays, one on the construction of his suspension bridge across the Ohio at Pittsburgh and the other on the proposed railroad from Philadelphia to Pittsburgh, appeared in 1846 and 1847. *ARJ*, 7:7–9, 330–338, 361–366 (July 1, Dec. 1, 15, 1838); 10:161–168, 264–265 (March 15, May 1, 1840); 11:66–68, 325–328 (Aug. 1, Dec. 1, 1840); 12:9–16, 66–68, 161–166, 193–196

(Jan. 1, Feb. 1, March 15, April 1, 1841); 13:196–197 (Oct. 1, 1841); 16:321–324 (Nov., 1843); 18:631, 648–649 (Oct. 2, 9, 1845); 19:376–377 (June 13, 1846); 20:122–125, 138–140, 155–156 (Feb. 20, 27, March 6, 1847).

18. *ARJ*, 4:737 (Nov. 28, 1835).

19. For example, see Carlo di Ghega, *Die Baltimore-Ohio-Eisenbahn . . .* (Vienna, 1844), pp. ix–xvi, 1–2; David Stevenson, *Sketch of the Civil Engineering of North America* (London, 1838), pp. 253–257; Franz Anton von Gerstner, "Railroads in the Kingdom of Belgium Compared with Those in the United States," *ARJ*, 9:5–6 (July 1, 1839).

20. Besides the works of di Ghega and Stevenson cited above, these European studies of American railroading in this period include, Franz Anton von Gerstner, *Die Innern Communicationen der Vereingten Staaten von Nordamerica*, 2 vols. (Vienna, 1842–1843); Michel Chevalier, *Les Voies de Communication aux États-Unis* (Paris, 1837); and Guilliaume Tell Poussin, *Chemins de Fer Americans . . .* (Paris, 1836). Significantly, the best studies on early American railroads were published in Vienna and Paris. The most thorough of these works was von Gerstner's.

21. *ARJ*, 17:18–20 (Jan. 1844); Ellet's comments on the collection and reliability of railroad statistics are in *ARJ*, 17:105 (April 1844); for von Gerstner's complaints see *ARJ*, 8:2–3 (Jan. 1, 1839); for Poussin's, *ARJ*, 18:744 (Nov. 20, 1845); for Stevenson's, his *Civil Engineering*, p. 256.

22. In the United States, there were very few professional schools until the 1850's and no effective national professional engineering societies until after the Civil War. During the late 1830's and 1840's prominent engineers like Benjamin Latrobe and the *Journal's* editor, Schaeffer, did their best to organize an American Society of Civil Engineers and to encourage the development of technical education. Latrobe's concerted but unsuccessful effort to found a national engineering society can be followed in detail in *ARJ* 8:153–157, 193–195, 225–232 (March 1, April 1, 15, 1839); 10:65–66, 81–84 (Feb. 1, 1840). After this attempt failed Latrobe wrote "that pen, ink, paper and the mails must, at last, be the grand medium of communicating among the Profession." He urged the engineers to assure the supply of and channel for technical information by subsidizing either the *American Railroad Journal* or the *Journal of the Franklin Institute*, *ARJ*, 16:334–337 (Nov. 1843). The engineers failed to take any action on Latrobe's suggestion.

23. Besides *Herapath's Railway Magazine* and the *Railway Times*, they included the *Railway Record* and the *Railway Register*, both monthlies, the *Railway Express*, whose intervals of publication are uncertain, and the *Railroad Monitor*, the *Economist's* railroad supplement.

24. *ARJ*, 17:352 (Nov. 1844).

25. For example, the enthusiastic support he gave John Alfred Poor's Atlantic and St. Lawrence; see *ARJ*, 18:156, 347–348, 602 (March 6, May 29, Sept. 18, 1845).

26. Hewson and the other assistant editor wrote for a small fixed salary and initialed their articles; see *ARJ*, 27:632 (Oct. 7, 1854). For Hewson's policies, see *ARJ*, 22:393, 395, 424 (June 23, July 7, 1849).

27. James G. Wilson and John Fiske, editors, *Appleton's Cyclopaedia of American Biography* (New York, 1887–1890), I, 682–683; *Transactions of the American Society of Mechanical Engineers* (1882), III, 37.

28. For example, "Concentration of Power; as Applied to the Leading New England Roads," beginning with *ARJ*, 27:102 (Feb. 18, 1854); and "The Economy of Railroads, as Affected by the Adoption of Locomotive Power —— Addressed to the Railroad Interests of New England," beginning *ARJ*, 27:193 (April 1, 1854).

29. *ARJ*, 33:89–90 (Feb. 5, 1859); *Railroad Advocate*, May 5, Dec. 1, 1855, Feb. 23, 1856.

30. *Railroad Advocate*, April 19, 1856.

31. For their financial difficulties and their attempt to sell the *Advocate* to Thomas S. Feron, editor of the *United States Railroad and Mining Register* (during its first year of publication it was entitled the *Pennsylvania Railroad and Mining Register;* hereafter cited as *Railroad Register*), see *Railroad Register,* 3:148 (Oct. 3, 1857); 4:32, 42 (Jan. 30, Feb. 6, 1858). Its editors then went to England, where they gathered material for comparative studies of the mechanical aspects of British and American railroading, which they published in 1859. Colburn remained in England, first writing for the *Engineer,* a technical paper founded in 1856, and then, after 1866, editing his own paper, *Engineering,* which soon became one of the best engineering papers in the world. Holley, after returning to the United States, turned his energies to introducing and developing the Bessemer steel process in the United States.

32. *Appleton's Mechanics Magazine and Engineers' Journal,* which was published only from 1851 to 1853, carried a number of articles on engineering subjects. For the decision of the American *Railway Times* to become an engineering paper see the issue of Dec. 24, 1859. Unless otherwise indicated a citation to the *Railway Times* will refer to the *American Railway Times* rather than the London *Railway Times.*

33. *ARJ,* 22:273 (May 5, 1849). For Hodge, see *Appleton's Cyclopaedia,* III, 224. Among other interesting articles Hodge gave in the *Journal* some of the first full length descriptions of the Lake Superior iron and copper mining regions.

34. Terms of purchase are in *ARJ,* 22:392 (June 23, 1849). After the founding of the *Mining Journal* in New York in 1847, Minor had added, "and Iron Manufacturers and Mining Gazette" to the title of his paper, but he did almost nothing to make this name valid. By the same token, the *Mining Journal* carried very little to justify the words "American Railroad Gazette" as part of its title.

35. Hodge helped Abram Hewett, John F. Winslow, and other iron manufacturers to organize conventions in 1849 and 1850, and to demand an increase in the tariff. He also represented the iron makers in Washington in 1850. See *ARJ,* 22:184, 753, 755, 791–792 (March 24, Dec. 1, 15, 1849); 23:470 (July 27, 1850).

36. This contact with the engineer also affected the content of his writings, for Poor, like Latrobe and Schaeffer, encouraged in his editorials the development of technical schools and societies.

37. For an example of an early bid for construction contracts see *ARJ,* 1:224 (March 31, 1832); contractors in these first years of railroading urged the companies to advertise their bids in the *Journal, ARJ,* 2:688 (Nov. 2, 1833).

38. For example, *ARJ,* 27:64 (Jan. 25, 1854).

39. *ARJ,* 28:115 (Feb. 24, 1855); also important is *ARJ,* 24:507 (Aug. 9, 1851). Occasionally firms advertised to supply railroads and contracting firms with reliable laborers and to forward these laborers to any desired location, for example, *ARJ,* 24:824, 832 (Dec. 27, 1851).

40. For advertising rates see *ARJ,* 22:112 (Feb. 17, 1849); 27:313 (May 20, 1854); 28:624 (Sept. 29, 1855); for the new unnumbered pages to take the increased advertising see *ARJ,* 24:8 (Jan. 4, 1851).

41. In 1854 the *Railway Times* charged $5.00 for a square of sixteen lines; the *Journal* charged $0.25 a line per month or $4.00 for sixteen lines, *Railway Times,* Oct. 16, 1854, *ARJ,* 27:313 (May 20, 1854). The amount of space in a square was smaller in the *Journal* than in the *Railway Times.* The *Railroad Record* of Cincinnati charged $4.00 a column and $10.00 a page when the *Journal* was asking $10.00 a column and $25.00 a page. *Railroad Record,* 1:59 (March 22, 1853). The rates listed in other railroad papers were about the same as the *Railroad Record.* For contemporary advertising rates in other periodicals, see Mott, *History of American Magazines,* II, 14.

42. The *Railroad Register* of Philadelphia at first charged $3.00, but almost at once lowered its price to $2.00, *Railroad Register,* 1:141 (Sept. 27, 1856); 3:4, 148 (May 30, Oct. 3, 1857); Mott, *History of American Magazines,* II, 13, gives the standard subscription price of this period at $3.00 a year,

43. For examples of complaints and special offers see *Railroad Record,* 1:817 (Feb. 23, 1854); *Railroad Advocate,* Dec. 30, 1854, Jan. 12, March 15, Sept. 13, 1856; *Railroad Register,* 1:141, 148 (Sept. 27, Oct. 4, 1856), 3:66 (Sept. 18, 1858), 6:162 (March 5, 1859).

44. Henry Poor to Mary Poor, March 5, 1849.

45. *ARJ,* 23:8 (Jan. 5, 1851); *ARJ,* 27:312–313 (May 20, 1854). The *Railway Times,* December 19, 1850, January 1, 1852, claimed 8,000 to 11,000 circulation; the *Railroad Record* claimed 16,000, but these claims may have referred to readers rather than subscribers. The leading English periodicals, *Herapath's Railway Magazine* (London) and *Railway Times* (London), claimed 1,570 and 2,180 respectively in 1842 at the beginning of the English railroad expansion. *Railway Gazette* (London), 79:521 (1943). Mott, *History of American Magazines,* II, 10, gives the average circulation of the weekly periodicals in the 1850's as 2,400 copies. Demaree, *American Agricultural Press,* p. 36, gives the size of the subscription list of Skinner's *American Farmer* at between 1,500 and 2,000.

46. It is almost impossible, given the available information, to estimate the costs of printing and publishing the *Journal* and, therefore, to estimate exactly the profits Poor and Schultz received and Poor's actual income. In 1843 Benjamin Latrobe estimated the cost of putting out 1500 copies of a periodical similar to the *Journal* at $6,588 a year (*ARJ,* 16:339–340 [Nov. 1843]). He divided this into $2,038 for printing, including "composition, press and paper"; $2,200 for publishing, including "advertising, commissions, envelopes, postage, etc."; and $2,350 for editing, including apparently the editor's salary and office expenses. These estimates fit closely with the partial estimates of cost made by John Alfred Poor to Henry Poor just before they purchased the paper (in fragment of letter in possession of Charles L. Chandler). If by the mid-fifties the number of copies of the *Journal* issued weekly was over 4,500 and since costs had risen quite rapidly in that decade, the cost of printing and publishing a paper like the *Journal* might be estimated at $13,000. The editor's salary was then $2,000, the salary of an editorial assistant was probably $1,000, and office rent and expenses $1,000 —— a total of $17,000. This would exclude payment to assistant editors or contributors. If the *Journal* had 4,000 subscribers, its annual income at this time would be $20,000. Add to this an estimated income of $9,000 to $10,000 from advertising. In such a case, the profit would be around $12,000 to $13,000. Of this Schultz received anywhere from one-third to two-thirds. Given these profits and his salary, Poor's annual income was somewhere between $6,000 and $10,000. This was a good income at a time when the general superintendent of the New York Central Railroad received a top salary of $4,000, *New York Central Railroad Company, Report of a Committee, October 24, 1855* (Boston, 1855), p. 38.

Chapter 3: Initial Editorial Policies

1. For New England prosperity in general and the boom in shipbuilding and textiles in particular see Thomas P. Kettell, "Debts and Finances of the States of the Union with Reference to Their General Condition and Prosperity: Chapter II, The New England States — Maine and Massachusetts," *Hunt's Merchants' Magazine* (hereafter cited as *Hunt's*) 17:572–587 (Dec. 1847); also *Hunt's,* 21:536 (Nov. 1849), 24:117 (Jan. 1851); and also Caroline F. Ware, *The Early New England Cotton Manufacture: a Study in Industrial Beginnings* (Boston, 1931), pp. 144, 151–152.

2. *ARJ,* 22:537 (Aug. 25, 1849); see also *ARJ,* 23:264 (April 27, 1850).

3. *ARJ,* 22:357, 487 (June 9, Aug. 4, 1849); 23:264, 521, 665 (April 27, Aug. 17, Oct. 19, 1850); 24:225–226, 513–514 (April 12, Aug. 15, 1851); 25:225–226 (April 10, 1852).

4. Examples of Maine railroad promotion are in *ARJ,* 23:438–439, 456–457, 504, 678 (July 13, 20, Aug. 10, Oct. 26, 1850); 24:1, 185, 234–235, 273–276,

280, 449–450 (Jan. 4, March 22, April 12, May 3, July 19, 1851); 28:17 (Jan. 13, 1855). For similar promotions by another railroad editor, see *Railway Times,* July 18, 1850. Poor was, however, more realistic than his brother about other Maine roads, as, for example, in *ARJ,* 23:217 (April 6, 1850).

5. *ARJ,* 22:580–581 (Sept. 15, 1849); see also *ARJ,* 22:537 (Aug. 25, 1849).

6. This and the following quotations are from *ARJ,* 22:502 (Aug. 11, 1849).

7. *ARJ,* 22:296 (May 12, 1849).

8. *ARJ,* 22:580 (Sept. 15, 1849); see also *ARJ,* 22:296 (May 12, 1849); 23:244 (April 27, 1850).

9. *ARJ,* 22:537 (Aug. 25, 1849); see also *ARJ,* 23:244 (April 27, 1850).

10. The low fare — high fare controversy is summarized in Edward C. Kirkland, *Men, Cities and Transportation* (Cambridge, Mass., 1948), I, 357–361. Poor gives his views in *ARJ,* 23:245 (April 20, 1850). He believed roads should charge extra fare on express trains, which were very costly to operate.

11. Poor makes critical analyses of the reports of the Cheshire, the Boston and Worcester, the New Haven and New London, the Boston and Maine, the Vermont and Canada, and the Vermont Central in *ARJ,* 22:344, 356-357, 360, 411, 535–537, 598 (June 2, 9, 30, Aug. 25, Sept. 22, 1849); 23:521, 665 (Aug. 17, Oct. 19, 1850).

12. *ARJ,* 22:581 (Sept. 15, 1849).

13. *ARJ,* 22:502 (Aug. 11, 1849).

14. *ARJ,* 23:790 (Dec. 14, 1850).

15. *ARJ,* 23:790 (Dec. 14, 1850); see also *ARJ,* 22:280–281 (May 5, 1849); 23:245–246 (April 20, 1850); 24:40 (Jan. 18, 1851).

16. This and the following quotation are from *ARJ,* 23:790 (Dec. 14, 1850). Latrobe mentions the obstacles to interchange of information in *ARJ,* 16:334–337 (Nov. 1843).

17. *Reports and Other Papers of the New England Association of Railroad Superintendents from the Commencement of the Society to January 1, 1850* (Boston, 1850), p. 35; also pp. iii–iv. The various aspects of the association's work are made clear in the reports printed in this pamphlet and in the reports and records of its meeting printed in *Records of the New England Association of Railway Superintendents* (Washington, 1910). The association appears to have been less used than later railroad associations to set and maintain rates.

18. This and the following quotations are from *ARJ,* 24:40 (Jan. 18, 1851); also *ARJ,* 23:790–791 (Dec. 14, 1850).

19. For views on need for better accounting and publicity see Kirkland, *Men, Cities and Transportation,* I, 283–284, 341–342 and letters printed in the *Railway Times,* May 16, 30, June 14, Sept. 22, 1850. For the railroad superintendents' demands for publicity of reports see *Reports . . . of the New England Association of Railroad Superintendents,* p. 33. For the British railroad reforms see *ARJ,* 22:440, 595–597 (July 14, Sept. 22, 1849).

20. A comparison of *Annual Reports of the Railroad Corporations in the State of Massachusetts for 1849* (Boston, 1850) and *Annual Reports of Railroad Corporations in the State of Massachusetts for 1855* (Boston, 1856) indicates that in both years only three roads provided information in this column. Some, however, included depreciation of specific items, usually just locomotives and rolling stock, under "working expenses," which soon became a standard way of accounting for depreciation. For improvements and changes made in accounting, required reports, and railroad commissions, see Kirkland, *Men, Cities and Transportation,* I, 281–284, 338–344, II, 232–237.

21. For examples of Haven's comments on accounting and publicity, see *Railway Times,* Jan. 2, May 1, 15, 1851.

22. The best summaries of the different Pacific railroad projects are, Robert R. Russel, *Improvement of Communication with the Pacific Coast as an Issue in American Politics, 1783–1864* (Cedar Rapids, Iowa, 1948), chs. 1–3; Nelson H. Loomis, "Asa Whitney: Father of Pacific Railroads," *Proceedings of the Mississippi Valley Historical Association,* 6:166–175 (1912–1913), Whitney's own

pamphlet, *A Project for a Railroad to the Pacific* (New York, 1849) gives additional details of his scheme.

23. Margaret L. Brown, "Asa Whitney and his Pacific Railroad Publicity Campaign," *Mississippi Valley Historical Review*, 20:209–224 (Sept. 1933); *ARJ*, 21:1 (Jan. 1, 1848).

24. *ARJ*, 22:519 (Aug. 18, 1849).

25. Poor's initial editorials against Whitney's plan are in *ARJ*, 22:424–425, 441–442, 456 (July 7, 14, 21, 1849). These are best amplified in *ARJ*, 22:519–520, 600–601, 678 (Aug. 18, Sept. 22, Oct. 27, 1849); 23:184–185, 710–712, 756–757 (March 23, Nov. 9, 30, 1850); 24:24–26, 167, 217, 728 (Jan. 11, March 15, April 5, Nov. 15, 1851). The significance of Poor's views are emphasized by comparing his editorials of July 1849 with that of James D. B. De Bow printed in *De Bow's Review*, 7:1–37 (July 1849) which reflects the optimistic views held by most of the press and public on the ease of constructing a transcontinental railroad.

26. *ARJ*, 24:24 (Jan. 11, 1851).

27. *ARJ*, 24:728 (Nov. 15, 1851). See also *ARJ*, 22:806 (Dec. 22, 1849).

28. *ARJ*, 22:424 (July 7, 1849).

29. *ARJ*, 22:647 (Oct. 13, 1849). For other comments on De Grand's plan, see *ARJ*, 22:628–629, 648–649, 663 (Oct. 6, 13, 20, 1849); 23:104–105, 131 (Feb. 16, March 2, 1850).

30. *ARJ*, 22:614 (Sept. 29, 1849). See also *ARJ*, 23:787–789 (Dec. 14, 1850).

31. *ARJ*, 22:614–615 (Sept. 29, 1849); the following quotations in this paragraph are from this editorial. See also *ARJ*, 22:647 (Oct. 13, 1849).

32. *ARJ*, 22:614 (Sept. 29, 1849).

33. Russel, *Improvement of Communication with the Pacific*, pp. 46, 52, 188; *ARJ*, 22:806–807 (Dec. 22, 1849); 23:228 (April 13, 1850).

34. *ARJ*, 23:185 (March 28, 1850). For the views of the three conventions see *ARJ*, 22:519–520, 708–710, 711, 822 (Aug. 18, Nov. 10, Dec. 29, 1849); 23:228–231, 233 (April 13, 1850).

35. For example, *Western Journal and Civilian*, 2:105–121 (Feb. 1849).

36. For example, *Hunt's*, 29:659–673 (Dec. 1853); 31:633–635 (Nov. 1854); 35:659–680 (Dec. 1856); 42:553–558 (May 1860); *Western Journal and Civilian*, 9:88–101 (Nov. 1852); 13:268–281 (March 1855); *De Bow's Review*, 12:99–101, 402–408 (Jan., April 1852); 15:535–537, 641–642 (Nov., Dec. 1852); 16:507–519 (May 1854); 19:336–341 (Sept. 1855); 21:469–490 (Nov. 1856); 22:509–513 (May 1857).

37. Good examples of Haven's views are *Railway Times*, Jan. 27, Feb. 10, Sept. 1, 1853, Jan. 5, 1854, Jan. 15, 1857; of Mansfield's are *Railroad Record*, 4:18, 50, 82, 99, 387–388, 401, 753–754 (March 6, 20, April 3, 10, Aug. 14, 21, 1856, Jan. 22, 1857).

38. Poor's later views on the Pacific railroad are best summarized in his article, "Railroad to the Pacific," *Bulletin of the American Geographical and Statistical Society*, vol. I, pt. 3:81–100 (1854). The editorials that best indicate the development of his ideas from 1853 to 1860 are in *ARJ*, 26:545–546, 635, 728, 762, 844–845 (Aug. 27, Oct. 1, Nov. 12, 26, Dec. 31, 1853); 27:186–187, 257–258, 273–274, 385–386, 451 (March 25, April 29, May 6, June 24, July 22, 1854); 28:2–4, 17–18, 148–149 (Jan. 6, 13, March 10, 1855); 29:65, 488, 792 (Feb. 2, Aug. 2, Dec. 13, 1856); 30:417 (July 4, 1857); 31:72–73, 360 (Jan. 30, June 5, 1858); 32:8, 808 (Jan. 1, Dec. 10, 1859); 33:36, 1049 (Jan. 14, Nov. 24, 1860).

39. This quotation and those in the following paragraph are from *ARJ*, 31:72–73 (Jan. 31, 1858).

40. For revival of trunk lines and other smaller roads in New York, New Jersey, and Pennsylvania, see Henry V. Poor, *The History of the Railroads and Canals of the United States of America* (New York, 1860), pp. 221, 378–379, 417–418.

41. Poor discusses the trunk lines in *ARJ*, 22:662 (Oct. 20, 1849); 23:377, 600–601, 758 (June 15, Sept. 21, Nov. 30, 1850).

42. *ARJ*, 23:360 (June 8, 1850). As Poor pointed out, the West lacked stone, asphalt, and other materials necessary for surfacing roads; see *ARJ*, 23:344–345 (June 1, 1850).

43. The financial history of these state ventures in transportation is well summarized by Thomas P. Kettell, "Debts and Finances of the States of the Union: with Reference to their General Condition and Prosperity," *Hunt's*, 21:147–163 (Aug. 1849) for Indiana; 21:389–410 (Oct. 1849) for Ohio; 22:131–145 (Feb. 1850) for Michigan. For Illinois, see Paul W. Gates, *The Illinois Central Railroad and Its Colonization Work* (Cambridge, Mass., 1934), pp. 21–24.

44. The best summary of the railroad situation in the Old Northwest in 1849 is Frederic L. Paxson, "The Railroads of the 'Old Northwest' before the Civil War," *Transactions of the Wisconsin Academy of Sciences, Arts, and Letters*, vol. XVII, pt. 1, no. 4, pp. 243–274. Additional information can be found in Wylie J. Daniels, *The Village at the End of the Road, A Chapter in Early Indiana Railroad History* (Indianapolis, 1938); Robert L. Black, *The Little Miami Railroad* (Cincinnati, 1940); Henry G. Pearson, *An American Railroad Builder, John Murray Forbes* (Boston, 1911); Alvin F. Harlow, *The Road of the Century* (New York, 1947); George H. Burgess and Miles C. Kennedy, *Centennial History of the Pennsylvania Railroad Company, 1846–1946* (Philadelphia, 1949); Richard C. Overton, *Burlington West: A Colonization History of the Burlington Railroad* (Cambridge, Mass., 1941); Balthasar H. Meyer, director, and Caroline E. MacGill, *History of Transportation in the United States before 1860* (Washington, 1917); and Gates, *Illinois Central Railroad.*

45. *ARJ*, 23:360 (June 8, 1850).

46. *ARJ*, 23:601 (Sept. 21, 1850). See also *ARJ*, 22:360, 476, 662 (June 9, July 28, Oct. 20, 1849); 23:120, 360, 377, 708, 727 (Feb. 23, June 8, 15, Nov. 9, 16, 1850).

47. *ARJ*, 23:120, 425 (Feb. 23, July 6, 1850); *Report of Israel D. Andrews Consul of the United States for Canada and New Brunswick on the Trade and Commerce of the British North American Colonies, and upon the Trade of the Great Lakes and Rivers* (Senate Document, 32nd Congress, 1st Session), pp. 286–287, 379–384. Poor wrote the section on railroads in this report.

48. Those particularly favored included the Ohio and Pennsylvania, the Madison and Indianapolis, the Bellefontaine and Indiana, the Indianapolis and Bellefontaine, the Terre Haute and Richmond, the Atlantic and Mississippi, and the Pacific Railroad of Missouri. For examples of articles describing these roads by Poor and their promoters, see *ARJ*, 22:553, 567, 758, 768–769 (Sept. 1, 8, Dec. 1, 8, 1849); 23:120, 201, 232, 293–294, 489–490, 535–536, 584, 593–594, 772, 799–800 (Feb. 23, March 30, April 13, May 11, Aug. 3, 24, Sept. 14, 21, Dec. 7, 21, 1850).

49. The quotation is from *ARJ*, 24:502 (Aug. 9, 1851).

50. The new roads included the Orange and Alexandria, the Richmond and Danville, the South Side, and the Virginia and Tennessee; and work was resumed on the Seaboard and Roanoke and on the extension of the old Louisa road under a new company, the Virginia Central, including the Blue Ridge road and tunnel. The best summary of railroad construction in Virginia and other Southern states is Milton S. Heath, "Public Cooperation in Railroad Construction in the Southern United States to 1861," a doctoral dissertation submitted at Harvard in 1937. The most useful published studies are, Ulrich B. Phillips, *A History of Transportation in the Eastern Cotton Belt to 1860* (New York, 1908); Howard D. Dozier, *A History of the Atlantic Coast Line Railroad* (Boston, 1920); Carlton J. Corliss, *Main Line of Mid-America* (New York, 1950); and Meyer and MacGill, *History of Transportation in the United States*, ch. 15.

51. The energetic group of Savannah merchants and Georgia planters who promoted and financed, with municipal aid, the state's two basic trunk lines,

in the late forties helped finance the branches and western connections of these two roads. In order to avoid paying the heavy cost of a road across the mountains, they appear to have engineered the state into constructing the Western and Atlantic. Until 1855, the cost of this road was almost the only state aid to Georgia roads.

52. *ARJ*, 24:502 (Aug. 9, 1851). See also *ARJ*, 23:689 (Nov. 2, 1850).

53. *ARJ*, 22:161, 247 (March 17, April 21, 1849).

54. *ARJ*, 24:696, 794–795 (Nov. 1, Dec. 13, 1851), 25:202 (March 27, 1852).

55. *ARJ*, 26:401–402 (June 25, 1853); 27:602 (Sept. 23, 1854); 28:673–674 (Oct. 27, 1855); 32:696–697 (Oct. 29, 1859).

56. *ARJ*, 23:312, 345, 536 (May 18, June 1, Aug. 24, 1850).

57. *ARJ*, 24:289–291, 314, 500–501 (May 10, 17, Aug. 9, 1851). In 1852, and again in 1854, New Orleans invested heavily in the New Orleans, Jackson and Great Northern and the New Orleans, Opelousas and Great Western. On the value of railroads to New Orleans Poor wrote at this time a good deal more than did New Orleans' most influential editor, James D. B. De Bow.

58. *ARJ*, 24:290, 668 (May 10, Oct. 18, 1851). See also *ARJ*, 23:689 (Nov. 2, 1850).

59. Good examples of promotional literature for these and other Southern railroads by Poor and their promoters are in *ARJ*, 22:293–294, 694–696, 799 (May 12, Nov. 3, Dec. 22, 1849); 23:147–149, 261–262, 279, 292–293, 341–342, 566, 583, 616 (March 9, April 27, May 4, 11, June 1, Sept. 7, 14, 28, 1850); 24:22, 682, 696 (Jan. 11, Oct. 25, Nov. 1, 1851); 25:337–338, 392, 394–395, 491, 680, 769–770, 776, 810–811 (May 29, June 19, July 31, Oct. 23, Dec. 4, 18, 1852).

60. *ARJ*, 23:148 (March 9, 1850), for the comment on the Virginia and Tennessee. Poor mentions his acquaintance with McDaniels and Boyd in Henry Poor to Mary Poor, July 11, 1852; April 18, 19, 22, 1867. Poor also helped United States Senator David Yulee raise capital in 1859 and 1860 for his Florida Railroad, Henry Poor to Mary Poor, Sept. 12, 1859, July 17, 31, 1860.

61. *ARJ*, 24:72 (Feb. 1, 1851).

62. *ARJ*, 22:293 (May 12, 1849). See also *ARJ*, 25:491 (July 31, 1852).

63. For De Bow's acquaintance with Poor, see *ARJ*, 23:693 (Nov. 2, 1850). A good example of De Bow's views on this subject is printed in *De Bow's Review*, 12:534–562 (May 1852). Maury and Poor often saw each other at the Geographical Society's meetings. Poor had asked James to be an assistant editor after reading his articles on cotton manufacturing in the South, parts of which were reprinted in *ARJ*, 22:277–278, 292–293 (May 5, 12, 1849); see also *ARJ*, 22:263 (April 28, 1849).

64. *ARJ*, 23:648 (Oct. 12, 1850). For other articles on the value of railroads and industry to the South, and their role in mitigating the sectional controversy, see *ARJ*, 22:248–249, 311, 420–421, 694–696 (April 21, May 19, July 7, Nov. 3, 1849); 23:72, 147–148, 279, 293, 312, 360, 425, 520–521, 536, 616, 631, 689, 693–694, 758 (Feb. 2, March 9, May 4, 11, 18, June 8, July 6, Aug. 17, 24, Sept. 28, Oct. 5, Nov. 2, 30, 1850). Poor also argued that land grants to Southern railroads, by aiding Southern economy, would help unite the nation; see *ARJ*, 23:312 (May 18, 1850).

65. *ARJ*, 23:265 (April 27, 1850). Daniels, *Village at the End of the Road*, pp. 57–58, emphasizes the value of the press in winning local support for the early Midwestern railroads. Oliver H. Smith's remarks in *Exhibit of the President of the Indianapolis and Bellefontaine Railroad Company, September 11, 1851* (Indianapolis, 1851), pp. 3–4, show how the promoters made use of the *Journal*.

Chapter 4: Representing the Railroads on Wall Street

1. *ARJ*, 23:726 (Nov. 16, 1850).

2. *ARJ*, 23:312–313, 582, 678, 799–800 (May 18, Sept. 14, Oct. 26, Dec.

21, 1850). Wylie J. Daniels, *The Village at the End of the Road, A Chapter in Early Indiana Railroad History* (Indianapolis, Indiana, 1938), pp. 40–43, 54–56, 88–89, emphasizes the heavy freight traffic of the Madison and Indianapolis and the effect the road had on the communities along its route.

3. Other towns which had financially aided railroads included Alton, Terre Haute, New Albany, Maysville, Salem, and Elkhart, *ARJ*, 23:247, 457, 472, 719, 727, 744 (April 20, July 20, 27, Nov. 16, Dec. 7, 1850); see also Daniels, *Village at the End of the Road*, pp. 66–67; Robert L. Black, *The Little Miami Railroad* (Cincinnati, 1940), p. 47.

4. *ARJ*, 23:249 (April 20, 1850).

5. *The First Annual Report of the President to Directors of the Indianapolis and Bellefontaine Railroad Company, March 6, 1849* (Indianapolis, 1849), p. 9; for the Indianapolis and Cincinnati, see extracts from its 1850 annual report in *ARJ*, 28:265 (April 28, 1855); for other examples of roads with stock subscriptions taken largely in land and materials, see Daniels, *Village at the End of the Road*, pp. 19–21, and Howard D. Dozier, *A History of the Atlantic Coast Line Railroad* (Boston, 1920), p. 89.

6. Thus when William Robinson, president of the Ohio and Pennsylvania, came East in the fall of 1850 he brought a $1,000,000 bond issue, one half to be used to pay for iron, chains, spikes, rails, locomotives, and cars and the other half to raise essential cash, *Third Annual Report of the President and Directors to the Stockholders of the Ohio and Pennsylvania Railroad Company* (Pittsburgh, 1851), pp. 13–14.

7. The following paragraphs are a summary of Alfred D. Chandler, Jr., "Patterns of Railroad Finance, 1830–1850," *Business History Review*, 28:248–263 (Sept. 1954) which gives the story in more detail and provides documentation.

8. Other New England railroads still under construction which made their first bond issue in 1848 or 1849 included the Cheshire, the Naugatuck, the Hartford, Providence and Fishkill, the Atlantic and St. Lawrence and its feeder the Androscoggin and Kennebec.

9. *Hunt's*, 21:535–536 (Nov. 1849).

10. *Hunt's*, 18:297–302, 403–412 (March, May 1848); 20:421 (April 1849); 21:535–536, 651 (Nov., Dec. 1849); 22:423, 549 (April, May 1850); 24:206 (Feb. 1851).

11. *Bankers' Magazine*, 2:200–205, 327–328, 453–455, 511–512, 705–709 (Oct., Nov. 1847, Jan., Feb., June 1848); 3:324, 384, 771–772, 866–868, 911–913 (Nov., Dec. 1848, March, April, May 1849); 4:579, 674, 1059–1060 (Jan., Feb., June 1850); 5:87–88, 178–180, 262, 432, 516 (Aug., Sept., Nov., Dec. 1850).

12. *ARJ*, 23:248 (April 20, 1850); see also *ARJ*, 23:536 (Aug. 24, 1850); 24:26–27, 152–153 (Jan. 11, March 8, 1851).

13. Details and documentation of the shift from Boston to New York can be found in Alfred D. Chandler, Jr., "The Pen in Business —— A Biography of Henry Varnum Poor," a doctoral dissertation submitted at Harvard University in 1951, pp. 242–243 and Appendix I. The Philadelphia, Wilmington and Baltimore was the only Boston-financed non-New England road which did not have to go to New York for funds after 1847.

14. *ARJ*, 23:632 (Oct. 5, 1850).

15. This and the following quotation are from *ARJ*, 24:8 (Jan. 4, 1851); see also *ARJ*, 24:504 (Aug. 9, 1851).

16. *ARJ*, 23:719 (Nov. 16, 1850).

17. Late in 1849, the Michigan Southern, as had the Reading, the Harlem, the Cumberland Valley, the Morris Canal, and possibly one or two other transportation companies in 1848 and 1849, tried to raise funds for construction and expansion of facilities by issuing long-term preferred stock. See *ARJ*, 28:458 (July 21, 1855); *Railway Times*, Dec. 1, 1849.

18. *Hunt's*, 20:530–531 (May 1849); 22:419 (April 1850); *Annual Report*

of the State Engineer and Surveyor Concerning the Returns of Railroads of the State of New York for 1850 (Albany, N. Y., 1850), Appendix B; Frank W. Stevens, *The Beginnings of the New York Central Railroad, A History* (New York, 1926), pp. 295–300.

19. *ARJ*, 23:424 (July 6, 1850); also *ARJ*, 23:280 (May 4, 1850); 25:122 (Feb. 21, 1852). In 1849 and 1850, municipal securities issued for railroads were marketed on a large scale in the Eastern money markets; *Hunt's*, 21:535–536 (Nov. 1849); see also citations given in footnote 3 of this chapter. Among the many Ohio and Indiana county issues placed in New York in 1849 and 1850 were: Ohio-Franklin County (for the Columbus and Xenia and the Cleveland, Columbus and Cincinnati), Greene County (for the Columbus and Xenia), Scioto County (for the Scioto and Hocking Valley), Shelby County (for the Cleveland and Pittsburgh and the Bellefontaine and Indiana), Stark County (for the Ohio and Pennsylvania), Richland County (for the Ohio and Pennsylvania), Delaware County (for the Cleveland, Columbus and Cincinnati), Champaign County (for the Columbus, Piqua and Indiana); Indiana-Vigo County (for the Terre Haute and Indianapolis), Lawrenceburg County (for the Indianapolis and Cincinnati), Decatur County (for the Indianapolis and Cincinnati). Most of these securities were marketed by Winslow, Lanier and Company; see the firm's advertisement and dividend notice in the New York *Tribune*, Jan. 3, July 12, 1851. Harry H. Pierce, *Railroads of New York, A Study in Government Aid, 1826–1875* (Cambridge, Mass., 1953) provides a revealing and thorough study of the larger story of public support in an Eastern setting.

20. *ARJ*, 24:67, 104, 120, 136, 200 (Feb. 1, 15, 22, March 1, 29, 1851).

21. For advice on convertibility of corporate and county bonds, see *ARJ*, 25:184–185, 200 (March 20, 27, 1852). Many of the first roads constructed in the West, such as the Cleveland and Pittsburgh, the Cleveland, Columbus and Cincinnati, the Columbus and Xenia, and the Little Miami, had nearly all their bonds converted before the depression of 1854; and, because of this, had a much lower debt throughout the rest of the decade than those roads built just a little later.

22. *ARJ*, 23:536–537, 584, 632, 703–704 (Aug. 24, Sept. 14, Oct. 5, Nov. 9, 1850); 24:26, 152–153 (Jan. 11, March 8, 1851).

23. *ARJ*, 23:584, 632 (Sept. 14, Oct. 5, 1850). See also *ARJ*, 24:26–27, 104, 137–138, 360 (Jan. 11, Feb. 15, March 1, June 7, 1851). For comments similar to Poor's on the dangers of excessive imports, see *Bankers' Magazine*, 5:599, 779, 1027 (Jan., March, June 1851); Ralph W. Hidy, *The House of Baring in American Trade and Finance* (Cambridge, Mass., 1949), p. 393; also Joshua Baker to John Ward, Jan. 3, 1851 and T. W. Ward to John Ward, Jan. 25, 1851, in the Thomas Wren Ward papers, Massachusetts Historical Society, Boston.

24. *ARJ*, 24:104 (Feb. 15, 1851).

25. *ARJ*, 23:703 (Nov. 9, 1850).

26. *ARJ*, 24:200 (March 29, 1851); for his advice to bring in securities, *ARJ*, 24:67–68, 104, 120 (Feb. 1, 15, 22, 1851).

27. *ARJ*, 24:328 (May 24, 1851).

28. *ARJ*, 24:360, 425, 472, 520 (June 7, July 5, 26, Aug. 16, 1851).

29. *ARJ*, 24:648 (Oct. 11, 1851). For similar comments, see *ARJ*, 24:728, 761 (Nov. 15, 29, 1851); for the development and culmination of the money stringency, see these citations and *ARJ*, 24:425, 488, 616 (July 5, Aug. 2, Sept. 27, 1851); *Bankers' Magazine*, 6:167, 250–252, 503–504 (Aug., Sept., Dec. 1851); Margaret G. Meyers, *Origin and Development of the New York Money Market* (New York, 1927), pp. 138–139; for New York's recovery, *ARJ*, 24:792 (Dec. 13, 1851); 25:24, 121 (Jan. 10, Feb. 21, 1852); *Bankers' Magazine*, 6:587–588, 671–672 (Jan., Feb. 1852).

30. U. S. Bureau of the Census, *Historical Statistics of the United States, 1879–1945* (Washington, 1949), p. 245.

31. *ARJ*, 24:776 (Dec. 6, 1851); see also *ARJ*, 24:26–27, 344, 376–377

(Jan. 11, May 31, June 15, 1851); 29:49–50 (Jan. 26, 1856); compare Poor's concern with gold as an export with comments in *Bankers' Magazine,* 6:251–252, 503–504 (Sept., Dec. 1851), *United States Economist,* 2:236 (Jan. 22, 1853). His emphasis was closer to that of the London *Economist,* see reprint in *ARJ,* 24:776 (Dec. 6, 1851). Hereafter the citation *Economist* will mean the *United States Economist.*

32. Ward and Company acted as agent for the sale of Erie bonds, Brown Brothers for the Vermont and Massachusetts, *Bankers' Magazine,* 3:451 (Jan., 1849); *ARJ,* 22:457 (July 21, 1849). Ward and Company did, however, serve as agent for the Boston-backed Mad River and Lake Erie, New York *Tribune,* Jan. 13, 1851.

33. *ARJ,* 24:328 (May 24, 1851). The names of these firms appear in notices and reports of sales in *ARJ* and the New York *Tribune* during 1851. Several purchasers of Western bonds at sealed bid sales in 1851 were listed on the stock books of the Mansfield and Sandusky Railroad, one of the very first Western roads to come to New York for funds; *Fourth Annual Report of the President and Directors of the Mansfield and Sandusky Railroad Company to the Stockholders* (New York, 1851), pp. 20–23. For purchases by brokerage houses of state securities in the 1840's, see *Hunt's,* 21:401 (Oct. 1849). Other stock and domestic exchange firms bidding for railroad bonds before 1852 included Carpenter and Vermilye, Clark, Dodge and Co., P. McMartin, E. C. McIntosh, Alfred Colvill, Corcoran and Riggs of Washington, D. C., and E. S. Whalen and Co. of Philadelphia.

34. For examples of sales by professional auctioneers, see *ARJ,* 25:269, 328, 409 (April 24, May 22, June 26, 1852); 26:88 (Feb. 5, 1853); *Railroad Record,* 1:825 (Feb. 23, 1854); New York *Tribune,* Jan. 6, 13, 24, Feb. 24, 27, 1851. For the sale of state securities by auction, see *Hunt's,* 21:400 (Oct., 1849); for municipal bonds *ARJ,* 25:537 (Aug. 21, 1852).

35. *ARJ,* 24:73 (Feb. 1, 1851). See also *ARJ,* 24:88, 680 (Feb. 8, Oct. 25, 1851).

36. *ARJ,* 24:6 (Jan. 4, 1851). See also *ARJ,* 24:744 (Nov. 22, 1851). For earlier and quite similar comments on speculation in the securities of unfinished roads, see *ARJ,* 15:41–43 (July 1, 1842).

37. *ARJ,* 24:73 (Feb. 1, 1851).

38. In this and the following quotation, Poor was referring specifically to railroad companies selling their county issues; *ARJ,* 23:424 (July 6, 1850). See also *ARJ,* 23:457 (July 20, 1850).

39. This and the following three quotations are from a long article on bond-selling in *ARJ,* 24:56–57 (Jan. 25, 1851). The business periodicals and daily papers of the day refer to such private sales of bonds to middlemen for resale as "negotiations." This is somewhat different from the terminology encountered by Fritz Redlich in his studies of sales of government securities where "negotiating" means sale on commission and "contracting" means buying blocks for resale, Fritz Redlich, *The Moulding of American Banking Men and Ideas* (Ann Arbor, Michigan, 1951), pp. 318, 348.

40. *ARJ,* 23:424 (July 6, 1850).

41. *ARJ,* 25:169 (March 13, 1852). See also *ARJ,* 23:424, 457 (July 6, 20, 1850).

42. *ARJ,* 25:169 (March 13, 1852). For further comments on fictitious bids, see *ARJ,* 24:56 (Jan. 25, 1851); 25:114, 425 (Feb. 21, July 3, 1852); 32:73 (Jan. 29, 1859).

43. The Erie Railroad used bids to sell its bonds in the late 1840's, *Bankers' Magazine,* 3:451 (Jan. 1849); *Hunt's,* 20:530 (May 1849). Sealed bids were first used to sell Western railroad bonds in late 1850, when Winslow, Lanier and Co., acting as agent, asked for bids on large issues of both Michigan Southern and Ohio and Pennsylvania bonds, *ARJ,* 24:664, 727, 789 (Oct. 19, Nov. 16, Dec. 14, 1850).

44. *ARJ,* 28:237 (April 14, 1855). The bids for the Michigan Central bonds in 1850 were to be opened at a specified hour "in the presence of Samuel Frothingham, president of the State Bank, Boston, and D. D. Williamson, President of the Farmers' Loan and Trust," New York *Tribune,* July 29, 1850.

45. Lanier's autobiography, *Sketch of the Life of J. F. D. Lanier* (New York, 1870), has a brief account of Lanier's business activities. For Winslow, see his obituary, written by Poor, in Lanier, *Sketch of the Life of Lanier,* pp. 60–62.

46. *ARJ,* 18:409 (June 26, 1845); Daniels, *Village at the End of the Road,* p. 30.

47. The different Western roads which Winslow, Lanier and Company served are indicated by the list in *ARJ,* 26:425–426 (July 2, 1856); Lanier, *Sketch of the Life of Lanier,* pp. 18–20. For a more detailed listing see Chandler, "The Pen in Business," Appendix I. Winslow, Lanier and Co. acted as agents for Southern roads as well as Western ones. In the summer of 1851, they marketed the bonds of the Seaboard and Roanoke, originally supported by Henshaw and Ward of Boston, and the Wilmington and Manchester, connecting Wilmington, N. C. to the South Carolina roads, *ARJ,* 24:360, 440 (June 7, July 12, 1851), *Exhibit of the Affairs of the Seaboard and Roanoke Railroad Company, March, 1851* (n.p., n.d.), p. 7. The firm also purchased rails for the Virginia Central, *ARJ,* 25:115 (Feb. 21, 1852).

48. For examples of how Winslow, Lanier and Co. performed these functions, see *ARJ,* 24:440, 617 (July 12, Sept. 27, 1851); 25:115 (Feb. 21, 1852); 26:331, 412 (May 21, June 25, 1853); *Railway Times,* June 27, 1850; *Exhibit of the Cleveland, Columbus and Cincinnati Railroad Company* (New York, 1849), pp. 10–13; *Third Annual Report of the President of the Indianapolis and Bellefontaine Railroad Company, February 10, 1851* (Indianapolis, 1851), pp. 6, 9–12; *Third Annual Report of the President and Directors to the Stockholders of the Ohio and Pennsylvania Railroad Company* (Pittsburgh, 1851), pp. 13–14; *Third Annual Report of the Directors to the Stockholders of the Columbus and Xenia Railroad Company* (Columbus, Ohio, 1853), pp. 13–14; *Fourth Annual Report of the Indiana Central Railroad Company, January 1856* (Indianapolis, 1856), p. 8; and a copy of the second mortgage of that road dated October 8, 1857, in same folder with its annual reports in the Baker Library, Cambridge, Mass.; *Ninth Annual Report of the Directors of the Little Miami Railroad for 1851* (Cincinnati, 1851), pp. 13–14; *Tenth Annual Report of the Directors of the Little Miami Railroad* (Cincinnati, 1852), p. 10; *Eleventh Annual Report of the Directors of the Little Miami Railroad* (Cincinnati, 1853), p. 18. For the Little Miami sales, see also *ARJ,* 26:432, 669 (July 2, Oct. 15, 1853). The firm also paid the interest and principal on the municipal and county bonds it sold, *ARJ,* 26:331 (May 21, 1853); 29:408, 414–415 (June 30, 1855).

49. For example see *ARJ,* 26:74 (Jan. 29, 1853); 27:632 (Oct. 7, 1854). In 1849 the *Journal's* office was at 54 Wall Street and Winslow and Lanier's at 52 Wall Street. During the fifties the firm became one of Poor's largest advertising accounts. This house, the first bond house to advertise its wares, also advertised in the *Railway Times* and in the New York daily press, especially the *Tribune.*

50. For the banker's views on the importance of popularizing Western bonds, see Lanier, *Sketch of the Life of Lanier,* p. 19.

51. *ARJ,* 23:424 (July 6, 1850). For comments on the lack of knowledge of and confidence in the new securities coming into the investment market, see New York *Tribune,* July 15, 1850.

52. This and the following quotations in this paragraph are from *ARJ,* 24:88 (Feb. 8, 1851). See also *ARJ,* 24:8 (Jan. 1, 1851).

53. For Poor's arguments, see *ARJ,* 24:56, 152, 280, 731–732, 785 (Jan. 25, March 8, May 3, Nov. 15, Dec. 13, 1851). Most of Poor's arguments appear in his numerous articles on the individual roads written in late 1850, 1851, and the first part of 1852.

54. *ARJ*, 25:296, 305–306 (May 8, 15, 1852), and particularly *ARJ*, 25:410 (June 26, 1852).

55. For the influx of Continental capital seeking safety in the United States in 1848 and 1849, see Jean B. H. R. Capefigue, *Histoire des Grandes Opérations Financières* . . . (Paris, France, 1854–1860), III, 315–316, and IV, chs. 18 and 19, *passim; Hunt's*, 19:634–635 (Dec. 1848); 20:193–194 (Feb. 1849); 23:653 (Dec. 1850); Hidy, *House of Baring*, pp. 384–388. In 1856 the Frankfort *Zeitung* estimated that $42,000,000 had been invested in American securities, including railroad bonds, between 1848 and 1851, *ARJ*, 29:458 (July 19, 1856).

56. *Bankers' Magazine*, 4:78, 83, 332 (July, Oct. 1849); 5:83, 95–96 (July 1850); 6:251 (Sept. 1851); *Hunt's*, 22:642 (June 1850); 23:91, 94, 318 (July, Sept. 1850); *ARJ*, 23:704 (Nov. 9, 1850).

57. *ARJ*, 24:152, 808–809 (March 8, Dec. 20, 1851); 25:40, 57, 185 (Jan. 17, 24, March 20, 1852); New York *Tribune*, May 19, 1851.

58. For bids by these houses on railroad issues, *ARJ*, 23:789 (Dec. 14, 1850); 24:27, 360, 392 (Jan. 11, June 7, 21, 1851); 25:217, 345, 360–361, 425, 681 (April 3, May 29, June 5, July 3, Oct. 23, 1852); *Bankers' Magazine*, 4:251 (Sept. 1849); New York *Tribune*, Jan. 24, 1851. These firms also bid on state issues; see, for example, bid on an Ohio state loan, *Bankers' Magazine*, 5:83 (July 1850).

59. In *Doggett's New York City Directory for 1850–1851* (New York, 1850), De Launay, Iselin and Clarke, De Coppet and Co., and Cammann, Whitehouse and Co. listed themselves as "brokers," and others as commission merchants. In the *New York Mercantile Union Business Directory . . . for 1850–1851* (New York, 1850), Cammann, Whitehouse and Co. and Philip Speyer and Co. are listed under brokers, with Speyer also listed under importing and commission merchants.

60. For the Iselins, *National Cyclopaedia of American Biography* (New York, 1895), XXII, 243; XXVI, 329–330; for De Coppet, Dumas Malone, ed., *Dictionary of American Biography* (New York, 1946), V, 190 (the firm after 1853 sent weekly bulletins on the New York investment market to Geneva and Paris which are printed in *ARJ*); for Speyer, Joseph E. Hedges, *Commercial Banking and the Stock Market before 1863* (Baltimore, 1938), p. 42; for De Rham and Moore, J. A. Scoville (Walter Barrett, pseud.), *The Old Merchants of New York City*, first series (New York, 1864); pp. 211–212; for Meyer and Stucken, *ARJ*, 27:723 (Nov. 18, 1854), Scoville, *Old Merchants of New York*, p. 129 (the two partners were, during the 1850's, consuls for Hanover); for Cammann, Whitehouse and Co., *National Cyclopaedia*, XIX, 353; XXVI, 253. As for Delano, Dunlevy and Co., Francis Dunlevy came from Cincinnati, and so, probably, did Columbus Delano; while Jacob Atwood, who replaced Delano in 1853, had apparently been a New York broker; see listings in H. Wilson, compiler, *Trow's New York City Directory, for 1854–1855* (New York, 1854); John Doggett, Jr., and J. A. Rode, compilers, *The New York City Directory, for 1851–1852* (New York, 1851).

61. I am indebted to Professor Leland H. Jenks for the information on the appearance on the Frankfort and later the London exchange of these and other American issues. Chandler, "The Pen in Business," Appendix I, lists nearly all bonds issued by Western railroads before 1853 indicating for each issue, when the data were available, the amount, price, type of sale, the fiscal agent, and where and when it first appeared abroad.

62. *ARJ*, 25:145 (March 6, 1852). See also *ARJ*, 25:26, 506–507 (Jan. 10, Aug. 7, 1852); 26:65–68, 168–169, 369–371, 401–402 (Jan. 29, March 12, June 11, 25, 1853).

63. *Report of Israel D. Andrews, Consul of the United States for Canada and New Brunswick, on the Trade and Commerce of the British North American Colonies, and upon the Trade of the Great Lakes and Rivers* (Senate Document 112, 32nd Congress, 1st Session), p. 382. One of Poor's aims in writing in 1852

the section on American railroads in this report was to indicate to foreigners the value of American railroads.

64. *Andrews Report*, p. 380.

65. *ARJ*, 26:395 (June 11, 1853). See also *ARJ*, 25:296, 689–690, 705–706, 728–729 (May 8, Oct. 30, Nov. 6, 13, 1852).

66. *ARJ*, 25:506 (Aug. 7, 1852).

67. *ARJ*, 25:232, 410–411, 506–507, 552, 689–690 (April 10, June 26, Aug. 7, 28, Oct. 30, 1852).

68. *ARJ*, 25:561–562, 600, 776 (Sept. 4, 18, Dec. 4, 1852).

69. *ARJ*, 25:305–306, 395–397, 433–437, 689–690, 705–706, 728–729 (May 15, June 19, July 10, Oct. 30, Nov. 6, 13, 1852).

70. For the British investor's dislike of American railroad bonds before 1852, *ARJ*, 23:17–18 (Jan. 12, 1850); *Bankers' Magazine*, 4:1024–1026 (June 1849); 5:948 (Feb. 1850); 6:671 (Feb. 1852); Hidy, *House of Baring*, pp. 392–393; and Muriel E. Hidy, "George Peabody, Merchant and Financier, 1829–1854," an unpublished doctoral dissertation submitted at Radcliffe College in 1939, pp. 345–346. In 1850 and 1851, Peabody was also writing that iron manufacturers were sending American railroad bonds to Switzerland, Germany, and New York for sale. For the change in the British view of American securities, see *Bankers' Magazine*, 6:924, 1019 (May, June 1852); *Economist*, 1:765 (Sept. 25, 1852); Hidy, *House of Baring*, pp. 409–411. The Rothschilds took some Erie issues before 1852, apparently for the English market; while Ward and Company took $2,500,000 worth of Erie bonds in 1850, "very many" of which, *Hunt's* reported, went to England; *Hunt's*, 23:88 (July 1850). However, many of these probably were sent from London to Germany, for toward the end of the 1850's German holdings in the Erie were estimated at $15,000,000; *Railroad Record*, 6:212 (June 24, 1858).

71. *ARJ*, 25:417 (July 3, 1852).

72. This and the following quotations in this paragraph are from *ARJ*, 25:417–418 (July 3, 1852). See also *ARJ*, 25:436–437 (July 10, 1852).

73. *ARJ*, 25:418 (July 3, 1852). See also *ARJ*, 28:113–114 (Feb. 24, 1855). In the spring of 1853, Poor made a tour of investigation of the Western roads with several representatives of Continental investors, including Messrs. C. G. Eschen of the banking firm of Meyer and Stucken; Schleiden, resident minister at Washington for Bremen; Rucker, chargé d'affaires for the city of Hamburg; and Delbruhe, a Prussian official from Berlin. "Their object was," Poor wrote, "to form a correct opinion, for themselves, and for the numerous class of German and Continental investors interested, as to the value and the commercial importance of our roads," *ARJ*, 26:747 (Nov. 19, 1853), also Henry Poor to Mary Poor, Oct. 20, 21, 23, 1853.

74. *ARJ*, 26:370 (June 11, 1853).

75. *ARJ*, 26:370 (June 11, 1853).

76. *ARJ*, 25:417–418 (July 3, 1852) for this and the following quotations in this paragraph. See also *ARJ*, 25:369–370 (June 11, 1852).

77. *ARJ*, 25:418 (July 3, 1852) for this and the following quotations in this paragraph. See also *ARJ*, 25:26 (Jan. 10, 1852).

78. *ARJ*, 25:418, 437 (July 3, 10, 1852).

79. For Poor's views on the speculative character of the Illinois Central, *ARJ*, 24:792, 827 (Dec. 13, 27, 1851); 25:26, 114, 418, 435 (Jan. 10, Feb. 21, July 3, 10, 1852).

80. *ARJ*, 24:792 (Dec. 13, 1851).

81. For views of financial and railroad men similar to those of Poor see Paul W. Gates, *The Illinois Central Railroad and Its Colonization Work* (Cambridge, Mass., 1934), pp. 69, 72–75 and Hidy, *House of Baring*, pp. 413–414, 595. For Kettell's support see *Economist*, 1:797–798 (Oct. 16, 1852); 2:2–3, 20–21, 36, 148, 218, 293, 326, 452 (Oct. 23, 30, Nov. 6, Dec. 18, 1852, Jan. 15, Feb. 12, 19, April 16, 1853). Kettell also considered the Erie issues "sound," *Economist*,

2:153 (Jan. 15, 1853). For the London *Times* and other London papers see reprints and comments in *ARJ*, 25:433–437 (July 10, 1852).

82. The comment is De Bow's, *De Bow's Review*, 8:86 (Jan. 1850). For Samuel Gray Ward's views of Kettell's financial articles see Hidy, *House of Baring*, p. 600.

83. *ARJ*, 25:409 (June 26, 1852).

84. *ARJ*, 25:88 (Feb. 7, 1852).

85. *ARJ*, 25:449–450, 617, 776 (July 17, Sept. 25, Dec. 4, 1852).

86. For bonds, *ARJ*, 25:137, 232–233, 409 (Feb. 28, April 10, June 26, 1852); for stocks, *ARJ*, 25:680, 729 (Oct. 23, Nov. 13, 1852), also *Economist*, 1:672–674 (Sept. 18, 1852).

Chapter 5: Warning Against Overconstruction

1. *ARJ*, 25:761 (Nov. 27, 1852); also *ARJ*, 26:136–137 (Feb. 26, 1853). For the comments of other business editors see *Bankers' Magazine*, 7:494, 590, 672, 751 (Dec. 1852, Jan., Feb., March 1853); *Hunt's*, 27:714 (Dec. 1852); 28:73 (Jan. 1853) and the *Economist*, 2:77, 96–97, 150 (Nov. 20, 27, Dec. 18, 1852).

2. This and the following quotations in this paragraph are from Poor's long editorial of Dec. 11, 1852 in *ARJ*, 25:785–787. For further elaboration of this policy see *ARJ*, 26:136–137, 305, 328, 481–482, 577–578 (Feb. 26, May 14, 21, July 30, Sept. 10, 1853) 27:8–9 (Jan. 7, 1854); 28:225–226 (April 14, 1855).

3. *ARJ*, 26:1 (Jan. 1, 1853).

4. *Bankers' Magazine*, 7:590 (Jan. 1853).

5. *ARJ*, 25:561 (Sept. 4, 1852). Other editorials on the significance of the closing up on the railroad system are *ARJ*, 25:168, 600–602, 679, 776 (March 13, Sept. 18, Oct. 23, Dec. 4, 1852).

6. *ARJ*, 25:600–602 (Sept. 18, 1852). See also *ARJ*, 25:776 (Dec. 4, 1852).

7. During 1852 both Homans of the *Bankers' Magazine* and Poor agreed Wall Street had clinched its position as the nation's financial capital. "Both Philadelphia and Boston assume the condition of the New York market as criterion for themselves," Homans admitted in the spring of 1852, "and as the rates rise and fall on Wall Street, so they rise and fall in other cities." That fall Homans, conceding completely New York's supremacy, moved his magazine from Boston to Wall Street. At the same time Poor was pointing out that the roads built to serve Philadelphia and Baltimore had to depend on New York for capital. He reported that the presidents of two of the Pennsylvania Railroad's primary feeders, the Ohio and Pennsylvania and the Springfield, Mount Vernon, and Pittsburgh, had told him if they had had to rely on Philadelphia for even a small portion of their funds, they would have had to suspend construction, *ARJ*, 25:170, 536, 682, 792 (March 13, Aug. 21, Oct. 23, Dec. 11, 1852), and *Bankers' Magazine*, 6:839 (April 1852).

8. A representative list of these houses is the list of bidders for an Erie issue in 1855, *ARJ*, 28:41 (Jan. 20, 1855). According to the listing in "Wilson's New York City Co-Partnership Directory," printed in Trow's *New York City Directory for 1854–1855* (New York, 1854), Von Hoffman and his partners were also partners in a German firm of the same name and G. Vombaur and Company were the New York partners of the Bank of Commerce and Industry in Darmstadt, Hesse. Joseph A. Scoville (Walter Barrett, pseud.), *Old Merchants of New York City*, first series (New York, 1864), pp. 131–132, gives Schuchardt and Gebhard's European connections. Before forming their partnership Marie had been a partner in De Coppet and Company and Kanz had been with Von Hoffman and Company, *Railroad Record*, 2:442 (Sept. 7, 1854). Fritz Redlich, *The Moulding of American Banking, Men and Ideas* (Ann Arbor, Michigan, 1951), II, 352 has a brief sketch of Duncan, Sherman and Company. H. Gelpcke who represented German bondholders in the reorganization of the Erie in 1859 was

probably connected with the Berlin banking firm of Breest and Gelpcke, while the close connections of Schall and Luling with German financed Western roads suggests that they had German banking connections.

9. Besides De Launay, Iselin and Clark and Delano, Dunlevy and Company, the foreign houses which were by 1852 fiscal agents of Western roads included Duncan, Sherman and Company, Cammann, and Whitehouse and Company, Carpenter and Vermilye, and G. S. Robbins and Son. De Launay's firm was agent for the Indianapolis and Cincinnati and the Junction, Delano's for the Milwaukee and Mississippi and the Springfield, Mt. Vernon, and Pittsburgh, Duncan's for the Galena and Chicago Union, Cammann's for the Evansville and Illinois and the Terre Haute and Alton, Carpenter's for the New Castle and Richmond and Robbins' for the Chicago and Aurora. Besides these, the following firms also acted as fiscal agents for Western roads during the 1850's: Schuchardt and Gebhard for the Covington and Lexington, the Sacramento Valley, and possibly the Marietta and Cincinnati; De Coppet and Company for the Milwaukee and Mississippi and the Logansport and Burlington; L. Von Hoffman and Company for the Chicago and Mississippi; Morris K. Jessup for the Joliet and Chicago and after 1859 the Pittsburgh, Fort Wayne and Chicago; Cammann and Company for the Toledo and Wabash, E. Whitehouse and Company for the Texas and New Orleans (both these firms were successors to Cammann, Whitehouse and Company), Churchman and Roberts for the Cincinnati, Peru and Chicago and Clark, Dodge and Company for the Peoria and Bureau Valley. This is an illustrative rather than a complete list. At least two incorporated banks, the Ohio Life and Trust Company and the Farmers' Loan and Trust Company, acted as fiscal agents for Western roads.

10. *ARJ*, 25:506 (Aug. 7, 1852).

11. The correspondence between Adrian Iselin and the officers of the Chicago, Burlington and Quincy Railroad (in the Burlington Archives, Newberry Library, Chicago, Illinois) concerning the bonds of the Northern Cross owned by the Duke of Brunswick, illustrates how a banking house served as an investor's representative. See also letters printed in the *Journal* by Gelpcke to Meyer and Stucken; *ARJ*, 27:723 (Nov. 18, 1854); 32:465–466 (July 23, 1859).

12. So also were bankers Herman Gelpcke, Charles and Theodore Moran, Edward Whitehouse, John Ferguson, Louis Von Hoffman, William M. Vermilye and merchants G. T. Oliphant, Henry Chauncy, and William S. Wetmore. Winslow was a director in the Madison and Indianapolis, the Indianapolis and Bellefontaine, and the Pittsburgh, Fort Wayne and Chicago; Lanier in the Madison and Indianapolis and (in 1862) the Pittsburgh, Fort Wayne and Chicago; Schuchardt in the New Albany and Salem and the Schuylkill and Susquehanna; Whitehouse in the Toledo and Wabash and the Lockport and Niagara Falls; Gebhard in the Illinois Central, the Dubuque and Pacific, and the Maysville and Lexington; Charles Moran in the Erie and the Buffalo and State Line; Theodore Moran in the New Albany and Salem; Ferguson in the Madison and Indianapolis; Robbins in the Chicago and Galena Union; Gelpcke in the Erie; Meyer in the New Albany and Salem, the Pittsburgh, Fort Wayne and Chicago, and the Maysville and Lexington; Von Hoffman in the Erie; Delano in the Cumberland and Pennsylvania; Stockwell in the Lafayette and Indianapolis; Oliphant in the Cleveland and Toledo; Vermilye in the Michigan Southern and the Cleveland and Toledo; and Butler in the Chicago and Northwestern. These names are taken from James W. Low, Jr., *Low's Railway and Telegraph Directory for 1858* (New York, 1858); Low and Burgess, *Low and Burgess' Railway Directory for 1859* (New York, 1859); and scattered references in *ARJ*. This is certainly only a partial list.

13. For the role of Winslow, Lanier, Von Hoffman, Ferguson, and Charles Moran in the reorganization of the Pittsburgh, Fort Wayne and Chicago, see Lanier, *Sketch of the Life of Lanier*, pp. 24–28; *Second Annual Report of the Board of Directors of the Pittsburgh, Fort Wayne and Chicago Railroad Company to the Stockholders* (Pittsburgh, 1859), p. 6; for the role of Von Hoffman, Meyer,

and William Schall in the reorganization of the Milwaukee and Mississippi, see *ARJ,* 33:764 (Sept. 1, 1860); for Meyer, Schall, and Charles Luling in that of the Jeffersonville Railroad, see *ARJ,* 31:745–746 (Nov. 20, 1858); for Charles Moran and Von Hoffman in the Erie, see Edward H. Mott, *Between the Ocean and the Lakes; the Story of the Erie* (New York, 1908), p. 116.

14. Redlich, *The Moulding of American Banking,* p. 326.

15. Reginald C. McGrane, *Foreign Bondholders and American State Debts* (New York, 1935), p. 7, estimates the states' indebtedness incurred during the decade of the 1830's at some $144,000,000. In January 1860 Poor estimated the cost of American railroads at close to $1,120,000,000; *ARJ,* 33:2 (Jan. 7, 1860). Of this amount, well over half of which came from sale of bonds in the Eastern commercial cities, only a little more than $200,000,000 was raised before 1850. A conservative estimate of the value of the securities disposed of by railroads, both municipal and corporate, between 1850 and 1853 might be $150,000,000, of which $45,000,000 went abroad. The United States Treasury Department in *Report of the Secretary of the Treasury in Answer to a Resolution of the Senate Calling for the Amount of American Securities Held in Europe and other Foreign Countries on the 30th June, 1853* (Senate Document 42, 33rd Congress, 1st Session) puts the securities issued by railroads at just over $400,000,000, of which $52,000,000 was held by foreigners. In this same report Winslow, Lanier and Company estimated that in three states alone — Ohio, Indiana, and Kentucky — counties had issued a total of $8,100,000 of which $5,000,000 went abroad. Both Thomas Wren Ward and the London *Times* considered these figures to be much too low, McGrane, *Foreign Bondholders,* pp. 277–278. In September 1854 Poor estimated that close to $150,000,000 of foreign capital had been invested in American railroads which represented close to one third of their total cost. By the end of 1857 *Hunt's* estimated that $160,000,000 of railroad securities had been sent to England alone, *Hunt's* 38:21 (Jan. 1858). For the same date the statistician Richard S. Fisher estimated the total state and federal debt at $265,-000,000, *ARJ,* 31:25 (Jan. 9, 1858).

16. *ARJ,* 26:209–210 (April 2, 1853); 27:586–587, 632 (Sept. 16, Oct. 7, 1854).

17. John M. Forbes to John W. Brooks, April 9, 1855, a letter in the archives of Michigan Central Railroad Company at the road's Terminal Building in Detroit, Michigan. I am indebted to Professor Thomas Cochran for this citation.

18. *ARJ,* 26:562 (Sept. 3, 1853); also *ARJ,* 26:513–514 (Aug. 13, 1853).

19. For editorials addressed after 1852 to investors, especially foreign investors, see *ARJ,* 26:97–98, 369–371, 401–402, 561–562, 586–587, 747–749 (Feb. 12, June 11, 25, Sept. 3, 10, Nov. 19, 1853); 27:32–33, 266, 315, 424–425, 572–573, 689–690 (Jan. 21, April 29, May 20, July 8, Sept. 9, Nov. 4, 1854); 28:17, 417–418, 561–562 (Jan. 13, July 7, Sept. 8, 1855). For comments on earnings see *ARJ,* 26:657–658, 761 (Oct. 15, Nov. 26, 1853); 27:456–458, 505 (July 22, Aug. 12, 1854); 28:392 (June 23, 1855); 29:568 (Sept. 6, 1856); for Winslow, Lanier and Company, *ARJ,* 26:425–426 (July 2, 1853); 28:1 (Jan. 6, 1855); 29:8, 12–13 (Jan. 5, 1856).

20. This and the following quotation are from *ARJ,* 27:762 (December 2, 1854).

21. *ARJ,* 26:827 (Dec. 24, 1853).

22. *ARJ,* 22:726 (Nov. 17, 1849); 27:762 (Dec. 2, 1854).

23. For comments on air lines and rival roads see *ARJ,* 24:56–57 (Jan. 25, 1851); 25:172, 648 (March 13, Oct. 9, 1852); 26:482, 828, 842–843 (July 30, Dec. 24, 31, 1853); 27:58, 89, 394, 513–514, 522, 550 (Jan. 28, Feb. 11, June 24, Aug. 19, Sept. 2, 1854).

24. *ARJ,* 26:8, 497–498 (Jan. 1, Aug. 6, 1853); 27:401–402 (July 1, 1854).

25. See especially *ARJ,* 27:365–366, 449–450 (June 10, July 22, 1854).

26. *ARJ,* 27:449 (July 22, 1854).

27. *ARJ,* 25:448–449, 617, 776 (July 17, Sept. 25, Dec. 4, 1852); 26:513–514 (Aug. 13, 1853); 27:248 (April 22, 1854).

28. *Annual Report of the Railroad Commissioners of the State of New York . . . for the Year Ending September 30, 1855* (Albany, 1856), I, p. xx.

29. Sarah F. Hughes, *Letters and Recollections of John Murray Forbes* (Boston, 1899), I, 162; for Jervis see John B. Jervis, *Railway Property* (New York, 1861), pp. 58, 60.

30. *Seventh Annual Report of the President and Directors of the Ohio and Pennsylvania Railroad Company, Pittsburgh, January 25, 1855* (Pittsburgh, 1855), p. 3. For similar views by another financier see *ARJ*, 30:553–557 (Aug. 29, 1857). For the demands by Forbes's operating managers for feeder lines see Thomas C. Cochran, *Railroad Leaders, 1845–1890* (Cambridge, Mass., 1953), pp. 268–269, 365–366. The story of Jervis' Michigan Southern can be pieced together from articles in *ARJ* cited below in footnote 59.

31. For examples of Poor's views on contracting see *ARJ*, 26:509 (Aug. 6, 1853); 27:330, 697–698, 762–763 (May 27, Nov. 4, Dec. 2, 1854); 28:33, 104–105, 273 (Jan. 20, Feb. 10, May 5, 1855). For similar comments by leading railroad men see Jervis, *Railway Property*, ch. 4; Hughes, *Letters of John Murray Forbes*, p. 163; and a letter printed in *ARJ*, 30:553–557 (Aug. 29, 1857).

32. Besides the contracts previously cited for the Atlantic and St. Lawrence and the Terre Haute and Alton, good examples of the gross contract and large contractors' operations can be found in Henry W. Farnam, *Henry Farnam* (New Haven, c. 1889), pp. 41–45, 54–55.

33. *ARJ*, 26:488 (July 30, 1853). Alvah C. Morton, who had recently become Seymour's partner, carried on the firm under the name of Seymour, Morton and Company. From 1855 to 1856 the firm advertised in the *Journal* that it was "prepared to contract for the construction and equipment of railroads in any part of the country; also to furnish corps of Engineers and Contractors; Locomotive Engines and Cars; Railroad Iron, Chairs, Spikes, Switch-irons, etc. They will also sell or negotiate loans on all kinds of Railroad Securities. . . . [and] have to dispose of at private sale, in amounts to suit persons desirous of investing, a large amount of valuable Railroad and other Securities," *ARJ*, 28:509 (Aug. 11, 1855). The firm listed regularly in the *Journal* the securities of the roads it was constructing that it had for sale.

34. *Bankers' Magazine*, 9:81 (Aug. 1854); Edward C. Kirkland, *Men, Cities and Transportation* (Cambridge, Mass., 1948), I, 260–266; *ARJ*, 26:328–329 (May 21, 1853); 27:405, 433–434 (July 1, 15, 1854).

35. *ARJ*, 28:82–83, 273–277 (Feb. 10, May 5, 1855). This operation made Poor increasingly skeptical of the Rock Island management, *ARJ*, 29:248, 625, 626, 817 (April 19, Oct. 4, Dec. 27, 1856). Poor referred to the sale of the Joliet cutoff to the Michigan Central as a similar "bogus operation," *ARJ*, 28:110 (Feb. 17, 1855). Poor later suspected that the construction of the Missouri and Mississippi Railroad and the Rock Island bridge by these same contracting directors was a similar sort of a job, *ARJ*, 31:57–58 (Jan. 23, 1858); 32:377, 408 (June 11, 25, 1859); 33:912–913 (Oct. 13, 1860).

36. *ARJ*, 27:167, 221–222, 225, 428 (March 18, April 8, 15, July 8, 1854); 28:33, 104–105, 168–169, 178–179, 401, 488, 776 (Jan. 20, Feb. 17, March 17, 24, June 30, Aug. 4, Dec. 8, 1855); also *Hunt's*, 32:209–210 (Feb. 1855) and *Railroad Record*, 5:226 (Jan. 4, 1857), and *Reports and Statistical Documents Pertaining to the Ohio and Mississippi Railroad; Extending from Cincinnati to St. Louis* (Cincinnati, 1853), pp. 3–9. Besides its faulty financing and the fact that it took bonds directly to London, Poor disapproved of the road's broad gauge.

37. See, for example, the list of railroads under construction in Illinois in 1854 in *ARJ*, 27:595–598 (Sept. 23, 1854).

38. *ARJ*, 26:786 (Dec. 11, 1852).

39. This and the following quotations are from *ARJ*, 26:786–787 (Dec. 11, 1852).

40. *Exhibit of the Conditions, Progress and Business of the Covington and Lexington Railroad Company, December 1852, March 1853* (New York, 1853).

Pages 1–13 include the report dated December 1852 which Poor criticized; pages 14–22, dated March 1853, include the second report which met with Poor's approval.

41. *ARJ*, 26:321 (May 21, 1853).

42. *ARJ*, 26:289 (May 7, 1853).

43. *Railway Times*, Dec. 30, 1852, Jan. 6, Feb. 24, 1853; *ARJ*, 26:74 (Jan. 29, 1853); New York *Tribune*, May 9, 10, 1853.

44. *ARJ*, 26:289–290, 310–311 (May 7, 14, 1853).

45. These men, as well as Thomas C. Durand and John Stryker, became directors in June 1853; compare list of directors in *Exhibit of the Terre Haute and Alton Railroad Company, November, 1852* (New York, 1852) and *First Annual Report of the President and Directors of the Terre Haute and Alton Railroad Company* (New York, 1853).

46. The information in this paragraph is from *The Second Annual Report of the President and the Directors of the Terre Haute and Alton Rail-Road Company to the Stockholders. . . . Presented January 1st, 1855* (New York, 1855), pp. 13, 15–16; *Report of Azariah C. Flagg, Trustee and Surviving Receiver, to the Bondholders of the Terre Haute, Alton and St. Louis Railroad* (New York, 1868), pp. 55, 57–59; *ARJ*, 28:364–365 (June 9, 1855); 31:88, 121 (Feb. 6, 20, 1858); Muriel E. Hidy, "George Peabody, Merchant and Financier, 1829–1854," an unpublished doctoral dissertation submitted at Radcliffe College in 1939, p. 339; Alvin F. Harlow, *The Road of the Century* (New York, 1947), pp. 364–365.

47. This and the following quotations are from *ARJ*, 26:74 (Jan. 29, 1853); for examples of Poor's earlier attacks on the "exclusive" policy of Illinois see, *ARJ*, 22:230–231, 822 (April 14, Dec. 29, 1849).

48. *ARJ*, 26:74 (Jan. 29, 1853). In this editorial Poor wrote "We have had sufficient experience to see and feel the advantage of being entirely independent, and we are fully satisfied that it is for our interest to remain so, to say nothing of the principle of the thing."

49. *ARJ*, 24:801–802 (Dec. 20, 1851); 26:747–749 (Nov. 19, 1853); 27:58–59, 119, 123–124, 315 (Jan. 28, Feb. 25, May 20, 1854); 28:561–562, 690 (Sept. 8, Nov. 3, 1855).

50. *ARJ*, 28:193 (March 31, 1855), also *ARJ*, 28:216 (April 7, 1855).

51. *ARJ*, 27:451 (July 22, 1854).

52. *ARJ*, 25:88 (Feb. 7, 1852). For reports meeting Poor's standards see *ARJ*, 28:245, 356 (April 21, June 9, 1855).

53. From an annual report of the Marietta and Cincinnati Railroad Company printed in *ARJ*, 24:369 (June 14, 1851); for similar statements see *Third Annual Report of the President and Directors to the Stockholders of the Ohio and Pennsylvania Railroad Company* (Pittsburgh, 1851), pp. 13–14; James F. Kirkwood, "Railroad Enterprises and Their Detractors," *Hunt's*, 32:405 (April 1855); *Annual Report of the Railroad Commissioners of New York for 1855*, I, xxvii.

54. So too were his criticisms of the Fort Wayne and Southern, the Atlantic and Pacific, the New Orleans, Jackson and Great Northern, and the Galveston, Houston and Henderson. For the Louisville and Nashville, see *ARJ*, 27:426–427, 437–438, 572 (July 8, 15, Sept. 9, 1854); for Fort Wayne and Southern, *ARJ*, 28:194, 233 (March 31, April 14, 1855); for Evansville, Indianapolis and Cleveland, *ARJ*, 28:7, 194, 216, 241–242, 280, 296–297, 461 (Jan. 6, March 31, April 7, 21, May 5, 12, July 21, 1855); Atlantic and Pacific, *ARJ*, 26:635, 728 (Oct. 1, Nov. 12, 1853); 27:395–396 (June 24, 1854); New Orleans, Jackson and Great Northern, *ARJ*, 26:449–450, 473 (July 16, 23, 1853); Galveston, Houston and Henderson, *ARJ*, 28:502, 625, 665 (Aug. 11, Oct. 6, 20, 1855).

55. *ARJ*, 26:482 (July 30, 1853); also *ARJ*, 26:778 (Dec. 3, 1853), 28:225–226 (April 14, 1855). For value of personal inspection see *ARJ*, 26:747–749 (Nov. 19, 1853); for printing articles sent in by promoters see *ARJ*, 25:183 (March 20, 1853), 28:264 (April 28, 1855). A letter from the publishers of the Cincinnati *Railroad Record* to Henry N. Day, dated March 30, 1853, indicates

that the printing of copy sent by promoters without making any changes was a standard practice. I am indebted to Dr. R. Richard Wohl for this citation.

56. *ARJ*, 30:136, 177–178, 209, 457 (Feb. 28, March 21, April 4, July 18, 1857).

57. *ARJ*, 30:418–419, 440–441 (July 4, 11, 1857).

58. *ARJ*, 30:456 (July 18, 1857); also *ARJ*, 30:488–489, 504–505, 520 (Aug. 1, 8, 15, 1857); 31:120, 156–157, 329 (Feb. 20, March 6, May 22, 1858); 32:344 (May 28, 1859).

59. For Poor's comments on the Michigan Southern's management before its breakdown see *ARJ*, 26:584, 763, 793 (Sept. 10, Nov. 26, Dec. 10, 1853); 27:41–42, 184, 497 (Jan. 21, March 25, Aug. 12, 1854), 28:264, 456, 744 (April 28, July 21, Nov. 24, 1855); 30:120–121, 214, 264–265 (Feb. 21, April 4, 25, 1857); for comments after the company's financial collapse, *ARJ*, 30:376–377, 441, 529–531, 600, 609–610 (June 13, July 11, Aug. 22, Sept. 19, 26, 1857), 31:218, 739–740 (April 3, Nov. 20, 1858); 32:360, 563, 568 (June 4, Sept. 3, 1859); 33:312, 360 (April 14, 28, 1860).

60. For examples, *ARJ*, 27:221, 225, 344 (April 8, 15, June 3, 1854); 28:241–242, 264, 280, 461, 568 (April 21, 28, May 5, July 21, Sept. 8, 1855); *Railway Times*, Feb. 23, Aug. 17, Oct. 12, Nov. 2, 1854; Feb. 8, May 31, June 21, 1855; *Railroad Advocate*, May 5, 1855; *Railroad Record*, 2:65–67 (March 30, 1854), 3:66, 131 (March 29, April 26, 1855), and supplement to Nov. 19, 1855 issue.

61. *Railway Times*, Oct. 12, 1854.

62. *Hunt's*, 27:206–207 (Aug. 1852).

63. *Railroad Record*, 1:785–787 (Feb. 6, 1854); 2:17–18, 65–66, 129–130 (March 9, 30, April 27, 1854); *ARJ*, 27:58–59, 119–120, 167, 218 (Jan. 28, Feb. 25, March 18, April 8, 1854).

64. *ARJ*, 27:119 (Feb. 25, 1854).

65. *Railroad Record*, 4:97–98, 497 (April 10, Oct. 2, 1856).

66. *Railway Times*, Aug. 18, Oct. 20, 1853; July 6, 20, Sept. 21, Nov. 30, 1854; Jan. 5, 1855; May 29, 1856. For articles on the financial promise of new roads projected and under construction in the Mississippi Valley, see *Railway Times*, Jan. 27, 1853; April 20, Sept. 28, Oct. 12, Nov. 2, 1854; Jan. 11, 18, Feb. 8, May 10, 1855.

67. For example, *Railway Times*, Sept. 28, 1854, Feb. 8, May 10, 1855. For Evans and the Indianapolis *Locomotive* see Harlow, *Road of the Century*, pp. 356–359.

68. The best editorial summarizing Poor's views on land grants after December 1852 is *ARJ*, 27:161–162 (March 18, 1854); compare this with Poor's earlier view favoring grants in *ARJ*, 25:58–59 (Jan. 24, 1852). For the similar views of John Murray Forbes on the inflationary influences of land grants see Henry G. Pearson, *An American Railroad Builder* (Boston, 1911), pp. 187–191.

69. *ARJ*, 27:161 (March 18, 1854).

70. *ARJ*, 30:1, 392, 472–473, 633 (Jan. 3, June 20, July 25, Oct. 3, 1857); 31:264 (April 24, 1858).

71. The quotations in this and the following sentence are from *ARJ*, 30:472–473 (July 25, 1857). See also, *ARJ*, 30:392 (June 20, 1857).

72. Two of the best editorials on Poor's views after December 1852 concerning municipal aid are *ARJ*, 26:346–347 (May 28, 1853); 27:449–450 (July 22, 1854), also compare *ARJ*, 24:289–291, 314 (May 10, 17, 1851) to *ARJ*, 26:449–450 (July 16, 1853).

73. *ARJ*, 27:449–450 (July 22, 1854).

74. For Poor's comments on state aid and on the Tennessee railroad law see *ARJ*, 27:602 (Sept. 24, 1854); 28:281, 673–675 (May 5, Oct. 27, 1855); 29:344 (May 31, 1856); 30:481 (Aug. 1, 1857); 31:792 (Dec. 11, 1858); 33:124 (Feb. 11, 1860). Poor was not quite clear on how the funds which were not provided locally were to be raised. If $20,000 to $25,000 a mile were raised locally, some $10,000 more would be needed to make the $35,000-a-mile figure which Poor

estimated was required to complete a road. He appears to have assumed that investors would accept second mortgage bonds up to $10,000 a mile on such a conservatively financed road.

75. *ARJ*, 30:392 (June 20, 1857); 31:265 (April 24, 1858). Minnesota's experience suggested a flaw in Poor's views on state credit. In hard times a new state like Minnesota had to sell its own securities at a heavy discount, thus defeating Poor's purpose for state credit, which was to obtain funds for railroad construction without the financial sacrifice usually involved in marketing the securities of new roads in recently opened areas. Poor's answer was that Minnesota should have withheld granting bonds to her railroads until the return of good times brought the value of these bonds up nearly to par. Her basic scheme was, he believed, proper enough; the error had come in its execution, see *ARJ*, 33:520–521 (June 16, 1860).

76. This comparison is well stated in *ARJ*, 30:481 (Aug. 1, 1857).

77. *ARJ*, 26:346 (May 28, 1853).

78. *ARJ*, 28:673 (Oct. 27, 1855).

79. Carter Goodrich, "The Revulsion Against Internal Improvements," *Journal of Economic History,* 10:168–169 (Nov. 1950); Milton S. Heath, "Public Co-operation in Railroad Construction in the Southern United States until 1861," an unpublished doctoral dissertation submitted at Harvard University in 1937, p. 49.

80. *Railway Times,* Feb. 15, 22, 1855. De Bow, surprisingly enough, says little about the merits of the Southern system of mixed enterprise. Kettell praised the conservative financing of Southern railroads but wrote little about state financial aid, Thomas Prentiss Kettell, *Southern Wealth and Northern Profits* (New York, 1860), pp. 86–88.

81. *ARJ*, 26:656–657 (Oct. 15, 1853); 27:24, 266, 296, 424–425, 456–458 (Jan. 14, April 29, May 13, July 8, 22, 1854); 28:392, 433 (June 23, July 14, 1855).

Chapter 6: Calling for Financial and Administrative Reform

1. *Annual Report of the Railroad Commissioners of New York . . . for the Year Ending September 30, 1855* (Albany, 1856), I, xlv–xlvi, II, 3–4.

2. The *Western Railroad Gazette,* the forerunner of one of the leading post-Civil War railroad papers, was founded in 1857. I have been unable to obtain the early volumes of the journal, but have read articles reprinted from it in the *American Railroad Journal.*

3. *Railroad Advocate,* April 19, 1856. In issuing a prospectus for his paper the *Railroad Register,* Thomas Fernon stressed that it would be a spokesman for the interests of Philadelphia, particularly those threatened by the "menace" of New York, *Register,* 1:172 (Oct. 28, 1856); also *Register,* 1:140 (Sept. 27, 1856).

4. *ARJ*, 28:145–146, 289–290, 443, 449–450, 705–706 (March 10, May 12, July 14, 21, Nov. 10, 1855); 29:1–2, 113, 728–729, 760–761, 777 (Jan. 5, Feb. 23, Nov. 15, 29, Dec. 6, 1856).

5. *ARJ*, 28:114, 145, 216–217, 233 (Feb. 24, March 10, April 7, 14, 1855); 30:449–450 (July 18, 1857); 31:312–313, 523–524 (May 15, Aug. 14, 1858); *Economist,* June 29, July 13, 1859.

6. *ARJ*, 29:424, 568 (July 5, Sept. 6, 1856); 30:680 (Oct. 24, 1857); 31:696 (Oct. 30, 1858); 33:212–213, 804–805 (March 10, Sept. 8, 1860). For a similar defense of the American railroads by a leading engineer and friend of Poor's see James P. Kirkwood, "Railroad Enterprises and Their Detractors," *Hunt's,* 36:403–413 (April 1855).

7. *ARJ*, 27:826 (Dec. 30, 1854); 28:8 (Jan. 6, 1855); 29:113 (Feb. 23, 1856); 30:633–634, 665 (Oct. 3, 17, 1857); 31:1 (Jan. 2, 1858); 32:34 (May 28, 1859).

8. *ARJ*, 28:657–658 (Oct. 20, 1855); 29:113, 728–729 (Feb. 23, Nov. 15, 1856).

9. See especially *ARJ*, 28:689–690, 705–706 (Nov. 3, 10, 1855). The first two quotations in the paragraph are from the first of the above citations; the last from the second. Poor also wrote a series of editorials on banking and currency in 1857, *ARJ*, 30:744, 760, 776, 792, 808–809, 824–825 (Nov. 21, 28, Dec. 5, 12, 19, 26, 1857).

10. *ARJ*, 29:568 (Sept. 6, 1856); 30:584–585 (Sept. 12, 1857); 31:312–313 (May 15, 1858); 32:392 (June 18, 1859).

11. *ARJ*, 27:574 (Sept. 9, 1854); 28:107–108 (Feb. 17, 1855); Edward Hungerford, *Men and Iron: the History of the New York Central* (New York, 1939), pp. 86–89. Sometimes the register and transfer accounts were kept in the same office, John J. Hill, *A Concise Method of Keeping the Accounts and Stock Transfers of Railroad and other Corporate Agencies in the City of New York* (New York, 1858), ch. 2.

12. *ARJ*, 31:136 (Feb. 27, 1858); also *ARJ*, 32:520 (Aug. 13, 1859). In this case Poor had a chance to practice what he preached. In September 1857 he agreed to act with Azariah C. Flagg as trustee for the Meadville Railroad, the Pennsylvania section of what was soon to be the Atlantic and Great Western Railroad. The editor quickly became disturbed by the speculative nature of the company. Unable to raise funds locally, the directors were planning to market large blocks of bonds in New York and London. Poor was also dissatisfied with the company's plans for spending the money. In February 1858 he wrote William Reynolds that he refused as trustee to permit the sale of bonds which he considered at the moment worthless. "I cannot allow my name to be used in any manner to mislead the public," he insisted, "nor will I consent to its use when I cannot see that all the monies raised in connection with it are applied properly. I take it the duties of a Trustee commence the instant he assumes his trust and are not delayed until the road gets into difficulty and breaks down." If the managers persisted in their plans, Poor wrote, he would have to sever all connections with the company. No changes were made, so Poor in mid-April resigned as trustee, and turned over the bonds which he had endorsed to Flagg who, at the editor's request, destroyed them. The story is made clear in letters from Henry Poor to William Reynolds, Feb. 25, March 18, May 16, 1858, William Reynolds to Henry Poor, April 7, 1858, George Church to William Reynolds, April 8, 20, 1858. All these letters are in the William Reynolds Collection, Allegheny College Library, Meadville, Pa.

13. *Seventh Annual Report of the President and Directors of the Ohio and Pennsylvania Railroad Company, Pittsburgh, January 25, 1855* (Pittsburgh, 1855), pp. 4–5, *ARJ*, 27:598–599 (Sept. 23, 1854).

14. *ARJ*, 27:723 (Nov. 18, 1854); Meyer's letters to Poor urging a sinking fund for the Erie are printed in *ARJ*, 27:586–587, 629 (Sept. 16, Oct. 7, 1854).

15. *ARJ*, 27:602 (Sept. 23, 1854); for other editorial comments on sinking fund see *ARJ*, 27:562, 577–579 (Sept. 9, 16, 1854).

16. See "Annual Circular of Messrs. De Coppet and Co.," printed in *ARJ*, 30:37 (Jan. 17, 1857); Hill, *Keeping the Accounts and Stock Transfers of Railroad . . . Agencies,* p. 21; James H. Whiton, *Railroads and Their Management* (Concord, N. H., 1856), pp. 24–25.

17. *ARJ*, 27:330–331 (May 27, 1854).

18. *ARJ*, 27:330–331, 374–375, 490, 697–698 (May 27, June 17, Aug. 5, Nov. 4, 1854). All the following quotations are from pages 330–331.

19. *ARJ*, 32:696–697 (Oct. 29, 1859), also *ARJ*, 32:771–772, 784 (Dec. 3, 1859).

20. For Pittsburgh, Fort Wayne and Chicago see *ARJ*, 33:392, 961 (May 12, Oct. 27, 1860); for the Erie *ARJ*, 32:592–593, 628–629, 694–695, 696 (Sept. 17, Oct. 1, 29, 1859). For use of preferred stock in the financial reorganization of the Milwaukee and Mississippi, which was managed in part by Lewis H. Meyer and Louis von Hoffman, see *ARJ*, 33:360, 380, 765 (April 28, May 5, Sept. 1, 1860). It was also used by Hessletine and Powell in the financial reorganization of the Marietta and Cincinnati in 1860, John E. Pixon, "The Marietta and

Cincinnati Railroad, 1875–1883" (an unpublished study written in 1954), pp. 51, 68–71.

21. Frederick A. Cleveland and Fred W. Powell, *Railroad Finance* (New York, 1912), p. 262. In the Middle Atlantic States, where bonds were used for construction, preferred stock, as more than a temporary financial device, came first into use in the financial reorganizations of the 1840's. It was used for this purpose by the Schuylkill Navigation Company in 1845, the Reading in 1848, the Morris Canal in 1849 and the Tioga in 1851. In New England, where prior to the 1850's stock was used to finance construction, it was first used by financially weak roads to complete construction or expand facilities. The preferred issues of the Housatonic, the Norwich and Worcester, the Hartford, Providence and Fishkill, the Cheshire, and the Cambridge and West Lexington are cases in point. It was also used for this purpose by the Cumberland Valley and the Harlem in 1848. The articles by George H. Evans on "The Early History of Preferred Stock in the United States," and "Preferred Stock in the United States, 1850–1878," *American Economic Review,* 19:43–58 (March 1929) and 21:56–79 (March 1931) are concerned largely with issues of preferred stock used as temporary financial devices for raising funds for construction.

22. *ARJ,* 28:56–57 (Jan. 27, 1855), also *ARJ,* 27:129–130 (March 4, 1854); 32:552 (Aug. 27, 1859). There are many references to the uses and abuses of the construction account in Poor's critical editorials on different railroads cited below in footnote 30.

23. *ARJ,* 27:129 (March 4, 1854).

24. John B. Jervis, *Railway Property* (New York, 1861), p. 304.

25. Besides *ARJ,* 27:129–130 (March 4, 1854), 28:56–57 (Jan. 27, 1855), Poor said much on the points covered in this paragraph in his analyses of railroad reports and in statistical studies cited in footnotes 28–30 below. For similar comments by contemporaries see Jervis, *Railway Property,* pp. 302–309 and the *Third Annual Report of the President and Directors of the Cleveland, Columbus and Cincinnati Railroad Company, January 11, 1854* (Cleveland, 1854), p. 8, and comments in the "Annual Report of the State Engineer of New York State for 1854" printed in *ARJ,* 28:67–68 (Feb. 3, 1855) and a similar report for 1857 printed in *ARJ,* 31:195–196 (March 27, 1858). In his 1858 questionnaire, which is discussed in Chapter VII, Poor asked whether the roads kept separate depreciation and renewal accounts; in the accounts to be submitted he asked for data on repairs and renewals which were to be listed under operating expenses; but he also asked for estimates of cost to maintain road and equipment in top operating condition, *ARJ,* 31:114, 131, 146 (Feb. 20, 27, March 6, 1858); see also Thomas C. Cochran, *Railroad Leaders, 1845–1890* (Cambridge, Mass., 1953), p. 88.

26. *ARJ,* 27:526–527 (Aug. 19, 1854); 28:9, 33 (Jan. 6, 20, 1855).

27. Quoted from the "Annual Report of the State Engineer of New York State for 1854," printed in *ARJ,* 28:67 (Feb. 3, 1855).

28. For the uses of cost accounting see *ARJ,* 26:403–405 (June 25, 1853); 27:102–103, 110 (Feb. 18, 1854); 28:497–499, 547, 817–818 (Aug. 11, Sept. 1, Dec. 29, 1855); 29:120, 229 (Feb. 23, April 12, 1856); 30:793 (Dec. 12, 1857); 31:584 (Sept. 11, 1858); 32:392, 408, 489, 534, 552, 568, 585, 600, 680 (June 18, 25, July 30, Aug. 20, Aug. 27, Sept. 3, 10, 17, Oct. 22, 1859).

29. *ARJ,* 32:504, 521, 536–538, 553–554, 568, 569–570, 600–601, 629–631, 646–648, 662–663 (Aug. 6, 13, 20, 27, Sept. 3, 17, Oct. 1, 8, 15, 1859).

30. For Michigan Central, *ARJ,* 27:682–683, 696–697 (Oct. 28, Nov. 4, 1854), 28:425, 472, 504, 552 (July 7, 28, Aug. 11, Sept. 1, 1855), 32:504 (Aug. 6, 1859); for Michigan Southern, *ARJ,* 31:216 (April 3, 1858), 32:360, 563, 568 (June 4, Sept. 3, 1859), 33:312, 360 (April 14, 28, 1860); for Delaware, Lackawanna and Western, *ARJ,* 31:616 (Sept. 25, 1858); for Lafayette and Indianapolis, *ARJ,* 31:473 (July 24, 1858); for Panama, *ARJ,* 26:27, 58, 72, 378–379 (Jan. 8, 22, 29, June 11, 1853), 27:776 (Dec. 9, 1854); the Rock Island, *ARJ,* 29:248, 625–626, 817 (April 19, Oct. 4, Dec. 27, 1856), 31:57–58, 729 (Jan.

23, Nov. 13, 1858), 33:912 (Oct. 13, 1860); the Camden and Amboy, *ARJ*, 28:785–786 (Dec. 15, 1855), 31:449 (July 17, 1858), 34:120–121 (Feb. 9, 1861); the New York and New Haven, *ARJ*, 27:601, 649, 733 (Sept. 23, Oct. 14, Nov. 18, 1854), 28:312 (May 19, 1855), 32:312 (May 14, 1859); for the New York and Harlem, *ARJ*, 27:529 (Aug. 26, 1854), 28:81–82 (Feb. 10, 1855); for Hudson River, *ARJ*, 25:40, 90–92, 344 (Jan. 17, Feb. 7, May 29, 1852), 26:104, 322, 625–627 (Feb. 12, May 21, Oct. 1, 1853), 27:434, 721–722, 776 (July 15, Nov. 18, Dec. 9, 1854), 30:457 (July 18, 1857); the New York Central, *ARJ*, 27:817 (Dec. 30, 1854), 31:312 (May 15, 1858), 32:584–585, 852–853 (Sept. 10, Dec. 24, 1859).

31. For Poor's first serious criticisms of the Erie, see *ARJ*, 25:17–19, 56, 401–402 (Jan. 10, 24, June 26, 1852); for his severe condemnation early in 1853, *ARJ*, 26:122–124, 145–147, 161–164, 177–182, 193–197, 209–212, 225–226, 392, 409–410, 417–418, 471, 530–531 (Feb. 19, March 5, 12, 19, 26, April 2, 9, June 18, 25, July 2, 23, Aug. 20, 1853); for its speculating directors, *ARJ*, 26:471, 488, 650, 826 (July 23, 30, Oct. 8, Dec. 24, 1853), 27:434 (July 15, 1854); for other comments, *ARJ*, 26:807–810, 826–827 (Dec. 17, 24, 1853), 27:56, 547–549, 561, 586–587 (Jan. 28, Sept. 2, 9, 16, 1854).

32. Both quotations from *ARJ*, 26:182 (March 19, 1853).

33. The directors' reply is reprinted in *ARJ*, 26:193–194 (March 26, 1853); for Greeley's comments, see New York *Tribune*, March 12, 29, 1853.

34. John Murray Forbes to John W. Brooks, July 21, 1855. Forbes's letter to Brooks on advertising in the *Journal* was dated April 9, 1855. Both letters are in the archives of the Michigan Central Railroad in the company's Terminal Building in Detroit, Michigan. I am indebted to Professor Thomas C. Cochran for these two citations. Poor's requests for information will be discussed below in chapter 9. His continuing criticism of the Central appears in *ARJ*, 28:472, 504, 552 (July 28, Aug. 11, Sept. 1, 1855).

35. A. C. Littleton, *Accounting Evolution to 1900* (New York, 1933), pp. 227–236. Edward C. Kirkland, *Men, Cities and Transportation* (Cambridge, Mass., 1948), I, 338–344; Cochran, *Railroad Leaders*, pp. 59, 88–89.

36. Cochran, *Railroad Leaders*, ch. 16. Poor's reforms for financial management are, for example, similar to those of the Eastern financiers mentioned in Hill, *Keeping the Accounts and Stock Transfers of Railroad . . . Agencies*, pp. 27–28. The editor appears to have been closer to the specialized investment bankers like Lanier and Meyer than the more "general entrepreneurs" like William E. Dodge, James Boorman, Edwin D. Morgan, and John C. Green. However, through the Geographical Society he became well acquainted with this type of businessman. Letters to and from Meyer, Powell, and other bankers appear in the *Journal;* examples are *ARJ*, 26:209–210 (April 2, 1853); 27:586–587, 629, 723 (Sept. 16, Oct. 7, Nov. 8, 1854); 28:648–649 (Oct. 13, 1855); 29:457 (July 19, 1856); 32:456–457, 465–466, 628–629 (July 16, 23, Oct. 1, 1859). Meyer once testified that "I know Poor's handwriting; have frequently seen it; have seen him write it," *In The Supreme Court of Pennsylvania, Prentiss* vs. *The Atlantic and Great Western Railroad Company, Penn* v. *the Same* (n.p., 1870), p. 8.

37. These persons and other reformers and intellectuals are mentioned in Mary Poor's diary.

38. Letters of interest and in support of Poor's policies from investors at home and abroad, besides those listed in footnote 36, may be found in *ARJ*, 28:234–235 (April 14, 1855); 29:456–457 (July 19, 1856); 30:690–691 (Oct. 31, 1857); 31:121–122, 641–643 (Feb. 20, Oct. 9, 1858); 32:33, 81–82, 113–114, 369–370, 529–530 (Jan. 15, Feb. 5, 19, June 11, Aug. 20, 1859).

39. Parts of the remainder of this chapter and some of the next chapter follow closely Alfred D. Chandler, Jr., "Henry Varnum Poor, Philosopher of Management," in William Miller ed., *Men in Business* (Cambridge, Mass., 1952), pp. 258–282.

40. These generalizations are made from data found chiefly in H. V. Poor,

History of the Railroads and the Canals of the United States (New York, 1860); (U. S.) Census Office, *Tenth Census, 1880, Report on the Agencies of Transportation* . . . (Washington, 1884) and from mileage and other figures in *ARJ.*

41. Compare, for example, the following operational statistics for the Western Railroad of Massachusetts, running between Albany and Worcester, one of the very largest operating units in the country in 1850, and those of the Erie in 1855. Data on the Western (including the Albany and West Stockbridge) is from *Annual Reports of Railroad Corporations in the Commonwealth of Massachusetts, 1850* (Boston, 1851), pp. 240–241; on the Erie from *Annual Report of the Railroad Commissioners of the State of New York . . . 1855* (Albany, 1856), II, 195, 209.

	The Western (1850)	*The Erie (1855)*
Miles run, passengers	256,758	1,464,839
Miles run, freight	453,111	1,676,500
No. of passengers carried in cars	467,086	1,033,922
Tons of freight carried in cars	261,296	842,054
Expenses	$607,549	$2,625,744
Salaries and wages paid in nearest thousand (excluding president, treasurer, and superintendent)	$175,000	$795,000

42. *Reports of the President and the Superintendent of the New York and Erie Railroad to the Stockholders for the Year Ending September 30, 1855* (New York, n.d.), p. 34. Moreover, as Henry Poor pointed out, the work of an operative on a railroad was on the whole much more skilled and required much more responsibility than that of a mill hand or canal lock tender, *ARJ*, 27:808 (Dec. 23, 1854).

43. *ARJ*, 26:609–611, 826–827 (Sept. 24, Dec. 24, 1853); 27:147–148 (March 11, 1854); also *Report of the Directors of the New York and Erie Railroad Company to the Stockholders, November, 1853* (New York, 1853), pp. 47–48.

44. For comments on Massachusetts roads see *ARJ*, 26: 609–610 (Sept. 24, 1853); and especially *ARJ*, 28:721–723 (Nov. 17, 1855).

45. *ARJ*, 27:147–148 (March 11, 1854). See also *ARJ*, 28:568 (Sept. 8, 1856); 29:264–265 (April 26, 1856).

46. *ARJ*, 28:568 (Sept. 8, 1855). See also *ARJ*, 28:129–130 (March 3, 1855). McCallum's brilliant organizing ability was put to good use during the Civil War when he was commissioned "director and superintendent" of all the Union railroads necessary for the successful prosecution of the war. Before the end of the war he was operating with great efficiency over two thousand miles of line, see sketch in Dumas Malone, *Dictionary of American Biography* (New York, 1946), and Carl R. Fish, "The Northern Railroads, April 1861," *American Historical Review*, 22:779, 790–793 (July 1917).

47. *ARJ*, 27:548–549 (Sept. 2, 1854), discusses fully McCallum's initial reforms. McCallum took office in May 1854 having previously been superintendent of the Erie's Susquehanna Division, Edward H. Mott, *Between the Ocean and the Lakes, the Story of the Erie* (New York, 1899), p. 115.

48. For McCallum's use of the telegraph for railroad operation and administration, see the *Erie Report, 1855*, pp. 45–51; for Poor's emphatic approval of this reform which he urged all roads to adopt see, besides the editorial cited in footnote 47, *ARJ*, 29:40–41, 473, 712 (Jan. 19, July 26, Nov. 8, 1856).

49. *ARJ*, 27:549 (Sept. 2, 1854).

50. This chart is described in *ARJ*, 29:280 (May 3, 1856). Poor noted that: "It was first suggested by McCallum for reference merely; but has been lithographed and is now offered for sale at . . . One Dollar." McCallum's system of organization, communication, and information is fully described in the *Erie Report, 1855*. For Poor's comments on this report, see *ARJ*, 29:225–226 (April 12, 1856); see also *ARJ*, 28:568 (Sept. 8, 1855).

51. *ARJ*, 29:184 (March 22, 1856). In this article Poor describes the carefully detailed organization of the Susquehanna repair shop; see also Colburn's *Railroad Advocate*, Oct. 27, 1855.

52. There was much controversy over the requirements to wear uniforms and insignia as unfitting in a democratic country. Poor's reply to an article in the *Railroad Record* of Cincinnati which disapproved of McCallum's uniform regulations gives a good picture of the requirements and the controversy; *ARJ*, 28:555–556 (Sept. 1, 1855).

53. *Erie Report, 1855*, p. 40.

54. *Erie Report, 1855*, p. 51.

55. *ARJ*, 28:675 (Oct. 27, 1855).

56. *Erie Report, 1855*, p. 52. McCallum's full account of his reporting system is in the *Erie Report, 1855*, pp. 34–35, 51–54. This reporting system, like the organization plan and the use of the telegraph, had been initiated in part on the Erie before McCallum became general superintendent (see *Erie Report, 1853*, pp. 46–53), but he systematized the initial plans and unified them so that they became all integral parts of one comprehensive operating scheme.

57. *Erie Report, 1855*, p. 53.

58. *ARJ*, 28:497–499, 817–818 (Aug. 11, Dec. 29, 1855); 29:161–163, 264–265 (March 15, April 26, 1856); 32:408 (June 25, 1859).

59. For comments on the value of engineering reports, see *ARJ*, 28:497–499, 547 (Aug. 11, Sept. 1, 1855); good examples of analyses of these reports are *ARJ*, 31:296–297 (May 8, 1858); 32:534 (Aug. 20, 1859). The *Advocate*, which claimed to speak for the engineers and other skilled laborers, favored monthly reports, stating that: "Although, perhaps, for a purely selfish purpose, the monthly reports acknowledge the full doings of each engineer, they still serve as an honorable stimulant to exertion," *Advocate*, Nov. 24, 1855.

60. Besides the Erie, monthly engine reports were printed in the newspapers by the New York Central, the Pennsylvania, the Baltimore and Ohio, the Illinois Central, and the Cleveland and Pittsburgh. See for examples and comment, *Advocate*, Oct. 13, 20, Nov. 17, Dec. 15, 1855, Jan. 12, 1856; such engine reports are scattered through *ARJ* from 1855 on.

Similar operating statistics used to determine fuel expenses showed emphatically the cheapness of coal as compared with wood and thus may have hastened the change to coal. During the 1850's Poor repeatedly urged the use of coal, *ARJ*, 26:360, 435–436 (June 4, July 9, 1853); 28:696 (Nov. 3, 1855); 30:777–778, 793 (Dec. 5, 12, 1857); 32:408 (June 25, 1859); 33:437–440, 481–483 (May 26, June 9, 1860).

61. For an excellent editorial on the need for understanding "the absolute and comparative cost of different kinds of traffic," as a basis for rate making, see *ARJ*, 28:817–818 (Dec. 29, 1855); see also *ARJ*, 29:161–163, 193–195, 225–226, 229 (March 15, 29, April 12, 1856); 30:456–457 (July 18, 1857); 32:680 (Oct. 22, 1859); and *Erie Report, 1855*, pp. 78–80.

62. There is a brief discussion of the high fare-low fare controversy in Kirkland, *Men, Cities and Transportation*, I, 357–361. The writings on this matter which received the most attention in *ARJ* were William Appleton and William H. Swift, *Massachusetts Railroads, 1842–1855* (Boston, 1856); E. B. Grant, *Boston Railways: Their Condition and Prospects* (Boston, 1856); James M. Whiton, *Railroads and Their Management* (Concord, N. H., 1856); and Elias H. Derby, "The Policy of Railways," in the *Railway Times*, January 18, 1855. For Poor's discussion of these writers, see *ARJ*, 29:145–146, 161–163, 177–179, 193–195, 264–265 (March 8, 15, 22, 29, April 26, 1856); compare these articles with *Railway Times*, March 20, 1856; Jan. 8, 1857; *Railroad Record*, 5:365, 553–554 (July 30, Oct. 22, 1857); see also *ARJ*, 28:721–723 (Nov. 17, 1855); 30:456 (July 18, 1857).

63. *ARJ*, 30:456 (July 18, 1857).

64. For this competition see Alvin F. Harlow, *The Road of the Century*

(New York, 1947), p. 229; Robert F. Black, *The Little Miami Railroad* (Cleveland, 1940), pp. 108, 114, 134; *ARJ*, 27:421–422, 543 (July 8, Aug. 26, 1854).

65. *Eighth Annual Report of the Directors of the Pennsylvania Railroad Company to the Stockholders, February 5, 1855* (Philadelphia, 1855), p. 13.

66. The conventions and their agreements are discussed in *ARJ*, 27:538–539, 605, 663, 810 (Aug. 26, Sept. 23, Oct. 21, Dec. 23, 1854). At these conventions many other problems besides rates and ticket-selling requiring solution for the efficient movement of through traffic were considered. For similar conventions, agreements and railroad associations in the South see *ARJ*, 28:197–198 (March 31, 1855).

67. *ARJ*, 28:249, 424 (April 21, July 7, 1855); 30:481–482 (Aug. 1, 1857); *Railroad Record*, 4:481–483 (Sept. 25, 1856); Hungerford, *Men and Iron*, pp. 110–115, also excerpts from letters of John W. Brooks, James F. Joy, James V. L. Pruyn, Dean Richmond, printed in Cochran, *Railroad Leaders*, pp. 269–274, 366, 452, 453.

68. *ARJ*, 31:753–755 (Nov. 27, 1858); *Railroad Record*, 6:361–362 (Nov. 18, 1858); *Proceedings of the Railroad Convention, Held at the St. Nicholas Hotel, in New York, September 25, 1858* (New York, 1858); Hungerford, *Men and Iron*, p. 115.

69. *ARJ*, 32:105, 280, 296, 312, 328, 344–346 (Feb. 12, April 30, May 7, 14, 21, 28, 1859); Hungerford, *Men and Iron*, pp. 115–116; Harlow, *Road of the Century*, pp. 277–278.

70. For the making and the details of the 1860 agreements see *ARJ*, 32:394 (June 19, 1859); 33:746 (Aug. 25, 1860); *American Railway Review*, 3:40, 72, 153 (July 26, Aug. 9, Sept. 13, 1860).

71. This and the following quotation are from *ARJ*, 32:105 (Feb. 12, 1859); see also Poor's remarks in *ARJ*, 27:298, 405, 421–422, 534, 808 (May 13, July 1, 8, Aug. 26, Dec. 23, 1854); 30:456, 504 (July 18, Aug. 8, 1857); 32:169, 200, 280, 296, 344 (March 12, 26, April 30, May 7, 28, 1859).

72. For examples of investors' agreement see letters printed in *ARJ*, 30:728–729 (Nov. 14, 1857); 32:465–466, 529–530 (July 23, Aug. 20, 1859); for similar comments by editors, *American Railway Review*, 3:101 (Aug. 23, 1860); *Railroad Record*, 5:318 (July 9, 1857), 229, 254 (July 8, 29, 1858), *Railroad Register*, 3:84, 204 (Aug. 8, Nov. 21, 1857).

73. Douglas Galton, *Report to the Lords of the Committee of the Privy Council for Trade and Foreign Plantations on the Railways of the United States* (London, 1857), pp. 20–23, 27; *Annual Report of the Railroad Commissioners of New York . . . 1855*, I, xxxii–xxxiv, xxxvii–xxxix; George L. Vose, *Handbook on Railroad Construction; for the Use of American Engineers* (Boston, 1857), ch. 26 and *Railway Times*, 13:476 (Dec. 28, 1861), Jervis, *Railway Property*, preface, and chs. 15, 22, 27; *Atlantic Monthly*, 2:641, 651–654 (Nov. 1858).

Chapter 7: The Problem of Management

1. See the *Report of the President of the New York and Erie Railroad to the Stockholders, for the Year Ending September 30, 1857* (New York, 1857), pp. 7–8; *ARJ*, 29:584, 641–642 (Sept. 13, Oct. 11, 1856); *Railroad Record*, 4:594 (Nov. 13, 1856); 5:36 (March 12, 1857). For somewhat similar strikes on the Baltimore and Ohio, see *Railroad Record*, 5:169, 185 (May 7, 14, 1857).

2. The call for the meeting is given in full in the *Railroad Record*, 4:689 (Dec. 25, 1856); see also *Railroad Record*, 4:722, 738 (Jan. 8, 15, 1857); and *Railroad Advocate*, October 27, November 3, December 8, 22, 1855, August 25, 1856.

3. *ARJ*, 29:641–642 (Oct. 11, 1856).

4. *ARJ*, 32:41 (Jan. 15, 1859). For further comments on labor relations see *ARJ*, 31:56–57 (Jan. 23, 1858); 32:72, 488 (Jan. 29, July 30, 1859).

5. *Railroad Record*, 4:721–722 (Jan. 8, 1857). The *Railway Times* referring

to the Erie strike of 1856 commented: "Reduce rational, immortal man, of aspiring genius to mere machines! Horrible! Intolerable! So they argued and spouted and got the sympathy of a good many fools," *Railway Times,* March 26, 1857; see also *Railway Times,* November 20, 1856, January 1, 1857.

6. *ARJ,* 32:424 (July 2, 1859). See also *ARJ,* 32:369–370 (June 11, 1859). In the 1830's Peter Lecount in one of the first books written on railroads made similar comments; so too did Charles E. Perkins and other American railroad managers fifty years later. Peter Lecount, *A Practical Treatise on Railways* (Edinburgh, 1834), p. 253; Thomas C. Cochran, *Railroad Leaders, 1845–1890* (Cambridge, Mass., 1953), p. 86.

7. This and the following quotations are from *ARJ,* 31:577 (Sept. 11, 1858). For other comments on bureaucratization of railroad management, see *ARJ,* 30:408–409 (June 27, 1857); 31:152–153, 561–562 (March 6, Sept. 4, 1858); 32:40–41, 369–370 (Jan. 15, June 11, 1859); for somewhat similar comments by American railroad managers, Cochran, *Railroad Leaders,* pp. 86–87, 272.

8. *ARJ,* 31:577 (Sept. 11, 1858).

9. For comments on leadership and responsibility of top management, see *ARJ,* 27:745–747 (Nov. 25, 1854); 28:721–723 (Nov. 17, 1855); 29:194 (March 29, 1856); 31:88, 104–105, 136–137, 153–154, 520, 561–562, 593–594 (Feb. 6, 13, 27, March 6, Aug. 14, Sept. 4, 18, 1858); 32:40–41, 369–370 (Jan. 15, June 11, 1859).

10. This and the following quotation are from *ARJ,* 31:561–562 (Sept. 4, 1858).

11. *ARJ,* 31:168 (March 13, 1858); see also *ARJ,* 27:808–809 (Dec. 23, 1854); 30:369–370, 408–409 (June 13, 27, 1857); 31:97–98, 104, 136–137, 152–153, 168, 577–578 (Feb. 13, 27, March 6, 13, Sept. 11, 1858); and an excellent letter from a British subscriber describing the same situation in England, *ARJ,* 31:641–643 (Oct. 9, 1858).

12. *ARJ,* 32:580–581 (Sept. 10, 1859); for examples of protests against reliance on "great names" and the need for technically trained railroad presidents, see *ARJ,* 23:264 (April 27, 1850); 30:712 (Nov. 7, 1857); 31:137, 152–153 (Feb. 27, March 6, 1858). However, in an editorial on the Rock Island, *ARJ,* 29:632 (Oct. 4, 1856), Poor shows an understanding of the power which commanding credit gave the financial entrepreneur.

13. This and the following quotations are from *ARJ,* 31:593 (Sept. 18, 1858). See also *ARJ,* 31:561–562 (Sept. 4, 1858); 32:369–370 (June 11, 1859).

14. Comments on the stockholder's position are scattered throughout the *Journal;* for some of the best articles see *ARJ,* 27:529, 536-537, 638, 692–693, 745–747 (Aug. 26, Oct. 7, Nov. 4, 25, 1854); 30:408–409, 526, 530, 568–569 (June 27, Aug. 22, Sept. 5, 1857); 31:97–99, 152–153 (Feb. 13, March 6, 1858); 32:369–370 (June 11, 1859).

15. See citations from *ARJ* in footnote 19 and also *Railroad Record,* 4:258, 433 (June 1, Sept. 4, 1856), and *Railway Times,* Dec. 22, 1857.

16. *ARJ,* 32:370 (June 11, 1859); also *ARJ,* 31:97 (Feb. 13, 1858); for recognition of the same situation in England see *ARJ,* 31:641–643 (Oct. 9, 1858).

17. *ARJ,* 30:584 (Sept. 12, 1857); also *ARJ,* 27:808–809 (Dec. 23, 1854); see also John B. Jervis, *Railway Property* (New York, 1861), pp. 55, 299.

18. *ARJ,* 31:562 (Sept. 4, 1858).

19. Poor's comments on the board of directors, like those on the stockholders, are scattered throughout the *Journal.* His best editorials are: *ARJ,* 27:433–434, 529, 692–693, 745–747 (July 15, Aug. 26, Nov. 4, 25, 1854); 28:104 (Feb. 17, 1855); 29:264–265 (April 26, 1856); 30:408–409, 536 (June 27, Aug. 22, 1857); 31:88, 104–105, 152–153 (Feb. 6, 13, March 6, 1858); 32:369–370 (June 11, 1859).

20. Emphasizing the differences between the effects of dishonest and incompetent directors, Poor wrote: "The speculations of the former are usually neces-

sarily small in amount, while the mistakes of the latter may, and often do, involve in ruin the entire sum invested in a road," *ARJ*, 31:152 (March 6, 1858).

21. *ARJ*, 32:370 (June 11, 1859); also *ARJ*, 31:136–137 (Feb. 27, 1858).

22. *ARJ*, 31:153 (March 6, 1858); also *ARJ*, 32:600 (Sept. 17, 1859).

23. *ARJ*, 30:568 (Sept. 5, 1857).

24. This and the following quotations are from *ARJ*, 31:153 (March 6, 1858); see also *ARJ*, 30:408–409 (June 27, 1857).

25. For examples see *Railway Times*, Jan. 13, March 14, April 11, 1850; Sept. 14, 1853; Oct. 12, 1854; July 14, 1855; Dec. 12, 1857; *Railroad Record*, 5:413 (Aug. 20, 1858); *Railroad Register*, 3:116, 148, 196 (Sept. 5, Oct. 3, Nov. 14, 1857; 4:46 (Feb. 12, 1858); *Hunt's*, 31:333–334 (Sept. 1854); 34:622–623 (May 1856); 39:750 (Dec. 1858); *De Bow's Review*, 14:145–151 (Feb. 1853); James M. Whiton, *Railroads and Their Management* (Concord, N. H., 1856), pp. 19–20, 32–33.

26. Jervis, *Railway Property*, particularly preface, chs. 4, 30.

27. *ARJ*, 30:409 (June 27, 1857). Many of the citations in footnote 19 mention these reforms; see also *ARJ*, 27:785–786 (Dec. 16, 1854); 30:376–377, 729 (June 13, Nov. 14, 1857); 32:440 (July 9, 1859). These reforms were in line with those already adopted in England, *ARJ*, 30:689–690 (Oct. 31, 1857).

28. *ARJ*, 27:808–809 (Dec. 23, 1854); for a full discussion of the contract or lease system see also *ARJ*, 27:692–693 (Nov. 4, 1854); 28:722 (Nov. 17, 1855); see also citations in footnotes 32 and 34, and *ARJ*, 32:408, 600 (June 25, Sept. 17, 1859). The contract plan seems to have been first suggested by one of Poor's Maine friends, F. O. A. Smith, the telegraph promoter, earlier that same year in *Hunt's*, 34:682–683 (June 1854).

29. *ARJ*, 27:809 (Dec. 23, 1854).

30. There is a detailed account of the operations of the contract system in John Butterick, "The Inside Contract System," *Journal of Economic History*, 12:205–221 (Summer, 1952).

31. *ARJ*, 22:392 (June 23, 1849), 27:630–631 (Oct. 7, 1854); the operation of locomotives by contract is described fully in *Herapath's Railroad and Commercial Journal* (London), 16:564–565, 577, 582–583 (June 3, 10, 1854).

32. For the importance of the trip to England on the development of Poor's views on the contract system see *ARJ*, 31:561–562, 577–578, 593–594 (Sept. 4, 11, 18, 1858).

33. *Railway Times*, Aug. 2, 1855; Whiton, *Railroads and Their Management*, p. 62. Both Haven and Whiton described the plan to contract out operations as a quite new and original idea. For comments on the use of premiums see, *Railroad Advocate*, Dec. 15, 1855, Jan. 5, 1856. Such premiums later became standard practice on American railroads, Frederick A. Cleveland and Fred W. Powell, *Railroad Finance* (New York, 1912), pp. 158–159.

34. *Twentieth Annual Report of the President and Directors to the Stockholders of the Philadelphia, Wilmington and Baltimore Railroad Company for the Year ending November 30, 1857* (Philadelphia, 1858), p. 17. Pages 17–19 of this report and page 15 of the *Nineteenth Annual Report* and pages 15–16 of the *Twenty-First Annual Report* give the best summary of the contract system in operation. For Poor's comments about the working of this system on Felton's road see *ARJ*, 31:488–489 (July 30, 1859); see also *ARJ*, 32:503, 504 (Aug. 6, 1859).

35. Cochran, *Railroad Leaders*, pp. 115, 248–249.

36. *ARJ*, 32:353, 376–377, 424 (June 4, 11, July 2, 1859). For fuller details of the contract see New York *Tribune*, June 8, 1859.

37. *ARJ*, 32:456–457, 472, 513–514, 520, 580–581 (July 16, 23, Aug. 13, Sept. 10, 1859); see also New York *Times*, June 30, 1859, New York *Tribune*, Aug. 11, 1859 and Edward H. Mott, *Between the Ocean and the Lakes, the Story of the Erie* (New York, 1899), p. 129.

38. *Twentieth Annual Report . . . of the Philadelphia, Wilmington and*

Baltimore Railroad Company . . . , November 30, 1857, pp. 17–18. The road gave up the contract plan in 1862 when, because of the war, the rapid rise in "the prices of the principal articles used in operating the road" made the fixing of a fair price on annual contracts almost impossible, *Twenty-Fifth Annual Report of the President and Directors to the Stockholders of the Philadelphia, Wilmington and Baltimore Railroad Company, October 31, 1862* (Philadelphia, 1863), p. 15. When after the war the road was consolidated into the Pennsylvania Railroad system, the new managers never attempted to revive the contract system.

39. *ARJ,* 32:600 (September 17, 1859).

40. *ARJ,* 30:568 (Sept. 5, 1857). Poor's editorials and comments on the need for and the effectiveness of publicity to reform railroad administration and operation appear constantly in the *Journal.* For the best of his views see *ARJ,* 27:638, 692–693, 777–778, 785–786, 817 (Oct. 7, Nov. 4, Dec. 9, 16, 30, 1854); 28:9, 105, 232–233 (Jan. 6, Feb. 17, April 14, 1855); 29:264–265, 626 (April 26, Oct. 4, 1856); 30:136, 392, 408–409, 568, 593 (Feb. 28, June 20, 27, Sept. 5, 19, 1857). In the last of these editorials, Poor wrote that the stockholders' "watchwords should be Honesty, Competency, Publicity." For comments in 1858 see citations in footnote 56 and also *ARJ,* 31:344 (May 29, 1858); for comments in 1859 and 1860 see footnote 61.

41. *ARJ,* 31:99 (Feb. 13, 1858).

42. *ARJ,* 31:137 (Feb. 27, 1858).

43. This and the following quotation are from *ARJ,* 31:152–153 (March 6, 1858).

44. *ARJ,* 30:392 (June 20, 1857).

45. Many of the editorials cited in footnote 40 asked for government legislation; see also the *Report of Israel D. Andrews, Consul of the United States for Canada and New Brunswick, on the Trade and Commerce of the British North American Colonies, and upon the Trade of the Great Lakes and Rivers* (Senate Document 112, 32nd Congress, 1st Session), pp. 388–389.

46. *ARJ,* 31:424 (July 3, 1858); see also *ARJ,* 31:232 (April 10, 1858); 33:272 (March 31, 1860).

47. *ARJ,* 33:272 (March 31, 1860). The reports of these states were printed in the *Journal* as soon as they were published.

48. The categories included: first, the road's financial structure, its stocks, bonds, and floating debt; second, the cost of the road and its equipment listed under such headings as masonry and gradation, bridges, superstructure, "stations, buildings, and fixtures," locomotives, rolling stock, and so forth; third, the road's characteristics, such as its length, trackage, weight of rail, maximum, minimum, and average grades and curves; fourth, its "doings of the year," that is, the miles run, passengers and tons of freight carried, rates of speed, but nothing on the fares charged; fifth, "the expenditures of the road" including the repair and maintenance of its plant and equipment, the amount paid for fuel, wages, and so forth; and finally, the income received from freight, passenger, and mail traffic and from rents.

Massachusetts first began publishing annual reports of railroads in 1837 in accordance with a recommendation of the Joint Committee on Railways and Canals submitted on February 6, 1837. It was not until the act passed on April 16, 1846, that full detailed and uniform regulations covering reports were set up and not until 1849 that abstracts and statistical summaries were made on these reports, see *Annual Reports of the Railroad Corporations in the State of Massachusetts,* for 1837, p. 1; for 1846, p. 1; for 1848, pp. iii–iv (these reports were printed in Boston in the year following the date submitted); see also *ARJ,* 29:162 (March 15, 1856). Poor in a questionnaire sent out to railroads in 1854 followed the pattern of the Massachusetts requirements quite closely, although he did ask for more details on financial and historical matters, see Appendix.

49. Although New York's first general requirements for the submission, collection, and publication of annual reports were embodied in a resolution of the assembly passed February 3, 1843, detailed data were not required until the passage of the New York general railroad law on April 3, 1850, *New York State, Report . . . relative to Railroad Statistics, March 11, 1844* (n.p., n.d.), p. 1 and accompanying tables; *Annual Report of the State Engineer and Surveyor covering the Returns of the Railroads of New York for 1850* (n.p., n.d.), pp. 1–5; for the 1855 law see *Annual Report of the Railroad Commissioners of the State of New York . . . for the Year ending September 30, 1855* (Albany, 1856), II, 3–5.

50. *ARJ*, 31:186 (March 20, 1858); see also *ARJ*, 23:201 (March 30, 1850); 28:274 (May 5, 1855); 30:392 (June 20, 1857).

51. *ARJ*, 26:642 (Oct. 8, 1853); also *ARJ*, 26:153 (March 5, 1853). Poor had the same criticism of the reports and audits required by Parliament in Britain. Until these statements were much more detailed, they were, in his opinion, of little value for railroad regulation or reform, *ARJ*, 31:561–562, 641–643 (Sept. 4, Oct. 9, 1858).

52. See *ARJ*, 26:153, 641–642 (March 5, Oct. 8, 1853); 30:217, 260, 536, 593 (April 4, 25, Aug. 22, Sept. 19, 1857); 32:658 (Oct. 15, 1859). The Southern roads included the Wilmington and Weldon, the South Carolina, the Georgia, the Georgia Central, and the Atlanta and La Grange.

53. *ARJ*, 29:264–265 (April 26, 1856); 31:97–98 (Feb. 13, 1858); 32:360 (June 4, 1859).

54. *ARJ*, 31:610 (Sept. 25, 1858).

55. *ARJ*, 31:610 (Sept. 25, 1858).

56. *ARJ*, 31:98 (Feb. 13, 1858). Poor's publicity plan was proposed and described in the February 13, 1858, issue of the *Journal*, pp. 97–99, 104–105, and was fully expounded in subsequent editorials of February 27, March 6, 13, 1858, pp. 136–137, 152–154, 161, 168. These editorials are the best Poor wrote on publicity as a major reform. A copy of the questionnaire in pamphlet form is in the possession of Charles L. Chandler. The "Interrogatories" are given by installments in *ARJ* from February 20 to March 13, inclusive.

57. *ARJ*, 31:98 (Feb. 13, 1858).

58. *ARJ*, 31:98 (Feb. 13, 1858).

59. *Railroad Register*, 4:58, 66 (March 6, 20, 1858). Poor, as will be described in the following chapter, had been actively fighting for a decrease in the tariff on rails.

60. See Frederick L. Allen, *The Great Pierpont Morgan* (New York, 1949), pp. 84–85, 88–93; E. G. Campbell, *The Reorganization of the American Railroad System, 1893–1900* (New York, 1938), ch. 5.

61. *ARJ*, 32:584–585, 600, 658 (Sept. 10, 17, Oct. 15, 1859); 33:766 (Sept. 1, 1860); 34:120–121 (Feb. 9, 1861).

62. See above, p. 140 and below, pp. 213–218.

63. *United States Congress. Select Committee on Interstate Commerce . . . Regulation of Interstate Commerce. Testimony* (Washington, D. C., 1886), II, p. 232.

64. *ARJ*, 23:726 (Nov. 16, 1850).

65. Poor expressed this view succinctly in a talk which he had with Robert Stephenson during his visit to England in 1858. In describing a "long conversation upon governmental policy in reference to Railroads" Poor wrote his wife that he told Stephenson: " 'If you leave the building of R.R. to the public, you must not interfere with it any more than with the building of a ship. The liberty to make a *bad* investment must be left at the choice of the individual just as much as the liberty of making a *good* one.' 'What is the remedy then?' he asked. 'To enlighten the public,' I replied, 'and to caution all not to invest in a work about which, or the parties managing, they know nothing,' " Henry Poor to Mary Poor, June 10, 1858.

66. In this connection Poor never considered the Pacific railroad as a purely "commercial enterprise." Instead he looked on it as a national project much in the same way as a later generation of government officials and businessmen did on the construction of the Panama Canal.

67. *Railway Times,* Nov. 10, 1853, Dec. 21, 1854, Jan. 17, 1856, April 10, May 8, 1858; *Railroad Record,* 3:34, 53 (March 15, 22, 1855); 4:33–34 (March 13, 1856); *Railroad Register,* 1:108 (Aug. 30, 1856); 4:70, 98 (March 27, May 15, 1858); Whiton, *Railroads and Their Management,* p. 66; *Annual Report of the Rail-Road Commissioners of the State of New York . . .* 1855, I, xlii–xliii. Besides the bankers who supported Poor's publicity plan, Charles Moran, leading New York investment banker who became president of the Erie, gave publicity his support, *ARJ,* 32:657–658, 673–674 (Oct. 15, 22, 1859).

68. *Railway Times,* 13:8, 18, 48, 168, 404, 412, 428, 436, 476 (Jan. 5, 12, April 27, Oct. 26, Nov. 2, Dec. 28, 1861).

69. Charles F. Adams, *Railroads: Their Origin and Problems* (New York, 1878), pp. 116–121, 138–143; *Charles Francis Adams, 1835–1915, an Autobiography* (Boston, 1916), p. 175.

70. Adams, *Railroads,* pp. 127–135. For a good summary of the Granger legislation which indicates the stress placed on publicity see *First Annual Report of the Railroad Commissioners of Wisconsin, 1874* (Madison, Wis., 1874), pp. 77–85.

71. William Diamond, *The Economic Thought of Woodrow Wilson* (Baltimore, 1943), pp. 79, 92–93.

Chapter 8: Spokesman for the Industry

1. For an excellent case study of the role of the trade journalist in defining an industry's stand on the tariff and in lobbying for its increase, see Harry Brown, "The Fleece and the Loom: Wool Growers and Wool Manufacturers during the Civil War Decade," *Business History Review,* 19:1–27 (March 1955).

2. *ARJ,* 22:753–754, 791–792 (Dec. 1, 15, 1849); 23:470 (July 27, 1850).

3. *ARJ,* 22:184, 280, 534, 550–551, 774 (March 24, May 5, Aug. 25, Sept. 1, Dec. 8, 1849); 23:248–249, 297 (April 20, May 11, 1850).

4. For the fluctuating price and amount of iron rails imported in the 1850's see *Railway Age Gazette,* 53:125 (July 19, 1912); also the appendix to Frank W. Taussig, "The Tariff, 1830–1860," *Quarterly Journal of Economics,* 2:379 (April 1888).

5. *ARJ,* 23:376–377 (June 15, 1850). In an editorial of April 20, 1850, pp. 248–249, Poor used both the home market argument and the need of tariff to prevent specie exports. In an editorial of May 11, 1850, p. 297, he used for the last time the need for a home market. From then on the tariff as a financial device remained his only argument, see *ARJ,* 23:376–377 (June 15, 1850); 24:25–26, 137–138, 721–723 (Jan. 11, March 1, Nov. 15, 1851). This argument appears to have found support in financial and mercantile New York, see *Bankers' Magazine,* 6:672 (Feb. 1852).

6. *ARJ,* 24:136 (March 1, 1851).

7. *ARJ,* 24:26 (Jan. 11, 1851).

8. *ARJ,* 25:664 (Oct. 16, 1852).

9. Lewis H. Haney, *A Congressional History of the Railways in the United States* (Madison, Wisconsin, 1910), II, 40.

10. *ARJ,* 25:641 (Oct. 9, 1852); for other editorials and comments on repeal of the tariff on rails, *ARJ,* 25:664, 673–674, 721–722, 753–754, 817–818 (Oct. 16, 23, Nov. 13, 27, Dec. 25, 1852).

11. For the meeting and the appointment of the committee, see *ARJ,* 27:121, 137, 320 (Feb. 25, March 4, May 27, 1854).

12. A letter in possession of Charles L. Chandler from Samuel Hanna to Henry Poor dated March 31, 1854 indicates the hearty approval of one Western

railroad president for proposals of Poor's committee. See also critical comments on the circular in *Railway Times,* May 18, 1854.

13. For his arguments on the need to repeal or reduce the tariff, see *ARJ,* 27:249–250, 321–323, 353–355, 450–451, 481–482 (April 22, May 27, June 10, July 22, Aug. 5, 1854); 28:24, 49–50, 209–210 (Jan. 13, 27, April 7, 1855). Mary Poor to Lucy Hedge, Feb. 28, 1855, and Mary Poor's diary both mention trips to Washington. *Railway Times,* May 18, Dec. 14, 1854, comments on the lobbying activities of the *Journal's* editor.

14. For failure of action in 1854 and 1855 Haney, *Congressional History of Railways,* 41–43; Allan Nevins, *Abram S. Hewitt: With Some Account of Peter Cooper* (New York, 1935), pp. 111–112, 154–156; a long letter from J. W. Williams to William B. Ogden printed in *ARJ,* 28:499–502 (Aug. 11, 1855); and *Railway Times,* April 27, 1854. The House bill to suspend the duties on rails was introduced by Alfred P. Edgerton of Ohio and strongly supported by Nathaniel P. Banks of Massachusetts.

15. *Railway Times,* March 27, 1856, Jan. 16, 1858.

16. *Railway Times,* March 1, 1855, March 12, April 16, 1857; Robert C. Procter, *Tariff Acts Passed by the Congress of the United States from 1787 to 1897* (Washington, D. C., 1898), p. 133.

17. For its arguments on the tariff see *Railway Times,* Dec. 23, 30, 1852; July 21, Oct. 27, 1853; April 13, 27, May 4, 11, 18, June 8, Aug. 24, Nov. 16, 1854; March 1, 1855. After 1857 Haven began to argue for an increase in the iron duties, especially on rails, see particularly *Railway Times,* Jan. 16, Oct. 28, Dec. 25, 1858.

18. For example, *Railroad Register,* 3:126, 150 (Jan. 1, Feb. 12, 1858). Colburn's *Railroad Advocate,* while saying little on the tariff, appears to have opposed reduction on rails, *Advocate,* May 1, 1855.

19. For example, *Railroad Record,* 2:337, 417, 486 (July 27, Aug. 31, Sept. 14, 1854). The *United States Economist* was another strong advocate of tariff reduction, particularly of the duties on rails, for example, the *Economist,* 2:147 (Dec. 18, 1852); 23:2 (Feb. 12, 1860).

20. At first several central New York lines were forbidden by their charters to carry freight. In 1844 all lines were permitted to carry freight when ice prevented the canal's operation, but all had to continue to pay tolls on freight. In 1847 they were allowed to carry freight in winter and summer and exempted from paying tolls on cattle, horses, sheep, and fresh meat. David M. Ellis, "Rivalry Between the New York Central Railroad and the Erie Canal," *New York History,* 46:270–300 (July 1948) has the best summary of New York legislation on tolls for railroad traffic.

21. For Poor's arguments against toll on railroads see *ARJ,* 24:217, 663, 824 (Apr. 5, Oct. 18, Dec. 27, 1851); 28:97–98, 169–170 (Feb. 17, Mar. 17, 1855); 31:184–186, 200 (Mar. 20, 27, 1858); 32:24, 432–436, 577–578, 616, 632 (Jan. 8, July 9, Sept. 10, 24, Oct. 1, 1859); 33:684–685 (Aug. 4, 1860).

22. *ARJ,* 28:169–170 (Mar. 17, 1855).

23. For comments on the pro-rata bill see *ARJ,* 33:66, 101, 102–103, 336–337 (Jan. 21, Feb. 4, Apr. 21, 1860). Analysis of the political and economic pressure groups mobilized in support of the pro-rata, toll, and other restrictive legislation is given in Frederick Merk, "Eastern Antecedents of the Grangers," *Agricultural History,* 23:1–8 (Jan. 1949). For attempts at somewhat similar action a little earlier in Ohio, see Ernest L. Bogart, "Early Canal Traffic and Railroad Competition," *Journal of Political Economy,* 31:66–68 (Jan. 1913).

24. For example, *Railway Times,* March 3, April 7, Dec. 29, 1853; Jan. 9, 1858, Jan. 28, Feb. 4, 1860. Kettell's *Economist* also joined in protesting state discrimination against railroads, *Economist,* 2:378 (March 19, 1853).

25. For Poor's protests against these instances of economic particularism see *ARJ,* 22:230, 822 (Apr. 14, Dec. 29, 1849); 24:186–187, 229–230, 321–322 (Mar. 22, Apr. 12, May 24, 1851); 25:161–162, 172, 264 (Mar. 13, Apr. 24,

1852); 26:264, 746–747 (Apr. 23, Nov. 12, 1853); 27:130 (Mar. 4, 1854). For protests against city officials in Chicago, Wheeling, and Macon, Georgia, for refusing to permit railroad tracks to cross their cities in order to reap profit by the transference of goods and passengers, see *ARJ*, 26:667–668 (Oct. 15, 1853); 27:774–775 (Dec. 9, 1854).

26. *ARJ*, 28:786 (Dec. 15, 1855); see also *ARJ*, 26:264 (Apr. 23, 1853); 29:24–25 (Jan. 12, 1856).

27. For examples of Pennsylvania's restrictive policies (besides those which led to the "Erie war") and Poor's attacks on them, see *ARJ*, 22:135–136 (Mar. 3, 1849); 23:615–616 (Sept. 28, 1850); 25:161–162 (Mar. 13, 1852); 28:177–178 (Mar. 24, 1855).

28. There is a good summary of the events at Erie in Alvin F. Harlow, *The Road of the Century* (New York, 1947), pp. 269–274.

29. *ARJ*, 27:98 (Feb. 18, 1854). Large extracts from Bigler's speeches are given here and in *ARJ*, 27:113–117 (Feb. 25, 1854).

30. Poor's many lengthy editorials on the affairs at Erie include *ARJ*, 26:840–842 (Dec. 31, 1853); 27:1–2, 17–18, 49–50, 65–66, 73, 90–91, 94, 97–99, 113–116, 130, 145–146 (Jan. 7, 14, 28, Feb. 4, 11, 18, 25, Mar. 4, 11, 1854); 28:723, 753–755 (Nov. 17, Dec. 1, 1855).

31. *ARJ*, 27:1–2 (Jan. 7, 1854).

32. Thomson's condemnation of the *Journal* which appeared in the Pittsburgh *Gazette* is printed in *ARJ*, 27:97–99 (Feb. 18, 1854); for the effect of Poor's comments on European investors see an article from the New York *Times* printed in *ARJ*, 27:74 (Feb. 4, 1854).

33. *ARJ*, 22:135–136 (March 3, 1849).

34. For Poor's advocacy of general railroad laws see *ARJ*, 23:393, 615–616, 726 (June 22, Sept. 28, Nov. 16, 1850); 25:216, 824 (Apr. 3, Dec. 25, 1852); 26:562–564 (Sept. 3, 1853); 27:130, 145–146, 641 (Mar. 4, 11, Oct. 14, 1854); 28:117 (Feb. 24, 1855); 29:609–610 (Sept. 25, 1858). The New York general railroad law is printed in full in *ARJ*, 25:209–214 (Apr. 3, 1852). The *Railway Times* also urged the adoption of general railway laws, *Railway Times*, July 28, 1853, Jan. 19, 1854.

35. *ARJ*, 29:312–313 (May 17, 1856); also *ARJ*, 28:473–474 (July 28, 1855).

36. *ARJ*, 29:313 (May 17, 1856).

37. Poor's views on the impact of superior railroad and canal transportation over river, of "artificial" over "natural" means of commerce, on the course of American trade are given in *ARJ*, 24:289–291, 294–295, 314, 731–732, 785 (May 10, 17, Nov. 15, Dec. 13, 1851); 25:66, 488, 609 (Jan. 31, July 31, Sept. 25, 1852); 27:314, 322–323 (May 20, 27, 1854); 28:609 (Sept. 29, 1855); 29:729 (Nov. 15, 1856). *ARJ*, 33:273, 829 (March 31, Sept. 15, 1860) indicate the validity of some of his predictions.

38. U. S. Census Office, *The Eighth Census of the United States, Agriculture of the United States* (Washington, 1864), cxlix. Louis B. Schmidt, "Internal Grain Trade of the United States, 1850–1860," *Iowa Journal of History and Politics*, 18:94–124 (Jan. 1920), summarizes the census findings on this subject.

39. *ARJ*, 25:360, 609, 746–747 (June 5, Sept. 25, Nov. 20, 1852); also *ARJ*, 24:630–631, 652 (Oct. 4, 11, 1851) and Robert L. Black, *The Little Miami Railroad* (Cleveland, 1940), p. 140.

40. *ARJ*, 32:808 (Dec. 10, 1859); for the movement of cotton and tobacco on the Pennsylvania see the *Annual Report(s) of the Directors of the Pennsylvania Central Railroad Company* dated Feb. 1, 1858, Feb. 7, 1859, Feb. 6, 1860 and Feb. 4, 1861 (all printed in Philadelphia), pp. 101, 103, 105, 108 respectively; for tobacco on the Baltimore and Ohio, see *Thirty-Fourth Annual Report of the President and Directors of the Baltimore and Ohio Railroad Company* (Baltimore, 1860), table X, pp. 104–105; for cotton on the Little Miami, the *Joint Annual Report(s) of the Directors to the Stockholders of the Little Miami and the Columbus and Xenia Railroad Companies* for 1857, 1858, 1859, 1860

(all printed in Cincinnati), pp. 31, 32, 36, 44 respectively. In the 1850's a hogshead of tobacco was usually 1200 pounds and a bale of cotton 400 pounds.

41. *ARJ*, 24:294, 714, 731–732 (May 10, Nov. 8, 15, 1851); 25:609 (Sept. 25, 1852); 28:217 (April 7, 1855).

42. *ARJ*, 24:291, 294–295 (May 10, 1851); 26:487 (July 30, 1853).

43. Ellis, "Rivalry Between the New York Central Railroad and the Erie Canal," pp. 274, 282, estimates that in 1856 only 23.2 per cent of New York City's Western trade was shipped by canal. Of the remainder 25.5 per cent went by the New York Central, 18.4 per cent by the Erie Railroad, 16.8 per cent by the Pennsylvania, and 16.1 per cent by the Baltimore and Ohio.

44. The railroads also carried more hides, horses, and whisky, see *ARJ*, 32:177–180, 194–197 (March 19, 26, 1859). Ellis, "Rivalry Between the New York Central Railroad and the Erie Canal," p. 274; *Eighth Census, Agriculture*, pp. cli–clii, emphasizes the growing grain traffic on the Pennsylvania and Baltimore and Ohio as well as the New York trunk lines.

45. *ARJ*, 33:404 (May 12, 1860). See also statistics given in footnote 66 below.

46. *Eighth Census, Agriculture*, p. clxv. According to the census, wheat production in the five states of the Old Northwest rose from 39,348,495 bushels in 1850 to 79,798,163 bushels in 1860; corn output for the same period went from 177, 320, 441 bushels to 280,268,862 bushels. These and similar statistics are listed in a section entitled "Influence of Railroads on Agriculture," pp. clxiv–clxix. For a summary of Poor's views on the impact of railroads on agriculture, see *Report of Israel D. Andrews . . . on the Trade and Commerce of the British North American Colonies*, Senate Document 112, 32nd Congress, 1st Session, pp. 379–386.

47. Henry V. Poor, "Pacific Railroad," *Bulletin of the American Statistical and Geographical Society*, I, pt. III (1854), 81.

48. The Georgia Railroad, for example, carried in 1841, the year it was completed, $73,504 worth of passengers and $121,697 worth of freight. By 1849 the road had earned $166,484 from passengers and $415,133 from freight, *Report of the Engineer in Chief of the Georgia Rail Road and Banking Co. to the Convention of Stockholders; May 9, 1842* (Athens, Ga., 1842), pp. 6–7, 9, 15; *Report of the Directors & C. of the Geo. R.R. and Banking Co.; To the Stockholders in Convention, May 15, 1849* (Augusta, 1849), statement 4. *The Semi-Annual Report of the Directors of the South Carolina Canal and Railroad Company to the Stockholders Oct. 31, 1834* shows that for the previous six months the road had earned $36,140 from passengers and $47,304 from freight. The succeeding semiannual reports indicate that, in general, freight receipts grew much more rapidly than passenger income. For the North-South lines see Howard D. Dozier, *History of the Atlantic Coast Line* (Boston, 1920), pp. 28–29, 87–88.

49. For Michigan Central see the first to thirteenth *Annual Report(s) of the Directors of the Michigan Central Rail Road Company to the Stockholders* (Boston, 1848–1861), pp. 28, 25, 21, 20, 21, 26, 28, 13, 30, 17, 30, 17, 14 respectively. From May 1847 until the road was completed in 1849 the road made more from freight than passengers. For the Michigan Southern see *Report of Directors of the Michigan Southern and Northern Indiana Railroad Company to the Stockholders* (New York, 1857), "Table of Earnings" and the "Table of Gross Earnings" in the company's annual reports dated March 1, 1860, and March 1, 1861; for the Cleveland, Painesville and Astabula, *ARJ*, 33:38 (Jan. 14, 1860); for Cleveland and Toledo, *ARJ*, 32:547 (Aug. 27, 1859); for Pittsburgh, Fort Wayne and Chicago, Henry V. Poor, *History of Railroads and Canals of the United States of America* (New York, 1860), p. 497 and *ARJ*, 28:65 (Feb. 3, 1855). An examination of the annual reports of other Western roads indicates that until 1855 the Little Miami, the Cleveland, Columbus and Cincinnati occasionally and the Mad River for just one year earned more from passengers than freight, although freight was the primary revenue producer for the over-all period

before 1855. After 1855 it remained the most important source of revenue on these roads.

50. Poor, *History of Railroads and Canals*, pp. 19, 287, 474, 584.

51. Poor, *History of Railroads and Canals*, pp. 93, 186, 194, 381.

52. Poor, *History of Railroads and Canals*, pp. 102, 104, 106, 147, 261, 278, 291. The New York Central in 1859 grossed $2,566,688 from passengers and $3,337,148 from freight.

53. See especially *ARJ*, 26:234–235, 561 (Apr. 9, Sept. 3, 1853); 27:824–825 (Dec. 30, 1854); 29:1 (Jan. 5, 1856); 30:633–639 (Oct. 3, 1857).

54. According to the census the iron produced in the United States in 1860 totaled in tons: railroad iron, 235,107; bar iron, 227,682; boiler and nail plate, 30,895; sheet, 11,200; miscellaneous, 4,200, U. S. Census Office, *The Eighth Census of the United States, Manufacturers of the United States in 1860* (Washington, 1865), p. clxxxiii.

55. Louis C. Hunter, "Influence of the Market upon the Techniques in the Iron Industry in Western Pennsylvania," *Journal of Economic and Business History*, 1:241–281 (Feb. 1929); Louis C. Hunter, "Iron Manufacturers, Financial Problems of Early Pittsburgh," *Journal of Economic and Business History*, 2:531–532. Nearly all the mills, Hunter points out, which first used coal or coke were also the first to manufacture rails. Indeed the great integrated rail mills at Johnstown, Pittsburgh, and the anthracite region of Pennsylvania, first built in the 1850's, became symbolic of the new industrial age which the railroads were helping to create.

56. This generalization comes chiefly from an analysis of advertisements in the *Railroad Journal* during the 1840's and 1850's. A study of the annual reports of early Midwestern roads indicates that, except for A. Harkness and Son, Eastern locomotive firms supplied their wants.

57. See especially *ARJ*, 25:360, 730 (June 5, Nov. 13, 1852); 26:289 (Apr. 30, 1853); 27:346, 361 (June 3, 10, 1854); 32:514–516 (Aug. 13, 1859).

58. Citations to these editorials which begin with the December 7, 1860, issue of the New York *Times* and continue into February 1861 will be normally given to the compilation of these editorials, *The Effect of Secession Upon the Commercial Relations Between the North and the South and Upon Each Other* (New York, 1861). The Library of Congress erroneously attributes this title to Daniel Lord. Lord wrote *The Legal Effects of the Secession Troubles on the Commercial Relations of the Country* (New York, 1861). In this compilation Poor's wording of some of the original editorials, none of which were signed, was slightly changed. Also some editorials which in content and style appear to be those of Poor were not included in the compilation. The most valuable of those were "A Businessman's View of the Political Crisis," "The Internal Trade of New York," and "The Exports of Produce of the Western States by Way of the Mississippi," New York *Times*, Dec. 17, 1860; Feb. 2, 7, 1861.

59. *ARJ*, 23:1049 (Nov. 24, 1860). For other editorials on the secession crisis in which Poor expresses his disbelief that the South would really sacrifice her economic interests for ideological convictions, see *ARJ*, 33:981, 1024–1025, 1092–1093, 1136–1137 (Nov. 3, 17, Dec. 8, 22, 1860); 34:36–37, 200 (Jan. 17, Mar. 9, 1861).

60. New York *Times*, Dec. 7, 1860.

61. *ARJ*, 33:1024–1025, 1093–1094 (Nov. 17, Dec. 8, 1860).

62. Poor, *Effect of Secession*, the editorials entitled "How the South Came by Their Mistaken Ideas," pp. 10–11; "Effect of Secession on the Direct Trade Between the Southern States and Europe," pp. 12–16; "On the Exchanges of the Country," pp. 16–17; "Southern Free Trade," pp. 54–57; also "Motives of Secession on the Part of the South," pp. 3–10. Much of what Poor discussed, especially in the last editorial, is more fully considered by Robert R. Russel, *The Economic Aspects of Southern Sectionalism* (Urbana, Ill., 1924). In "The Effect of Secession on the Material Interests of the South," pp. 48–58, Poor

emphasized that secession would cut the South off from the major supply of capital necessary to build railroads so essential even to her agricultural prosperity.

63. Poor, *Effect of Secession*, p. 15.

64. Poor, *Effect of Secession*, p. 11, in an editorial entitled "The Cotton States Must Continue to Push the Production of Their Staple to the Fullest Extent"; also pp. 22–23 in "The Past Commercial Relations Between the North and the South Must Be Continued."

65. Poor, *Effect of Secession*, pp. 58–59, 63–65 in an editorial entitled "The Lesson of the Census."

66. Poor, *Effect of Secession*, p. 35. This quotation and the statistics in this paragraph are from an editorial entitled, "The Mouths of the Mississippi — Where Are They?" pp. 32–42. Of these shipments eastward the Erie Canal in 1860 carried 1,367,563 tons of breadstuffs valued at $48,183,044. The Erie and the Central carried nearly 500,000 tons of breadstuffs worth $25,000,000. The two railroads brought 425,185 tons of animal food worth an estimated $85,037,000; the canal transported 12,574 tons of pork, beef, and other animal food products valued at $2,766,694. Poor estimated the total value of vegetable and food products brought East by the Erie Canal, the Central, Erie, Pennsylvania, and Baltimore and Ohio Railroads to be over $200,000,000.

67. Poor, *Effect of Secession*, p. 39. According to the *Report of the Select Committee on Transportation Routes to the Seaboard* (Senate Report 307, pt. 2, 43rd Congress, 1st Session), p. 848, the export of flour from New Orleans to United States and foreign ports dropped from 141,494 barrels in 1856–1857 to 10,862 in 1859–1860.

68. Poor, *Effect of Secession*, pp. 23–31 in an editorial called the "Relative Degree of Wealth and Means of Production, North and South," see also editorial entitled "Northern and Southern Industrial Skill," p. 31.

69. Poor, *Effect of Secession*, p. 29.

70. Poor, *Effect of Secession*, p. 31.

71. Statement on the frontispiece of *Effect of Secession;* also Henry Poor to Mary Poor, June 3, 1861.

72. The nation's largest gunpowder producer, E. I. Du Pont de Nemours and Company, found that the plant expansion made from 1850 to 1859 to meet the requirements of the railroads and the growing coal industry was enough to handle the war orders. Foundries which handled railroad equipment took over most of the heavy ordnance production. Such shops included the West Point Foundry, Algar and Company, Hinckley and Williams, the Scott Foundry, and the Portland Company. Victor S. Clark, *History of Manufactures in the United States, 1607–1914* (New York, 1929), II, 16–19, 35; B. G. Du Pont, *E. I. Du Pont de Nemours and Company. A History, 1802–1902* (New York, 1920), pp. 80–81; *U. S. Navy Department; Bureau of Ordnance, Annual Report for 1862* (Washington, 1863), p. 4; *U. S. Navy Department; Bureau of Ordnance, Annual Report for 1863* (Washington, 1864), p. 9; Nevins, *Hewitt*, pp. 199–214.

73. For statistics and chart on value added by manufacturing see Chester W. Wright, *Economic History of the United States* (New York, 1941), p. 707; for statistics on coal, pig iron, copper, and lead production, see U. S. Bureau of the Census, *Historical Statistics of the United States, 1789–1949* (Washington, 1949), pp. 142, 148, 149, 151; for iron imports, *Report of the Secretary of the American Iron and Steel Institute for Year 1871* (Philadelphia, 1872), pp. 29–30; Swank, *History of Iron*, p. 387; for coal, Howard N. Eavenson, *The First Century and a Quarter of the American Coal Industry* (Pittsburgh, 1942), table of coal production opposite p. 418. Paul H. Cootner, "Transport Innovation and Economic Development: The Case Study of the U. S. Steam Railroad," a doctoral dissertation submitted at the Massachusetts Institute of Technology, 1953, chapters 5–6, provides a beginning of a systematic analysis of the thesis suggested by these statistics. Emerson D. Fite, *Social and Industrial Conditions in the North During the Civil War* (New York, 1910), includes little that contradicts the

theory that the Civil War retarded rather than stimulated basic American industrial growth.

74. Bureau of Census, *Historical Statistics,* pp. 100, 104, 106–107. The information for the intermediate years emphasizes the slow growth during the 1860's.

Chapter 9: Providing Business Information

1. For Poor's view and that of the investor on the *Journal's* role as an investors' paper see *ARJ,* 27:312–313, 744 (May 20, Nov. 25, 1854).

2. *ARJ,* 27:441, 459, 503 (July 15, 22, Aug. 12, 1854); 28:105 (Feb. 17, 1855); 29:424 (July 5, 1856); 31:744, 782 (Nov. 20, Dec. 11, 1858). Poor, of course, urged the roads to keep full faith with the investors, for example, *ARJ,* 29:248–249 (April 19, 1856).

3. For example, *ARJ,* 26:65–68, 528 (Jan. 29, Aug. 20, 1853); 27:818 (Dec. 30, 1854); 28:257 (April 28, 1855).

4. In 1861 Isaiah H. Sylvester was "the law reporter for the *Journal,*" *ARJ,* 34:840 (Nov. 30, 1861). Before 1853 Poor reported on cases involving railroad law, but not in a regular column.

5. Minor's list first appeared in *ARJ,* 18:7–9 (Jan. 2, 1845).

6. Poor's list first appeared in *ARJ,* 22:309 (May 19, 1849) and was somewhat enlarged very shortly thereafter. Schaeffer's table was printed in *ARJ,* 20:169 (March 17, 1847). Schaeffer, in turn, relied heavily on data supplied by Franz Anton von Gerstner, *Die Innern Communicationen der Vereingten Staaten von Nordamerica,* 2 vols. (Vienna, 1842–1843). Gerstner's data are far more complete than those given in the best known early compilation by an American — Henry S. Tanner, *A Brief Description of Canals and Rail Roads of the United States: Comprehending Notices of All the Most Important Works of Internal Improvement Throughout the Several States* (Philadelphia, 1834).

7. This list first appeared in *ARJ,* 26:473 (July 26, 1851).

8. This list first appeared in *ARJ,* 26:376–377 (June 11, 1853).

9. A copy of the questionnaire is printed below as an appendix.

10. This list appeared for the first time in *ARJ,* 28:520–521 (Aug. 18, 1855); the bond list made its first appearance in the next issue, August 25, on p. 535.

11. For about six months after October, 1858 Poor regularly ran a letter from William Lance on the British market for American securities. This feature began with *ARJ,* 31:697 (Oct. 30, 1858). During his trip to Britain Poor had arranged with Lance to write this column.

12. The complete revised share and bond list appeared in *ARJ,* 32:784 (Dec. 3, 1859). As the different pages were completed, they appeared in the paper beginning with the October 29 issue.

13. These summaries first appeared in *ARJ,* 33:100 (Feb. 4, 1860). This list was expanded in *ARJ,* 33:474 (June 2, 1860).

14. *ARJ,* 33:980–981 (Nov. 3, 1860).

15. The first quotation is from *ARJ,* 33:380 (May 5, 1860) and the second is from *ARJ,* 30:427 (July 4, 1857). See also Henry V. Poor, *History of the Railroads and Canals of the United States of America, Exhibiting Their Progress, Cost, Revenues and Expenditures and Present Condition* (New York, 1860), p. v.

16. The only attempt made by the government to collect railroad statistics on any comprehensive scale was the compilation made by William H. Jones in the *Report of the Secretary of Treasury on the State of the Finances for the Year ending June 30, 1856* (House Document 2, 34th Congress, 3rd Session). Jones sent a questionnaire to the railroads which asked for somewhat less data than Poor's questionnaire of 1854 and asked for information for only the previous year. As the department failed to give the final report wide publication or to keep the returns up to date, this government effort was of comparatively little value to businessmen or statisticians. The fact that James Guthrie, the Secretary

of Treasury from 1853 to 1857 was an active railroad promoter and manager may have helped the national government make this one effort to collect railroad statistics. One other report of the Treasury Department, made at the request of the Senate, included very brief but valuable information on railroad finance. This was the *Report of the Secretary of Treasury Department in Answer to a Resolution of the Senate Calling for the Amount of American Securities Held in Europe and other Foreign Countries on the 30th June, 1853* (Senate Document 42, 33rd Congress, 1st Session). Both these reports used information from the *Journal* to supplement the data they received from railroad companies.

17. *Report of Israel D. Andrews, Consul of the United States for Canada and New Brunswick, on the Trade and Commerce of the British North American Colonies, and Upon the Trade of the Great Lakes and Rivers* (Senate Document 112, 32nd Congress, 1st Session), p. 3. Both De Bow and Mansfield of the *Railroad Record* served as statisticians in public positions. De Bow as superintendent of the census of 1850 and Mansfield in the late 1850's as Ohio's commissioner of statistics. The railroad press advocated the creation of national and state bureaus of commercial and industrial statistics, see particularly *ARJ*, 25:720 (Nov. 20, 1852) and *Railway Times*, May 8, 1858.

18. De Bow took his data in the census of 1850 on railroads from the *American Railroad Journal, Report of the Superintendent of the Census for December 1, 1852* (Washington, 1853), pp. 101–102. Joseph C. G. Kennedy, superintendent of the census of 1860, does not give the source of his railroad statistics, but they are close to Poor's. The figures on mileage and cost of railroads in 1860 printed in Joseph C. G. Kennedy, *Preliminary Report of the Eighth Census, 1860* (Washington, 1862), pp. 214–231, are very close to those in *ARJ*, 34:2–6 (Jan. 5, 1861), while the comments on railroads, pp. 103–104, are much in Poor's style of thought and prose.

19. *Andrews Report*, pp. 11, 275–405.

20. *Andrews Report*, p. 405 and Henry V. Poor, *Manual of the Railroads of the United States, for 1869–1870* (New York, 1869), p. xxiv.

21. The maps which Poor published on cloth and mounted on rollers for $3.00 and on paper in "pocket form with cover" for a dollar and which were sent free of charge to subscribers of the *Journal*, though varying slightly, were usually about 35" by 40" in size, *ARJ*, 27:726 (Nov. 18, 1854); 28:6 (Jan. 6, 1855); 30:785 (Dec. 12, 1857); 31:9 (Jan. 2, 1858); 33:856 (Sept. 20, 1860).

22. The questionnaire is printed above as an appendix. This and the following quotations are from the questionnaire.

23. *ARJ*, 27:648 (Oct. 14, 1854).

24. For examples of Poor's efforts to compile information on roads which failed to answer his questionnaire see *ARJ*, 27:682, 684 (Oct. 28, 1854); 28:337–340 (June 2, 1855). The first was a reference to the Michigan Central, the second to the Mad River and Sandusky and the Sandusky, Mansfield and Newark.

25. On the folder to his railroad map of 1854 Poor solicits orders for his "Railways and Canals, United States and Canada, A Concise History of Each Enterprise, from its Charter to the Present Time, Illustrated with Statistical Tables and Maps," which was to be issued in 1855.

26. Poor, *History of Railroads and Canals*, p. vi. Examples of Fisher's statistical compilations in the *Journal* are *ARJ*, 31:24–25, 306–307, 312, 517, 667, 746 (Jan. 9, May 15, Aug. 21, Oct. 16, Nov. 20, 1858). Fisher published, among other things, *The Book of the World* (New York, 1849), revised in 1851 and 1852; *A New and Complete Statistical Gazetteer of the United States* (New York, 1853), revised 1855; *The Progress of the United States of America, Geographical, Statistical and Historical* (New York, 1854); *A Statistical Account of the West India Islands* (New York, 1855); *The Progress of the Republic* (New York, 1856). He was also editor of *Colton's Traveler and Tourist Guide-Book Through the United States* (New York, 1857), and several editions of Colton's atlases.

27. Poor, *History of Railroads and Canals*, p. vi; *ARJ*, 33:938 (Oct. 20, 1860).

28. Poor, *History of Railroads and Canals*, p. vi.

29. Poor, *History of Railroads and Canals*, p. vi.

30. *ARJ*, 33:849 (Sept. 22, 1860) and the maps themselves.

31. Poor, *History of Railroads and Canals*, p. v.

32. *Railway Times*, 12:408 (Oct. 13, 1860).

33. *Bankers' Magazine*, 15:404 (Nov. 1860). For comments by other periodicals and newspapers see *American Railway Review*, 3:264 (Nov. 1, 1860) and *ARJ*, 33:969 (Nov. 3, 1860).

34. Henry Poor to Mary Poor, July 15, 1860. Poor dedicated his volume "To the American Geographical and Statistical Society, this work, a contribution to the objects of the society, is respectfully inscribed by a member."

35. The supplier was George C. Dunbar; the financier, Frederic H. Stow, who in 1859 compiled *Stow's Capitalist Guide;* the engineers and contractors, Charles B. Stuart, Samuel McElroy, and Alexander L. Holley. The officers of the bureau are listed and its purposes and functions are described in each issue of the *American Railway Review*, during its first months of publication. In 1851 Duff Green, Southern railroad promoter and politician, with Benjamin E. Green and Richard H. Clarke organized a similar type of consulting office in New York and Washington which apparently was even more short-lived than the American Railway Bureau, *ARJ*, 24:677 (Oct. 25, 1851).

36. The banker was Samuel Gray Ward, Ralph W. Hidy, *The House of Baring in American Trade and Finance, 1763–1861* (Cambridge, Mass., 1949), p. 600.

37. According to the jubilee issue of the *Dry Goods Economist* (1896), p. 14 and Nathan H. Smith, *Twenty Years Among the Bulls and the Bears of Wall Street* (Hartford, Conn., 1870), p. 523, Kettell who began writing the financial column for the *Herald* in 1835, the year Bennett founded the paper, was the first financial editor of a daily paper in this country.

38. These generalizations are based on comments on the history of the financial columns of the New York papers in Smith, *Twenty Years Among the Bulls and Bears*, pp. 520–530 and an examination in the Lamont Library of Harvard University and the New England Deposit Library in Boston, Mass., of the New York *Times, Tribune, Herald, Post, Journal of Commerce,* and *Commercial Advertiser.* I. Smith Homans, editor of the *Bankers' Magazine*, was also financial editor during the 1850's of the *Courier and Enquirer*, Frank L. Mott, *A History of American Magazines* (Cambridge, Mass., 1938), II, 94. The leading German-language newspaper in the country, the *New Yorker Handels-Zeitung*, devoted much space to financial matters sending weekly reports on American securities and business conditions to readers in Frankfurt, Berlin, Hamburg, Bremen, and elsewhere, *ARJ*, 2:207 (April 1, 1854).

39. For comments on *Tribune*, see *ARJ*, 27:221–222, 371–372 (April 8, June 3, 1854); on *Herald, ARJ*, 27:371–372 (June 10, 1854).

40. Poor's awareness of the need for accurate business information may have been increased by the fact that his wife's uncle, Lewis Tappan, founded and during the 1840's operated the first commercial credit agency in the United States.

41. *Railroad Record*, 4:98 (April 10, 1856); for the earlier protests of the *Record* and other papers see chapter 7 above.

42. See any issue of *Herapath's Railway and Commercial Journal* from 1845 until well into the 1850's.

43. Poor was accused of being a tool of Winslow, Lanier and Company, see chapter 6 above, and he, in turn, accused the *Tribune's* financial editor and the editor of the *Railroad Record* of being in the pay of the Ohio and Mississippi, *ARJ*, 27:221–222, 344, 345 (April 8, June 3, 1854), but such accusations were actually very rarely made in spite of the heated debates the *Journal* and other

papers had over the merits of individual railroad companies. The only paper which may have been subsidized by a railroad promoter was the Indianapolis *Locomotive*, which appears to have been the spokesman for railroad promoter Oliver H. Smith. I have not seen a copy of this paper since it is not listed in the *Union List of Serials*, but is mentioned in the *Journal* and by Alvin F. Harlow, *The Road of the Century* (New York, 1947), p. 358.

44. The best summary of the *Journal's* later history is in *Railway Mechanical Engineer*, 106:385ff. (Oct. 1932).

45. Arthur T. Hadley, *Railroad Transportation* (New York, 1886), p. iv.

46. *National Cyclopedia of American Biography* (New York, 1892–1938), XX, 129. These generalizations on the *Gazette* come from a brief examination of the periodical for the period from 1870 to 1900, and they can be made for almost every individual volume during that period.

47. After Freeman Hunt's death in 1858, Kettell became editor of *Hunt's Merchants' Magazine*, as well as editor of the *United States Economist*. From April 1861 until February 1862 Homans and William B. Dana edited it jointly and then, until he stopped its publication in 1870, by Dana alone.

48. For examples of Dana's views in one volume on railroad speculation and malpractices see *Commercial and Financial Chronicle*, 6:38–39, 325–326, 358–359, 614, 677, 711–712 (June 11, 1868, March 7, 21, May 15, 19, June 5, 1869). Cleveland and Powell indicate the value of the information and analyses and editorial policies of the *Chronicle*, and, after the turn of the century, the *Wall Street Journal*, Frederick A. Cleveland and Fred W. Powell, *Railroad Finance* (New York, 1912), pp. 355–356, 364.

Chapter 10: Wall Street and Washington

1. Henry Poor to Mary Poor, June 7, 1861.

2. Henry Poor to Mary Poor, June 7, 1861. Schultz's name first appears as a coeditor in the issue of July 27, 1861. Poor's name as editor last appears August 23, 1862.

3. Henry Poor to Mary Poor, Aug. 16, 30, 1861. Reprints of the contents of Hallett's circular appear regularly in the *American Railroad Journal* until the fall of 1862. In June 1862 he wrote that, "I still get out Hallett's circular, though I have no other relations with him," Henry Poor to Mary Poor, June 15, 1862.

4. Henry Poor to Mary Poor, June 24, 27, July 20, 1862.

5. Barney, Collector of the Port of New York, in the summer of 1861 had obtained a customs house job for Poor which involved very little work, Henry Poor to Mary Poor, June 6, Sept. 8, 15, 1861. His trip to Washington on currency legislation will be considered in more detail in part II of this chapter.

6. Cabel B. Smith to Henry Poor, July 4, 1862, a letter belonging to Mr. Charles L. Chandler.

7. For an account of the meeting and Poor's election see *ARJ*, 35:719–722 (Sept. 20, 1862). Poor received 51 votes to 10 for B. F. Camp of New York and 6 for J. R. Robinson of California.

8. The canvassing and other work is mentioned in Henry V. Poor, *The Pacific Railroad. The Relations Existing Between It and the Government of the United States* (New York, 1871), pp. 37–38 and is described in more detail in Poor's letters to his wife during the summer of 1863. Especially good are those dated June 19, July 5, 10, 16, Aug. 19, 29, 31, Sept. 14, 24, 1863. In one, Aug. 29, he stated he was being paid $10,000 for his work by the railroad company. Examples of his occasional articles for the road are New York *Times*, Aug. 18, 1863, and the *Proceedings of the American Geographical and Statistical Society*, 2:3–40 (1863–1864).

9. "Affairs of the Union Pacific Railroad Company" (*House Report No. 78*, 42nd Congress, 3rd Session), pp. 599–600, 740–742; *ARJ*, 36:925–926 (Oct. 3, 1863). Henry K. White in his *History of the Union Pacific Railway* (Chicago,

1895), p. 18 credits Thomas C. Durant for raising most of this subscription. However Durant's name does not appear in Poor's correspondence to his wife.

10. *ARJ*, 36:1047–1048 (Nov. 7, 1863).

11. The refusal of responsible men to take part in the road's affairs after Durant became active in its management in the winter of 1863–1864 is stressed in the debates in Congress on the Pacific Railroad bill during June, 1864. Especially good are Senator Elihu B. Washburne's remarks on June 21, 1864, printed in *Pacific Railroad —— Congressional Proceedings in the 37th, 38th and 41st Congresses* (West Chester, Pa., 1875), p. 284. As neither Poor nor his wife left New York from September 1863 to April 1864, their correspondence has nothing in it about the reasons for Poor's resignation.

12. Henry Poor to Mary Poor, June 15, 1862, also Henry Poor to Mary Poor, Sept. 3, 9, 1863.

13. Mary Poor's diary in the Poor collection, April 18, 20, 26, 28, 1864; Henry Poor to Mary Poor, May 4, 10, 12, 1864.

14. Poor's work as a partner in Fitch and Company is mentioned in Henry Poor to Mary Poor, May 10, 18, Aug. 23, Sept. 25, Oct. 26, 1864; April 10, July 20, Oct. 9, 24, 1865; March 9, 1866; Nov. 16, 17, 1867. His lobbying against the tariff on rails is described in part III of this chapter.

15. Henry Poor to Mary Poor, Jan. 6, Feb. 2, 4, 8, 10, 12, 1866. After making his report Poor was sent by Lanier to represent the New York directors and to vote their proxies, Henry Poor to Mary Poor, March 18, 19, 1866; *Fourth Annual Report of the Board of Directors of the Pittsburgh, Fort Wayne and Chicago Railway Company . . .* (Pittsburgh, 1866), pp. 6, 14.

16. Henry Poor to Mary Poor, March 17, April 16, 18, 22, 27, 29, May 4, 6, 1867. On this trip, Poor, owing to a train accident in which he was injured, spent several days in Lynchburg with his old friend John Robert McDaniel with whom he talked over the refinancing of the Virginia and Tennessee.

17. The Erie claims for $120,000 are mentioned in Henry Poor to Mary Poor, June 18, 19, 21, July 2, 1866; the car spring company's taxes in Henry Poor to Mary Poor, June 6, 29, 1866.

18. John Alfred Poor's plans and their development are summarized in Edward C. Kirkland, *Men, Cities and Transportation* (Cambridge, Mass., 1948), I, 470–474. Laura Poor, *The First International Railroad* (New York, 1890), pp. 80–88 adds many details. John A. Andrews, wartime governor of Massachusetts and a close friend of Henry Poor, had been influential in getting Massachusetts to hand over her claims to the European and North American. Henry Poor's activities in behalf of his brother's road are described in many of his letters to his wife, particularly Henry Poor to Mary Poor, May 1, June 1, 5, 8, 15, July 8, 1866, Jan. 2, 11, 13, 24, 1867. The Poors were never able to take advantage of the congressional aid Henry Poor helped win because in 1868 John Alfred was ousted from the road's presidency, Kirkland, *Men, Cities and Transportation*, I, 473; and John A. Poor to Henry Poor, April 28, 29, 1870. The first of these letters belongs to Charles L. Chandler; the second is in the Poor collection. There is also much correspondence on the European and North American Railroad in the John A. Andrews collection in the Massachusetts Historical Society, Boston, Massachusetts.

19. Poor's work on the Gold Contract Bill is described in part III of this chapter.

20. Henry Poor to Mary Poor, Nov. 15, 16, 17, 19, 1867. In two letters written on the seventeenth Poor told of his losses and described the details of the type of work the new firm would do.

21. Henry Poor to Mary Poor, Jan. 4, 28, 1866; Jan. 1, Feb. 10, 1867; Dec. 1, 9, 1868; Henry William Poor to Henry Poor, Nov. 30, 1868.

22. Henry Poor to Mary Poor, Nov. 4, 1868; Aug. 8, Nov. 11, 1869; Jan. 19, 26, Feb. 11, March 3, 18, 26, April 3, 13, 1870; Dec. 12, 1871; Jan. 17, Feb. 15, 1872; April 17, 1873. In a letter dated March 18, 1870 Poor wrote

that in the past few months the firm with Habicht's assistance had sold 20,000 tons of rails grossing close to $1,300,000 at an estimated profit of $2.00 a ton.

23. Henry V. Poor, *Manual of the Railroads of the United States for 1870–71* (New York, 1870), pp. 408–409. Letters in which Poor describes his work with the Selma and Gulf are those to his wife dated Aug. 8, 1869; Jan. 28, Aug. 9, Oct. 24, Nov. 16, 21, 29, Dec. 7, 1870; March 17, 1871; Dec. 18, 1872; May 3, 1873 and letters to William dated Aug. 13, 16, 1869.

24. Henry Poor to Mary Poor, Jan. 28, April 21, 27, 29, May 22, June 22, 25, Aug. 21, 1870; Philip Dorf, *The Builder, a Biography of Ezra Cornell* (New York, 1952), 386–387, 434.

25. Since the Poors accepted the responsibility of marketing the road's bonds in New York and London as well as its building, there are many letters in the Poor collection written by Poor to his wife during 1871 and 1872 from Ithaca, Courtland, and Horseheads telling of the problems and progress of both the railroad's construction and of its financing.

26. Henry Poor to Mary Poor, May 1, 1873.

27. Negotiations for the sale of the contract back to Cornell are mentioned in Henry Poor to Mary Poor, Dec. 5, 1872; Jan. 6, 8, 12, 15, 1873; the difficulties of collecting from Cornell in Henry Poor to Mary Poor, April 5, 17, May 7, June 17, July 1, 8, 9, Sept. 8, 17, 18, 1873; also Dorf, *The Builder*, p. 418.

28. Henry Poor to Mary Poor, Sept. 19, 1873.

29. For the history of the Utica, Ithaca, and Elmira after 1873, see Dorf, *The Builder*, 434, 441; Henry V. Poor, *Manual of the Railroads of the United States for 1875–76* (New York, 1875); p. 765; Henry V. Poor, *Manual of the Railroads of the United States for 1876–77* (New York, 1876), pp. 817–818; Henry V. Poor, *Manual of the Railroads of the United States for 1877–78* (New York, 1877), pp. 751–753; Henry V. Poor, *Manual of the Railroads of the United States for 1878* (New York, 1878), pp. 217–218; Henry V. Poor, *Manual of the Railroads of the United States for 1879* (New York, 1879), p. 217. The continuing connection of the Poors with the road is also mentioned in Henry Poor to Mary Poor, Feb. 15, March 9, April 14, 19, May 12, 17, June 16, Nov. 30, Dec. 6, 8, 19, 29, 1876; Dec. 12, 1882, June 26, 1883.

30. The first partners, besides the two Poors, were two men of William's age of old New York lineage, James L. Anthony and James H. Oliphant. By 1882 both these men had dropped out and J. H. White joined the firm. In 1884 John Greenough, William's very close friend and classmate, became a partner. White left the firm at the same time as the elder Poor in 1888. The history of the firm can be traced in Henry Poor to Mary Poor, Jan. 15, 22, March 14, 20, April 10, 17, 1878, Dec. 7, 1881, May 9, 1883, April 16, 1884, Aug. 12, 1886, and in printed prospectuses for the firm in the Poor collection. An example of his work for the firm was the negotiations he carried on for the sale of a block of stock of the Hannibal and St. Joseph Railroad to John Murray Forbes and the Chicago, Burlington and Quincy Railroad. These negotiations may be traced in Henry Poor to John Murray Forbes, June 23, 25, 26, 1879 in the Burlington Archives in the Newberry Library, Chicago, Illinois and also in a letter from John Murray Forbes to Henry Poor, June 24, 1879, in the possession of Charles L. Chandler. Poor's and Coe's Texan interests are mentioned in Henry Poor to Mary Poor, May 22, 1871, May 20, 21, 23, 28, 1878, June 5, 1883. The contract with the English Association is mentioned in Henry Poor to Mary Poor, May 5, 6, July 10, 15, 1885; also see Henry V. Poor, *Manual of the Railroads of the United States for 1887* (New York, 1886), p. 58.

31. Since Poor's editorials were unsigned, I have cited only those which can positively be identified as his. These include twenty which were clipped and saved and are now part of the Poor collection. These were all written in the first months of 1861. Also cited are some of a number which Poor mentioned in his letters to his wife. Poor wrote on political as well as economic matters. Among his best editorials on political topics are: "Secession and reconstruction,"

Jan. 21, 1861; "Secession —— what has already been gained," Feb. 18, 1861; "Inaugural of President Davis," Feb. 19, 1861; "The great question," March 30, 1861.

32. See particularly New York *Times* editorials: "Direct trade with the South," March 19, 1861; "Our Revenue Policy," March 23, 1861; "Free trade of the South with Europe," April 4, 1861.

33. See especially New York *Times* editorials: "The new nation of Mississippi," Jan. 29, 1861; "Finances of the Confederate States," March 16, 1861; "Difference of authorities —— Jeff. Davis and A. H. Stephens," May 7, 1861; "Confederate finances and folly," July 16, 1861; "Confederate finances," Aug. 13, 1861.

34. "The crisis of the country and the duty of the government," April 19, 1861.

35. Poor's views are best summarized in New York *Times* editorials "No British interference," May 20, 1861; "Relation of England to the war," May 23, 1861; "England recognizes the blockade," May 25, 1861, "The blockade," July 13, 1861.

36. Poor's views on war finance are spelled out in his writing in Hallett's circular, reprinted in *ARJ*, 34:697–698, 817–818, 825–826, 859–860 (Oct. 5, Nov. 23, 30, Dec. 14, 1861); also New York *Times* editorials written in the summer, especially July 22, Aug. 6, 14, 15, 16, 17, 1861.

37. The background of the financial crisis and the resulting developments are well covered in Don C. Barrett, *The Greenbacks and the Resumption of Specie Payments* (Cambridge, 1931), ch. 1; Wesley C. Mitchell, *A History of the Greenbacks* (Chicago, 1903), ch. 2; Elbridge G. Spaulding, *History of the Legal Tender Paper Money Issued during the Late Rebellion* (Buffalo, 1869), pp. 1–152.

38. Henry V. Poor and others, *Report on the Financial Credit of the United States. How It Can Be Sustained* (New York, 1862). This report was made to the American Geographical and Statistical Society on January 16, 1862 by a committee chaired by Poor which included Charles Gould, Archibald Russell, I. Smith Homans of the *Bankers' Magazine,* and William C. H. Waddell. The report, which set forth a specific plan for the raising of funds through long-term bond issues and demand notes backed by tax revenue, summarized the views Poor expressed on public financial policy in Halletts' circular reprinted in *ARJ*, 34:729–730, 745–746, 809–810, 893, 900 (Oct. 19, 26, Nov. 23, Dec. 28, 1861); 35:15, 35–36, 53–54 (Jan. 4, 18, 25, 1862). Editorials, most probably written by Poor, which took the same line of argument, appeared in New York *Times* of Jan. 1, 8, 9, 13, 16, 1862.

39. Poor, *Report on the Financial Credit of the United States,* p. 3.

40. Poor, *Report on the Financial Credit of the United States,* p. 7.

41. Henry Poor to Mary Poor, Jan. 24, 1862; New York *Times,* Jan. 22, 1862.

42. Henry Poor to Mary Poor, Jan. 28, 1862; also Henry Poor to Mary Poor, Jan. 29, 1862.

43. Mitchell, *History of Greenbacks,* p. 75; Spaulding, *History of Legal Tender Paper Money,* pp. 52, 92–94; Henry Poor to Mary Poor, Jan. 30, 1862.

44. Mitchell, *History of Greenbacks,* p. 75; also Henry Poor to Mary Poor, Feb. 5, 6, 1862. While Poor was helping to devise compromise measures, Raymond had come out in favor of the legal tender bill as an unsatisfactory, but for the moment the most practical emergency measure. Even so the *Times* insisted that the legal tender notes issued must not exceed tax revenue collected, New York *Times,* Jan. 18, 27, 31, Feb. 3, 5, 7, 1862.

45. The tariff rates on iron rails, plates, rods, and so on, are summarized in "Rates of Duty on Imports into the United States from 1789 to 1890 Inclusive. . . ." (*Senate Report,* No. 2130, 51st Congress, Second Session), pp. 196–199; more detailed listings can be found in Robert G. Proctor, *Tariff Acts Passed by the Congress of the United States from 1789 to 1897* (Washington, 1898).

A good general survey of the tariff history of these years is Frank W. Taussig, *The Tariff of the United States* (New York, 1898), ch. 2.

46. Henry Poor to Mary Poor, June 10, 12, 16, 19, 25, 1864; March 5, 1865; a printed circular signed by the presidents of twelve major roads dated June 25, 1866, in the Poor collection. In 1864 Poor was paid $1,000 in cash for going to Washington and received a second thousand on the successful conclusion of his mission.

47. At a meeting held June 25, 1866, the representatives of the railroad companies appointed the presidents of the following companies "to confer with and obtain the cooperation of other Companies, for the purpose of securing and maintaining the duty on imported rails at reasonable rates." The companies listed were the New York Central, the Michigan Southern and Northern Indiana, the Cleveland and Toledo, the Ohio and Mississippi, the Quincy and Toledo, the Toledo and Wabash, the Dubuque and Sioux City, the Chicago and Alton, the Little Miami, the Milwaukee and St. Paul, the Cincinnati, Hamilton and Dayton, and the Hartford and New Haven, listed in the printed letter dated June 25, 1866, in the Poor collection. A printed letter dated December 21, 1868, which Poor sent out urging railroad and other businessmen to write their congressmen and sign a memorial protesting the proposed rates was signed by A. S. Biven, vice-president of the Erie, J. F. Tracy, president of the Chicago, Rock Island and Pacific, Russell Sage, vice-president of the Milwaukee and St. Paul, and William D. Bishop, president of the New York and New Haven. This letter is also in the Poor collection.

48. Poor describes his fight against the tariff between 1866 and 1868 in Henry Poor to Mary Poor, June 26, 28, 29, July 3, 7, 8, 1866; Jan. 2, 4, 9, 17, 27, Feb. 16, 1867; Jan. 10, 13, Feb. 12, 1868.

49. Printed circular dated Dec. 21, 1868 and a four-page printed circular, undated, entitled "Duties on Steel and Steel Rails," both in the Poor collection. Poor tells of his work on the steel rates in Henry Poor to Mary Poor, Jan. 11, 14, Feb. 2, 3, 1869; Feb. 9, March 21, 22, 24, April 3, 4, 7, 9, 14, 24, 28, 29, May 4, 1870.

50. Henry Poor to Mary Poor, Dec. 29, 1871; Feb. 13, 27, 1872.

51. *Argument of Henry V. Poor on the Reduction of the Duty on Steel Rails. Delivered Before the Committee of Ways and Means of the House of Representatives, February 3, 1880* (New York, 1880); printed circular signed by Poor dated 1879 in the Poor collection; Henry Poor to Mary Poor, Feb. 5, 8, June 9, 1880; also undated newspaper clippings in Poor collection. Poor was paid by the Chicago, Burlington and Quincy at a rate of $.25 for each mile operated, an entry in the Chicago, Burlington and Quincy Railroad Record Book, Number 1, dated Jan. 3, 1880. I am indebted to Dr. Richard C. Overton for this citation.

52. The information for this paragraph comes from letters, newspaper clippings, and circulars in the Poor collection, nearly all of which have been already cited.

53. His arguments are summarized in the New York *Post,* Jan. 9, 1869; New York *Times,* March 15, April 4, 10, 1870 (these citations are from clippings in the Poor collection); and printed circular entitled "Duties on Steel and Steel Rails," cited above.

54. New York *Times,* March 15, 1870, a clipping in the Poor collection.

55. Henry Poor to Mary Poor, April 10, 1870.

56. Good examples of the types of petitions, circulars, and letters used by representatives of the iron and steel industry in the fight to increase rates, and the arguments used to make their case can be found in the *Bulletin of the American Iron and Steel Institute,* 4:121, 137, 153, 209–210, 241, 249–250, 321 (Dec. 22, 1869; Jan. 5, 19, March 9, April 6, 13, June 15, 1870).

57. *Duty on Steel Rails. The Case for the Manufacturers at the Hearings of the Ways and Means Committee of the House of Representatives, at Washington, Feb. 3, 4, and 5, 1880* (Philadelphia, 1880), *passim.*

58. *Bulletin of the American Iron and Steel Institute,* 4:153 (Jan. 19, 1870).

59. *Report of the Secretary of the American Iron and Steel Association read at the Regular Annual Meeting of the Association at Philadelphia, March 5, 1868* (Philadelphia, 1868), p. 31. The operation of the association's tariff committee is made clear in this report and the pages of the association's weekly *Bulletin,* and the industry's leading trade journal, the *Iron Age.* Besides the American Iron and Steel Association, the industry had at least two other trade organizations active in the tariff fight, the National Association of Iron Manufacturers and the American Pig Iron Manufacturing Association. These two small associations did not have as large or effective Washington organization as did the American Iron and Steel Association.

60. *Report of the Secretary of the American Iron and Steel Association, March 5, 1868,* pp. 3–10.

61. James F. D. Lanier, *Sketch Life of J. F. D. Lanier* (New York, 1870), pp. 44–55, 65; Poor tells of his role in Henry Poor to Mary Poor, Oct. 28, 31, 1865; background information can be found in Barrett, *Greenbacks and the Resumption of Specie Payments,* pp. 161–165.

62. Barrett, *Greenbacks and the Resumption of Specie Payments,* pp. 165–168.

63. Henry V. Poor, "On Sound Principles of Banking," *Bankers' Magazine,* 22:841–868. The article, dated December 25, 1867, appeared in pamphlet form in January, Henry Poor to Mary Poor, Jan. 14, 1868. Coe's more specific formulation of this plan can be found in the summary of his "The Natural Road to Specie Payment," in the *Commercial and Financial Chronicle,* 6:134 (Feb. 1, 1868).

64. The Gold Contract Bill, given in full in a circular in the Poor collection, is summarized in the *Commercial and Financial Chronicle,* 6:709, 742–743 (June 6, 13, 1868).

65. Henry Poor to Mary Poor, Jan. 10, 19, 29, 31, Feb. 4, 1868; John Murray Forbes to Henry Poor, May 5, 1868, a letter belonging to Mr. Charles L. Chandler.

66. Henry Poor to Mary Poor, June 5, 10, 27, 28, July 17, 18, 1868; *Commercial and Financial Chronicle,* 6:709, 742–743 (June 6, 13, 1868).

67. Barrett, *Greenbacks and the Resumption of Specie Payments,* p. 171; John Sherman, *Selected Speeches and Reports on Finance and Taxation* (New York, 1879), p. 192; *Bankers' Magazine,* 23:611–612 (February 1869).

Chapter 11: The Manual

1. Henry Poor to Mary Poor, Nov. 17, 1867, June 30, 1868.

2. The first directory of this kind in this country was published in 1856 by Homans, editor of the *Bankers' Magazine,* and is described in *Hunt's,* 35:118 (July, 1856). From 1858 until 1865 James F. Low and Josiah J. Burgess, who were partners in a New York railroad supply house, published sometimes individually and sometimes jointly an annual directory with the possible exception of the years 1860 and 1863. The full title for the different volumes varies only slightly from that of 1859 which is *Low and Burgess' Railway Directory for 1859 Containing a Correct List of All Officers and Directors of the Railroads of the United States and Canada Together with Their Financial Condition.* In 1867 two directories with somewhat similar titles were being published, one by John Ashcroft, the other by A. H. King, a railroad equipment maker.

3. The first British manual was Henry Tuck's *Railway Shareholders' Manual* begun before 1845. It was replaced as the standard manual in the 1850's by *Bradshaw's* which had started before 1840 as a guide to railway schedules and fares. Frederick H. Stow, New York merchant and banker and a founder of the American Railway Bureau and its *American Railway Review,* published an imitation of *Bradshaw's* in 1859 in New York, a *Capitalist Guide and Railway Annual.* He never printed a second annual volume.

4. Henry Poor to Mary Poor, Nov. 17, 1867, April 6, 1868.

5. The information on compiling and publishing the first manual comes from Henry Poor to Mary Poor, Jan. 8, 10, Feb. 17, March 5, April 6, 24, May 15, 21, June 2, 7, 9, 14, 17, 24, 26, 1868, and Henry Poor to William Poor, April 4, 1868.

6. From a letter of Henry Poor to Amasa Stone, president of the Lake Shore Railroad, Feb. 20, 1868, which is in possession of the Standard and Poor's Corporation, New York, N. Y.

7. The full title was *Manual of the Railroads of the United States for 1868–69, Showing Their Mileage, Stocks, Bonds, Cost, Earnings, Expenses, and Organizations; with a Sketch of Their Rise, Progress, Influence, etc.; Together with an Appendix Containing a Full Analysis of the Debts of the United States and of the Several States.* In this chapter the *Manual* will be cited as Poor, *Manual* with date except for the volumes after 1893, when Poor's name was no longer on its title page; then it will be cited as *Poor's Manual* with date.

8. *Commercial and Financial Chronicle,* 6:716 (June 6, 1868); see also *Railway Gazette,* 4:272–273 (June 29, 1872). Poor later printed his favorable press notices on the back of the questionnaires he sent the roads for information.

9. Henry Poor to Mary Poor, April 20, June 9, 17, 26, 27, Sept. 2, 1868.

10. The full title of Lyle's first manual was *Official Railway Manual of the Railroads of North America for 1869–70; Showing Their Financial Condition, Mileage, Cost, Earnings, Expenses and Organization; Together with a List of the Railroads of the World;* and of Vernon's, *American Railroad Manual for the United States and the Dominions. The Manual of Statistics. Railroads, Grain and Produce, Cotton, Petroleum, Mining Dividends, etc., etc.* published annually from 1881 until 1924 (except for the years 1885 and 1886, when it was published semiannually) was the closest thing to a competitor before Moody began publication. As the title indicates, these volumes carried much more information on subjects other than railroads. Information about individual railroads was much less than in Poor's *Manual.*

11. Until 1883 Poor's European agent was Samson, Low and Company, 188 Fleet Street, London. After that his agent was Effingham Wilson, Royal Exchange, London. For a short time in the early 1870's H. V. and H. W. Poor had their own London offices at 4 Grace Church Street.

12. The information on sales, costs, advertising, and profits comes from the letters of Henry Poor to his wife dated April 20, May 14, 1868, Feb. 16, March 24, 1869, May 10, 1871, April 17, 1878, July 28, 1880, May 20, Aug. 2, 1881, March 30, 1888. In 1868 Poor sold the back cover for $500.00 to the Adams Express Company (Henry Poor to Mary Poor, May 14, 1868), who continued to buy the space regularly for several years.

13. The number of pages of text, excluding the introduction and advertising, increased from 404 in 1868 to 504 in 1870, then to 1028 in 1878 and 1055 in 1883. From the first the *Manual* included data on Canadian roads.

14. Stone is mentioned in Henry Poor to Mary Poor, June 7, 1873; Hand's name appears on the firm's stationery as the officer in charge of advertising.

15. Charles L. Chandler has a set of filled-out questionnaires from the Kansas Pacific Railroad from 1872 through 1878 in his collection of materials concerning his grandfather.

16. This and the following quotation is from Poor, *Manual . . . for 1873–74,* p. xxvii. See also Poor, *Manual . . . for 1871–72,* p. xxxi.

17. This and the following quotation is from Poor, *Manual . . . for 1871–72,* p. xxxi. See also Poor, *Manual . . . for 1872–73,* p. xxxi, Poor, *Manual . . . for 1872–73,* p. xxviii.

18. Poor, *Manual . . . for 1872–73,* pp. xxxiv–xlvii.

19. Poor, *Manual . . . for 1871–72,* p. xxxi. See also Poor, *Manual . . . for 1879,* p. i. John Moody in an interview on Dec. 10, 1948 reported that the comment "information refused" printed in his *Manual* usually resulted in a call from

the company or its fiscal agent pointing out that it was an unintentional oversight.

20. William K. Vanderbilt to Henry Poor, April 16, 1870, a letter in the possession of Charles L. Chandler.

21. Poor, *Manual . . . for 1873–74,* p. xxvii. See also Poor, *Manual . . . for 1871–72,* p. xxxi, Poor, *Manual . . . for 1872–73,* p. xxi.

22. Henry Poor to Mary Poor, February 16, March 24, May 25, 1869, Feb. 11, April 27, 1870, May 10, 22, June 26, 28, 1871, June 6, 7, 17, 18, July 9, 1873.

23. Henry Poor to Mary Poor, April 17, June 5, July 9, Aug. 2, 1878, March 3, 1881.

24. Poor, *Manual . . . for 1878,* pp. 1012–1027.

25. Henry Poor to Mary Poor, May 25, 1881; also Henry Poor to Mary Poor, April 13, May 20, 1881, Feb. 3, March 14, 15, 16, April 18, May 12, 1882.

26. Henry Poor to Mary Poor, May 20, 25, June 2, 10, 1881, July 29, Aug. 1, 1883.

27. Henry Poor to Mary Poor, Dec. 12, 1882.

28. Henry Poor to Mary Poor, July 30, 1883; other letters on the training of his staff are May 12, June 22, 1882; July 29, Aug. 1, 1883.

29. Henry Poor to Mary Poor, Aug. 1, 1883.

30. Henry Poor to Mary Poor, April 16, July 1, 1884.

31. Henry Poor to Mary Poor, June 30, July 8, 10, 15, 16, Aug. 15, 16, 1885.

32. *Railroad Gazette,* 16:536 (Aug. 21, 1885); compare to highly favorable comments in *Railroad Gazette,* 14:461 (July 28, 1882), 15:544–545 (Aug. 17, 1883).

33. Henry Poor to Mary Poor, Aug. 15, 1885.

34. *Poor's Handbook of Investment Securities; for the Use of Bankers, Investors and Trust Institutions and Railroad Officials,* was published annually from 1890 to 1893 when the depression of that year apparently cut the demand for it. Because Meany did not revive this volume, which included a large number of industrials and other securities not listed in the *Manual,* John Moody decided to do so and in this way issued in 1900 a successful competitor to Poor's *Manuals;* interview with John Moody, December 10, 1948.

35. Interview with John Moody, December 10, 1948.

36. The decision to issue a supplementary volume resulted not only in meeting the demand for a more convenient book for firms like railroad suppliers that primarily needed names and addresses of railroad officials, but also in cutting down the *Manual,* whose increasing size was making it too bulky for convenient handling. For this latter reason data on street railways were included in the *Directory, Poor's Manual . . . for 1887,* p. ix.

37. According to John Moody, Meany was not permitted to send the copy to the printer until it had been sent to Brookline and had been approved by "the old man," interview with John Moody, December 10, 1948.

38. The data for the following come primarily from the letters of Henry Poor to his wife about the *Manual,* particularly those written in 1881 to 1883, and also from some letters, questionnaires, and other items belonging to Charles L. Chandler.

39. Poor, *Manual . . . for 1873,* p. li, Poor, *Manual . . . for 1891,* p. xi.

40. Poor, *Manual . . . for 1891,* p. xi. The evidence on when Poor began this practice is uncertain.

41. The introductions to the *Manuals* for 1871–72 and 1872–73 include briefer historical descriptions which are summaries of the three previous ones. Several of the introductions were reprinted in pamphlet form. Those reprinted include the introductions to the volumes for 1868–69, 1869–70, 1873–74, 1874–75, 1875–76, 1876–77, 1880, 1881, 1882, 1885, and 1890. There were probably more which I have been unable to locate.

42. Poor, *Manual . . . for 1868–69,* p. 26; Poor, *Manual . . . for 1869–70,* pp. xvii, xxxi; Poor, *Manual . . . for 1871–72,* pp. xxvii–xxviii; Poor, *Manual*

. . . *for 1872–73,* pp. xxix–xxx; Poor, *Manual . . . for 1881,* pp. xlvi–xlvii; Poor, *Manual . . . for 1889,* pp. xxi–xxii, xxiv–xxv.

43. Poor, *Manual . . . for 1870–71,* p. xl.

44. Poor, *Manual . . . for 1888,* p. xix; also Poor, *Manual . . . for 1889,* p. xxiv. For the effects of the railroads on the recovery from the Civil War and on the national finances in general, see Poor, *Manual . . . 1868–69,* pp. 27–28; Poor, *Manual . . . for 1869–70,* p. xlix; Poor, *Manual . . . for 1870–71,* p. xl; Poor, *Manual . . . for 1871–72,* pp. xvii–xxix.

45. Poor, *Manual . . . for 1883,* p. iii; Poor, *Manual . . . for 1889,* pp. xii–xv.

46. This and the following quotation are from Poor, *Manual . . . for 1889,* pp. xiii–xiv.

47. Poor, *Manual . . . for 1874–75,* p. 30; Poor, *Manual . . . for 1875–76,* p. 30.

48. Poor, *Manual . . . for 1873–74,* pp. lii–liii; Poor, *Manual . . . for 1874–75,* pp. 30–31; Poor, *Manual . . . for 1883,* pp. iii–iv; Poor, *Manual . . . for 1885,* p. iv–v; Poor, *Manual . . . for 1889,* pp. xiv–xv.

49. Poor, *Manual . . . for 1874–75,* p. 32; Poor, *Manual . . . for 1883,* pp. iii–iv; Poor, *Manual . . . for 1885,* pp. iv–v.

50. Poor, *Manual . . . for 1870–71,* pp. xli–xlii; Poor, *Manual . . . for 1882,* pp. i–ii. In 1871 and 1872 Poor praised the making of land grants, Poor, *Manual . . . for 1871–72,* pp. xxx–xxxi; Poor, *Manual . . . for 1872–73,* pp. xxx–xxxi.

51. Poor, *Manual . . . for 1873–74,* pp. lii–liii; Poor, *Manual . . . for 1883,* pp. iii–iv.

52. Poor, *Manual . . . for 1874–75,* pp. 31–32; Poor, *Manual . . . for 1875–76,* p. 31; Poor, *Manual . . . for 1876–77,* p. xv; Poor, *Manual . . . for 1877–78,* p. viii; Poor, *Manual . . . for 1883,* pp. v, vii.

53. Poor, *Manual . . . for 1875–76,* p. 31; Poor, *Manual . . . for 1877–78,* p. viii; Poor, *Manual . . . for 1879,* p. ii. In the 1870's Poor further suggested that the unhealthy currency situation delayed recovery. In the 1880's he also blamed hostile regulatory legislation, Poor, *Manual . . . for 1874–75,* p. 32; Poor, *Manual . . . for 1889,* p. xx.

54. The arguments Poor made against rate regulation are all given in the introduction to the 1881 *Manual,* entitled "Sketch of the Rise and Progress of the Internal Improvements, and of the Internal Commerce, of the United States; with a Review of the Charges of Monopoly and Oppression Made Against Railroad Corporations." These arguments he repeated in later introductions, particularly those of 1882 and 1889, in his testimony before the Cullom committee (see footnote 68 below) and in a short pamphlet entitled *Interstate Commerce Bill* (New York, 1887).

55. Poor, *Manual . . . for 1881,* p. xlviii.

56. In the introduction to the 1881 *Manual,* Poor praised the general railroad laws much as he had done in editorials in the *Journal,* in the earlier introductions, and also protested as he had done in the 1850's against the taxes New Jersey and Maryland continued to levy on railroad traffic passing through their states, Poor, *Manual . . . for 1868–69,* pp. 31–32; Poor, *Manual . . . for 1869–70,* pp. xxix–xxx; Poor, *Manual . . . for 1870–71,* pp. xxxi–xxxiii; Poor, *Manual . . . for 1871–72,* p. xxv.

57. Poor, *Manual . . . for 1889,* p. xx.

58. For the high operating costs of American roads and the cost-cutting improvements he urged, see Poor, *Manual . . . for 1868–69,* pp. 29–30; Poor, *Manual . . . for 1869–70,* pp. xliii–xlvi; Poor, *Manual . . . for 1883,* p. iii.

59. Poor, *Manual . . . for 1869–70,* p. xvi.

60. Poor, *Manual . . . for 1868–69,* p. 28.

61. Poor, *Manual . . . for 1868–69,* pp. 30–32; Poor, *Manual . . . for 1869–70,* pp. xxxi, xli; Poor, *Manual . . . for 1870–71,* p. xxxiii; Poor, *Manual*

. . . *for 1871–72,* p. xlii. For similar later comments, see Poor, *Manual . . . for 1884,* p. iii; Poor, *Manual . . . for 1885,* p. v.

62. Poor, *Manual . . . for 1883,* pp. iv–v; Poor, *Manual . . . for 1884,* pp. i, iii–iv; Poor, *Manual . . . for 1885,* p. v.

63. Poor, *Manual . . . for 1883,* p. iii.

64. Poor, *Manual . . . for 1868–69,* p. 30.

65. Poor, *Manual . . . for 1869–70,* p. xxxi.

66. Poor, *Manual . . . for 1885,* pp. iv–vi.

67. Poor, *Manual . . . for 1871–72,* p. xxxi; also Poor, *Manual . . . for 1879,* p. i.

68. *United States Congress. Senate. Select Committee on Interstate Commerce . . . Regulation of Interstate Commerce by Congress. Testimony. . . .* (Washington, D. C., 1886), II, p. 232.

69. Poor, *Manual . . . for 1891,* p. xxi, and repeated in the introductions of the succeeding *Manuals.* In 1886 Poor praised the "much greater fullness and uniformity in railroad reports . . . secured through the efforts of 'Railroad Commissioners' now appointed for most of the states," but lamented the slowness of the publication by the states of the compilations of the reports, Poor, *Manual . . . for 1886,* p. ix.

70. For Adams' work as given in the annual reports of the Interstate Commerce Commission and of its Bureau of Statistics, see particularly *Second Annual Report of the Interstate Commerce Commission, December 1, 1888* (Washington, 1889), pp. 236–247; *Second Annual Report on the Statistics of Railways in the United States, 1889* (Washington, 1890), pp. 2–7; *Fifth Annual Report on the Statistics of Railways in the United States, 1892* (Washington, 1893), pp. 85–92; also Henry C. Adams, "Administrative Supervision of Railways Under the Twentieth Section of the Act to Regulate Commerce," *Quarterly Journal of Economics,* 12:364–383 (May, 1908).

71. *Second Annual Report of the Interstate Commerce Commission, 1888,* pp. 246–247; *Seventeenth Annual Report of the Interstate Commerce Commission, December 15, 1903* (Washington, 1904), pp. 17, 31; *Fifth Annual Report on the Statistics of Railways, 1892,* pp. 89–91. A plan similar to Poor's seems to have been tried again by private individuals, for Adams wrote on page 91 of this last report: "An attempt was made a few years ago to establish upon a private basis a bureau of examination into the operations of great business corporations, the purpose of which was to give such information to the public that capital might be invested judiciously and the speculative element in market quotations reduced to a minimum. This attempt came to nothing on account of the reluctance of corporations to open their accounts to inspection, but it is a pertinent question whether Government has not a duty to perform in this regard."

72. I. Leo Sharfman, *The Interstate Commerce Commission: a Study in Administrative Law and Procedure* (New York, 1931), I, 117–121; Adams, "Administrative Supervision of Railways," pp. 365–367.

73. The first table was published for the first time in the 1872–73 volume, the second in the 1873–74 volume. The mileage table was included from the first volume on.

74. Poor, *Manual . . . for 1873–74,* pp. l-li; Poor, *Manual . . . for 1886,* p. ix.

75. For the problem of duplication, see Poor, *Manual . . . for 1883,* p. ii; for that of the fiscal year, Poor, *Manual . . . for 1873–74,* p. li; Poor, *Manual . . . for 1874–75,* p. l; Poor, *Manual . . . for 1890,* p. xv; Poor, *Manual . . . for 1891,* p. v.

76. Poor, *Manual . . . for 1873–74,* pp. l-li.

77. Poor, *Manual . . . for 1873–74,* p. l.

78. Poor, *Manual . . . for 1873–74,* p. xxvii.

79. Frederick L. Paxson, "The Railways of the Old Northwest before the

Civil War," *Transactions of the Wisconsin Academy of Arts and Sciences,* XVII, pt. 1 (1914), pp. 268–274. The census figures are from Armin E. Shuman, "Statistical Report of the Railroads in the United States," *Report on the Agencies of Transportation in the United States* (Washington, 1883), pp. 289–290. Poor's statistics come from the table in Poor, *Manual . . . for 1868–69,* pp. 25–29.

80. Henry Poor to Mary Poor, Aug. 1, 1883.

81. Henry Poor to Mary Poor, July 29, 1883.

82. Poor, *Manual . . . for 1883,* p. ii.

83. This and the following quotation are from *Railroad Gazette,* 15:544–545 (Aug. 17, 1883).

84. *Railroad Gazette* 17:536 (Aug. 21, 1885); 18:582 (Aug. 20, 1886); *Railroad Age,* 14:533 (Aug. 16, 1889).

85. *First Annual Report on the Statistics of Railways in the United States, 1888* (Washington, 1889), pp. 345–353; *Third Annual Report on the Statistics of Railways in the United States, 1890* (Washington, 1891), pp. 10–11, 15, 95–100; *Fifth Annual Report on the Statistics of Railways, 1892,* pp. 85–89.

86. *Poor's Manual . . . for 1897,* p. v. Since Adams reported for the fiscal year ending June 30, and Poor for the calendar year ending December 31, Poor's figures are naturally a little higher.

87. *Second Annual Report on Statistics of Railways, 1889,* pp. 42–45.

88. There are good comparisons of the statistics in the *Manual* to those collected by Adams' *Statistics of Railways in Railroad Gazette,* 21:45, 542–547 (Jan. 18, Aug. 16, 1889); 22:605 (Aug. 29, 1890); *Railway Age,* 14:521 (Aug. 16, 1889); see Arthur T. Hadley, "American Railroad Statistics," *Publications of the American Statistical Association* 1:241–253 (June 1889).

89. Printed in New York. Henry Poor in a letter to Mary Poor, Dec. 28, 1868, stated that: "The Pacific Railroad people paid me $500 for my memorial."

90. Printed in New York. Useful background material for the controversies between the Pacific railroads and the government can be found in Homer Cummings and Carl McFarland, *Federal Justice* (New York, 1937), ch. 14.

91. *The Pacific Railroads, and the Relations Existing Between Them and the Government of the United States* (New York, 1879). Poor wrote this in February 1879, Henry Poor to Mary Poor, Feb. 25, 1879.

92. "The Pacific Railroad," *North American Review,* 128:664–680 (June 1879).

93. This was reprinted in pamphlet form.

94. The article was printed in Boston.

95. Fritz Redlich gives an excellent description of George S. Coe's activities and ideas in *The Moulding of American Banking, Men and Ideas* (New York, 1951), II, 424–467.

96. *Bankers' Magazine,* 22:841–868 (May 1868).

97. *North American Review,* 122:3–55 (Jan. 1874). The following quotation is from p. 55.

98. Its full title was *Money and Its Laws: Embracing a History of Monetary Theories and a History of the Currencies of the United States* (New York, 1877).

99. See particularly Poor, *Money and Its Laws,* pp. 585–601. Poor believed that, since there was no central bank, it was the duty of the government through the Treasury Department to take on some central banking functions, particularly in providing currency in a money stringency through the issuing of Treasury notes, increasing deposits in national banks and other devices, "The Relation of the Railroad System of the United States to the Present Monetary Situation," a letter by Henry Poor to the New York *Times.* Sept. 21, 1887 and reprinted by the firm of Poor and Greenough.

100. Henry Poor to Mary Poor, Dec. 19, 1877; Jan. 9, 10, 11, 25, 30, Feb. 3, 6, 1878; Redlich, *Moulding of American Banking,* p. 448. 10,000 copies of the memorial were taken by the different clearing house associations. Poor dedicated *Money and Its Laws* to Coe, and his correspondence shows that he saw

the New York banker often after the two went to Washington to lobby for the Gold Contract Bill in 1868.

101. *The Silver Question. Memorial to Congress, January, 1878* (New York, 1878). The resolutions of the New York Clearing House Association which preface the memorial describe Coe's organizing activities.

102. Henry Poor to Mary Poor, Jan. 30, Feb. 3, 1878.

103. *North American Review* 127:117–131 (July–Aug. 1878); Henry Poor to Mary Poor, March 14, 1878.

104. Bland, "Debtor and Creditor, Part I," p. 119.

105. The full title is *Resumption and the Silver Question: Embracing a Sketch of Coinage and Legal Tender Currencies of the United States and other Nations. A Handbook for the Times* (New York, 1878). A second edition was printed in the same year.

106. Published first in New York in 1896 with a second and slightly larger edition published in 1897 and a third in 1898. Poor wrote one other campaign document besides this book and those on the tariff. The title of that pamphlet written for the 1876 campaign indicates its contents. It was called *The Three Secession Movements in the United States. Samuel J. Tilden, the Democratic Candidate for the Presidency; the Advisor, Aider and Abettor of the Great Secession Movement of 1860; and One of the Authors of the Infamous Resolution of 1864. His Claims as a Statesman and Reformer Considered* (Boston, 1874).

107. This was published in New York by H. V. and H. W. Poor as were all of Henry Poor's books, though not his pamphlets.

108. The quotation is from Poor, *Twenty Two Years of Protection,* p. 63.

109. Henry Poor to Mary Poor, Sept. 26, Oct. 3, 11, 1888.

110. This was published in New York in 1892.

Index